I0273310

Tommaso Alpina

Subject, Definition, Activity

Scientia Graeco-Arabica

Herausgegeben von
Marwan Rashed

Band 28

Tommaso Alpina

Subject, Definition, Activity

Framing Avicenna's Science of the Soul

DE GRUYTER

This book has been written under the aegis of the project "Animals in Philosophy of the Islamic World", which has received funding from the European Research Council (ERC) under the European Union's Horizon 2020 research and innovation programme (grant agreement No. 786762).

ISBN 978-3-11-110924-4
e-ISBN (PDF) 978-3-11-070684-0
e-ISBN (EPUB) 978-3-11-070695-6
ISSN 1868-7172

Library of Congress Control Number: 2020941884

Bibliographic information published by the Deutsche Nationalbibliothek
The Deutsche Nationalbibliothek lists this publication in the Deutsche Nationalbibliografie; detailed bibliographic data are available on the Internet at http://dnb.dnb.de.

This volume is text- and page-identical with the hardback published in 2021.
Printing and binding: CPI books GmbH, Leck

www.degruyter.com

Ἡ περὶ τῆς ἀληθείας θεωρία τῇ μὲν χαλεπὴ τῇ δὲ
ῥᾳδία. σημεῖον δὲ τὸ μήτ' ἀξίως μηδένα δύνασθαι θιγεῖν
αὐτῆς μήτε πάντας ἀποτυγχάνειν, ἀλλ' ἕκαστον λέγειν τι
περὶ τῆς φύσεως, καὶ καθ' ἕνα μὲν ἢ μηθὲν ἢ μικρὸν ἐπιβάλλειν αὐτῇ,
ἐκ πάντων δὲ συναθροιζομένων γίγνεσθαί τι μέγεθος·
Aristotle, *Metaph.*, II, 1, 993 a30 – b4

Allerdings muß sich die Darstellungsweise formell von der Forschungsweise unterscheiden. Die Forschung hat den Stoff sich im Detail anzueignen, seine verschiednen Entwicklungsformen zu analysieren und deren innres Band aufzuspüren. Erst nachdem diese Arbeit vollbracht, kann die wirkliche Bewegung entsprechend dargestellt werden. Gelingt dies und spiegelt sich nun das Leben des Stoffs ideell wider, so mag es aussehn, als habe man es mit einer Konstruktion a priori zu tun.
K. Marx, *Das Kapital*, I, *Nachwort* [1873], MEGA II/6, 709

Τὸ προοίμιον τοῦ προκειμένου βιβλίου τοῦ Ἀριστοτέλους
τὸν παρ' Ὁμήρῳ μάντιν ἐκμιμούμενον,
ὃς ᾔδη τά τ' ἐόντα τά τ' ἐσσόμενα πρό τ' ἐόντα,
τοῖς τρισὶ χρόνοις συμπαραθέον ἀναμιμνήσκει τῶν
φθασάντων, προανακρούεται τὰ μέλλοντα,
ἐκδιηγεῖται τὰ παρόντα.
Olympiodori *In Aristotelis Meteora commentaria*, 1.5 – 9

Acknowledgments

This book is the revised version of my Ph.D. dissertation ("Subject, Definition, Activity. The Epistemological Status of the Science of the Soul in Avicenna's *Kitāb al-Nafs*", Scuola Normale Superiore, November 2016). I wish to express here my sincere gratitude to Amos Bertolacci for the constant attention, outstanding competence, and friendly support with which he has guided me along the path of Graeco-Arabic studies and supervised my research since my second year as an undergraduate student. I am also deeply grateful to Marwan Rashed for reading and discussing with me several textual and interpretative aspects of this book and thus saving me from many errors, for his constant support and encouragement, and for believing in this book right from the beginning. My profound gratitude also goes to Peter Adamson for giving me many comments and advice, which improved the first draft of this book. My interest in Aristotle and his medieval interpreters dates back to 2005 when, just admitted at the Scuola Normale Superiore of Pisa, I met the late Francesco Del Punta, who taught me to combine philological accuracy with philosophical interpretation. I will always treasure his teaching. I wish to thank Gianfranco Fioravanti, who supervised my BA and MA thesis at the University of Pisa and whose lectures on Augustine and Thomas Aquinas instilled in me the curiosity for Medieval philosophy. I also wish to thank all the members of the board of my Ph.D. viva for their insightful comments, remarks, and suggestions: Dag N. Hasse, Concetta Luna, Ivana Panzeca, Francesco Pelosi, Marwan Rashed, Ayman Shihadeh.

This research started at the Scuola Normale Superiore of Pisa, where I was first an undergraduate and graduate student, and then a postdoctoral fellow within the ERC project "Philosophy on the Border of Civilizations and Intellectual Endeavours: Towards a Critical Edition of the *Metaphysics* (*Ilāhiyyāt of Kitāb al-Šifā'*) of Avicenna (Ibn Sīnā)", led by Amos Bertolacci, and ended up finally at MUSAPh (Munich School of Ancient Philosophy), where I am currently a postdoctoral fellow within the ERC project "Animals in Philosophy of the Islamic World", led by Peter Adamson. Here I wish to express my deep gratitude to the principal investigators of both projects, who allowed me to pursue my research, and to the members of both research groups for all the discussions on the topic we had (in alphabetical order): Alessia Astesiano, Niccolò Caminada, Gaia Celli, Gholamreza Dadkhah, Sarah de Mendonça Virgi, Stefano Di Pietrantonio, Silvia Di Vincenzo, Rotraud Hansberger, Daniele Marotta, Ivana Panzeca, Bethany Somma.

At the Scuola Normale, I met excellent researchers who contributed considerably to my education. I wish to thank, in particular, Laura M. Castelli, Cristina Cerami, Matteo di Giovanni, Gabriele Galluzzo, Concetta Luna.

I was not always able to explain to my family what the soul about which I was so curious exactly *is*. Despite that, they never failed to give me their unconditional support. Here I want to express my profound love to them all. During the first year of my Ph.D. studies, my beloved grandfather Saverio Covelli passed away: he will always

https://doi.org/10.1515/9783110706840-001

hold a special place in my heart. I wish to thank Emanuela and Ilaria for being always there for me. Over the past fifteen years, I realized how lucky I am to have them in my life. I also wish to thank Marie-Odile Volpoët for making me feel at home away from home.

Alberto supported and encouraged me through this long and sometimes hard journey. He taught me what being loved every moment of every day means, and made my life truly happy. I dedicate this book to him.

Contents

Introduction — 1

Chapter One — 6

Avicenna's *Kitāb al-Nafs:* Nature, Content, Sources — **6**

Introduction — **6**

Nature — **6**

Content — **9**

Sources — **15**

The Text of Aristotle's *De anima* in Arabic Translation — **16**

Greek Commentaries on the *De anima* in Arabic Translation: Direct and Indirect Evidence — **19**

Supplementing Aristotle with Aristotle and Other Sources — **20**

The Arabic Text of Avicenna's *Nafs* — **24**

Avicenna's *Nafs* between East and West — **27**

Chapter Two — 29

The Science of the Soul: An Attempt at Contextualization — **29**

Introduction — **29**

How It All Began — **30**

From Alexandria to Athens to Baghdad — **40**

An All-Natural Perspective — **42**

Culmination of Natural Philosophy and Anticipation of Metaphysics — **44**

Staying in the Middle — **50**

Taking a Breath — **56**

Chapter Three — 58

Subject: *Psychologia generalis* vs. *psychologia specialis* — **58**

Introduction — **58**

Grounding the Investigation of the Soul: Part 1 — **60**

Knowing the Soul from Knowing Oneself: The Prologue to *Nafs* — **64**

The Transition to the Essence-Inquiry: The *Flying Man* Argument — **68**

The Soul is Substance insofar as it is the Form of the Body: the Ascertainment of the Essence of Sublunary Soul — **74**

The *a posteriori* Proof of the Essence of the Human Rational Soul — **77**

Grounding the Investigation of the Soul: Part 2 — **86**

Conclusion — **93**

Chapter Four — 96
Definition: An Attempt at Unification — **96**
Introduction, or Dialectic is the Way — **96**
Giving a Name or Pointing at the Quiddity? Form (*ṣūra*) vs. Perfection (*kamāl*) — **98**
Which Return to Aristotle? — **106**
Does Avicenna Formulate a Definition of the Soul? — **112**
Which Body for which Soul? Reception (*qubūl*) vs. Relation (*nisba*) — **117**
Conclusion on a Tightrope — **128**

Chapter Five — 130
Activity: A Clue to the Twofold Nature of the Human Soul — **130**
Introduction — **130**
Abstraction & Emanation: Which One do You Side with? — **131**
Immaterial Forms, Abstracted Forms, and Recovered Forms — **139**
How do We Intellect Material Forms? *Nafs*, V, 5 — **144**
The Epistemological Role of the Active Intellect in First Acquisition of an Intellectual Form — **146**
The Ontological Role of the Active Intellect in Recovering an Intellectual Form already Acquired — **155**
Conclusion — **157**

Chapter Six — 158
Avicenna's Psychology: A Diachronic Perspective — **158**
Introduction — **158**
K. al-Maǧmūʿ or al-Ḥikma al-ʿArūḍiyya (The Compilation or Philosophy for ʿArūḍī) — **159**
ʿUyūn al-Ḥikma (Elements of Philosophy) — **160**
K. al-Hidāya (The Guidance) — **162**
K. al-Naǧāt (The Salvation) — **164**
Dānešnāme-ye ʿAlāʾī (Philosophy for ʿAlāʾ al-Dawla) — **166**
Al-Mašriqiyyūn or al-Ḥikma al-Mašriqiyya (The Easterners or Eastern Philosophy) — **168**
K. al-Išārāt wa-l-tanbīhāt (Pointers and Reminders) — **170**
Conclusive Considerations — **173**
Synoptic table — **177**
Psychology in Classificatory Writings — **181**

Conclusion, or Explaining Avicenna by Way of Avicenna — 184

Appendix — 190
Translation of Avicenna's *Kitāb al-Nafs* — **190**

Introduction

This book investigates the reception and reworking of the theory of the soul expounded in Aristotle's *De anima* (Περὶ ψυχῆς) in the *Kitāb al-Nafs* (*Book of the Soul*), which is an influential work by Avicenna (Ibn Sīnā, ca. 980–1037 AD), one of the most eminent figures of Islamic philosophy.

Subject, *definition*, *activity* represent the concepts on which this research focuses. *Subject* is the *soul* (*nafs*), i.e. the subject-matter of psychology, or science of the soul (*ʿilm al-nafs*). It is the most fundamental concept: it is the ground on which this science is built, it confers unity upon science, and distinguishes it from other sciences. However, determining the subject-matter of psychology is not as easy as it might seem *prima facie*. For within and outside of the *De anima* Aristotle himself, who can be considered the pioneer of a global science of the soul, seems hesitant to assign to the natural philosopher engaging in psychology the investigation of the entirety of the soul. In all likelihood, the reason for Aristotle's hesitation is the rational (part of the) soul, because it seems to be the actuality of no body and, consequently, separable from it. Therefore, its investigation seems to exceed the boundaries of natural philosophy and to spill over into metaphysics. Most Late Ancient and early Arabic exegetes of the *De anima* built their own interpretation of Aristotelian psychology precisely on the undetermined claims that Aristotle made about the nature of the human rational soul. Their intentions were to present a *reformed* psychology according to new agendas, in particular the necessity of granting some kind of ontological independence to the human soul. Aristotle's psychology (and its reformed version) seems to be then at an impasse: either it is a unitary science that is placed within natural philosophy but does not investigate its entire subject-matter (the separable soul properly pertaining to metaphysics), or it investigates the entire soul but at the expense of its internal unity. In his *Kitāb al-Nafs* Avicenna undertakes to determine the subject-matter and, consequently, the place of psychology in his system of science, by following both the *real* Aristotle of the *De anima* and the *virtual* Aristotle of the commentators, in an attempt to integrate an overall physical account of the soul and a specific, not entirely physical approach to the essence of the human rational soul.

Definition refers to the formula that delineates the subject-matter of psychology by qualifying the soul as the perfection (*kamāl*) of the body. Defining the proper subject-matter of psychology is crucial to demarcating the boundaries of this science and, at the same time, conferring unity upon it, especially since considering the entire soul as its subject-matter poses some problems for its unity. In order to solve the unity issue, Avicenna firstly revises the theoretical tools put in place by his predecessors to account for the soul (terminology and standard definition). He concentrates in particular on Philoponus, with whom he shares the concern to acknowledge the separability of the human rational soul. Following his legacy, Avicenna makes use of the notion of *perfection* to refer to the soul, since it is broad enough to encompass also

https://doi.org/10.1515/9783110706840-002

separable entities and allows him to focus on the soul as the operational principle of activities. However, the dialectical discussion on a nonessential characteristic of the soul (its being an operational principle *qua* perfection) is not Avicenna's final goal. Rather, he also aims to found the application of the term *perfection* to the soul on the quidditative level independently of its being defined as perfection. Once the substantiality of the soul has been demonstrated, the term *kamāl* passes from designating the soul insofar as it has a relation to the body (operational level) to designating it unequivocally insofar as it is a substance (ontological level). Having provided psychology with a strong focal unity, Avicenna moves on to deal with the faculties (and the consequent activities) for which the soul is responsible, in line with *De anima*, II, 2 where Aristotle moves from investigating what is clearer in itself (the soul) to investigating what is clearer and more familiar to us (the faculties of the soul and their activities) as a better way to get knowledge of what is clearer in itself. Avicenna's philosophical psychology thus turns out to be a faculty psychology like Aristotle's.

Activity does not generically refer to the activities for which the soul is responsible, but rather to the peculiar activity of the theoretical intellect (*ʿaql naẓarī*) or the theoretical faculty (*quwwa naẓariyya*) of the soul, i. e. intellectual conceptualization. Focusing on the peculiar activity of the theoretical intellect reveals the distinctiveness of the human rational soul with respect to all the other instances of the sublunary soul. This distinctiveness concerns the human rational soul's relation to the body and clearly emerges from the account of intellectual conceptualization: unlike all other psychic activities, intellectual conceptualization can be performed with no need of a bodily organ. According to the medieval adage *operari sequitur esse*, the nature of something can be inferred from the activity of that something; therefore, from the soul's capability to perform an activity independently of the body the independence of the soul from the body can be inferred. Thus, Avicenna's doctrine of human intellection shows the amphibious status of the human rational soul and, consequently, the intermediate status of psychology between natural philosophy and metaphysics. Human intellection involves two opposite movements: a movement *downwards*, i. e. the human soul's examination of the particulars acquired through the lower perceptive faculties, which operate through the body, and its consequent abstraction of intellectual forms from those particulars, and a movement *upwards*, i. e. the human soul's contact with the Active Intellect above it and the consequent emanation of something from it. These two movements, far from being incompatible, seem to account perfectly for, on the one hand, the soul's need for a relation to (not a reception in) the body and, on the other hand, its independence of that body in performing its own activity.

Subject, *definition*, *activity* can be therefore glossed, respectively, as *soul*, *perfection*, *intellection*. These three concepts, which form the cornerstone of Avicenna's writing, have been chosen to disclose through their examination the twofold consideration of the soul in Avicenna's psychology. Besides the *general approach* to the *soul of* sublunary living beings which, in line with Aristotle's *De anima*, is the *formal principle* of the body, immanent to it, Avicenna's psychology also exhibits a *specific ori-*

entation towards the *soul in itself*, i.e. the human rational soul that, considered in isolation from the body, is a *self-subsistent substance*, identical with the theoretical intellect and capable of surviving severance from the body. These two investigations demonstrate the coexistence in Avicenna's psychology of a more specific and less physical science (*psychologia specialis*) within a more general and overall physical one (*psychologia generalis*).

The issue of the epistemological status of psychology in Avicenna's system of science seems to be crucial to engaging in any further inquiry into specific psychological issues. However, apart from some occasional forays into this issue, none of the available studies devoted to the *Kitāb al-Nafs* directly tackles it. The *Kitāb al-Nafs* is one of the better-studied texts in the Avicennian oeuvre. Its text has been edited four times over the past century, though none of these is a proper critical edition, and some of the issues dealt with in it have aroused the interest of historians of philosophy. However, these have mostly focused on three topics: the doctrine of internal senses (with particular attention to the faculty of estimation, *wahm*), which develops and supplements Aristotle's doctrine of φαντασία; the theory of human intellection, which combines abstraction and emanation in an apparently problematic way; and the so-called "metaphysics of the rational soul", which considers the doctrine of soul's return to the celestial realm after death (*maʿād*) as the pinnacle of metaphysics. By contrast, this study (with the exception of the theory of human intellection) largely avoids raking over well-trodden ground like that mentioned above, focusing instead on a previously unexplored methodological issue: what is, for Avicenna, the place of psychology within the sciences, and on what basis can we say that psychology is a unified science?

The present study has some limits, however. The first limit directly concerns Avicenna's thinking with regard to the scope and depth of this research. As to the scope, the present study deals primarily with the first and the fifth treatise of Avicenna's *Kitāb al-Nafs*, where the major theoretical issues concerning psychology are treated. The topics of the second, third, and fourth treatises are marginal with respect to the purpose of the present investigation and, consequently, have been taken into account only selectively. Moreover, the psychological sections of Avicenna's other *summae* have been taken into consideration. These sections have been compared with the *Kitāb al-Nafs* because they belong to the same literary genre, cover the whole period of Avicenna's philosophical activity and, unlike the works on particular subjects and topics in psychology, offer a general exposition of the science of the soul, which might make it possible to evaluate the development of Avicenna's thought. As to the depth of the investigation, this project deals only with a chapter of the complex history of the relationships between psychology and the other sciences, that is, its relation to natural philosophy and metaphysics. The goal of this trajectory is to establish to which branch of theoretical philosophy psychology belongs. However, this research does not take into consideration other, crucial chapters of this history such as, for example, the relation of psychology to medicine, which is pointed out by many cross-references. For instance, the first book of the *Kitāb al-Qānūn fī l-ṭibb* (*Canon of Medicine)* contains a discussion of philosophers' and physicians' psychologies, and there Avicenna repeatedly refers to soul as the principle responsible for cognition and voluntary motion; conversely, in psychology Avicenna refers several times to his medical books. The relation of psychology to medicine represents a field of research on its own, which deserves a specific study.

The second limit concerns the philosophical tradition before and after Avicenna. As to the tradition before Avicenna, the present study is intended to offer not so much a new interpretation of Aristotle and of the Late Ancient and early Arabic interpreters of Aristotelian psychology, but rather a survey of their positions concerning the epistemological status of psychology, in order to provide the theoretical and historical background of Avicenna's elaboration of his own psychology. In this connection, the debate involving philosophers and theologians contemporary to Avicenna concerning the human being and the nature of his soul deserves more attention. As to the later philosophical tradition, it has not been taken into consideration, even though it could have greatly contributed to the interpretation of Avicenna's major tenets, and to the evaluation of their impact on the subsequent philosophical tradition, which approaches Avicenna's philosophy in a both critical and conciliatory manner. However, the investigation of both these philosophical traditions goes beyond the scope of the present work.

The third limit concerns the translations provided as an appendix to the present book. The English translation of the relevant chapters of the *Kitāb al-Nafs* is based on the Arabic text edited by Fazlur Rahman in 1959. Although the text has occasionally been emended and improved on the basis of direct inspection of some of the manuscripts used by the editor as well as other manuscripts, a systematic revision and a critical edition of it are beyond the scope of the present endeavour. All the aforementioned limits amount to further directions along which inquiry into Avicenna's psychology might (and perhaps should) be conducted in the near future in order to bolster our knowledge on this topic.

* * *

This book consists of six chapters and one appendix.

Chapter 1 contains an outline of Avicenna's *Kitāb al-Nafs*. In particular this chapter focuses on the nature of the writing, its content, its sources, and its impact on the subsequent philosophical tradition both in the East and in the West.

Chapter 2 reconstructs the vicissitudes of the science of the soul from its foundation and its first most comprehensive exposition in Aristotle's *De anima*, which was intended to provide the theoretical framework for the quintessentially "natural" texts on zoology, to the Late Ancient and early Arabic exegesis of the Aristotelian treatise, which transformed and adulterated Aristotle's psychology according to new concerns, especially the independence of the human rational soul from the body and its consequent survival after death.

Chapters 3–5 contain the core of the book. Chapter 3 is devoted to the subject-matter of Avicenna's *Kitāb al-Nafs*. In particular, it evaluates how a more general and overall physical investigation of the soul (*psychologia generalis*), and a more specific and less physical one (*psychologia specialis*) can coexist in one and the same science according to the system of science outlined by Avicenna in metaphysics. In this chapter, I have used some excerpts from my article "The *Soul of*, the Soul *in itself*, and the *Flying Man* Experiment", *Arabic Sciences and Philosophy*, 28.2, 2018, 187–224.

Chapter 4 deals with Avicenna's definition of the soul as a way to delineate the subject-matter of psychology and confer unity upon the science. In this chapter, Avicenna's dialectical approach to his predecessors' terminology and standard definition to refer to the soul is contrasted with his positive account of the soul. Then, Avicenna's focus on the faculties and the activities ensuing from the soul is shown.

Chapter 5 tackles Avicenna's theory of human intellection as a litmus test for verifying the conclusions of Chapter 3 and 4 about the intermediate place of psychology between natural philosophy and metaphysics with regard to a part of its subject-matter, i.e. the human rational soul. For its specific activity, i.e. intellectual conceptualization, reveals the distinctiveness of the human rational soul from any other instance of sublunary soul. This chapter is a revised version of my article "Intellectual Knowledge, Active Intellect and Intellectual Memory in Avicenna's *Kitāb al-Nafs* and Its Aristotelian Background", *Documenti e studi sulla tradizione filosofica medievale*, 25, 2014, 131–183.

Chapter 6 approaches Avicenna's psychology in a diachronic perspective by providing a survey of the contents of the psychological section of Avicenna's other *summae.*

The Appendix contains an annotated translation of the following chapters from Avicenna's *Kitāb al-Nafs:* prologue; I, 1; I, 3; I, 5; V, 2; and V, 5. These chapters, some of which are translated into a modern language in their entirety here for the first time, represent the textual foundation of this research. For this reason, it seemed appropriate to make them available to the reader.

Chapter One

Avicenna's *Kitāb al-Nafs:* Nature, Content, Sources

Introduction

The *Kitāb al-Nafs* (*Liber de anima seu Sextus de Naturalibus* in Latin, *Book of the Soul* in English, henceforth *Nafs*) is the sixth section of the second part of the *Kitāb al-Šifāʾ* (*Liber sufficientiae/Sufficientia* in Latin,[1] *Book of the Cure/Healing* in English, henceforth *Šifāʾ*), Avicenna's most comprehensive philosophical *summa*, where he undertakes an exhaustive inquiry into the soul, carrying out for the first time in Arabic philosophy an enterprise similar to the one Aristotle pursued in his *De anima*.

According to the information that can be drawn from his biography,[2] Avicenna composed the entire *Šifāʾ* in approximately eight years, beginning it in Hamadān around 411/1020 at the request of Abū ʿUbayd ʿAbd al-Wāḥid ibn Muḥammad al-Ğūzğānī (*fl.* XI c.), his disciple and secretary, and completing it at the latest by 418/1027, when he was en route to Sābūr Ḫwāst. On the basis of the same pieces of information, the composition of the *Nafs*, together with that of the preceding five sections of natural philosophy and of the metaphysical part, can be safely situated in Hamadān between 412/1022 and 414/1024.[3] In the following pages the nature, the content, the sources, and the *fortuna* of Avicenna's *Nafs* will be outlined.

Nature

Avicenna's *Šifāʾ* consists of four parts (*ğumal*, s. *ğumla*), covering a great deal of the philosophical legacy, especially Aristotelianism, inherited from Antiquity. The four main areas this massive work encompasses are: logic (*al-manṭiq*), natural philosophy (*al-ṭabīʿiyyāt*), mathematics (*al-riyāḍiyyāt*), and metaphysics (*al-ilāhiyyāt*). The part on natural philosophy is divided, in turn, into eight sections (*funūn*, s. *fann*) corresponding to the works which make up the Aristotelian physical *corpus* (with the ad-

---

[1] For a study of the reason why Latin translators rendered the Arabic word *Šifāʾ* as *Sufficientia*, see G. Saliba, "Avicenna's *Shifāʾ* (*Sufficientia*): in Defense of Medieval Latin Translators", *Der Islam. Journal of the History and Culture of the Middle East*, 94.2, 2017, 423–433.

[2] Avicenna started to write his autobiography but then, after meeting al-Ğūzğānī, he entrusted him with its composition.

[3] See *The Life of Ibn Sina. A Critical Edition and Annotated Translation*, W. E. Gohlman, ed., State University of New York Press, Albany, NY 1974, 56.9–67.4. For a commentary on this passage of Avicenna's biography, see D. Gutas, *Avicenna and the Aristotelian Tradition. Introduction to Reading Avicenna's Philosophical Works. Second, Revised and Enlarged Edition, Including an Inventory of Avicenna's Authentic Works*, Brill, Leiden-Boston 2014, 103–109.

dition of Nicolaus of Damascus' *De plantis*).[4] The eight books of the part on natural philosophy deal with the following topics: the so-called *communia naturalia*, namely the principles and the causes of perishable things (*Samāʿ ṭabīʿī*, first section); the heavens and the celestial bodies (*Samāʾ wa-ʿĀlam*, second section); generation and corruption and the nature of elements (*Kawn wa-Fasād*, third section); the activities and affections of the primary qualities and the mixtures resulting from these qualities (*Afʿāl wa-Infiʿālāt*, fourth section); mineralogy, geology, and meteorology (*Maʿādin wa-Āṯār ʿulwiyya*, fifth section); psychology (*Nafs*, sixth section); botany (*Nabāt*, seventh section); zoology (*Ḥayawān*, eighth section).[5]

In the sixth section, like Aristotle, Avicenna aims at providing a general account of the sublunary soul that might fit every kind of soul, be it vegetative, animal, or human. Thus, as becomes clear from the way in which Avicenna arranges the sections of the *Šifāʾ* on natural philosophy, the study of the soul has been conceived – at least at the theoretical level – as preliminary to the specific treatment of plants and animals, which are the subjects of the seventh and the eighth sections, again the botanical and the zoological sections.[6]

A quick glance at the general structure and content of the book enables the reader to evaluate Avicenna's peculiar approach to the Aristotelian source as it is described in his introduction to the entire *summa*.[7] There, he said that his purpose in the composition of this book was "to set down in it the gist of what we have ascertained with respect to the fundamental principles contained in the philosophical sciences attributed to the ancients (*lubāb mā taḥaqqaqnāhu min al-uṣūl fī l-ʿulūm al-falsafiyya al-mansūba ilà l-aqdamīna*, 9.8–9) and based on methodical and verified theoretical analysis (*al-mabniyya ʿalà l-naẓar al-murattab al-muḥaqqaq*, 9.9), and the fundamental principles discovered by [a series of] acts of comprehension cooperating in the attainment of the truth, which was diligently pursued for a long time (*wa-l-uṣūl al-mustanbaṭa bi-l-afhām al-mutaʿāwina ʿalà idrāk al-ḥaqq al-muǧtahad fīhi zamānan ṭawīlan*, 9.9–10) until it culminated in such a body [of principles] (*ḥattà istaqāma āḫiruhū ʿalà ǧumlatin*, 9.10–11)".[8] In order to accomplish this goal, Avicenna

4 On the possible existence of an Aristotelian writing on plants, see Chapter 2, n. 10.

5 For a survey of the sections making up the natural philosophy of the *Šifāʾ*, see *Nafs*, prologue, 1.4–2.1 [9.4–10.21]. More on this in Chapter 3. The quotations from Avicenna's *Nafs* are usually followed by the reference to the page and the line number of the corresponding passage in the Latin translation in square brackets. The same quotation scheme is followed in the case of other sections of the *Šifāʾ* whose Latin translation is edited in the Avicenna Latinus series.

6 See *Nafs*, prologue, 2.1–3.11 [10.21–13.62]. More on this in Chapter 3.

7 *Madḫal*, I, 1, 9–10. For the English translation of this introduction, see D. Gutas, *Avicenna and the Aristotelian Tradition*, 41–46.

8 *Madḫal*, I, 1, 9.8–10. The English translation is that provided in Gutas, *Avicenna and the Aristotelian Tradition*, 42, with minor modifications. Avicenna's focus on the fundamental principles, or cornerstones, of his sources, disregarding any accessory element, seems to echo the axiomatic procedure, inferred from Euclid's *Elements*, which Proclus had already used in metaphysics. On this, see

uses two complementary procedures: (1) setting down most of the discipline, indicating where ambiguity may occur, and solving it by setting forth clearly the correct answer;[9] and (2) supplying corollaries (*furūʿ*, lit. *branches*, 9.13) along with the fundamental principles, with the exception of what is self-evident,[10] a method which is in line with the mainstay of Avicenna's conception of the praxis of philosophy, that is, the idea of the process of the accumulation of knowledge by successive philosophers, each contributing his act of comprehension (*fahm*), with a special role reserved for Avicenna himself.[11]

Thus, Avicenna's adherence to Aristotelianism is genuine without being slavish. For, on the one hand, Avicenna assimilates all the Aristotelian philosophy that was available in Arabic translations, exhibiting dependence on and deference to his source: he refers to Aristotle by using the epithet *First Teacher* (*al-muʿallim al-awwal*) and to his works as *First Teaching* (*al-taʿlīm al-awwal*),[12] where Aristotle's being *first* refers not only to his chronological priority but also to his philosophical primacy.[13] By contrast, Avicenna shows a critical attitude towards Aristotle, and Ar-

---

Avicenna (Ibn Sīnā), *Libro della Guarigione. Le cose divine*, a cura di A. Bertolacci, Unione Tipografico-Editrice Torinese (Utet), Torino 2007, 32.

9 *Madḫal*, I, 1, 9.12–13.

10 *ibidem*, 9.13–14.

11 On Avicenna's conception of the praxis of philosophy, see Gutas, *Avicenna and the Aristotelian Tradition*, 249–266. For a clearer insight about Avicenna's idea that true principles are extracted over a long period of time by the cooperative activity of philosophers' understanding (*afhām*), see M.E. Marmura, "Plotting the Course of Avicenna's Thought", *Journal of the American Oriental Society*, 111/2, 1991, 333–342, in part. 338–339. For the Aristotelian background of this idea, see *Metaphysics*, II, 1, 993 a30–b4: "The investigation of truth is in one way hard, in another easy. An indication of this is found in the fact that no one is able to attain truth adequately, while, on the other hand, no one fails entirely [to attain it], but everyone says something true about the nature of things, and while individually (καθ'ἕνα) they contribute little or nothing to the truth, by the union of all (ἐκ πάντων δὲ συναθροιζομένων) a considerable amount is amassed" (tr. J. Barnes).

12 For the occurrence of these epithets in *Nafs*, see III, 5, 126.6; III, 7, 149.20, where Avicenna shares in Aristotle's theory of vision, notably the necessity of a transparent medium conveying the object of sight and the intromission model of vision. For Avicenna's use of these epithets, see G. Endress, "La 'Concordance entre Platon et Aristote'. L'Aristote arabe et l'émancipation de la philosophie en Islam médiéval", in B. Mojsisch and O. Pluta eds., *Historia Philosophiae Medii Aevi.* Studien zur Geschichte der Philosophie des Mittelalters (Festschrift K. Flash), Amsterdam – Philadelphia 1991, 237–257; id., "'Der erste Lehrer'. Der arabische Aristoteles und das Konzept der Philosophie im Islam", in U. Tworuschka ed., *Gottes ist der Orient. Gottes ist der Okzident. Festschrift für Abdoldjavad Falaturi zum 65. Geburtstag*, Böhlau, Köln-Wien 1991, 151–181; id., "L'Aristote arabe. Réception, autorité et transformation du Premier Maître", *Medioevo*, 23, 1997, 1–42; Gutas, *Avicenna and the Aristotelian Tradition*, 325, nn. 12–13.

13 For a list of the occurrences of these epithets in the *Šifāʾ*, see Avicenna (Ibn Sīnā), *Libro della Guarigione*, 36, n. 83. For the occurrence of these epithets in the *Ilāhiyyāt*, i.e. the metaphysical part of *Kitāb al-Šifāʾ*, see A. Bertolacci, *The Reception of Aristotle's* Metaphysics *in Avicenna's* Kitāb al-Šifāʾ. *A Milestone of Western Metaphysical Thought*, Brill, Leiden-Boston 2006, 318–334 and 560–561.

istotelianism.[14] In general, he does not limit himself to taking over Aristotelian philosophy, but he also attempts to systematize it in an original manner in order to provide it with a coherent structure and a demonstrative procedure.

The combination of these two complementary attitudes towards Aristotle, that is, *assimilation* and *critical sensibility*, can also be detected in the *Nafs* by looking at its table of contents.

Content

The following table provides the table of contents of the *Nafs*, and the *loci paralleli* in the Aristotelian source.[15]

Chapters	*Kitāb al-Nafs*	*De anima*
	[Prologue]	
	First Treatise	
I, 1	[Chapter] on establishing the [existence of the] soul and defining it insofar as it is soul	II, 1–2
I, 2	[Chapter] on what the ancients said about the soul and its substance, and its refutation	I, 2–5
I, 3	[Chapter] on the fact that the soul falls under the category of substance	II, 1
I, 4	[Chapter] on showing that the difference among the activities of the soul is due to the difference among its faculties	II, 3
I, 5	[Chapter] on the enumeration of the faculties of the soul by way of classification	II, 3; III, 12
	Second Treatise	
II, 1	[Chapter] on the verification of the faculties attributed to the vegetative soul	II, 4
II, 2	[Chapter] on the verification of the kinds of perceptions belonging to us	[II, 5]; II, 12; III, 8
II, 3	[Chapter] on the sense of touch	II, 11; [III, 13]
II, 4	[Chapter] on taste and smell	II, 9–10

14 As an example of this attitude in the *Nafs*, see *Nafs*, I, 1, 8.8–9.18 where, unlike some Peripatetics, Avicenna argues against the equation of perfection with substance. More on this *infra*.

15 References in square brackets point at thematic similarities, not at direct dependence. As for the Arabic version of Aristotle's *Parva naturalia* that was at Avicenna's disposal, see *Supplementing Aristotle with Aristotle and other Sources* below.

Continued

Chapters	*Kitāb al-Nafs*	*De anima*
II, 5	[Chapter] on hearing	II, 8
	Third Treatise	II, 7; [*De sensu et sensibilibus*]
III, 1	[Chapter] on the light, the transparent, and the color	
III, 2	[Chapter] on the fact that luminosity is not a body, but a quality that comes into being in it, and on the doctrines and doubts about luminosity and rays	
III, 3	[Chapter] on the accomplishment of the refutation of the doctrines denying that luminosity is something different from the manifest color, and the discourse on the transparent and the luminous	
III, 4	[Chapter] on the reflection about doctrines dealing with colors and their coming into being	
III, 5	[Chapter] on the difference among the doctrines about sight and the refutation of false doctrines in accordance with the things themselves	
III, 6	[Chapter] on the refutation of their doctrines according to the things said in their doctrines	
III, 7	[Chapter] on the solution of the doubts that they set forth, and on the accomplishment of the discourse on the visible things that occupy different positions among rough and smooth things	
III, 8	[Chapter] on the reason why one single thing is seen as two things	
	Fourth Treatise	
IV, 1	[Chapter] in which there is a general discourse on the internal senses belonging to animals	III, 1–2
IV, 2	[Chapter] on the activities of the form-bearing and the cogitative faculties among these internal senses, and containing the discourse on sleep, wakefulness, the veridical and the false dream, and a mode of the properties of prophecy	[III, 3; *De somno et vigilia*; *De insomniis*; *De divinatione per somnum*]
IV, 3	[Chapter] on the activities of the recollective and the estimative faculties and on the fact that the activities of all these faculties are [performed] through bodily organs	III, 7; [*De memoria et reminiscentia*]
IV, 4	[Chapter] on the states of the locomotive faculties and a mode of prophecy connected with them	III, 9–11
	Fifth Treatise	

Continued

Chapters	*Kitāb al-Nafs*	*De anima*
V, 1	[Chapter] on the properties of the activities and the affections belonging to the human being, and on the clarification about the faculties of contemplation and action belonging to the human soul	
V, 2	[Chapter] on establishing that the rational soul does not subsist as something impressed in corporeal matter	[III, 5]
V, 3	[Chapter] including two issues: (i) how the human soul makes use of the senses, and (ii) establishing the temporal origination of the soul	
V, 4	[Chapter] on the fact that human souls neither corrupt, nor transmigrate	I, 3–4
V, 5	[Chapter] on the Intellect Active upon our souls and the intellect that is affected through our souls	III, 4–5
V, 6	[Chapter] on the degrees of the activities of the intellect and their highest degree, namely the sacred intellect	[III, 6–8]
V, 7	[Chapter] on the enumeration of the doctrines inherited by the ancients about the state of the soul, its activities, and whether the soul is one or many, and the confirmation of the true discourse on it	
V, 8	[Chapter] on the clarification of the instruments belonging to the soul	

The Aristotelian skeleton is immediately detectable in Avicenna's writing, since in the structure of the Avicennian investigation of the soul three instances of sublunary souls can also be isolated, namely the vegetative, the animal, and the human soul. At the same time, however, it is also apparent that Avicenna attempts to bring Aristotle's teaching to completion through the procedure of deriving corollaries (*tafrī'*, lit. *ramification*)[16] from the fundamental principles.[17] In the *Nafs* Avicenna's completion of Aristotle's teaching in *De anima* happens in essentially two ways: (i) *expansion* of the Aristotelian treatment of the soul, and (ii) *integration* of philosophical, mainly Aristotelian, knowledge with other forms of knowledge which are connected with religious beliefs.

(i) *Expansion* of the Aristotelian treatment of the soul is observable in three major cases. (i.i) The theoretical framework of the investigation of the soul, which Aristotle provides in *De an.*, II, 1–3 in order to situate the inquiry into the soul within the framework of his investigation of the principles of composite substances, is substantially enlarged in Avicenna's *Nafs*: for it is more articulated and occupies the entire first treatise with the exclusion of chapter I, 2, which contains a doxography of the opinions of the predecessors about the soul (we shall discuss about *Nafs*, I in the following chapters). (i.ii) The imposing treatment of vision occupies the entire third treatise,[18] which represents a third of the Avicennian work, whereas in Aristotle the treatment of the same subject, far from being exhaustive, is limited to one chapter, i.e. II, 7, and is supplemented by *De sensu et sensibilibus*, 3, where more pieces of information are provided, for example about the physiology of the eye. The reason

---

16 It has already been pointed out that Avicenna refers to *furū'*, in *Madḫal*, I, 1, 9.13. The reference to the process of derivation of corollaries from the fundamental principles (*tafrī' 'alà l-uṣūl*) with relation to Avicenna's *Šifā'* can be found in a passage from the *Letter to Kiyā* (in *Arisṭū 'inda l-'Arab*, ed. 'A. Badawī, Maktabat al-nahḍa al-miṣriyya, Cairo 1947, 1978², 119–122; in part. 121, 6–8; for the English translation and a study of it, see Gutas, *Avicenna and the Aristotelian Tradition*, 53–58). The same idea can be found in Avicenna's reworking of Ptolemy's *Harmonica* (*Mūsīqà*, I, 1, 3.7–9, where Avicenna uses the terms *mutafarri'*, l. 8, and *furū'*, l. 9). Lastly, the term *furū'* in order to refer to Avicenna's procedure of derivation of corollaries occurs many times in *Memoirs of a Disciple writing from Rayy* (see Y. Mahdavī, *Fihrist-i nusḫahā-yi muṣannafāt-i Ibn-i Sīnā*, Intišārāt-i Dānišgāh-yi Tihrān, Tehran 1333/1954, 209, 12–13; the English translation is provided in Gutas, *Avicenna and the Aristotelian Tradition*, 59–67).

17 The fact that in the natural philosophy of the *Šifā'* Avicenna noticeably diverges from Aristotle is pointed out by Avicenna himself, in *Madḫal*, I, 1, 11.3–4; and by his biographer al-Ğūzğānī who, however, explains it by resorting to an apologetic tone, explaining it as the result of the unavailability of the Aristotelian physical works while he was composing that part of the *Šifā'*, and of his consequent reliance on memory. See *The Life of Ibn Sina*, 57.6–59.8. For the same explanation, see also al-Ğūzğānī's introduction to the *Šifā'*: *Madḫal*, 2.16–3.2. For a thorough analysis of al-Ğūzğānī's Introduction, his intentions in writing it, and Avicenna's Prologue to the *Šifā'*, see A. Bertolacci, S. Di Vincenzo, "On Avicenna's Prologue and Ğūzğānī's Introduction to the *Kitāb al-Šifā'* (*Book of the Cure/of the Healing*)", forthcoming.

18 In some manuscripts this treatise bears the title *Fī l-ibṣār* (*De visu* in some Latin manuscripts).

for this expansion might be that at his time several opinions about vision circulated[19] and, therefore, Avicenna might have decided to settle the issue by analysing the elements involved in the process of vision (color, light, and transparent), outlining and refuting the opinions on vision that he deemed wrong, and presenting his own theory. What is more, this detailed treatment of vision is announced in *Maʿādin*, II, 2, where the verification that even Aristotle wavered on this issue might have prompted Avicenna to tackle this topic directly in the place that he deemed more appropriate for it, that is, the *Nafs*.[20] (i.iii) The discussion on the internal senses, which covers the

---

19 Avicenna groups these opinions in three major groups, each of them having further internal subdivisions (*Nafs*, III, 5, 115.20 – 1 [212.32 – 3]: "We say: the well-known doctrines about this topic (*sc.* vision) are three, even though each of them has [internal] subdivisions (*wa-in kāna yatafarraʿu* [*habeat subdivisiones*])"). The first two groups endorse the extramission (or emission) theory of vision (the first group holds that the ray emitted from the eye actually performs vision, whereas the second group holds that the ray uses the air – or any other transparent medium – as an instrument in order to perform vision), whereas the third group endorses the Aristotelian intromission theory of vision. On Avicenna's presentation and refutation of these theories of vision, see D. C. Lindberg, *Theories of Vision from Al-Kindi to Kepler*, University of Chicago Press, Chicago-London 1976, 43 – 52. For a similar grouping of the major theories of vision, see *Maʿādin*, II, 2 (40.11: "The doctrines reckoned of some importance concerning the visual perception (*idrāk al-baṣar*) of these apparitions (*ašbāḥ*) are three"). More on this text in following footnote.

20 See *Maʿādin*, II, 2, 43.3 – 6: "This is the reason why the First Teacher (*sc.* Aristotle) did not distance himself [from this theory] in this place of his book (*fī hāḏā l-mawḍiʿ min kitābihī*, i.e. *Meteorology*, III, 4, 373 a35 – b10); rather, he made use of the reflection of sight (*inʿkās al-baṣar*, i.e. ἀνάκλασις), since that [theory] was more famous and better known, and since the discourse on the sense and what is sensed (*al-qawl fī l-ḥiss wa-l-maḥsūs*) had not been made clear yet. He then conformed to what was well-known. The verification (*taḥqīq*) of this entire [issue] [will be found] in the section that follows this section (*fī l-fann allaḏī yalī hāḏā l-fann*, *sc.* in the *Nafs*)". Aristotle seemed to waver on the explanation of the process of vision: for, in *De anima*, II, 7 and *De sensu*, 3 he endorses an intromission theory of vision, which primarily focuses on a physical explanation based on the role of the transparent and the light in the visual process, and on the physiology of the eye. In *Meteorology*, III, 2 and 4, by contrast, he provided a theory of vision based on the mathematical rules of optics and on the concepts of sight-streams and reflection (ἀνάκλασις) in order to explain optical phenomena such as halo, rainbow, and mock sun. In this connection, the quotation from *Maʿādin* offers two interesting elements: (i) Avicenna seems to believe that Aristotle provides his accomplished exposition of his theory of vision in the *Parva naturalia* (*al-qawl fī l-ḥiss wa-l-maḥsūs* has to be interpreted as an explicit reference to the Aristotelian writing that in Arabic tradition was named after the first treatise of Aristotle's collection, i.e. *De sensu et sensibilibus*); (ii) Avicenna defers the settlement of this issue to the following section, which is precisely the *Nafs*, because he seems to deem it irrelevant to the meteorological investigation. Consequently, it seems fair to conclude that in the *Nafs* Avicenna intends to provide the most exhaustive treatment of this topic by adding elements drawn from the Arabic version of Aristotle's *Parva naturalia*. Furthermore, it seems to be no accident that the only two occurrences of *al-muʿallim al-awwal* are found in *Nafs*, III in connection with the defence of the intromission theory of vision, namely Aristotle's mature and accomplished theory of vision. See, for instance, *Nafs*, III, 7, 149.19 – 22 [266.96 – 00]: "In general, how good was the discourse of the First Teacher (*sc.* Aristotle) when he said: for what is seen to stretch from the wideness to the narrowness, then to come together therein, is more helpful to the verification of its (*sc.* of what is seen) form than for what sees to go out of the eye expanding in the wideness". For the fact that the investigation of vision belongs to different

first three chapters of the fourth treatise, is more complex and more structured than what can be considered the corresponding discussion in Aristotle's *De anima.* For Aristotle devotes the first three chapters of the third book of *De anima* respectively to the common sense (III, 1), the relationship between sense and sensible thing and the awareness of perception (III, 2), and φαντασία (both retentive and compositive imagination), a faculty that will be included among internal senses later on (III, 3), and he writes another independent writing on memory, which will be also included among internal senses, namely *De memoria et reminiscentia*, which is part of the collection of *Parva naturalia.*

In all the aforementioned cases, Avicenna's *expansion* of Aristotle's *De anima* seems to be based both on other Aristotelian treatises belonging to the constellation of his biological writings, like the block of treatises known as *Parva naturalia*, and on the works of Greek commentators of Aristotle available in Arabic translation, which supplemented, refined, or corrected Aristotelian theory.[21] As a further example of expansion there might be added the treatment of the cardiac pneuma as the primary vehicle (*maṭiyya, markab*)[22] of the psychic faculties in *Nafs*, V, 8, which combines Aristotle's doctrine of innate vital heat, which is expounded in his zoological writings, and medical (primarily Galenic) discoveries about pneuma, and connects the global investigation of the soul with the investigation of its material counterpart, i.e. the inquiry into animal body and its properties (anatomy).[23]

---

disciplines, i.e. natural philosophy and mathematics, in different respects, see *Maʿādin*, II, 2, 46.13–4: "These things are then like premises and preliminary steps (*ka-muqaddimāt wa-tawṭiʾāt*). Some of them depend on the discipline of geometry (*ʿalà ṣināʿat al-handasa*); some of them [depend] on optics (*ʿalà ʿilm al-baṣar*), and we shall deal with it in its [proper] place (*wa-naḥnu natakallamu fīhi fī mawḍiʿihī*); and some of them [depend] on the examination by means of sense (*ʿalà l-imtiḥān bi-l-ḥiss*)". On Aristotle's different opinions about vision, see P. Lettinck, *Aristotle's* Meteorology *and its Reception in the Arab World. With an Edition and Translation of Ibn Suwār's* Treatise on Meteorological Phenomena *and Ibn Bājja's* Commentary on the Meteorology, Brill, Leiden-Boston-Köln 1999, in part. 243–46.

21 See T. Alpina, "Retaining, Remembering, Recollecting. Avicenna's Account of Memory and Its Sources", in V. Decaix, C. Thomsen Thörnqvist eds., *Aristotle's* De memoria et reminiscentia *and Its Reception*, Brepols Publishers, Studia Artistarum, Turnhout forthcoming.

22 See *Nafs*, III, 7, 144.2 [*markab, vehiculum*, 257.50], and V, 8, 263.9 [*maṭiyya, vehiculum*, 175.50].

23 In this connection in *Nafs*, V, 8 there are four references to the *Kitāb al-Ḥayawān* (*Liber De animalibus* in Latin, *Book of Animals* in English, henceforth *Ḥayawān*), the eighth section of the natural part of the *Šifāʾ*, by means of which Avicenna intends to connect the psychological discourse with its anatomical counterpart. In particular, in these four places of the *Ḥayawān* highly controversial anatomical issues (the origins of blood vessels and nerves, the male and female role in reproduction, and the anatomy and function of the heart) are discussed, and Aristotelian teachings are supplemented and, in some cases, corrected by medical discoveries made by Galen (see Chapter 3, n. 121). Moreover, the strong connection between Avicenna's psychology and his medical doctrines is testified, for example, by the explicit reference to not further specified "medical books" (*fī kutubinā l-ṭibbiyya*, *Nafs*, IV, 4, 201.13), which prompted al-Ǧūzǧānī to insert an excerpt from Avicenna's medical treatise *Maqāla fī l-adwiya al-qalbiyya* (*De Medicinis cordialibus*, or *De Viribus cordis* in Latin, *On Cardiac Remedies* in English, henceforth *Adwiya Qalbiyya*) between the end of the fourth treatise and the beginning of

(ii) As for the *integration* of the philosophical knowledge with other forms of knowledge connected with religious beliefs, two crucial examples have to be taken into account: (ii.i) Avicenna's doctrine of prophecy, to which there are devoted chapters IV, 2 ("imaginative prophecy"), IV, 4 ("operative prophecy"), and V, 6 ("intellectual prophecy"). There, Avicenna brings the discourse on prophecy onto the philosophical ground by relating it to the treatment of the psychic faculties belonging to the prophet insofar as he is a human being possessing a soul, though unordinary; and (ii.ii) Avicenna's treatment of the quiddity of the human rational soul in chapters V, 2–4, which goes beyond the theoretical framework provided in the first treatise, and seems to meet a different theoretical need, that is, the necessity to ensure the human soul's individual immortality. In the first case the cause of the process of integration is evident: a religious subject is dealt with within a philosophical framework, and is, therefore, legitimated on a rational basis (in addition to that, the metaphysical foundation of the psychological treatment of prophecy, and the demonstration of the prophet-legislator's necessary existence are provided in *Ilāhiyyāt*, X, 1–2). By contrast, the context of the second case is more complex. On the one hand, Avicenna's treatment of the quiddity of the human rational soul, and the demonstration of its immortality *a parte post*, was almost certainly influenced by Neoplatonic commentaries on Aristotle's *De anima*, which combined Aristotelian teaching (and hesitations) on this topic with the Platonic doctrine of the immortality of the soul *a parte ante*, in some cases because of adherence to the Christian faith, as in the case of Philoponus.[24] On the other hand, this integration might also reveal a concern extraneous to Aristotle and Aristotelianism and, perhaps, Avicenna's involvement in the debate about the nature of man and the quiddity of human soul, which occurred between the IX and X centuries and involved both philosophers and theologians.[25]

Sources

The completion and consequent transformation of Aristotle's teaching of psychology allow us to point out the main sources of Avicenna. Obviously, his main sources are Aristotle's *De anima* and the subsequent exegesis of it.

In Ibn al-Nadīm's *Kitāb al-Fihrist* (*The Catalogue*, henceforth *Fihrist*) we read the following entry about what was available in Syriac and Arabic translation of Aristotle's *De anima* and of the Late Ancient commentaries on it: "Discourse on the *De anima* (*al-kalām ʿalà kitāb al-nafs*). It consists of three books (*ṯalāṯ maqālāt*, *lit.*

---

the fifth treatise of the *Nafs*. On this excerpt, see T. Alpina, "Al-Ǧūzǧānī's Insertion of *On Cardiac Remedies* in Avicenna's *Book of the Soul:* the Latin Translation as a Clue to his Editorial Activity on *the Book of the Cure?*", *Documenti e studi sulla tradizione filosofica medievale*, 28, 2017, 365–400.

24 More on this in Chapter 2.

25 More on this in Chapter 2.

three treatises). Ḥunayn [ibn Isḥāq] translated (*naqalahū*) all of it into Syriac; Isḥāq [ibn Ḥunayn] translated all but a small part of it. Then, Isḥāq made another translation of it in its entirety by improving it. Themistius wrote an exposition (*šaraḥa*) of this book in its entirety: the first book (*lit.* treatise) in two books (*lit.* treatises), the second in two, and the third in three. There is a Syriac commentary (*tafsīr*) by Olympiodorus, which I read in the handwriting of Yaḥyà ibn ʿAdī. There is a good Syriac commentary (*tafsīr ǧayyid...suryānī*) that is attributed to Simplicius, who made it for Aṯāwālīs. There is an Arabic [version of it]. The Alexandrians had an epitome (*talḫīṣ*) of this book, about a hundred leaves. Ibn al-Biṭrīq had summaries (*ǧawāmiʿ*) of this book. Isḥāq said: 'I translated this book into Arabic from a poor manuscript and, after thirty years, I found a manuscript in the best possible condition. Then I collated (*fa-qābaltu*) the first translation (*sc.* the incomplete one) with it, and this was Themistius' exposition (*šarḥ*)'".[26]

Despite the difficulty of correctly interpreting some of Ibn al-Nadīm's references, the following pieces of information can be derived from his overview.

The Text of Aristotle's *De anima* in Arabic Translation

As for the text of Aristotle's *De anima*, it attests a complete Syriac translation made by Ḥunayn ibn Isḥāq (d. 873),[27] and apparently two translations, one incomplete and one complete, made by his son Isḥāq (d. 910).[28] However, after the list of Late Ancient commentaries on Aristotle's treatise that were available in Syriac and Arabic translation, Ibn al-Nadīm reports a statement attributed to Isḥāq according to which he worked initially with a deficient copy of the *De anima* (in either a Greek or Syriac version) and, thirty years later, upon the discovery of an excellent (presumably Greek) manuscript of Themistius' paraphrase of this work, he used it to produce a revised translation of the Aristotelian text. This statement is rendered problematic by the last sentence ("*and this was Themistius' exposition*"), whose reference has been variously interpreted even by other bio-bibliographers quoting Ibn al-Nadīm's

---

26 Ibn al-Nadīm, *Kitāb al-Fihrist*, G. Flügel, J. Rodiger, A. Müller eds., 2 vols., Leipzig 1871–1872, 251.11–18. The English translation is that provided by B. Dodge with minor modifications; Ibn al-Nadīm, *The Fihrist. A Tenth-century Survey of Muslim Culture*, ed. and transl. by B. Dodge, New York-London 1970, 604–605. For a thorough analysis of Ibn al-Nadīm's entry, see F. E. Peters, *Aristoteles Arabus. The Oriental translations and commentaries on the Aristotelian Corpus*, coll. "Monographs on Mediterranean Antiquity" 2, Brill, Leiden 1968, 40–45.

27 For information about Ḥunayn ibn Isḥāq, see A. Z. Iskandar, *Ḥunayn ibn Isḥāq*, in H. Selin ed., *Encyclopaedia of the History of Science, Technology, and Medicine in Non-Western Cultures*, Springer, New York 2008, 1081–1083, and the bibliography quoted therein.

28 For information about Isḥāq ibn Ḥunayn, see G. M. Cooper, *Isḥāq ibn Ḥunayn*, in T. Hockey et alii eds., *The Biographical Encyclopedia of Astronomers*, Springer, New York 2007, 578, and the bibliography quoted therein.

entry:[29] for instance, almost two hundred and fifty years later, Ibn al-Qifṭī reports a modified version of the last sentence, having Isḥāq revise an earlier translation of both Aristotle and Themistius.[30] Ibn al-Nadīm's entry and, in particular, its final sentence have produced a proliferation of translations: Ibn al-Nadīm and Ibn al-Qifṭī considered Isḥāq the Arabic translator of both Aristotle's *De anima* and Themistius' paraphrase, though whether one or both received a later recension by him is not clear.[31]

The evidence of the extant manuscripts supplements the information provided by the bio-bibliographers: at least two Arabic translations of Aristotle's *De anima* seem to be attested.[32] In 1954 ʿA. Badawī published the only extant integral Arabic translation of Aristotle's *De anima*, and attributed it to Isḥāq, considering it his second complete translation of the Aristotelian writing.[33] However, though arguing for the existence of a second complete translation of the *De anima* by Isḥāq, Badawī wonders why it has been ignored by Avicenna who, almost a hundred and twenty years later, in his *al-Taʿlīqāt ʿalà ḥawāšī kitāb al-nafs li-Arisṭāṭālīs* (*Marginal Glosses on Aristotle's* De anima)[34] uses an incomplete translation until the lemma 431 a14 of

29 Modern scholars are inclined to interpret this final sentence as a gloss of the preceding "*a manuscript in the best possible condition*", and to understand it as a reference to the discovery of a good manuscript of Themistius' paraphrase which served as a means for emending the poor text of the *De anima* then currently available. See Peters, *Aristoteles Arabus*, 41.

30 Ibn al-Qifṭī, *Taʾrīḫ al-ḥukamāʾ*, ed. J. Lippert, Leipzig 1903, 41.12–13: "Isḥāq translated into Arabic that which Themistius has composed, from a poor manuscript, then he amended it, after thirty years, by means of a collation with a good manuscript".

31 To these two bibliographers Ibn Ǧulǧul, Ibn al-Nadīm's contemporary, can be added. He cryptically reported that Isḥāq "translated the philosopher Aristotle's book *De anima* in seven chapters which he found in Themistius' commentary" (Ibn Ǧulǧul, *Ṭabaqāt al-aṭibbāʾ wa-l-ḥukamāʾ*, ed. F. Sayyid, Cairo 1955, 69). He apparently means that Isḥāq composed, or revised, his translation with the help of Themistius' seven-chapter (book?) paraphrase. On this information, see A. L. Ivry, "The Arabic Text of Aristotle's *De anima* and Its Translator", *Oriens*, 36, 2001, 59–77, in part. 59.

32 See Ivry, "The Arabic Text of Aristotle's *De anima*", 59.

33 ʿA. Badawī, *Arisṭāṭālīs, Fī l-Nafs [...]. Rāǧaʿahā ʿalà uṣūlihā l-yūnāniyya wa-šaraḥahā wa-ḥaqqaqahā wa-qaddama lahā ʿAbdurraḥmān Badawī*, coll. "Dirāsāt Islāmiyya" 16, Cairo 1954, reprinted Bayrūt 1980. Badawī's edition is based on the ms. Istanbul, Süleymaniye Kütüphanesi, Ayasofya 2450, where the translation is attributed to Isḥāq. The identification of the author of this translation with Isḥāq was provisionally accepted by L. Minio-Paluello; see L. Minio-Paluello, "Le texte du *De Anima* d'Aristote: la tradition latine avant 1500", in *Autour d'Aristote : recueil d'études de philosophie ancienne et medievale offert à Monseigneur A. Mansion*, coll. "Bibliothèque philosophique de Louvain" 16, Publications Universitaire de Louvain, Louvain 1955, 217–243; reprinted in *Opuscula. The Latin Aristotle*, A. M. Hakkert, Amsterdam 1972, 250–276, in part. 250, n. 2.

34 Ibn Sīnā, *al-Taʿlīqāt ʿalà ḥawāšī kitāb al-nafs li-Arisṭāṭālīs*, in *Arisṭū ʿinda l-ʿArab*, ed. ʿA. Badawī, Maktabat al-nahḍa al-miṣriyya, Cairo 1947, 1978^2, 75–116. On Avicenna's *Marginal Glosses*, and on the fact that they were originally glosses, and not part of Avicenna's lost *Kitāb al-Inṣāf* (*Book of the Fair Judgement*), as S. Pines ("La 'Philosophie Orientale' d'Avicenne et sa polémique contre les Bagdadiens", *Archives d'Histoire Doctrinale et Littéraire au Moyen Age*, 27, 1952, 5–37) and J. Finnegan ("Avicenna's Refutation of Porphyrius", Avicenna Commemoration Volume, Iran Society, Calcutta 1956, 187–203) assumed, see D. Gutas, "Avicenna's Marginal Glosses on *De Anima* and the Greek Commen-

the Aristotelian text and, from that point onwards, probably where the first translation – Isḥāq's incomplete one? – interrupts, another translation.[35] Starting from this unanswered question, R. Frank conducted a rigorous philological examination of the translation published by Badawī and concluded that it was not by Isḥāq.[36] According to Frank, Isḥāq made only one incomplete and unrevised translation of the *De anima*, whose fragments are preserved in Avicenna's glosses. Furthermore, he identified the other Arabic translation used by Avicenna from the lemma 431 a14 onwards and the excerpts of the *alia translatio* attested in the Latin version of Averroes' *Long Commentary* on the *De anima* with the translation published by Badawī, but argued against the identification of the main translation used by Averroes with the one made by Isḥāq and used by Avicenna.[37]

Therefore, at least two Arabic translations of Aristotle's *De anima* are attested: 1) an incomplete translation preserved in Avicenna's *Marginal Glosses*, which is Isḥāq's first (or, according to Frank, only) incomplete translation; and 2) the anonymous translation by pseudo-Isḥāq, published by Badawī, whose fragments are referred to in Averroes' *Long Commentary* as *alia translatio*. Besides these two translations, there is the translation preserved in Latin in the lemmata of Averroes' *Long Commen-*

tatorial Tradition", *Philosophy, Science and Exegesis in Greek, Arabic and Latin Commentaries*, 2, 2004, 77–88; and id., *Avicenna and the Aristotelian Tradition*, 153–154.

35 Badawī, 109, n. 1: "In the margin of the manuscript on the top of this folio there is what follows: 'the transcript of the lemma (*nusḫat al-faṣṣ*) [of the *De anima*] up to this point is the translation of Isḥāq ibn Ḥunayn, whereas from this point [onwards] it is another translation with many improvements by the commentator (*li-l-mufassir*)'". What is immediately evident from this note is that the author of the other translation cannot be Isḥāq ibn Ḥunayn: in all likelihood the reference is to Themistius' paraphrase.

36 R. Frank, "Some Fragments of Isḥāq's Translation of the *De Anima*", *Cahiers de Byrsa*, 9, 1958–59, 231–251. According to Frank, the translation published by Badawī is based on a defective Greek manuscript.

37 H. Gätje does not agree with Frank's conclusion about the main translation of Aristotle's *De anima* used by Averroes. According to Gätje, Frank's examples are not conclusive in proving that the Aristotelian lemmata appearing in Averroes' *Long Commentary* are not those of Isḥāq's translation. However, in line with Frank, he considers the *alia translatio* as having been published by Badawī. See H. Gätje, *Studien zur Überlieferung der aristotelischen Psychologie im Islam*, coll. "Annales Universitatis Saraviensis, Philosophische Fakultät", 11, Winter, Heidelberg 1971, in part. 35–44. What is more, following Gätje, A. Ivry argues for Isḥāq ibn Ḥunayn as the common source for most of the *De anima* quotations and paraphrases given by Avicenna, Averroes, and Zeraḥyah, who translated Aristotle's *De anima* from Arabic into Hebrew in 1284; see Ivry, "The Arabic Text of Aristotle's *De anima*", 64. Ivry's position is in conflict with that of G. Bos, the editor of Zeraḥyah's Hebrew translation of the *De anima*, who believes that the same Arabic source of both the Latin translator of the lemmata in Averroes' *Long Commentary* (presumably Michael Scot) and Zeraḥyah was the tenth century Abū ʿAlī ʿIsā ibn Isḥāq ibn Zurʿa, a pupil of the better known Yaḥyà ibn ʿAdī; see G. Bos, *Aristotle's* De Anima, translated into Hebrew by Zeraḥyah Ben Isaac ben Shealtiel Ḥen. A critical edition with an introduction and index by G. B., coll. "Aristoteles Semitico-latinus" 6, Brill, Leiden 1994. For the identification of Abū ʿIsā with ibn Zurʿa, on which Bos relies, see M. Steinschneider, *Die hebräischen Übersetzungen des Mittelalters und die Juden als Dolmetscher*, Berlin 1893, 146.

tary and in the Hebrew translation of Zeraḥyah, which according to Frank is anonymous, whereas according to Ivry it is based on Isḥāq's translation, that is, on the same translation preserved in Avicenna's glosses.[38]

Greek Commentaries on the *De anima* in Arabic Translation: Direct and Indirect Evidence

As for the bulk of Late Ancient commentaries on Aristotle's *De anima* in Arabic (and Syriac) tradition,[39] Ibn al-Nadīm lists the following items: (a) an exposition (*šarḥ*) by Themistius, which is in all likelihood a reference to his paraphrase of the Aristotelian work preserved both in Greek and in Arabic;[40] (b) a Syriac[41] translation of a commentary (*tafsīr*) by Olympiodorus, which however is no longer extant either in Greek or in Syriac; (c) a Syriac and Arabic translation of a commentary (*tafsīr*) that Simplicius is said to have written for a not further specified Aṯāwālīs, which is however no longer extant;[42] (d) an epitome (*talḫīṣ*) attributed to not further specified Alexandrians,[43] which however might be a reference to Alexander of Aphrodisias' own commentary;[44] and (e) summaries (*ǧawāmiʿ*) attributed to Ibn al-Biṭrīq, which seem to refer

38 Other contributions, essential to reconstructing the vicissitudes of the Arabic translation of Aristotle's *De anima*, are the following: A. Elamrani-Jamal, "De anima. *Tradition arabe*", in *Dictionnaire des Philosophes Antiques.* Publié sous la direction de R. Goulet. Supplement, avec la collaboration de J.-M. Flamand, M. Aouad, Editions du CNRS, Paris 2003, 346–358; and, R. Walzer, "New Light on the Arabic Translations of Aristotle", *Oriens*, 6, 1953, 91–142.

39 For an exhaustive study of the Arabic translations of Late Ancient commentaries on Aristotle, see C. D'Ancona, "Commenting on Aristotle. From Late Antiquity to the Arab Aristotelianism", in W. Geerlings, C. Schulze eds., *Der Kommentar in Antike und Mittelalter.* Vol. 1. *Beiträge zu seiner Erforschung*, Brill, Leiden 2002, 200–251.

40 Themistius, *In libros Aristotelis De anima paraphrasis*, *Commentaria in Aristotelem Graeca*, vol. 5.3, ed. R. Heinze, G. Reimer, Berlin 1899. For the edition of its Arabic translation, see Ṯāmisṭiyūs, *Kitāb al-nafs li-Arisṭūṭālīs. An Arabic Translation of Themistius' Commentary on Aristotle's* De Anima, M. Lyons ed., Oriental Studies II, Cassirer, Oxford 1973.

41 Here Ibn al-Qiftī has *ǧayyid* (*good*) instead of *suryānī* (*Syriac*); see al-Qifṭī, *Taʾrīḫ*, 41.9.

42 A commentary attributed to Simplicius is preserved in Greek. See Simplicius, *In libros Aristotelis De anima commentaria*, ed. M. Hayduck, *Commentaria in Aristotelem Graeca*, vol. 11, G. Reimer, Berlin 1882. Its authorship is, however, disputed. For its attribution to Priscianus Lydus (*fl.* VI century), see F. Bossier, C. Steel, "Priscianus Lydus en de 'In De anima' van pseudo(?)-Simplicius", *Tidschrift voor Filosofie*, 34, 1972, 761–822, and Priscian, *On Theophrastus on Sense-Perception*, within Simplicius, *On Aristotle's On the Soul* 2.5–12, trans. by P. Huby and C. Steel, in collaboration with J. O. Urmson; notes by P. Lautner, Duckworth, London 1997. For its attribution to Simplicius, see I. Hadot, *Le problème du néoplatonisme alexandrin: Hiéroclès et Simplicius*, Etudes Augustiniennes, Paris 1978, Appendice, 193–202, and ead., "Simplicius or Priscianus? On the Author of the Commentary on Aristotle's *De anima*", Mnemosyne, 55/2, 2002, 159–199.

43 Here Ibn al-Qiftī has *Iskandar* (*Alexander* [*of Aphrodisias*]) instead of *Iskandarāniyyūna* (*Alexandrians*); see al-Qifṭī, *Taʾrīḫ*, 41.9.

44 Alexander's own *De anima* has been proved to depend on materials from his lost commentary on the Aristotelian work. See P. Donini, "Testi e commenti, manuali e insegnamento. La forma sistema-

to the anonymous paraphrase of Aristotle's *De anima* preserved both in Arabic and in Persian, whose redaction has been attributed to Ibn al-Biṭrīq.[45]

Ibn al-Nadīm as well as other bio-bibliographers do not attest an Arabic translation of Philoponus' commentary on the *De anima*;[46] however, given the echoes of his doctrines in Arabic authors such as al-Kindī and Avicenna, the hypothesis has been formulated that it circulated in the Arabic world,[47] though in what form it is not clear.[48]

On the basis of this information, we can conclude that Avicenna had at his disposal at least two translations of Aristotle's *De anima*, namely the one preserved in his *Marginal Glosses* until *lemma* 431 a14, and the one used from *lemma* 431 a14 onwards. In addition to these two, Avicenna very likely knew the Arabic translation of Themistius' paraphrase and the anonymous paraphrase attributed to Ibn al-Biṭrīq.

Supplementing Aristotle with Aristotle and Other Sources

Aristotle's *De anima* and the Late Ancient exegesis of it, however, were not the only literature on psychology available to Avicenna. A complement to these works is represented by the so-called *Parva naturalia*, a collection of treatises which Aristotle himself conceived as a supplement to his treatment of psychic faculties in the *De*

---

tica e i metodi della filosofia in età postellenistica", in W. Haase, H. Temporini eds., *Aufstieg und Niedergang der römischen Welt*, II 36.7, Berlin-New York 1994, 5027-5100, in part. 5045–5056. For the edition of this treatise, see Alexander of Aphrodisias, *Praeter commentaria scripta minora. De anima liber cum mantissa, Quaestiones, De Fato, De Mixtione*, ed. I. Bruns, Reimer, Berlin 1887–1892.

45 For the edition of this paraphrase, which contains Philoponian materials, see R. Arnzen, *Aristoteles'* De anima. *Eine verlorene spätantike Paraphrase in arabischer und persischer Überlieferung. Arabischer Text nebst Kommentar, quellengeschichtlichen Studien und Glossaren*, Brill, Leiden 1998; and id., De anima. *Paraphrase arabe anonyme*, in *Dictionnaire des Philosophes Antiques*, 359–365.

46 Philoponus, *In Aristotelis De anima libros commentaria*, ed. M. Hayduck, *Commentaria in Aristotelem Graeca*, vol. 15, G. Reimer, Berlin 1897. For the debate about the authorship of the commentary on the third book of the *De anima*, see H. J. Blumenthal, "John Philoponus and Stephanus of Alexandria: Two Neoplatonic Christian Commentators on Aristotle?", in D. J. O'Meara ed., *Neoplatonism and Christian Thought*, State University of New York Press, Albany 1982, 54–63; P. Lautner, "Philoponus, In De Anima III: Quest for an author", *Classical Quarterly*, 42, 1992, 510–22; and R. Sorabji, *Philoponus and the rejection of Aristotelian science*, Duckworth, London 1987 (where the author prudently speaks of "disputed Greek commentary on book 3"). Recently, Pantelis Golitsis has supported Philoponus' authorship of this part of the commentary, see "John Philoponus on the third book of Aristotle's *De anima*, wrongly attributed to Stephanus", in R. Sorabji ed., *Aristotle Re-Interpreted. New Findings on Seven Hundred Years of the Ancient Commentators*, Bloomsbury Publishing, London 2016, 393–412.

47 See J. Jolivet, *L'Intellect selon Kindī*, Brill, Leiden 1971, in part. 50–73; D. Gutas, "Philoponos and Avicenna on the Separability of the Intellect", *The Greek Orthodox Theological Review*, 31, 1986, 121–129; and id., "Avicenna's Marginal Glosses"; R. Wisnovsky, *Avicenna's Metaphysics in Context*, Cornell University Press, Ithaca, NY 2003, in part. 113–114, 137.

48 For the Arabic tradition of Philoponus' works, see E. Gannagé, "Jean Philopon. Tradition arabe", in *Dictionnaire des Philosophes Antiques*, 503–563.

anima.[49] The entry of the *Fihrist* about what was available in Arabic translation of the *Parva naturalia* is extremely meagre and not entirely clear: "Discourse on *De sensu et sensato* (*al-kalām ʿalà kitāb al-ḥiss wa-l-maḥsūs*). It consists of two books (*maqālatā-ni, lit.* two treatises). No translation (*naql*) which can be relied upon is known or mentioned. What is mentioned is a small portion [of it] that al-Ṭabarī derived from Abū Bišr Mattà ibn Yūnus".[50]

Two preliminary considerations about this entry can be made. Firstly, the *Parva naturalia* seems to have been known in the Arabic tradition by the title of *Kitāb al-Ḥiss wa-l-maḥsūs* (*Book of Sense Perception and What is Sensed*), which is the title of the first treatise of Aristotle's original collection. Secondly, it is said to consist of two books. However, this description of the work fits with neither the global structure of the *Parva naturalia* (it consists of nine treatises), nor the internal organization of the *De sensu et sensibilibus* (it consists of seven chapters). The pieces of information provided in this entry seem to attest that very little was known about the *Parva naturalia* in Arabic tradition, as is stated in the second part of the entry. However, Arabic philosophers must have somehow known this work (or at least some parts of it), since in their writings they show a certain acquaintance with it.[51] Advancements have been

49 Aristotle, *De sensu*, 1, 436 a1–6: "Having now considered the soul, by itself, and its several faculties, we must make a survey of animals and all living things, in order to ascertain what functions are peculiar, and what functions are common, to them. What has been already determined respecting the soul must be assumed throughout. The remaining parts of our subject must be now dealt with, and we may begin with those that come first" (tr. J. I. Beare). The treatises making up the *Parva naturalia* are: (i) *De sensu et sensibilibus* (436a1–449b3); (ii) *De memoria et reminiscentia* (449b3–453b11); (iii) *De somno et vigilia* (453b11–458a32); (iv) *De insomniis* (458a33–462b11); (v) *De divinatione per somnum* (462b12–464b18); (vi) *De longitudine et brevitate vitae* (464b19–467b9); (vii.a) *De iuventute et senectute*, and (vii.b) *De vita et morte* (467b10–470b5); (viii) *De respiratione* (470b6–480b30). The *De spiritu* (481a1–486b4), which is sometimes added to them, is spurious. It seems that we owe the label "*Parva naturalia*" to Giles of Rome (d. 1316). More information on this in B. Bydén, "Introduction: The Study and Reception of Aristotle's *Parva naturalia*", in *The Parva naturalia in Greek, Arabic and Latin Aristotelianism. Supplementing the Science of the Soul*, eds. B. Bydén, F. Radovic, Springer, Cham 2018, 1–50, in part. n. 12.

50 Ibn al-Nadīm, *Fihrist*, 251.19–20. For a thorough analysis of Ibn al-Nadīm's entry, see Peters, *Aristoteles Arabus*, 45–47. Al-Qifṭī reports the same information provided by Ibn al-Nadīm with the exception of the name of al-Ṭabarī; see al-Qifṭī, *Taʾrīḫ*, 41.14–16.

51 It should be noted that both al-Kindī and al-Fārābī refer to the *Parva naturalia* in their list of Aristotle's writings. In particular, in the *Treatise on the Quantity of Aristotle's Books and What is Required for the Attainment of Philosophy* (*Risāla fī kammiyya kutub Arisṭāṭālīs wa-mā yuḥtāğu ilayhi fī taḥṣīl al-falsafa*, ed. Guidi-Walzer) al-Kindī mentions *De sensu et sensato* (*al-Ḥiss wa-l-maḥsūs*), *De somno et vigilia*, and *De longitudine et brevitate vitae*, together with the *De anima*, among the psychological writings (this reflects the contents of the *Kitāb al-Ḥiss wa-l-maḥsūs*). By contrast, in al-Fārābī's *Philosophy of Aristotle* (*Falsafat Arisṭūṭālīs*, ed. Mahdi) *Parva naturalia* are said to encompass the following topics: (i) the condition of health and disease (*De sanitate et morbo*); (ii) the different ages (*De iuventute et senectute*); (iii) the length and shortness of life (*De longitudine et brevitate vitae*); (iv) life and death (*De vita et morte*); (v) the senses, the sensory organs, and sensible objects (*De sensu et sensibilibus*); (vi) the types of local motion (*De incessu animalium*); (vii) respiration (*De respira-*

made in our knowledge of the vicissitudes of the *Parva naturalia* in Arabic tradition by H. Daiber, who discovered a copy of the *Kitāb al-Ḥiss wa-l-maḥsūs* preserved in one single, acephalous, and rather late manuscript, i.e. MS Rampur, Raza Library, Ar. 1752,[52] of which R. Hansberger is currently preparing the critical edition. It is more an adaptation than a proper translation, where excerpts from the Aristotelian text are combined with Neoplatonic and Galenic materials, perhaps due to the adaptor's own concerns. The adaptation, which seems to be related to al-Kindī's circle (IX century), consists of three treatises (*maqāla*), encompassing respectively the topics of external senses, their organs, and their objects (I); memory and recollection, sleep, dreams, and divination (II); length and shortness of life (III).[53] It is very likely that, like his predecessors, Avicenna had access to this reworking of the Aristotelian text.

The direct acquaintance with Galen's writings in Arabic translation certainly influenced Avicenna. Even though this influence is more clearly detectable in his medical works, in particular though not exclusively in the *Kitāb al-Qānūn fī l-ṭibb* (*Liber canonis* in Latin, *Canon of Medicine* in English, henceforth *Qānūn*), and in writings more directly connected with medicine, like the *Ḥayawān*, where Galen is referred to by the epithet *The excellent among physicians* (*fāḍil al-aṭibbāʾ*), or *The excellent physician* (*al-ṭabīb al-fāḍil*),[54] in *Nafs* the use of Galenic concepts and terminology,[55] as well as explicit references to medical works depending on Galen are attested.[56]

tione); (viii) the status of sleep and wakefulness, dreams and dream-visions (*De somno et vigilia*; *De insomniis*; *De divinatione per somnum*); (ix) memory and recollection (*De memoria et reminiscentia*). Al-Fārābī's list of topics seems to depend on the introductory lines of Aristotle's *De sensu*, 1, 436 a7–b1.

52 See H. Daiber, *Salient Trends of the Arabic Aristotle*, in G. Endress, R. Kruk eds., *The Ancient Tradition in Christian and Islamic Hellenism: Studies on the Transmission of Greek Philosophy and Sciences* dedicated to H. J. Drossaart Lulofs on his ninetieth birthday, Brill, Leiden 1997, 29–41, in part. 36–41.

53 For the text and the contents of the Arabic adaptation of Aristotle's *Parva naturalia* see R. E. Hansberger, "Length and Shortness of Life Between Philosophy and Medicine: The Arabic Aristotle and his Medical Readers", in P. Adamson, P. E. Pormann eds., *Philosophy and Medicine in the Islamic World*, The Warburg Institute, London, 2018, 48–74; ead., "Representation of Which Reality? "Spiritual Forms" and "*maʿānī*" in the Arabic Adaptation of Aristotle's *Parva naturalia*", in B. Bydén, F. Radovic eds., *The Parva naturalia in Greek, Arabic and Latin Aristotelianism. Supplementing the Science of the Soul*, Springer, New York 2018, 99–121; ead., "Plotinus Arabus Rides Again", *Arabic Sciences and Philosophy*, 21, 2011, 57–84; ead., "*Kitāb al-Ḥiss wa-l-maḥsūs:* Aristotle's *Parva naturalia* in Arabic Guise", in C. Grellard, P.-M. Morel eds., *Les* Parva naturalia *d'Aristote: Fortune antique et médiévale*, Paris, 2010, 143–162; ead., "How Aristotle Came to Believe in God-given Dreams: The Arabic Version of *De divinatione per somnum*", in L. Marlow ed., *Dreaming Across Boundaries: The Interpretation of Dreams in Islamic Lands*, Ilex Foundation and Center for Hellenic Studies, Washington-Cambridge, MA 2008, 50–77; ead., *The Transmission of Aristotle's* Parva naturalia *in Arabic*, Unpublished DPhil diss., University of Oxford 2007.

54 The epithet by which Avicenna refers to Galen is similar to the epithets by which he refers to Alexander of Aphrodisias, namely *fāḍil al-qudamāʾ al-mufassirīna* ("the excellent among the ancient commentators", *Nafs*, III, 7, 149.5 [265.78]), and *fāḍil al-mutaqaddimīna* ("the excellent among the predecessors", *Ilāhiyyāt*, IX, 3, 393.16–17 [464.92–93]). This can be considered as a sign of the

Moreover, for the place assigned to the human soul in his cosmology, Avicenna seems to be in debt to Neoplatonic metaphysics and, in particular, to the so-called *Theologia Aristotelis* (a sort of paraphrase of Plotinus' *Enneads* IV-VI), and to *Liber de causis* (a reworking of Proclus' *Elementatio Theologica*),[57] whereas, for his noetics, he might have been influenced by Themistius' paraphrase of Aristotle's *Metaphysics*

high esteem in which Avicenna held Galen, who seems to be equated with one of the most important and admired philosophers of the Peripatetic tradition.

55 Besides the anatomical issues contained in *Nafs*, V, 8, see *Nafs*, I, 5, 50.13–51.16 [99.79–102.15] (for a parallel passage, see *Naǧāt*, 341.11–343.9, ed. Danišpazuh). There, Avicenna arranges the psychic faculties into a hierarchy by using the categories of 'ruling' (*ra'usa* [*imperare*]) and 'serving' (*ḫadama* [*deservire/famulari/servire/subesse*]) drawn from Galen. Moreover, there he mentions the Galenic "four natural faculties" (*al-quwà l-ṭabī'iyya al-arba'* [*quattuor virtutes naturales*]), that is, digestive (*hāḍima, digestiva*), attractive (*ǧāḏiba, attractiva*), retentive (*māsika, retentiva*), expulsive (*dāfi'a, expulsiva*). Cf. *Qānūn*, I, i, vi, 1. More on this topic in T. Alpina, "Is Nutrition a Sufficient Condition for Life? Avicenna's Position between Natural Philosophy and Medicine", in R. Lo Presti, G. Korobili eds., *Nutrition and Nutritive Soul in Aristotle and Aristotelianism*, De Gruyter – Topics in Ancient Philosophy, Berlin-Boston 2020, 221–258; and R. E. Hall, "Intellect, Soul and Body in Ibn Sina: Systematic Synthesis and Development of the Aristotelian, Neoplatonic and Galenic Theories", in J. McGinnis ed., with the assistance of D. C. Reisman, *Interpreting Avicenna: Science and Philosophy in Medieval Islam. Proceedings of the Second Conference of the Avicenna Study Group*, Brill, Leiden-Boston 2004, 62–86.

56 Besides the mention of *medical books* in *Nafs*, IV, 4 (see n. 23 above), there are two other mentions of *medical books*, which in all likelihood refer to the *Qānūn:* 1) II, 4, 76.20 [146.21] (*fī l-kutub al-ṭibbiyya*) in connection with the classification of flavors (see *Qānūn*, III, vi, I, 2); and 2) III, 8, 156.15 [275.60] (*fī kutub al-ṭibb*) in connection with the causes of vertigo (see *Qānūn*, III, i, V, 1). Furthermore, in *Nafs*, III, 8, 151.18–19 [268.43–4], Avicenna explicitly defers the discussion of the physiology of the optic nerves to the anatomical investigation (*fī l-tašrīḥ*). In all likelihood, he is referring to *Qānūn*, III, iii, I, 1, where he deals with the physiology of the eye.

57 See Plotino, *L'immortalità dell'anima IV 7[2]. Plotiniana Arabica* (*Pseudo-Teologia di Aristotele, capitoli I, III, IX*). Introduzione, testo greco, traduzione e commento, testo arabo, traduzione e commento di C. D'Ancona, Pisa University Press, Pisa 2017; Plotino, *La discesa dell'anima nei corpi* (*Enn.* IV 8 [6]). *Plotiniana Arabica* (*Pseudo-Teologia di Aristotele, capitoli 1 e 7; "Detti del Sapiente Greco"*), ed. C. D'Ancona, Il Poligrafo, Padova 2003, 229–230; and C. D'Ancona Costa, "Avicenna and the *Liber de Causis:* A Contribution to the Dossier", *Revista Española de Filosofía Medieval*, 7, 2000, 95–114. Avicenna might also have known the treatise *Maqāla li-Furfūriyyūs fī l-nafs*, preserved in Arabic, which is attributed to Porphyry, and to which Avicenna seems to polemically refer in *Nafs*, V, 6, 240, 3–6 ("The one who has done most to confuse people concerning this [issue] is the one who composed (*ṣannafa*) for them the *Isagoge* (*Īsāġūǧī*, *sc.* Porphyry), desirous of saying confuse, poetic and mystic statements, which confine himself and others to the imaginative faculty. His books *On the intellect and the intelligibles* and his books *On the soul* (*kutubuhū fī l-'aql wa-l-ma'qūlāt wa-kutubuhū fī l-nafs*) indicate that to those provided with discernment"). For the edition of Porphyry's treatise, see W. Kutsch, "Ein Arabisches Bruchstück aus Porphyrios (?) und die Frage des Verfassers der 'Theologie des Aristoteles'", *Mélanges de l'Université St. Joseph*, 31, 1954, 263–286. It has been carefully analyzed in Jolivet, *L'Intellect*, 74–80.

Λ.[58] It is worth recalling here that Avicenna wrote a commentary both on *Theologia Aristotelis* and on *Metaphysics* Λ.[59]

Lastly, the denial of the corporeal nature of the human soul, even if in the form of an indivisible entity like an atom, which is the position of the majority of Muʿtazilites, and, by contrast, its characterization as a simple substance that does not undergo corruption, might reveal the influence on Avicenna of, if not his direct involvement in, the debate on the essence of man and the nature of the human soul, which was animated by al-Kindī, al-Nawbaḫtī, and the theologians between the IX and the X centuries.[60] Furthermore, al-Fārābī's reflection on the epistemological status of the science of the soul, and the distinction between an elementary principle of animation and the actual soul, i.e. the human rational soul, might very likely have been a source of Avicenna.[61]

The Arabic Text of Avicenna's *Nafs*

According to present knowledge, the Arabic text of Avicenna's *Nafs* is preserved in a hundred and thirty manuscripts dated from the XII to the XX centuries, whose places of copy include Turkey, Iran, Iraq, and India.[62] This impressive number of witnesses

---

58 See Thémistius, *Paraphrase de la* Métaphysique *d'Aristote: livre lambda*, traduit de l'hébreu et de l'arabe, introduction, notes et indices par R. Brague, Vrin, Paris 1999.

59 For Avicenna's commentary on *Theologia Aristotelis*, see Ibn Sīnā, *Šarḥ Kitāb Uṯūlūǧiyā l-mansūb ilà Arisṭū*, in ʿA. Badawī ed., *Arisṭū ʿinda l-ʿArab*, Maktabat al-nahḍa al-miṣriyya, Cairo 1947, 1978², 35–74. It is worth noticing that in a passage of the *Letter to Kīyā* (121.16–22 ed. Badawī), where the only reference to the *Theologia Aristotelis* is contained, Avicenna seems to have doubts about the authorship of this work. An analysis of this text can be found in Bertolacci, *The Reception of Aristotle's* Metaphysics, 47–50. On the impact of *Theologia Aristotelis* on Avicenna's thought, see G. Vajda, "Les notes d'Avicenne sur la 'Theologie d'Aristote'", *Revue Thomiste*, 51, 1951, 346–406; P. Adamson, "Correcting Plotinus: Soul's Relationship to Body in Avicenna's Commentary on the *Theology of Aristotle*", in P. Adamson, H. Baltussen, M.W. F. Stone eds., *Philosophy, Science and Exegesis in Greek, Arabic and Latin Commentaries*, in honor of Richard Sorabji, 2 vols., Supplement to the Bulletin of the Insititute Of Classical Studies 83.1–2, London 2004, 59–75; id., "Non-Discoursive Thought in Avicenna's Commentary on the *Theology of Aristotle*", in J. McGinnis ed., with the assistance of D. C. Reisman, *Interpreting Avicenna: Science and Philosophy in Medieval Islam. Proceedings of the Second Conference of the Avicenna Study Group*, Brill, Leiden-Boston 2004, 87–111. For Avicenna's commentary on *Metaphysics*, book Λ, see Avicenne (Ibn Sīnā), *Commentaire sur le livre lambda de la* Metaphysique *d'Aristote (chapitres 6–10)*. Edition critique, traduction et notes par M. Geoffroy, J. Janssens et M. Sebti, Vrin, Paris 2014. On this possible influence, see C. D'Ancona Costa, "The *Timaeus'* Model for Creation and Providence: An Example of Continuity and Adaptation in Early Arabic Philosophical Literature", in G. J. Reydams-Schils ed., *Plato's* Timaeus *as Cultural Icon*, University of Notre Dame Press, Notre Dame, IN 2003, 206–237, in part. 237, n. 80.

60 More on this in Chapter 2.

61 More on this in Chapter 2.

62 For a complete inventory of the manuscripts preserving Avicenna's *Nafs*, see Alpina, "Al-Ǧūzǧānī's Insertion of *On Cardiac Remedies*", 392–399.

has so far deterred scholars from the realization of a critical edition of the Arabic text; therefore, our knowledge of this work depends on a very limited portion of this tremendous manuscript tradition.

Five complete printed versions of Avicenna's *Nafs* are currently available, but none of them is a proper critical edition.

(1) The Tehran lithography, which was published in Tehran in 1303H/1885–6. It contains the natural philosophy and the metaphysics of the *Šifāʾ*, and is based on manuscript(s) whose number and identity however have not been established yet.[63]

(2) The edition made by Ján Bakoš in 1956,[64] which is based on five manuscripts and the Tehran lithography.

(3) The edition made by Fazlur Rahman in 1959,[65] which is based on eight manuscripts, the Tehran lithography, a manuscript containing the Latin translation of the work accomplished in Toledo in the mid-twelfth century, and the Venice edition of the Latin text (1508).

(4) The edition made by G. C. Anawati and S. Zayed at Cairo in 1975,[66] which is based on the same manuscripts used by the two precedent editors with the addition of two more manuscripts.

(5) Lastly, the edition published in Qum in 1417H/1997 by Ḥ. al-Āmulī; however, it is not clear on which manuscripts it is based.[67]

The aforementioned editions (with the exclusion of the Tehran lithography and the Āmulī edition), as well as the witnesses on which they are based, are listed in the table below.

Manuscripts	**Bakoš ed.**	**Rahman ed.**	**Anawati-Zayed ed.**
Egypt, Cairo, Maktabat Al-Azhar al-Šarīf, Beḫīt 331 *falsafa* (*ḫuṣūṣiyya*), 44988 (*ʿumūmiyya*)		x	x
Egypt, Cairo, Dār al-Kutub wa-l-Waṯāʾiq al-Qawmiyya (form.: Dār al-Kutub al-Miṣriyya), 262 *ḥikma wa-falsafa*		x	x

63 *Al-Ṭabīʿiyyāt min al-Šifāʾ li-Šayḫ al-Raʾīs Abī ʿAlī Ḥusayn Ibn ʿAbd Allāh Ibn Sīnā maʿa taʿlīqāt*, copyist ʿA. al-K. al-Šarīf al-Šīrāzī, editor Āqā Mīrzā Ḥusayn Ibn Āqā Mīrzā ʿAbbās, Madrasa Dār al-Funūn, Tehran 1303H/1885, vol. II.

64 *Psychologie d'Ibn Sīnā (Avicenne), d'après son oeuvre al-Shifāʾ*, Texte arabe vol. I, traduction annotée vol. II, J. Bakoš ed., Travaux de l'Académie Tchécoslovaque des Sciences. Section de linguistique et de littérature, Prague 1956.

65 *Avicenna's De Anima (Arabic Text), being the Psychological Part of Kitāb al-Shifāʾ*, F. Rahman ed., Oxford University Press, London-New York-Toronto 1959; repr. 1970.

66 *Al-Shifāʾ, al-Ṭabīʿiyyāt*, vol. 6: *al-Nafs*, eds. G. C. Anawati, S. Zayed, revised edition by I. Madkour, Al-Hayʾa al-miṣriyya al-ʿāmma li-l-kitāb, Cairo 1975.

67 Avicenna, *al-Nafs min kitāb al-Shifāʾ*, ed. Ḥ. al-Āmulī, Maktabat al-Iʿlām al-Islāmī, Markaz al-Nashr, Qum 1417H/1997.

Continued

Manuscripts	Bakoš ed.	Rahman ed.	Anawati-Zayed ed.
Egypt, Cairo, Dār al-Kutub wa-l-Waṯāʾiq al-Qawmiyya (form.: Dār al-Kutub al-Miṣriyya), 894 *falsafa*			x
Turkey, Istanbul, Süleymaniye Kütüphanesi, Damad İbrahim Paşa 822		x	x
The Netherlands, Leiden, Universiteitsbibliotheek, Or. 4 (Golius Collection) (Catalogue CCO, nr. 1444)		x	x
The Netherlands, Leiden, Universiteitsbibliotheek, Or. 84 (Golius Collection) (Catalogue CCO, nr. 1445)		x	x
UK, London, British Library, Oriental and India Office Collections (ex: British Museum), Ar. 1796 (Loth's catalogue, 476)	x	x	x
UK, London, British Library, Oriental and India Office Collections (ex: British Museum), Or. 2873 (British Museum Suppl. 711)	x		x
UK, London, British Library, Oriental and India Office Collections (ex: British Museum), Or. 7500			x
UK, Oxford, Bodleian Library, Pococke 114 (Uri's catalogue I, 467)	x		x
UK, Oxford, Bodleian Library, Pococke 116 (Uri's catalogue I, 471)	x	x	x
UK, Oxford, Bodleian Library, Pococke 125 (Uri's catalogue I, 435)	x	x	x
Tehran lithography	x	x	x
Swiss Confederation, Basel, Öffentliche Bibliothek der Universität Basel, D III 7 (Latin)		x	x
Venice edition (Latin)		x	x

All the aforementioned semi-critical editions are somehow deficient: none of them provides a *stemma codicum*; the editors do not choose either a manuscript or a group of manuscripts as the basis of their editions; and the variant readings seem to have been arbitrarily chosen.[68] Furthermore, the inspection of the manuscripts seems to be on the whole inaccurate: in some cases the critical apparatus does not faithfully reproduce the text transmitted by the manuscripts.[69] Lastly, in some cases the Arabic text is unsatisfactory.

68 See, for example, an excerpt from *Nafs*, I, 3, 32.19 in Rahman's edition. Here Avicenna maintains that the soul is perfection *qua* substance, not *qua* accident. However, in spite of the manuscript evidence (with the exception of ms. UK, London, British Library, Oriental and India Office Collections, Ar. 1796) and the doctrinal coherence, F. Rahman decides not to print the second element of the alternative ("*qua* accident"). In this edition there are many cases similar to this one.

69 See, for example, the crucial passage in which Avicenna provides the Aristotelian definition of the soul (*Nafs*, I, 1, 15.9 – 10 Bakoš ed.; 12.6 – 8, Rahman ed.; 10.18 – 19 Cairo ed.). Bakoš edition has no

Avicenna's *Nafs* between East and West

Avicenna's *Nafs* had an extraordinary circulation both in the East and in the West. We have already pointed at the tremendous manuscript dissemination of the Arabic text. However, the Latin tradition of this work is also impressive: its translation is attested in fifty manuscripts, of which thirty-five were copied in the XIII century, fourteen in the XIV century, and one in the XV century.[70] As can be inferred from the prologue to this translation,[71] it was produced in Toledo by Avendauth Israelita, who has been identified with the Jewish philosopher and historiographer Abraham Ibn Daūd (Avendauth in Latin, d. ca. 1180), and the archdeacon Dominicus Gundisalvi, or Gundissalinus (d. after 1181), the translator of other parts of Avicenna's *Šifāʾ*.[72] The trans-

variant for this passage, even though at a close examination at least one manuscript used by Bakoš, namely ms. Oxford, Bodleian Library, Pococke 116, has a different reading. F. Rahman makes some confusion about the text transmitted in the manuscripts and in the Tehran lithography. Lastly, the Cairo edition has no variant for this passage, even though it uses the same manuscripts used by Rahman, which attest different readings. For a detailed discussion of this passage, see Chapter 4. Another example is al-Ǧūzǧānī's insertion of the excerpt from the *Adwiya Qalbiyya*, which is attested in some manuscripts of Avicenna's *Nafs*. In the critical apparatus of their editions, Bakoš and Rahman note that between the fourth and fifth treatise of the text of Avicenna's *Nafs*, some of the manuscripts on which their editions are based attest the presence of an excerpt from the *Adwiya Qalbiyya* (Bakoš ed.: 197, n. 6; Rahman ed., 201, n. 11.). However, after having verified that this insertion was extraneous to the text of *Nafs*, they both decided not to print it. What happened in the Cairo edition is more baffling: although some of the manuscripts consulted attest the presence of the insertion – as the direct inspection of these manuscripts discloses – the editors did not even record its presence in their apparatus (Cairo ed.: 178.). More on this in Alpina, "Al-Ǧūzǧānī's Insertion of *On Cardiac Remedies*", 381–387.

70 For the description of the manuscripts containing the Latin translations of Avicenna's philosophical works see M.-Th. D'Alverny, S. van Riet, P. Jodogne, *Avicenna Latinus. Codices*, E. Peeters – Brill, Louvain-Leiden 1994.

71 For the critical edition of the Latin translation of Avicenna's *Nafs*, see Avicenna Latinus, *Liber de anima seu sextus de naturalibus IV-V*, édition critique de la traduction latine médiévale par S. van Riet, introduction sur la doctrine psychologique d'Avicenne par G. Verbeke, E. Peters – Brill, Louvain-Leiden 1968; Avicenna Latinus, *Liber de anima seu sextus de naturalibus I-II-III*, édition critique de la traduction latine médiévale par S. van Riet, introduction sur la doctrine psychologique d'Avicenne par G. Verbeke, E. Peeters – Brill, Louvain-Leiden 1972. For the prologue of the Latin translation see Avicenna Latinus, *Liber de anima seu sextus de naturalibus I-II-III*, 3.4–6.69 (3.4–4.26: the genesis of the translation (occasion, method, etc.); 4.27–6.69: the table of contents of Avicenna's work).

72 On Abraham Ibn Daūd, see M.-Th. D'Alverny, "Avendauth?", in *Homenaje a Millas-Vallicrosa*, I, Barcelona, 1954, 19–43, esp. 34. (repr. in M.-Th. D'Alverny, *Avicenne en Occident. Recueil d'articles de Marie-Thérèse d'Alverny réunis en hommage à l'auteur*, Vrin, Paris 1993, n. VIII); R. Fontaine, "Abraham Ibn Daud", *The Stanford Encyclopedia of Philosophy* (Spring 2015 Edition), Edward N. Zalta ed., URL = http://plato.stanford.edu/archives/spr2015/entries/abraham-daud/; and G. Freudenthal, "Abraham Ibn Daud, Avendauth, Dominicus Gundissalinus and Practical Mathematics in Mid-Twelfth Century Toledo", *Aleph*, 16.1, 2016, 61–106. On Domenicus Gundissalinus, see M. Alonso Alonso, "Notas sobre los traductores toledanos Domingo Gundisalvo y Juan Hispano", *Al-Andalus*, 8, 1943, 155–188; N. Polloni, "Gundissalinus and Avicenna: Some Remarks on an Intricate Philosophical Con-

lation was ordered and supported by John, the Archbishop of Toledo, to whom it is dedicated. The dedication of the translation to John, the archbishop of the seat of Toledo and the primate of the lands of Spain (*Iohanni reverentissimo Toletanae sedis archiepiscopo et Hispaniarum primati*, 3.1–2), allows us to situate this translation both chronologically and geographically. It was accomplished in Toledo (Spain) between 1152 and 1166, since John of Castellmoron became archbishop of Toledo in 1152 by succeeding Raymond de La Sauvetat (1125–1152) and remained in office until his death in 1166.[73]

This translation is extremely important for at least two reasons: firstly, because, apart from the references to psychological issues in the first book of the *Qānūn*, it was the only Avicennian work on psychology available in Latin in the XII and XIII centuries;[74] and secondly, because it was the first *exposition* on Aristotle's *De anima* available in Latin before the translation of Averroes' *Long Commentary* on the Aristotelian work (1220–1235).

Avicenna's *Nafs* can therefore be considered an extraordinary case-study of re-elaboration and systematization of the Aristotelian psychology in the Middle Ages, for Avicenna's peculiar approach to this subject-matter, the impressive operation of filtering of all the preceding philosophical traditions, and the impact of this work on subsequent thinkers.

---

nection", *Documenti e studi sulla tradizione filosofica medievale*, 28, 2017, 515–552; id. "Elementi per una biografia di Dominicus Gundisalvi", *Archives d'histoire doctrinale et littéraire du Moyen Âge*, 1, 2015, 7–22; id., "The Toledan Translation Movement and Gundissalinus: Some Remarks on His Activity and Presence in Castile", in Y. Beale-Rivaya, J. Busic eds., A *Companion to Medieval Toledo. Reconsidering the Canons*, Brill, Leiden-Boston 2018, 263–280.

73 For a thorough analysis of the prologue, see Avicenna Latinus, *Liber de anima seu sextus de naturalibus I-II-III*, 91*-103*; C. Burnett, "The Coherence of the Arabic-Latin Translation Program in Toledo in the Twelfth Century", *Science in Context*, 14 (1/2), 2001, 249–288, in part. 251; D. N. Hasse, "The social conditions of the Arabic-(Hebrew-)Latin translation movements in medieval Spain and in the Renaissance", in A.Speer, L. Wegener eds., *Wissen über Grenzen. Arabisches Wissen und lateinisches Mittelalter*, Miscellanea Mediaevalia 33, Berlin-New York 2006, 68–86; A. Bertolacci, "A Community of Translators: The Latin Medieval Versions of Avicenna's *Book of the Cure*", in C. J. Mews, J. N. Crossley eds., *Communities of Learning: Networks and the Shaping of Intellectual Identity in Europe 1100–1500*, Brepols, Turnhout 2011, 37–54. In particular, the articles by Hasse and Bertolacci focus on the social context promoting the translation enterprise of Avicenna's *Nafs* in Toledo. For the Latin translation of the sections of Avicenna's *Šifā'* see the special issue of the journal *Documenti e studi sulla tradizione filosofica medievale*, 28, 2017, vii-584, which I edited with Amos Bertolacci.

74 See D. N. Hasse, *Avicenna's* De Anima *in the Latin West. The Formation of a Peripatetic Philosophy of the Soul 1160–1300*, The Warburg Institute – Nino Aragno Editore, London-Turin 2000, 3.

Chapter Two

The Science of the Soul: An Attempt at Contextualization

> Die Bücher des Aristoteles *über die Seele* mit seinen Abhandlungen
> über besondere Seiten und Zustände derselben sind deswegen
> noch immer das vorzüglichste oder einzige Werk
> von spekulativem Interesse über diesen Gegenstand
> G. W. F. Hegel, *Enzyklopädie der philosophischen Wissenschaften im Grundrisse* (1830)

Introduction

The judgment that G. W. F. Hegel formulated about Aristotle's *De anima* shows the long-lasting legacy of the Aristotelian theory of the soul: even after more than two thousand years it has been considered the best and unparalleled treatment of the soul in terms of accuracy and speculative interest. This is even more true for the philosophers who came after Aristotle. By them he was rightfully considered the pioneer of a new discipline, that is, the *scientia de anima*, where the principle of all instances of organic life is thoroughly investigated. However, the hylomorphic model, which Aristotle uses to account for the soul as the form of an organic body, coming to be and passing away together with it, raises some problems with respect to the human rational soul. For the human rational soul seems not to be a form in the proper sense, since it does not make use of any bodily organ in order to perform its activity, i.e. intellection. Therefore, since the very essence of something can be inferred from its peculiar activity, the human rational soul seems to be separable from the body, due to its capacity for performing its activity independently of it. Hence the human soul seems to fall outside the Aristotelian hylomorphic paradigm, and not to be accounted for through it. As we shall see, in his *De anima* as well as elsewhere, Aristotle seems to be aware of the peculiar ontological status of the human soul but, apart from scattered considerations, he never directly tackles this issue.

However, the heterogeneity of the human soul might jeopardize the unity of psychology, since the unity of a science rests on the unity of its subject-matter, of the soul in this case. The followers of Aristotle, both in Greek and Arabic tradition, attempt to solve this major tension that challenges the claim of psychology to be a unitary science.

This chapter aims to reconstruct the Late Ancient and early Arabic exegetical vicissitudes of Aristotle's *De anima*, which paved the way for Avicenna's reworking of Aristotelian psychology as part of his global refoundation of Aristotle's system of science.

https://doi.org/10.1515/9783110706840-004

How It All Began

Reflections upon the subject-matter of psychology, together with those upon the place of this science and its boundaries, are found in Aristotle's *De anima*, where a new, autonomous discipline of the soul is established. For there, for the first time, a comprehensive study of the soul considered as a whole is undertaken.[1] In the prologue to this writing, before outlining the *agenda* of what is going to follow in the rest of the treatise (*De an.*, I, 1, 402 a23–b16), Aristotle provides some insightful remarks about the epistemological status of psychology: on the one hand, he emphasizes the importance of engaging in such a study, since a comprehensive knowledge of the soul would contribute to extending our knowledge in general and, in particular, in the domain of nature since the soul is the principle of *animal* life.[2] On the other hand, he distinguishes his enterprise from that of his predecessors, who focused almost exclusively on the human soul, leaving aside the wider context in which the human soul and its study should be placed.[3] Thus, the main innovation of the Aristotelian project is an interest in life in all its forms and manifestations, which caused Aristotle to be concerned with the soul: for he is persuaded that, in order to study life optimally, it is necessary to engage in the study of the principle of life, i.e. the soul.[4]

1 It is noteworthy that Plato's *Phaedo* was also known as *On the Soul.* However, there Plato's investigation of the soul is primarily an investigation of the human soul or, better, of the soul without qualification, identical with the soul belonging to human beings. In this connection, see the passage quoted in n. 3 below. *De an.*, I, 1, 402 a1–4: Τῶν καλῶν καὶ τιμίων τὴν εἴδησιν ὑπολαμβάνοντες, μᾶλλον δ' ἑτέραν ἑτέρας ἢ κατ' ἀκρίβειαν ἢ τῷ βελτιόνων τε καὶ θαυμασιωτέρων εἶναι, δι'ἀμφότερα ταῦτα τὴν περὶ τῆς ψυχῆς ἱστορίαν εὐλόγως ἂν ἐν πρώτοις τιθείημεν. For an introduction to Aristotle's investigation of the soul, see A. Falcon, "Aristotle on the Scope and Unity of the *De anima*", in G. Van Riel, P. Destrée eds., *Ancient Perspectives on Aristotle's* De anima, Leuven University Press, Leuven 2010, 167–181; M. Burnyeat, "Is an Aristotelian Philosophy of Mind Still Credible? A Draft", in M. C. Nussbaum, A. O. Rorty eds., *Essays on Aristotle's* De anima, Clarendon Press, Oxford 1992, 15–26; M. Frede, "On Aristotle's Conception of the Soul", in M. C. Nussbaum, A. O. Rorty eds., *Essays*, 93–107.

2 *De an.*, I, 1, 402 a4–7: δοκεῖ δὲ καὶ πρὸς ἀλήθειαν ἅπασαν ἡ γνῶσις αὐτῆς μεγάλα συμβάλλεσθαι, μάλιστα δὲ πρὸς τὴν φύσιν· ἔστι γὰρ οἷον ἀρχὴ τῶν ζῴων. For a recent study of the soul as the principle of life and of biological unity see D. Quarantotto, "Aristotle on the Soul as a Principle of Biological Unity", in S. Föllinger ed., *Was ist Leben? Aristoteles' Anschauungen zur Entstehung und Funktionsweise von Leben*, Franz Steiner Verlag, Stuttgart, 2010, 35–54, and ead., "Che cosa fa di una forma un'anima: L'organizzazione anatomo-fisiologica dei viventi e la sede della *psuche*", in A. Fermani, M. Migliori eds., *Attività e virtù: anima e corpo in Aristotele* (Macerata, 24–6 marzo 2004), Vita e Salute, Milano 2009, 367–381.

3 *De an.*, I, 1, 402 b1–5: σκεπτέον δὲ καὶ εἰ μεριστὴ ἢ ἀμερής, καὶ πότερον ὁμοειδὴς ἅπασα ψυχὴ ἢ οὔ· εἰ δὲ μὴ ὁμοειδής, πότερον εἴδει διαφέρουσα ἢ γένει. νῦν μὲν γὰρ οἱ λέγοντες καὶ ζητοῦντες περὶ ψυχῆς περὶ τῆς ἀνθρωπίνης μόνης ἐοίκασιν ἐπισκοπεῖν. Aristotle might be polemically referring to Plato and the Platonists.

4 For an introductory study on the soul as the principle of life, see S. Mansion, "Soul and Life in Aristotle's *De anima*", in G. E. R. Lloyd, G. E. L. Owen eds., *Aristotle on Mind and the Senses. Proceed-*

The scope of psychology – as Aristotle puts it – is, therefore, to grasp the nature and the essence of the soul and, subsequently, the accidents belonging to it, some of which seem to be affections proper to the soul itself, while some others belong to the composite *animal* due to its soul.[5] Nonetheless, the fact that in the first ten lines of the text Aristotle refers twice to animals (ζῷα) instead of to living beings in general (ζῶντα) seems to assign to psychology a *zoological orientation*,[6] according to which the *De anima* would primarily provide the explanatory resources and the conceptual framework for an optimal study of animal life.[7] The fact that the soul is said to be the principle of animals, however, does not exclude *ipso facto* that plants have soul (a position that would be in conflict with Aristotle's own words);[8] rather, it might simply mean that the scope of the *De anima* is limited to animal life, and that, consequently, the *De anima* should be understood primarily as a treatise on animal psychology.[9] Moreover, the fact that Aristotle did not write a specific treatise on

ings of the Seventh Symposium Aristotelicum, Cambridge University Press, Cambridge-London-New York-Melbourne 1978, 1–20.

5 *De an.*, I, 1, 402 a7–10: ἐπιζητοῦμεν δὲ θεωρῆσαι καὶ γνῶναι τήν τε φύσιν αὐτῆς καὶ τὴν οὐσίαν, εἶθ' ὅσα συμβέβηκε περὶ αὐτήν· ὧν τὰ μὲν ἴδια πάθη τῆς ψυχῆς εἶναι δοκεῖ, τὰ δὲ δι'ἐκείνην καὶ τοῖς ζῴοις ὑπάρχειν.

6 This expression was used for the first time by G. E. R. Lloyd in his article "Aspects of the Relationship between Aristotle's Psychology and his Zoology", in M. Nussbaum, A. Rorty eds., *Essays*, 147–167, in part. 148.

7 For a different interpretation of Aristotle's reference to ζῷα in *De an.*, I, 1, see Falcon, "Aristotle on the Scope", 168–169. Falcon maintains that at the outset of his investigation Aristotle cannot say that the study of the soul is preliminary only to the study of animals, because "the first, crucial step in his project is to provide an argument for the view that animals are a distinct class of living beings and animal life is a form of life distinct from plant life. Consequently, by translating ζῷα as animals from the very beginning the strategic importance of the *De anima* is not only overlooked; it is implicitly denied". Falcon upholds a broader reading of ζῷα by recalling Rodier's interpretation according to which "il faut probablement prendre ζῷα dans son sens le plus extensif d'être vivant" (169, n. 6). For Rodier's interpretation, see Aristote, *Traité de l'Ame*. Traduit et annoté par G. Rodier, Ernest Leroux Editeur, Paris 1900, vol. II, 6.

8 Cf. *De an.*, I, 5, 411 b27–28: ἔοικε δὲ καὶ ἡ ἐν τοῖς φυτοῖς ἀρχὴ ψυχή τις εἶναι; and *De an.*, II, 4.

9 The study of human soul somehow derives from that of animal soul, since thinking (τὸ νοεῖν) can be considered a further elaboration of perception (τὸ αἰσθάνεσθαι). P. Pellegrin offers a similar interpretation of the opening lines of the *De anima* in his article "Le *De anima* et la vie animale. Trois remarques", in *Corps et âme. Sur le* De anima *d'Aristote*, sous la direction de G. Romeyer Dherbey, études réunies par C. Viano, Vrin, Paris 1996, 465–492. In this article P. Pellegrin recognizes a sharp distinction between "animals" and "living beings" in Aristotle's use of ζῷα and ζῶντα, respectively. Moreover, he claims that in the *De anima* Aristotle reduces the general notion of soul to the animal soul: for instance, in *De an.*, III, 3, 427 a17–19 Aristotle says that the soul is primarily defined by locomotion and perception, the latter being the general capacity of discriminating (Ἐπεὶ δὲ δύο διαφοραῖς ὁρίζονται μάλιστα τὴν ψυχήν, κινήσει τε τῇ κατὰ τόπον καὶ τῷ νοεῖν καὶ φρονεῖν καὶ αἰσθάνεσθαι [...]). Locomotion and perception are the powers by which the animal is defined. Therefore, the *De anima*, Pellegrin concludes, is neither a treatise of general biology which deals with all the instances of sublunary life progressively more articulated, nor a treatise whose ultimate subject is the human soul; rather, it is a treatise of general zoology or "psychologie naturelle" (470–471). For

plants could provide further ground in support of this interpretation.[10] For it would be the case that in the *De anima* Aristotle deals with plants not because of a genuine interest in plant life, but because of the functional analogy with animals that plants exhibit on the physiological level:[11] in fact both plants and animals share in nutrition, growth, and reproduction.[12]

In mapping out his inquiry into the soul, Aristotle abides by the formal conditions laid down in the *Posterior Analytics* for all sciences: the task of the inquirer is to delimit the subject-matter of the science, to define it, and to deduce its *per se* properties.[13] Accordingly, psychology must define the essence of the soul (*De an.*, II, 1–3), from which its *per se* properties can be conveniently deduced, namely the faculties of the soul and their activities (the rest of the treatise deals with some corollaries: *De an.*, II, 12 is about sensation in general, and *De an.*, III, 12–13 deal with the teleology of animal faculties).[14] As for the *per se* properties of the soul, here also referred to as πάθη, Aristotle introduces the distinction between *peculiar* and *common* πάθη in discussing the ninth problem (ἀπορία) that arises in the investigation of the soul,[15] in order to ascertain the ontological status of the soul. For, if there is a *per se* property belonging exclusively to the soul, the soul will be an ontologically independent, separate substance; otherwise, the soul will be always bound up with the body and will not exist apart from it.[16] Examples of πάθη common to body and soul, which are the majority, are anger, courage, appetite, and, in general, sensation;

---

the central role played by sensation in Aristotle's *De anima*, see also G. R. Giardina, "'Se l'anima sia entelechia del corpo alla maniera di un nocchiero rispetto alla nave'. Plotino IV 3, 21 su Aristotele *De anima* II. 1, 413 a8–9", in M. Di Pasquale Barbanti, D. Iozzia eds., *Anima e libertà in Plotino.* Atti del Convegno Nazionale (Catania, 29–30 gennaio 2009), CUEM, Catania 2009, 70–112, in part. 76, n. 7.

10 Aristotle mentions several times a specific treatise on plants; see, for instance, *Hist. an.*, V, 1, 539 a21; *Gen. an.*, I, 2, 716 a1; 23, 731 a29–30. In *In De sensu*, 87, 11–12 Alexander of Aphrodisias implies that, even if Aristotle had actually written a treatise on plants, at his time that work was not extant anymore (καὶ ἔστι Περὶ φυτῶν Θεοφράστῳ πραγματεία γεγραμμένη· Ἀριστοτέλους γὰρ οὐ φέρεται). Theophrastus' botanical writings seem to have filled this gap.

11 L. Repici, *Uomini capovolti. Le piante nel pensiero dei Greci*, Editori Laterza, Roma-Bari 2000, 17.

12 The undeniable possibility of detecting in the "capacity for receiving something" a general pattern that provides the treatment of the sublunary instances of soul with a sort of unity does not imply that in the *De anima* plants are dealt with for their own sake. By the "capacity for receiving something" I refer to living beings' capacity for receiving the form at various degrees, inextricably linked to matter in the case of plants, with some of its material attributes in the case of animals, completely abstracted from matter in the case of human beings.

13 *Post. An.*, I, 7, 75 a38–b2.

14 *De. an.*, I, 1, 402 b25–403 a2: πάσης γὰρ ἀποδείξεως ἀρχὴ τὸ τί ἐστιν, ὥστε καθ' ὅσους τῶν ὁρισμῶν μὴ συμβαίνει τὰ συμβεβηκότα γνωρίζειν, ἀλλὰ μηδ' εἰκάσαι περὶ αὐτῶν εὐμαρές, δῆλον ὅτι διαλεκτικῶς εἴρηνται καὶ κενῶς ἅπαντες.

15 *De an.*, I, 1, 403 a3–5: ἀπορίαν δ'ἔχει καὶ τὰ πάθη τῆς ψυχῆς, πότερόν ἐστι πάντα κοινὰ καὶ τοῦ ἔχοντος ἢ ἔστι τι καὶ τῆς ψυχῆς ἴδιον αὐτῆς.

16 It is worth recalling here the well-known medieval adage "*operari sequitur esse*", already mentioned in the introduction to the present book, according to which from the peculiar activity of something the very essence of that something can be inferred.

while the only example of πάθη peculiar to the soul seems to be thinking. According to Aristotle, however, even thinking exhibits a connection with the body, since thinking involves images, and images are the remains of sensory activity.[17] Therefore, Aristotle concludes that all the *per se* properties of the soul are also common to the body,[18] because these πάθη are enmattered forms (λόγοι ἔνυλοι), namely forms that are always embodied and inseparable from their material substratum.[19]

The study of the soul and its *per se* properties is therefore said to pertain to the φυσικός since the task of the natural philosopher is precisely the investigation of the sensible substances and their constituents, i.e. matter and form,[20] and the soul seems to be a form that needs to be always instantiated in a bodily matter in order to perform its activities.[21] This picture, however, has to be refined: even though Aristotle seems definitively to have argued that thinking is also a πάθος common to body and soul and that the study of the soul is incumbent upon the natural philosopher, he still seems to doubt that the inquiry into the soul without qualification concerns natural philosophy. At the end of the prologue, in ascribing the inquiry into the soul to the natural philosopher, Aristotle seems to leave room for the possibility that the natural philosopher has to investigate not the soul in its entirety, but a certain

---

17 *De an.*, I, 1, 403 a8–10: εἰ δ'ἐστὶ καὶ τοῦτο (*sc.* τὸ νοεῖν) φαντασία τις ἢ μὴ ἄνευ φαντασίας, οὐκ ἐνδέχοιτ'ἂν οὐδὲ τοῦτ'ἄνευ σώματος εἶναι; III, 3, 427 b14–16: φαντασία γὰρ ἕτερον καὶ αἰσθήσεως καὶ διανοίας, αὕτη τε οὐ γίγνεται ἄνευ αἰσθήσεως, καὶ ἄνευ ταύτης οὐκ ἔστιν ὑπόληψις.

18 *De an.*, I, 1, 403 a16–19: ἔοικε δὲ καὶ τὰ τῆς ψυχῆς πάθη πάντα εἶναι μετὰ σώματος, θυμός, πραότης, φόβος, ἔλεος, θάρσος, ἔτι χαρὰ καὶ τὸ φιλεῖν τε καὶ μισεῖν· ἅμα γὰρ τούτοις πάσχει τι τὸ σῶμα.

19 *De an.*, I, 1, 403 a24–25: εἰ δ'οὕτως ἔχει, δῆλον ὅτι τὰ πάθη λόγοι ἔνυλοί εἰσιν.

20 Aristotle endorses the same view in *Physics*, I, 7. In that chapter Aristotle introduces the concept of form and the correlative notion of subject/matter in order to outline the ontological structure of change and to identify a metaphysical pattern which every kind of change, be it unqualified (i.e. substantial) or qualified (i.e. accidental), instantiates. Subject and form are the terms of change: the subject is the continuant, the persisting matter, the previously existing thing which undergoes the change, while the form is the something the matter comes to be. As a result of the analysis of change, Aristotle maintains that the matter and the form are not merely the principles of the different types of change, but also turn out to be the principles of the thing that emerges from the change (I, 7, 190 b17–20: φανερὸν οὖν ὡς, εἴπερ εἰσὶν αἰτίαι καὶ ἀρχαὶ τῶν φύσει ὄντων, ἐξ ὧν πρώτων εἰσὶ καὶ γεγόνασι μὴ κατὰ συμβεβηκὸς ἀλλ' ἕκαστον ὃ λέγεται κατὰ τὴν οὐσίαν, ὅτι γίγνεται πᾶν ἔκ τε τοῦ ὑποκειμένου καὶ τῆς μορφῆς). For a lucid and exhaustive analysis of this chapter (including a survey of the linguistic machinery afforded by the verb "to come to be"), see M. J. Loux, *Nature, Norm and Psyche. Explorations in Aristotle's Philosophical Psychology*, Pubblicazioni della Classe di Lettere e Filosofia, 32, Edizioni della Scuola Normale Superiore, Pisa 2004, especially Ch. 1: *Matter and Form*, 3–19. Furthermore, an overview of Aristotle's theory of sensible substances can be found in M. Frede, "The definition of sensible substances", in D. Devereux, P. Pellegrin eds., *Biologie, logique et métaphysique chez Aristote*, Les Editions du CNRS, Paris 1990, 113–129.

21 *De an.*, I, 1, 403 b17–18: ἐλέγομεν δὴ ὅτι τὰ πάθη τῆς ψυχῆς οὕτως ἀχώριστα τῆς φυσικῆς ὕλης τῶν ζῴων. It is noteworthy that at the end of the prologue to the *De anima* Aristotle refers once again to ζῷα rather than to ζῶντα. The soul is defined accordingly: εἰ δή τι κοινὸν ἐπὶ πάσης ψυχῆς δεῖ λέγειν, εἴη ἂν ἐντελέχεια ἡ πρώτη σώματος φυσικοῦ ὀργανικοῦ (*De an.*, II, 1, 412 b4–6).

part of it, namely that part of the soul which cannot exist without matter.[22] Thus, there seems to be a part of the soul that could exist without inhering in a material substratum, whose treatment is apparently deferred to another investigation and, perhaps, to another science. The best candidate for such a part is the theoretical intellect/part of the soul, whose exceptional ontological status in comparison to the other parts of the soul is pointed out at least three times in the treatise and seems to require a different approach.[23]

This first boundary of Aristotelian psychology seems to be confirmed by two crucial passages outside the *De anima:*[24] i) *Metaphysics,* VI, 1, 1026 a4–6; and ii) *De partibus animalium,* I, 1, 641 a17–b10. In the first passage, after having thoroughly spoken about natural philosophy as one branch of theoretical science, Aristotle clarifies that only that inquiry into the soul that cannot be without matter is incumbent upon the natural philosopher.[25] In the second passage, after having established that the inquiry into animals has to begin with the determination of their formal cause, i.e. the soul, Aristotle wonders whether the natural philosopher has to investigate the entire soul or some part of it,[26] expressing a quandary similar to the one expressed at the end of *De anima*, I, 1.[27]

---

22 *De an.*, I, 1, 403 a27–8: καὶ διὰ ταῦτα ἤδη φυσικοῦ τὸ θεωρῆσαι περὶ ψυχῆς, **ἢ πάσης ἢ τῆς τοιαύτης** (emphasis mine).

23 *De an.*, II, 1, 413 a3–5: ὅτι μὲν οὖν οὐκ ἔστιν ἡ ψυχὴ χωριστὴ τοῦ σώματος, ἢ μέρη τινὰ αὐτῆς, εἰ μεριστὴ πέφυκεν, οὐκ ἄδηλον; II, 2, 413 b24–7: περὶ δὲ τοῦ νοῦ καὶ τῆς θεωρητικῆς δυνάμεως οὐδέν πω φανερόν, ἀλλ'ἔοικε ψυχῆς γένος ἕτερον εἶναι, καὶ τοῦτο μόνον ἐνδέχεσθαι χωρίζεσθαι, καθάπερ τὸ ἀΐδιον τοῦ φθαρτοῦ; II, 3, 415 a11–12: περὶ δὲ τοῦ θεωρητικοῦ νοῦ ἕτερος λόγος. It is noteworthy that these passages are all from the first three chapters of the second book of the *De anima*, where Aristotle provides the theoretical framework of his investigation of the soul.

24 I deliberately leave aside the problematic notion of νοῦς θύραθεν (the intellect [coming] from outside) of *De generatione animalium,* II, 3, because that would lead us astray from the present investigation: for it involves the difficult, though fascinating, theory of generation and, in particular, of the kinds of soul that are present in the semen and foetus.

25 *Metaphysics,* VI, 1, 1026 a4–6: δῆλον πῶς δεῖ ἐν τοῖς φυσικοῖς τὸ τί ἐστι ζητεῖν καὶ ὁρίζεσθαι, καὶ διότι καὶ **περὶ ψυχῆς ἐνίας** θεωρῆσαι τοῦ φυσικοῦ, ὅση μὴ ἄνευ τῆς ὕλης ἐστίν (emphasis mine). Aristotle occasionally suggests that the immateriality of νοῦς, that is, the fact that it has no particular organic basis, could provide grounds for the exclusion of its study from psychology intended as a part of natural philosophy (*De an.*, II, 1, 413 a4–9; II, 2, 413 b24–7; III, 5, 430 a17–27). On the immateriality of νοῦς as a reason for its exclusion from the psychology, see J. Lennox, "The Place of Mankind in Aristotle's Zoology", *Philosophical Topics*, 27/1, 1999, 1–16, in part. 2.

26 *De part. an.*, I, 1, 641 a32–4: Ἀπορήσειε δ' ἄν τις εἰς τὸ νῦν λεχθὲν ἐπιβλέψας, πότερον περὶ πάσης ψυχῆς τῆς φυσικῆς ἐστι τὸ εἰπεῖν ἢ περί τινος.

27 In commenting upon this chapter J. G. Lennox writes: "In the immediately preceding discussion (cf. *De part. an.*, I, 1, 641 a17–8: Εἰ δὴ τοῦτό (*sc.* εἶδος) ἐστι ψυχὴ ἢ ψυχῆς μέρος ἢ μὴ ἄνευ ψυχῆς [...]; 641 a28: Τοιοῦτον (*sc.* οὐσία) δὲ τοῦ ζῴου ἤτοι πᾶσα ἡ ψυχὴ ἢ μέρος τι αὐτῆς) Aristotle has been hinting that there are reasons to doubt whether the *entire* soul should be an object of natural study" (Aristotle, *On the Parts of Animals. Translated with a Commentary by* J. G. Lennox, Clarendon Press, Oxford 2001, 142). Those vague suggestions reveal now a particular concern about νοῦς and its place within natural philosophy. In particular, in *De part. an.*, I, 1 Aristotle directly argues in favour of

In addition, a second boundary is detectable in the inquiry into the soul pertaining to natural philosophy: the investigation of the soul of celestial bodies seems to be ruled out. In the *De anima* there is evidence of Aristotle's exclusion of the soul of celestial bodies from the investigation of the soul he is engaging in: at least a couple of times Aristotle explicitly limits his investigation to the soul of *perishable living beings.*[28] The theoretical justification for this restriction, that is, for Aristotle's decision to focus exclusively on sublunary life, can be found in *De anima,* II, 3 where the relationship existing among sublunary souls is accounted for through the analogy between souls and rectilinear figures. In general terms, the analogy is meant to show (not without problems) that just as rectilinear figures are ordered in a series beginning with the triangle, so are souls beginning with the nutritive (or vegetative, θρεπτική) soul (414 b20 – 1). Thus, just as the triangle exists potentially in the rectangle, so the capacity for nutrition, growth, and decay exists potentially in the capacity for perception; and this crucially depends on the fact that self-nutrition, growth, and decay are constitutive activities of perishable life. The pivotal assumption here is that souls are ordered in a series, so that the lower soul can be found potentially in the higher one.[29] If the reconstruction of the argument is correct, Aristotle does not deliberately embark on the study of celestial souls because no serial relationship exists between perishable and celestial souls, and there is no serial relationship be-

---

the exclusion of νοῦς from the province of natural philosophy by using two different arguments. For a reconstruction of these arguments, see Aristotle, *On the Parts of Animals*, 142 – 44; S. Broadie, "*Nous* and Nature in *De anima* III", in J. J. Cleary ed., *Proceedings of the Boston Area Colloquium in Ancient Philosophy*, 12, 1996, 163 – 76, in part. 169 – 73 (on the first argument); W. Charlton, "Aristotle on the place of mind in nature", in A. Gotthelf, J. G. Lennox eds., *Philosophical Issues in Aristotle's Biology*, Cambridge University Press, Cambridge 1987, 408 – 423, in part. 410 – 11; Lennox, "The place of mankind".

28 *De an.*, II, 2, 413 a31 – 2: χωρίζεσθαι δὲ τοῦτο μὲν τῶν ἄλλων δυνατόν, τὰ δ' ἄλλα τούτου ἀδύνατον ἐν τοῖς θνητοῖς; *De an.*, II, 3, 415 a8 – 9: οἷς μὲν γὰρ ὑπ άρχει λογισμὸς τῶν φθαρτῶν, [...]. We shall see a similar boundary in Avicenna (*Nafs*, I, 1). More on this in Chapter 3.

29 I owe this argument to Falcon, *Aristotle and the Science of Nature*, 89 – 97. That the souls are ordered according to priority and posteriority, and that the higher is contained potentially in the lower, emerges from *De an.*, II, 3, 414 b28 – 32: παραπλησίως δ' ἔχει τῷ περὶ τῶν σχημάτων καὶ τὰ κατὰ ψυχήν· ἀεὶ γὰρ ἐν τῷ ἐφεξῆς ὑπάρχει δυνάμει τὸ πρότερον ἐπί τε τῶν σχημάτων καὶ ἐπὶ τῶν ἐμψύχων, οἷον ἐν τετραγώνῳ μὲν τρίγωνον, ἐν αἰσθητικῷ δὲ τὸ θρεπτικόν. On this aspect, see also Philoponus, *In De anima*, 206.28 – 30: καὶ ἄλλως ἔστιν ἐν ταῖς ψυχαῖς τὸ πρότερον καὶ τὸ ὕστερον· ἔνθα μὲν γὰρ ἡ λογική, ἐκεῖ πάντως καὶ αἱ λοιπαί, οὐκέτι μέντοι καὶ ἔμπαλιν. On the idea that serial organization prevents the vertical unity of souls, allowing only horizontal unity, namely the unity of the parts of the soul belonging to one and the same species of living being, see T. K. Johansen, *The Powers of Aristotle's Soul,* Oxford Aristotle Studies, Oxford University Press, Oxford 2012, 67. For the idea that souls are ordered in series, and the analogy between souls and rectilinear figures, see P. Ward, "Souls and figures: Defining the soul in the *De anima* II 3", *Ancient Philosophy*, 16, 1996, 113 – 128; and A. C. Lloyd, "Genus, species and ordered series in Aristotle", *Phronesis*, 7, 1962, 67 – 90. The discontinuity detectable within the natural, sensible world between the celestial and the sublunary realm, due to which celestial and sublunary natures cannot be explained in the same terms, clearly emerges from Aristotle's classification of substance in *Metaphysics*, XII, 1, 1069 a30 – b2.

tween them because the celestial substances are not engaged in any of the activities that are minimally constitutive of sublunary life (namely self-nutrition, growth, decay, and – at least according to the mature Aristotle – even perception). Therefore, this gap between the two realms prevents the notion of soul at work in the *De anima* from being referred to both the sublunary and celestial entities, except by equivocation.[30]

Nonetheless, if the exclusion of celestial soul is unproblematic since Aristotle does not even mention it in the *De anima*, the case of the exclusion of νοῦς is undoubtedly problematic. For, although Aristotle's firm decision of excluding the theoretical intellect from the subject of the natural philosopher's investigation emerges from external and internal pieces of textual evidence, he does devote to this topic a substantial part of the third book of his treatise, where its peculiar nature is accounted for. The inclusion of νοῦς within the programme of the *De anima* breaks the unity of its subject[31] – unity that guarantees the unity of the science[32] – and brings about a short circuit in Aristotle's theory of scientific inquiry and, in particular, in his partition of theoretical sciences whose distinction is based precisely on the identification

---

30 Aristotle does not explicitly speak of equivocity/homonymy, though he seems to be conscious of the difficulty of referring the same definition of soul to both sublunary and celestial entities. See, for example, *De an.*, I, 1, 402 b2–9, where Aristotle wonders whether the definition of soul is univocal, like the definition of "animal", or equivocal, like the definition of "animal" when it is referred to heterogeneous kinds of animal like horse, dog, human being, and star. It is telling that in the latter case, Aristotle hints at the possible equivocity of the definition of "animal" and, consequently, of "soul", by gathering together three instances of sublunary life (horse, dog, and human being) and one instance of celestial life (star). By contrast, in his own *De anima,* Alexander of Aphrodisias explicitly pointed out that the same notion of soul can be predicated of both sublunary and celestial souls *only by equivocation*; see *De anima* 28, 25–28: γίνεται δὲ ἡμῖν ὡς προεῖπον ὁ λόγος περὶ ψυχῆς τῆς τῶν ἐν γενέσει καὶ φθορᾷ· ταύτης γὰρ καὶ ὁ προειρημένος ὁρισμός· ἡ γὰρ **τῶν θεῶν** ψυχή, εἰ καὶ ταύτην δεῖ ψυχὴν καλεῖν, **ὁμωνύμως** ἂν ταύτῃ ψυχὴ λέγοιτο (emphasis mine). It is noteworthy that in the Aristotelian passage quoted above, equivocation is a problem that, in principle, might concern the relationship among all sublunary souls.

31 I consider νοῦς part of the subject of Aristotle's *De anima* as well as the vegetative and the animal soul, and not as a mere issue treated therein, by following what Aristotle says in *De an.*, II, 2. Since the definition of the soul provided in *De an.*, II, 1 is not satisfying because it does not allow inference of the features of the different kinds of soul, not the soul in general, but the different kinds of soul themselves and, in particular, their activities (intellection included) turn out to be the subject of Aristotle's investigation of the soul (cf. *De an.*, II, 2, 413 b11–13: νῦν δ' ἐπὶ τοσοῦτον εἰρήσθω μόνον, ὅτι ἐστὶν ἡ ψυχὴ τῶν εἰρημένων τούτων ἀρχὴ καὶ τούτοις ὥρισται, θρεπτικῷ, αἰσθητικῷ, διανοητικῷ, κινήσει; 414 a12–13: ἡ ψυχὴ δὲ τοῦτο ᾧ ζῶμεν καὶ αἰσθανόμεθα καὶ διανοούμεθα πρώτως). Furthermore, if Aristotle had not considered the treatment of νοῦς in the *De anima* part of the subject of psychology, he would not have bothered to point out that the treatment of some part of the soul does not pertain to the natural philosopher's task, as he seems to suggest in *Metaphysics*, VI, 1, and *De partibus animalium*, I, 1.

32 On the issue of the unity of the object of definition and its close relationship with the issue of the unity of the science to which that object belongs, see G. Galluzzo, "Il problema dell'oggetto della definizione nel commento di Tommaso d'Aquino a *Metafisica* Z 10–11", *Documenti e studi sulla tradizione filosofica medievale*, 12, 2001, 417–465.

of the kinds they are about. Consequently, since Aristotle's partition of the theoretical sciences into natural science, mathematics, and metaphysics/theology is meant to be exhaustive, psychology seems to enjoy a special status in the Aristotelian system because it does not seem to fall completely under any of them.[33]

A possible way out of this difficulty would be to isolate the soul *qua* formal principle of the activities observable in bodies as the main subject of Aristotle's *De anima*, regardless of its mode of existence and, consequently, of how its peculiar activities are performed. Aristotle seems to suggest this approach to the investigation of the soul at the beginning of *De an.*, II, 2. For, though the definition of the soul provided in II, 1 is the most comprehensive Aristotle could formulate, it is unsatisfactory – just a sketch, as Aristotle himself says[34] – since it describes rather than properly defines the soul because of its high level of generality. In order to overcome the difficulties raised by such a general account of the soul, which is unable to say anything about a specific kind of soul,[35] in II, 2 a fresh start of the investigation is provided. Here Aristotle argues for the necessity of providing another definition of the soul that is better able to explain the causal relationship between each soul and its specific body. From the beginning of this chapter, in line with what he has maintained in *Posterior Analytics*,[36] Aristotle insists that a definition (τὸν ὁριστικὸν λόγον) must show not only the fact (τὸ ὅτι), but also the reason why (τὴν αἰτίαν) something is what it is. So, with respect to the definition of the soul, Aristotle tries to focus on what can be gained from defining the soul as the first actuality of a natural, organic body, namely on what this definition says about the role of the soul.

The definition of the soul as the first actuality leads Aristotle into the "capacity-exercise" scheme or, to make this point clearer, into the framework of the "potentiality (to do something)-actualization (of such a potentiality)" scheme.[37] Since the soul is a first actuality, it is endowed with a set of unexercised capacities; but when the soul wishes, it can exercise these capacities by passing from the first to the second actuality, namely from the state of having acquired a disposition to its actual exercise. Therefore, to maintain that the soul is the first actuality of an appropriate kind of body brings out the fact that the soul is an ἐντελέχεια essentially directed towards the exercise of the capacities which are listed in II, 2 from the lowest (nutri-

---

33 See Falcon, *Aristotle and the Science of Nature*, 21. On the issue of subordination in natural science, see J. G. Lennox, "Aristotle's Nature Science: The Many and the One", *Apeiron* (Special issue: *From Inquiry to Demonstrative Knowledge: New Essays on Aristotle's* Posterior Analytics, J. H. Lesher ed.), 43, 2010, 1–23. See also L. Judson, "Aristotle and Crossing the Boundaries between the Sciences", *Archiv für Geschichte der Philosophie*, 101.2, 2019, 177–204.

34 *De an.*, II, 1, 413 a9–10: τύπῳ μὲν οὖν ταύτῃ διωρίσθω καὶ ὑπογεγράφθω περὶ ψυχῆς.

35 This is precisely the point made by Philoponus in his commentary on this chapter of Aristotle's *De anima*. See Philoponus, *In De anima*, 205.30–206.1: ὥστε ὁ λόγος ὁ ἀποδεδομένος ἐνταῦθα περὶ πάσης ψυχῆς ὑπογραφή ἐστι καὶ οὐχ ὁρισμός.

36 See *An. Post.*, II, 1–10.

37 For a general outline of the capacity-exercise scheme and for how this scheme is an instance of the more general potentiality-actuality scheme, see *Metaph.*, IX, 1–8.

tion, growth and decay) to the highest ones (perception, movement, desire, and intellection).[38] Thus, a more precise account of the soul should point at the various activities for which it is a power, by having as a model the potentiality-actuality scheme formulated in chapter II, 1: the soul as a first actuality is the principle of a set of capacities in virtue of which the composite exercises all the psychic functions.[39] Beginning the investigation of the soul with the activities and their correlative objects, which are more familiar to us, instead of with the parts of the soul responsible for them, is a suggestion made in *De an.*, I, 1.[40] According to this approach the νοῦς also would be a capacity of the human soul, which in turn is the formal principle of the human body. Thus, the subject of the treatise might be provided with the sufficient unity that is required by an Aristotelian science.

This solution, however, does not remove the unavoidable difficulty raised by the introduction of a kind of divine element in psychology which, here as well as in metaphysics[41] (and in ethics), seems to be an inalienable part of Aristotle's picture of

38 *De an.*, II, 1, 412 b11–413 a3: τοῦτο δὲ τὸ τί ἦν εἶναι τῷ τοιῳδὶ σώματι, καθάπερ εἴ τι τῶν ὀργάνων φυσικὸν ἦν σῶμα, οἷον πέλεκυς· ἦν μὲν γὰρ ἂν τὸ πελέκει εἶναι ἡ οὐσία αὐτοῦ, καὶ ἡ ψυχὴ τοῦτο· χωρισθείσης δὲ ταύτης οὐκ ἂν ἔτι πέλεκυς ἦν, ἀλλ'ἢ ὁμωνύμως, νῦν δ'ἔστι πέλεκυς. οὐ γὰρ τοιούτου σώματος τὸ τί ἦν εἶναι καὶ ὁ λόγος ἡ ψυχή, ἀλλὰ φυσικοῦ τοιουδί, ἔχοντος ἀρχὴν κινήσεως καὶ στάσεως ἐν ἑαυτῷ. θεωρεῖν δὲ καὶ ἐπὶ τῶν μερῶν δεῖ τὸ λεχθέν. εἰ γὰρ ἦν ὁ ὀφθαλμὸς ζῷον, ψυχὴ ἂν ἦν αὐτοῦ ἡ ὄψις· αὕτη γὰρ οὐσία ὀφθαλμοῦ ἡ κατὰ τὸν λόγον (ὁ δ' ὀφθαλμὸς ὕλη ὄψεως), ἧς ἀπολειπούσης οὐκέτ'ὀφθαλμός, πλὴν ὁμωνύμως, καθάπερ ὁ λίθινος καὶ ὁ γεγραμμένος. δεῖ δὴ λαβεῖν τὸ ἐπὶ μέρους ἐφ'ὅλου τοῦ ζῶντος σώματος· ἀνάλογον γὰρ ἔχει ὡς τὸ μέρος πρὸς τὸ μέρος, οὕτως ἡ ὅλη αἴσθησις πρὸς τὸ ὅλον σῶμα τὸ αἰσθητικόν, ᾗ τοιοῦτον. ἔστι δὲ οὐ τὸ ἀποβεβληκὸς τὴν ψυχὴν τὸ δυνάμει ὂν ὥστε ζῆν, ἀλλὰ τὸ ἔχον· τὸ δὲ σπέρμα καὶ ὁ καρπὸς τὸ δυνάμει τοιονδὶ σῶμα. ὡς μὲν οὖν ἡ τμῆσις καὶ ἡ ὅρασις, οὕτω καὶ ἡ ἐγρήγορσις ἐντελέχεια, ὡς δ' ἡ ὄψις καὶ ἡ δύναμις τοῦ ὀργάνου, ἡ ψυχή· τὸ δὲ σῶμα τὸ δυνάμει ὄν· ἀλλ' ὥσπερ ὀφθαλμὸς ἡ κόρη καὶ ἡ ὄψις, κἀκεῖ ἡ ψυχὴ καὶ τὸ σῶμα ζῷον.

39 Cf. *De an.*, II, 2, 413 b11–13: νῦν δ'ἐπὶ τοσοῦτον εἰρήσθω μόνον, ὅτι ἐστὶν ἡ ψυχὴ τῶν εἰρημένων τούτων ἀρχὴ καὶ τούτοις ὥρισται, θρεπτικῷ, αἰσθητικῷ, διανοητικῷ, κινήσει.

40 *De an.*, I, 1, 402 b9–16: ἔτι δέ, εἰ μὴ πολλαὶ ψυχαὶ ἀλλὰ μόρια, πότερον δεῖ ζητεῖν πρότερον τὴν ὅλην ψυχὴν ἢ τὰ μόρια. χαλεπὸν δὲ καὶ τούτων διορίσαι ποῖα πέφυκεν ἕτερα ἀλλήλων, καὶ πότερον τὰ μόρια χρὴ ζητεῖν πρότερον ἢ τὰ ἔργα αὐτῶν, οἷον τὸ νοεῖν ἢ τὸν νοῦν, καὶ τὸ αἰσθάνεσθαι ἢ τὸ αἰσθητικόν· ὁμοίως δὲ καὶ ἐπὶ τῶν ἄλλων. εἰ δὲ τὰ ἔργα πρότερον, πάλιν ἄν τις ἀπορήσειεν εἰ τὰ ἀντικείμενα πρότερον τούτων ζητητέον, οἷον τὸ αἰσθητὸν τοῦ αἰσθητικοῦ, καὶ τὸ νοητὸν τοῦ νοῦ. See also *De an.*, II, 4, 415 a14–22.

41 It might be argued that in *Metaphysics* Aristotle provides a general, unitary account of νοῦς, be it human, celestial, or divine, and not only the specific account of divine thinking. *Metaphysics*, XII, 7, and 9 seem to provide ground in support of such an interpretation. In outlining the διαγωγή of the first unmoved mover in *Metaph.*, XII, 7, 1072 b14–30, Aristotle identifies the first unmoved mover with νοῦς. This passage, however, does not bear specifically on the intellect of the unmoved mover, but on human intellect as well, since the latter serves explicitly as a model for thinking about the former (on intellect in general as the subject of *Metaph.*, XII, 7, 1072 b14–30, see A. Laks, "*Metaphysics* Λ 7", in M. Frede, D. Charles eds., *Aristotle's* Metaphysics *Lambda*, 207–243, in part. 231–237). In particular, here Aristotle contrasts human and divine intellect which exhibit a *similarity in kind*, despite the superiority of the divine intellect in terms of temporal continuity (the expression εἰ δὲ μᾶλλον at 1072 b25 also seems to claim an intrinsic, not further specified superiority for the divine intellect): for both

are νοῦς, that is, a substance capable of thinking, however the former brings that capacity to actuality only episodically, whereas the latter is always thinking in actuality; and the exercise of that capacity is something divine in human intellect (XII, 7, 1072 b22–4: τὸ γὰρ δεκτικὸν τοῦ νοητοῦ καὶ τῆς οὐσίας νοῦς, ἐνεργεῖ δὲ ἔχων, ὥστ' ἐκείνου μᾶλλον τοῦτο ὃ δοκεῖ ὁ νοῦς θεῖον ἔχειν, καὶ ἡ θεωρία τὸ ἥδιστον καὶ ἄριστον). Unlike *Metaphysics*, XII, 7, which mainly focuses on the similarity between human and divine intellect, *Metaphysics*, XII, 9 is officially devoted to the discussion of some difficulties concerning the intellect in general, for instance the existence and identification of its object and the features of its activity (XII, 9, 1074 b15–17: Τὰ δὲ περὶ τὸν νοῦν ἔχει τινὰς ἀπορίας· δοκεῖ μὲν γὰρ εἶναι τῶν φαινομένων θειότατον, πῶς δ'ἔχων τοιοῦτος ἂν εἴη, ἔχει τινὰς δυσκολίας); it is only at 1075 a6–10 that a clear distinction between human and divine intellect is made (XII, 9, 1075 a6–10: ἢ ἀδιαίρετον πᾶν τὸ μὴ ἔχον ὕλην—ὥσπερ ὁ ἀνθρώπινος νοῦς ἢ ὅ γε τῶν συνθέτων ἔχει ἔν τινι χρόνῳ (οὐ γὰρ ἔχει τὸ εὖ ἐν τῳδὶ ἢ ἐν τῳδί, ἀλλ' ἐν ὅλῳ τινὶ τὸ ἄριστον, ὂν ἄλλο τι)— οὕτως δ' ἔχει αὐτὴ αὑτῆς ἡ νόησις τὸν ἅπαντα αἰῶνα). That chapter XII, 9 is primarily concerned with intellect in general has been argued in M. Frede, "Introduction", in M. Frede, D. Charles eds., *Aristotle's* Metaphysics *Lambda. Simposium Aristotelicum*, Clarendon Press, Oxford 2000, 1–52, in part. 18–26, 36–37; and in E. Berti, "Il libro *Lambda* della *Metafisica* di Aristotele tra fisica e metafisica", in G. Damschen, R. Enskart, A. Vigo eds., *Platon und Aristoteles – sub ratione veritatis. Festschrift für Wolfgng Wieland zum 70. Geburgstag*, Vandenhoek & Ruprecht, Gottingen 2003, 177–193, in part. 179–180 (repr. in E. Berti, *Nuovi studi aristotelici. II – Fisica, antropologia e metafisica*, Morcelliana, Brescia 2004, 471–487); and by J. Brunschwig in his "*Metaphysics* Λ 9: A Short-Lived Thought-Experiment?", in M. Frede, D. Charles eds., *Aristotle's* Metaphysics *Lambda*, 245–306, in part. 277, 296–297). Therefore, it might be argued that in *Metaphysics*, XII, 7 and 9 Aristotle is neither exclusively nor mainly concerned with the divine intellect; rather, he provides a *typological analysis* of νοῦς in general, of which divine and human intellect are just instances. Furthermore, given the analysis of νοῦς and, in particular, of its activity in *Metaphysics*, XII one could be tempted to detect there a *pros hen* predication of νοῦς that would be primarily posited of divine intellect and only derivatively of human intellect. Though intriguing, this hypothesis is difficult to prove due to the lack of textual evidence of the language of *pros hen* predication in *Metaphysics*, XII, 7 and 9 and, more generally, in the entire book. Against this interpretation of *Metaphysics*, XII, 7 and 9, see Falcon, *Aristotle and the Science of Nature*, 96, n. 18: "On the one hand, Aristotle seems to be confident that a unified account of thinking, that is an account that includes human, celestial and divine thinking, is possible. On the other hand, he never engages in an attempt to provide this unified account". Michael V. Wedin too has argued against the possibility of a unitary account of thinking in Aristotle's *Metaphysics*, and the isomorphism between human and divine intellect in chapters 5 and 6 of his *Mind and Imagination in Aristotle*, Yale University Press, New Haven-London 1988. However, in spite of Wedin's thorough scrutiny of the *De anima* text, "his relentlessly naturalistic interpretation of *nous poiētikos* cuts against the grain of the text" and "some features of the autonomy of thinking" resist his explication, as C. Shields notes in his "Some Recent Approaches to Aristotle's *De anima*", in Aristotle, *De Anima. Books II and III (with passages from Book I)*, Translated with Introduction and Notes by D. W. Hamlyn, with a Report on Recent Work and a Revised Bibliography by C. Shields, Clarendon Aristotle Series, Clarendon Press, Oxford 1993, 176. That human and divine thinking share the same nature is firmly rejected by S. Menn, who radically distinguishes between νοῦς as a theoretical virtue, which is identified with the first unmoved mover, and νοῦς as a psychic faculty, which is identified with human intellect; consequently, in Menn's interpretation the first unmoved mover is by no means an intellect (see S. Menn, "Aristotle and Plato on God as *Nous* and as the Good", *The Review of Metaphysics*, 45/3, 1992, 543–573). In my opinion, Menn's distinction is, however, difficult to reconcile with Aristotle's distinction between potential and productive intellect in the *De anima*.

man's life and knowledge.[42] What is more, though being a part of the soul, νοῦς has a proper name, which seems to confer upon it a different status from that of the soul.[43] Consequently, all exegetes of Aristotle's *De anima* struggled with the presence of an explicit treatment of theoretical intellect within the Aristotelian naturalistic account of the soul and, therefore, provided their own solutions to harmonize it with *De anima*'s global inquiry into sublunary souls *qua* forms of organic bodies.

From Alexandria to Athens to Baghdad

In the opening lines of an article that appeared in 1997, H. J. Blumenthal wonders whether we can determine what Aristotle's intentions in writing the *De anima* actually were.[44] In raising this question Blumenthal's primary concern was not Aristotle's intentions themselves, but rather what an investigation of the soul precisely means for its Late Ancient commentators and, consequently, whether Aristotle's intentions were overlooked or forgotten in Late Antiquity. The fortune of the *De anima* in the subsequent philosophical tradition provides essential evidence to reconstruct which version of the Aristotelian psychology Avicenna had at his disposal: for it was not the genuine one but rather a mixture of *real* and *virtual* Aristotelianism, i.e. an Aristotelianism transformed and adulterated by the mediation of Late Ancient and early Arabic exegesis.[45] In this connection, the major trends of Late Ancient interpretation of Aristotle's *De anima* are also detectable in Arabic authors' writings on the soul or on the classification of sciences in which psychology is included.

In approaching both the Late Ancient and the early Arabic exegesis of Aristotle's *De anima* and of psychology as an autonomous science, it is therefore crucial to distinguish preliminarily between reflection on the place of the treatise *De anima* within Aristotle's *libri naturales* and, in general, in the scholastic curriculum, and theoretic reflection on the epistemological status of the science of the soul. Though intertwined, these reflections are two distinct issues for Aristotle's exegetes.[46]

---

42 On Aristotle's problematic introduction of a divine element in metaphysics, psychology, and ethics, see P. Donini, *La* Metafisica *di Aristotele. Introduzione alla lettura,* La Nuova Italia Scientifica, Roma 1995, in part. 159–162.

43 As we shall see, this aspect was noticed by Philoponus in his commentary on the *De anima.*

44 H. J. Blumenthal, "Were Aristotle's Intentions in writing the *De anima* forgotten in Late Antiquity?", *Documenti e studi sulla tradizione filosofica medievale*, 8, 1997, 143–157.

45 On this aspect of Aristotle's reception in the Late Antiquity, see *Aristotle's Transformed: The Ancient Commentators and Their Influence,* R. Sorabji ed., Duckworth, London 1990.

46 An example of such a distinction is provided by the prologue of Philoponus' commentary on Aristotle's *Physics* (but it is reasonable to extend it to other Late Ancient commentators). In that prologue (Philoponus, *In Aristotelis Physicorum libros tres priores commentaria*, ed. H. Vitelli, *Commentaria in Aristotelem Graeca*, vol. 16, Reimer, Berlin 1887, 1.1–2.13) Philoponus seems to accept Aristotle's distinction of things into eternal things and things undergoing generation and corruption, and assigns to *De caelo* the investigation of the former without questioning it. However, Philoponus'

In tracing back the aforementioned reflections formulated in the post-Aristotelian philosophical exegetical tradition, three types of writings will be taken into account: (1) commentaries on Aristotelian works; (2) classificatory writings; and (3) original treatises. The first type is mainly (though not exclusively)[47] used in Late Ancient exegesis of Aristotle;[48] the second type, on the other hand, namely that of *inventories* (or classifications) of sciences, is a peculiar genre of writings in which early Arabic encyclopaedism expressed itself.[49] Nonetheless, these writing kinds, which amount to different literary genres, are not to be conceived as mutually exclusive. For instance, it is not uncommon to find a classificatory section in writings belonging to the first type, notably in introductions.[50]

---

own position, expressed in his commentary on *De caelo*, rejects the eternity of heavenly bodies. Therefore, the preliminary classification of Aristotelian treatises, proper to the *prolegomena* and patterned after the division of existing things, seems not to entail discussion of the epistemological status (place, subject, and boundaries) of the sciences mentioned in that classification. In other words, in commenting on Aristotle's treatises, commentators feel forced to reconstruct the wider Peripatetic order of his scientific production without directly addressing the issue of the status of each particular science he has written about.

47 It is worth mentioning here that al-Fārābī wrote commentaries on Aristotle's *De interpretatione*, *Prior Analytics* (fragments), *Rhetoric*, *Categories* (fragments), and *Nicomachean Ethics* (lost). See Th.-A. Druart, *Al-Farabi*, 15 July 2016, https://plato.stanford.edu/entries/al-farabi/.

48 See D'Ancona, "Commenting on Aristotle"; P. Donini, "Testi e commenti, manuali e insegnamento".

49 For the use of the word "encyclopaedism" rather than "encyclopaedia" in this context, see D. Gutas, "The Greek and Persian Background of Early Arabic Encyclopedism", in G. Endress ed., preface by A. Filali-Ansary, *Organizing Knowledge: Encyclopædic Activities in the Pre-Eighteenth Century Islamic World*, Brill, Leiden – Boston 2006, 91–101, in part. 91, n. 1. For an overview of Arabic encyclopaedias of the rational sciences, see H. H. Biesterfeldt, "Arabisch-islamische Enzyklopädien: Formen und Funktionen", in C. Meier ed., *Die Enzyklopädie im Mittelalter vom Hochmittelalter bis zu frühen Neuzeit*, Wilhelm Fink, München 2002, 43–83; and id., "Medieval Arabic Encyclopedias of Science and Philosophy", in S. Harvey ed., *The Medieval Hebrew Encyclopedias of Science and Philosophy*, Kluwer, Boston 2000, 77–98; G. Endress, "The Cycle of Knowledge: Intellectual Traditions and Encyclopædias of the Rational Sciences in Arabic Islamic Hellenism", in G. Endress ed., *Organizing Knowledge*, 103–133. See also D. Gutas, "Aspects of Literary Form and Genre in Arabic Logical Works", in C. Burnett ed., *Glosses and Commentaries on Aristotelian Logical Texts: The Syriac, Arabic and Medieval Latin Traditions*, The Warburg Institute of the University of London, London 1993, 29–76.

50 This is the case of the introduction to the commentaries on Aristotle's *Categories* by Ammonius, Simplicius, Philoponus, Olympiodorus, and David (Élias), where before approaching the Aristotelian text, each of the five commentators provides a biography of Aristotle and an introduction to his philosophy, structured in ten points (the second point is usually devoted to the classification of Aristotle's writings). For an exhaustive and unequalled study on the Late Ancient prolegomena, see J. Mansfeld, *Prolegomena. Questions to be settled before the study of an author, or a text*, Brill, Leiden 1994. For the Neoplatonic introductions to Aristotle's philosophical writings, see Simplicius, *Commentaire sur les Catégories*. Traduction commentée sous la direction de Ilsetraut Hadot, Fascicule I, Introduction, Première partie. Traduction de Ph. Hoffmann (avec la collaboration de I. et P. Hadot). Commentaire et notes à la traduction par I. Hadot avec des appendices de P. Hadot et J.-P. Mahé, Philosophia Antiqua, Brill, Leiden 1990, in part. 44–45.

What is more, from the comparison and the combination of the elements of this threefold classification of writings three major positions on both the place of Aristotle's *De anima* in the scholastic curriculum and of psychology in the global system of science emerge: (a) *De anima* as an entirely physical work and psychology as a science belonging to natural philosophy for all intents and purposes; (b) *De anima* as a writing bringing to completion the *corpus* on natural philosophy and psychology as the science in which natural philosophy culminates and which at the same time protrudes into metaphysics; and (c) *De anima* as a treatise whose subject-matter is neither entirely physical nor entirely metaphysical and psychology as a science taking a middle rank between natural philosophy and metaphysics.

An All-Natural Perspective

That *De anima* is a treatise belonging to Aristotle's physical works, and that psychology entirely and uncontroversially falls within the province of natural philosophy seems to have been maintained by Alexander of Aphrodisias.[51] In default of Alexander's commentary on *De anima*,[52] we can read his commentary on the prologue to *Meteorology*, where Aristotle's outline of the investigation of nature gives the cue for a discussion on the order of his *libri naturales* and, accordingly, on the arrangement of sciences.[53] There, after briefly recalling the subject-matter of the previous treatises on natural philosophy and providing the agenda of the meteorological investigation on which he is embarking, Aristotle touches upon the subsequent inquiry into the sublunary world by which the investigation of nature is brought to completion, namely the study of animals and plants, both in general and separately (περὶ ζῴων καὶ φυτῶν, καθόλου τε καὶ χωρίς). Here Aristotle makes no reference to *De anima* (as he does also in the case of the other natural, special sciences) and – what is more important – to the notion of soul. However, the absence of a reference to *De anima* or to its topic at the beginning of *Meteorology*, which might be explained by appealing to the programmatic nature of the prologue, prompts both Ancient exegetes and modern interpreters of Aristotle[54] to tackle the issue explicitly, since *De*

51 Themistius could also be included in this group; however, his paraphrase of *De anima* does not allow us to infer precisely his own position about the place of *De anima* among Aristotelian writings and the status of psychology in the system of science.

52 See Chapter 1, n. 44.

53 Aristotle, *Meteor.*, I, 1, 338 a20 – 339 a9: Περὶ μὲν οὖν τῶν πρώτων αἰτίων τῆς φύσεως καὶ περὶ πάσης κινήσεως φυσικῆς, ἔτι δὲ περὶ τῶν κατὰ τὴν ἄνω φορὰν διακεκοσμημένων ἄστρων καὶ περὶ τῶν στοιχείων τῶν σωματικῶν, πόσα τε καὶ ποῖα, καὶ τῆς εἰς ἄλληλα μεταβολῆς, καὶ περὶ γενέσεως καὶ φθορᾶς τῆς κοινῆς εἴρηται πρότερον. λοιπὸν δ'ἐστὶ μέρος τῆς μεθόδου ταύτης ἔτι θεωρητέον, ὃ πάντες οἱ πρότεροι μετεωρολογίαν ἐκάλουν· [...] διελθόντες δὲ περὶ τούτων, θεωρήσωμεν εἴ τι δυνάμεθα κατὰ τὸν ὑφηγημένον τρόπον ἀποδοῦναι περὶ ζῴων καὶ φυτῶν, καθόλου τε καὶ χωρίς· σχεδὸν γὰρ τούτων ῥηθέντων τέλος ἂν εἴη γεγονὸς τῆς ἐξ ἀρχῆς ἡμῖν προαιρέσεως πάσης.

54 In outlining the formation of Aristotle's physio-biological *corpus* and the hesitation concerning his own conception of animate substance (is it an aggregate of parts, or a *synolon* with the form acting

anima is meant to provide the explanatory resources and the conceptual framework for an optimal study of life, notably of animal life, of which soul is the formal principle.

In commenting upon this passage of the Aristotelian text, Alexander spells out Aristotle's cumulative reference to plants and animals by providing two lists of works.[55] In the first list Alexander mentions *De anima, De sensu et sensibilibus, De memoria et reminiscentia, De somno et vigilia, De divinatione per somnum, De senectute et iuventute, De longitudine et brevitate vitae,* and all treatises dealing to some extent with animals. In the second list the commentator distinguishes between treatises dealing with animals in general (*Historia animalium, De generatione an., De partibus an., De incessu an., De motu an.*) and treatises dealing with them in a particular respect (*De memoria et reminiscentia, De somno et vigilia, De divinatione per somnum*).

Alexander refers to *De anima* and *De sensu*, a sort of introduction to the block of treatises generically known as *Parva naturalia*, only in the first list and in a hesitant way (τάσσοι δ' ἂν ἐν τῇ περὶ ζῴων θεωρίᾳ καὶ τὴν Περὶ ψυχῆς, ἔτι τε τὴν Περὶ αἰσθήσεώς τε καὶ αἰσθητῶν, [...]). Here Alexander puts *De anima* and *De sensu* in the first

as its *vinculum substantiale?*), M. Rashed discusses the opening lines of Aristotle's *Meteorology* and suggests two possible reasons why Aristotle does not there refer to the *De anima:* 1) that the investigation of the soul is part of his general biology was clear to such an extent that Aristotle may have considered it superfluous to refer to it explicitly; or 2) at the time of the composition of *Meteorology*, Aristotle still had a mereological conception of biology and, since the soul is not a part of the animal, he decided not to mention its investigation there. For this illuminating contribution, see M. Rashed, "Agrégat de parties ou *vinculum substantiale?* Sur une hésitation conceptuelle et textuelle du corpus aristotélicien", in A. Laks, M. Rashed eds., *Aristote et le mouvement des animaux: Dix études sur le* De motu animalium, Presses universitaires du septentrion, Villeneuve d'Ascq 2004, 185–202. On the contrary, M. Burnyeat does not see any problem in the opening lines of *Meteorology.* According to him, actually there is a reference to the *DA:* "This is a large scale map of Aristotle's natural philosophy, beginning with the *Physics*, going on to the *DC* and the *GC*, pausing here for the *Meteorologica*, looking forward to the *DA* and the biological works"; see M. Burnyeat, "Aristotle and the foundation of sublunary physics", in J. Mansfeld, F. J. de Haas eds., *Aristotle. On Generation and Corruption,* I. *Proceeding of the 15th Symposium Aristotelicum,* Oxford University Press, Oxford 2004, 7–24, in part. 13.

55 *In Meteorologicorum*, I, 1, 3.32–4.11 (ed. M. Hayduck): διελθόντες δὲ περὶ τούτων. τίνα πάλιν μετὰ τὴν μετεωρολογικὴν πραγματείαν ἐστὶ τῆς φυσικῆς πραγματείας, προστίθησι· περὶ γὰρ ζῴων, φησί, καὶ φυτῶν, καθόλου τε καὶ χωρίς. τάσσοι δ' ἂν ἐν τῇ περὶ ζῴων θεωρίᾳ καὶ τὴν Περὶ ψυχῆς, ἔτι τε τὴν Περὶ αἰσθήσεώς τε καὶ αἰσθητῶν, ἔτι τὴν Περὶ μνήμης καὶ ὕπνου καὶ τῆς καθ'ὕπνον μαντικῆς, ἔτι τὸ Περὶ γήρως καὶ νεότητος, μακροβιότητός τε καὶ βραχυβιότητος, καὶ ὅσα ἄλλα αὐτῷ γέγραπται ἔχοντα τὴν ἀναφορὰν ἐπὶ τὰ ζῷα· ὧν τὰ μὲν κοινὴν περὶ πάντων τῶν ζῴων τὴν θεωρίαν ἔχει, ὥσπερ ἥ τε Περὶ ζῴων ἱστορία, καὶ τὰ Περὶ ζῴων γενέσεώς τε καὶ μορίων, ἔτι δὲ τὰ Περὶ ζῴων πορείας τε καὶ κινήσεως, τὰ δὲ ἴδια, ὡς τὰ Περὶ μνήμης καὶ ὕπνου καὶ τῆς καθ' ὕπνον μαντικῆς· τῶν γὰρ ἐν τούτοις λεγομένων τὰ πλεῖστα ἀνθρώπῳ μόνῳ ὑπάρχει. τὴν δὲ ἐξ ἀρχῆς προαίρεσιν λέγει τὸ τὴν φυσικὴν θεωρίαν πᾶσαν ἐπεξελθεῖν· τοῦτο γὰρ ἦν τὸ προκείμενον. κατὰ δὲ τὸν ὑφηγημένον τρόπον εἶπεν, ὅτι μὴ ἱστορίαν τινὰ παρέδωκεν ἐν τοῖς πρὸ τούτων ψιλήν, ἀλλὰ μετὰ τοῦ τὰς οἰκείας αἰτίας ἑκάστου τῶν λεγομένων ζητεῖν τε καὶ ἀποδιδόναι καὶ μετὰ ἀποδείξεως τὴν περὶ αὐτῶν ποιεῖσθαι θεωρίαν. οὕτως οὖν ἀξιοῖ καὶ τὸν περὶ τῶν ῥηθησομένων γενέσθαι λόγον.

and second position respectively, after *Meteorology*, as a sort of introduction to the following, properly biological, treatises.[56] However, in the second list the reference to *De anima* disappears. The reason for Alexander's silence on this issue might be that, apart from a cursory hint at *De anima*, he considered the issue of the place of the treatise unproblematic and, consequently, deliberately eluded its discussion when his commentary comes to deal with more specific questions.

It is, therefore, reasonable to conclude that Alexander's reference to the *De anima-De sensu* block at the beginning of his overview (i.e. first list) of Aristotle's treatises dealing in general with organic life, notably with animals, might suggest that he considers *De anima* (and its supplement in the *De sensu*) to be a general introduction to all Aristotelian biology, namely a sort of *general biology*, dealing with the form of perishable living beings, a perspective that perfectly fits with his *essentialism*, namely with his primary concern with the form, which is the cornerstone of his entire philosophical system.[57] This might also be the reason why Alexander does not mention this treatise in his second list: it is not necessary since the role of *De anima* is clear, and the second list primarily refers to the internal subdivision of the investigation of animals into a general and a specific study respectively.[58]

Culmination of Natural Philosophy and Anticipation of Metaphysics

The position according to which *De anima* is a writing placed on the edge of natural philosophy and psychology an amphibious science in which natural philosophy culminates and which at the same time protrudes into metaphysics, was held by Alexandrian commentators (Ammonius, Philoponus, Olympiodorus), and acknowledged,

---

56 It is, however, noteworthy that in the *explicit* of Alexander's commentary, the inquiry into homeomerous parts, just accomplished in the *Meteorology*, is linked with the inquiry into anhomeomerous parts, i.e. plants and animals, made in *De partibus animalium*, which he considers to come immediately after the *Meteorology*; see *In Meteor.*, 227.15–19: γνωρίμων δὲ τούτων τῶν ὁμοιομερῶν οὕτως γενομένων, δεῖν φησιν ὁμοίως μετὰ ταῦτα περὶ τῶν ἀνομοιομερῶν μορίων λέγειν, εἶθ' οὕτω περὶ τῶν ἐκ τούτων συνεστώτων, ἅπερ ἐστὶ τά τε φυτὰ καὶ τὰ ζῷα. τῷ δὲ βιβλίῳ τούτῳ ἕπεσθαι δοκεῖ τὰ Περὶ ζῴων μορίων. It is worth recalling here that in the prologue to his commentary on Aristotle's *De sensu* Alexander explicitly relates the inquiry he is embarking on to the previous one, accomplished in *De anima* (*In De sensu*, 1.3–18). In the *explicit* of the same work, Alexander makes reference to *De memoria* and *De somno* as the treatises that come immediately after *De sensu* (*ib.*, 173.10–2).

57 For a thorough and detailed study of Alexander's essentialism, see M. Rashed, *Essentialisme. Alexandre d'Aphrodise entre logique, physique et cosmologie*, De Gruyter, Berlin 2007.

58 I have deliberately kept out of the picture Alexander's *Peri nou* and its tradition. However, the existence of this separate treatment seems to suggest that Alexander does consider noetics to fall outside the project of the *De anima*; and this fits perfectly with his physical approach to the treatise. For the influence of the *Peri nou* on the development of Arabic noetics, see M. Geoffroy, "La tradition arabe du *Περὶ νοῦ* d'Alexandre d'Aphrodise et les origines de la théorie farabienne des quatres degrés de l'intellect", in C. D'Ancona, G. Serra eds., *Aristotele e Alessandro di Afrodisia nella tradizione araba*. Atti del colloquio *La ricezione araba ed ebraica della filosofia e della scienza greche* (Padova, 14–15 maggio 1999), Il Poligrafo, Padova 2002, 191–231.

among Arabic philosophers, by al-Fārābī. Examples of this shared position can be found in different passages of Alexandrian commentators' commentaries on Aristotle. In his commentary on Aristotle's *Metaphysics*, which is preserved in the *reportatio* by his pupil Asclepius, Ammonius of Hermias maintains that Aristotle 'theologizes' (θεολογεῖ), i.e. speaks about God, not only in *Metaphysics* but also in the conclusive parts of some of his works on natural philosophy, such as *De generatione et corruptione* (perhaps, at the end of the second book), *Physics* VIII (the reference to the last book of this writing is explicit), and *De anima* (perhaps, in the third book).[59] Basically, Ammonius' idea is that, while remaining in the domain of nature, Aristotle lifts himself up to the transcendent causes of natural things in places and with respect to topics that seem to allow and require this disciplinary trespassing, as happens in *De anima*.

In their works Philoponus and Olympiodorus, Ammonius' pupils, expressed the same idea as their master. In the prologue of his commentary on Aristotle's *De anima*, like Ammonius, Philoponus says that in *De anima*, arguably in the third book, while inquiring into the rational soul, Aristotle crosses the borders of natural philosophy and protrudes into the domain of metaphysics, just as he does at the end of *Physics* (probably a reference to VIII, 6), where he looks for the primary cause of motion, and in *De generatione et corruptione* (probably a reference to II, 9–11).[60] It is worth mentioning that Philoponus' prologue is a chef-d'oeuvre of dialectic[61] in which the author offers his own interpretation of the goal of the Aristotelian treatise and, in doing so, explicitly draws out a substantial agreement between Plato and Aristotle, because both philosophers are said to concentrate primarily on rational soul and its separability from the body.[62] What is more, in commenting upon the respect in which

---

59 See Asclepius, *In Aristotelis Metaphysicorum libros A-Z commentaria*, ed. M. Hayduck, *Commentaria in Aristotelem Graeca*, vol. 6.2, Reimer, Berlin 1888, 1.22–2.3: καὶ ἐν ταῖς φυσικαῖς δὲ αὐτοῦ πραγματείαις καὶ μάλιστα πρὸς τοῖς πέρασι θεολογεῖ καὶ ἀνάγει ἑαυτόν. φησὶ γὰρ πρὸς τῷ τέλει τῆς Περὶ γενέσεως καὶ φθορᾶς "τῷ λειπομένῳ τρόπῳ ἀνεπλήρωσε τὸ ὅλον ὁ θεὸς ἐνδελεχῆ ποιήσας τὴν γένεσιν". ὁμοίως δὲ καὶ ἐν τῷ ὀγδόῳ λόγῳ τῆς Φυσικῆς ἀκροάσεως καὶ ἐν τῇ Περὶ ψυχῆς πραγματείᾳ καὶ ἐν πάσαις αὐτοῦ ταῖς φυσικαῖς πραγματείαις τοῦτο πεποίηκε. On this passage see also Bertolacci, *The Reception of Aristotle's* Metaphysics, in part. 79–80, n. 26.

60 Philoponus, *In De anima*, 20.31–4: ὥσπερ δ'εἴωθεν ἐν πάσαις ταῖς φυσικαῖς πραγματείαις ποιεῖν, πρὸς τοῖς τέλεσιν τῶν πραγματειῶν ἀνάγειν ἑαυτὸν ἐπὶ τὰς ἐξῃρημένας τῶν φυσικῶν πραγμάτων αἰτίας, οὕτω καὶ ἐνταῦθα ποιεῖ.

61 On the internal division of this proemium, see J. Dudley, "Johannes Grammaticus Philoponus Alexandrinus, " *in Aristotelis De anima proemion* ". Translated from the Greek", *Bulletin de philosophie médiévale édité par la société internationale pour l'étude de la philosophie médiévale*, 16–17, 1974–1975, 62–85.

62 In order to support his claim, Philoponus selects twelve Aristotelian passages in which Aristotle seems to argue for the separability of the rational soul from its bodily substratum and arranges them in order to show that, like Plato, Aristotle believes that the rational soul is separable from the body and, therefore, immortal. See Philoponus, *In De anima*, 11.25–29: ὥστε χωριστὸν αὐτὸν βούλεται εἶναι τοῦ σώματος καὶ μὴ μετὰ σώματος ἐνεργεῖν καὶ ἔτι ἀίδιον εἶναι. πολλῶν δὲ ὄντων ὧν δυνατὸν ἦν παραθέσθαι δεικνύντας ὅτι ἀθάνατον οἶδε τὴν λογικὴν ψυχὴν ὁ Ἀριστοτέλης καὶ χωριστὴν παντὸς

Aristotle says that the knowledge of the soul contributes to grasping the truth about nature, Philoponus clarifies the nature of the investigation of the soul: by being different from natural philosophy with respect to the nature of its subject, the study of the soul can really contribute to it by providing the formal, efficient, and final cause of living beings; by contrast, in virtue of a similarity in kind between the subject-matter of metaphysics and ethics and that of psychology, psychology reveals a substantial continuity with both disciplines.[63]

As for Olympiodorus, presumably a late pupil of Ammonius, in commenting upon the prologue to Aristotle's *Meteorology* and discussing the position occupied by *De anima* within Aristotle's natural books, as Alexander did, he lists it after writings on plants and animals and, in order to refine this position, immediately adds the following remark: "And that is where the treatise *De anima* will have been put (καὶ οὕτω τετάξεται ἡ Περὶ ψυχῆς). For this [treatise] is like an amphibious animal (αὕτη γὰρ ἀμφιβίῳ ζῴῳ ἔοικε) and can precede and follow. It can precede because *De anima* deals with physical matters, while it can follow because it is also a theological [treatment]. We must learn first about physical matters and thus [move to]

σώματος, ἱκανὰ καὶ τὰ εἰρημένα. What is more, within the survey of the opinions of his predecessors (9.3–12.9), Philoponus classifies the position according to which the soul is the entelechy of the bodily substratum among the opinions of those who maintain that the soul is an incorporeal, but inseparable principle; however, he omits to ascribe this opinion to Aristotle, whose name appears in connection with this position only later on, when Philoponus is commenting on the first difficulty raised by the inquiry into the soul (33.2–4: οἱ δὲ ὑπὸ τὸ ποιόν, ὧν εἰσιν καὶ οἱ ἰατροὶ κρᾶσιν εἶναι λέγοντες· τοιοῦτοι δ'ἂν εἶεν καὶ οἱ ἐντελέχειαν λέγοντες τοιαύτην· μαθησόμεθα γάρ, πῶς φησιν αὐτὴν ἐντελέχειαν ὁ Ἀριστοτέλης). Nonetheless, the sentence "μαθησόμεθα...ὁ Ἀριστοτέλης" seems to suggest that for Philoponus there is a sense of the term ἐντελέχεια, peculiar to Aristotle, that will be clarified later. See 203.1–207.14 (the prologue to the commentary on the second book of *De anima*), where Philoponus explains that the term ἐντελέχεια, qualified by the adjective "first", can be properly referred to both separable and inseparable souls. In the prologue, by contrast, Aristotle is mentioned, together with Plato, as the advocate of the true opinion on the soul, namely that according to which, in general, the soul is an incorporeal principle and, in particular, the vegetative and the irrational souls are inseparable from the body, whereas the rational soul is separable from it.

63 Philoponus, *In De anima*, 25.2–29. In this passage Philoponus distinguishes "what contributes" and "that to which something contributes" (τὸ συμβαλλόμενον ἕτερόν ἐστι τοῦ ᾧ συμβάλλεται) in order to argue that, while in truth belonging to ethics and metaphysics, the study of the soul only contributes to natural philosophy, from which the study of the soul/psychology is actually distinct. For, on the one hand, in engaging in theology, the soul returns to its own origin within the intelligible realm, whereas, on the other hand, in dealing with ethics, it studies concepts and orders of virtue, thereby once more discussing its own capacities and dispositions. By contrast, there is no link of the same kind between the study of the soul and natural philosophy: nature is one thing, soul is another. Here we see that in Neoplatonism the methodological ambiguity matches the twofold nature of the soul itself, which has a relation to both realms. On this aspect, see P. Lautner, "Status and Method of Psychology according to the Late Neoplatonists and their Influence during the Sixteenth Century", in C. Leijenhorst, C. Lüthy, J. M. M. H. Thijssen eds., *The Dynamics of Aristotelian Natural Philosophy from Antiquity to the Seventeenth Century*, Brill, Leiden-Boston-Köln 2002, 81–108, in part. 91–2.

deal with divine things".[64] Thus, according to Olympiodorus, *De anima* might either precede specific writings on plants and animals because it deals with their principle and, consequently, offers a more general account of them and their principle or follow them because it includes materials on a higher level of being (in all likelihood it is a reference to νοῦς), in which natural philosophy culminates and which protrudes into metaphysics.[65] This position, however, does not seem to lead Olympiodorus to question that *De anima* is a treatise of natural philosophy:[66] for, just as the eighth book of *Physics* is still part of natural philosophy, though talking about the intellect and the perpetual movement of the stars, which are not properly physical matters, likewise the "theological" part of *De anima* is still part of the physical realm.

In the Arabic context, Abū Naṣr Muḥammad ibn Muḥammad ibn Ṭarḫān ibn Awzaluġ (or Uzluġ) al-Fārābī (d. 950/1) seems to have been the first collector of this position concerning the place of *De anima* and the nature of the science of the soul. As for the first issue, al-Fārābī tackles it in his *Maqāla fī Iḥṣāʾ al-ʿulūm* (*Treatise on the Enumeration of the Sciences*),[67] a work whose goal is to provide a synthesis of knowledge (*ʿilm*) that encompasses the secular Aristotelian disciplines as well as Arab-Islamic science. In particular, in the fourth part of the writing al-Fārābī presents natural science and metaphysical (or divine) science (*al-ʿilm al-ṭabīʿī wa-l-ʿilm al-ilāhī*) and their divisions. The subject-matter of natural philosophy is said to be natural

---

64 Olympiodorus, *In Meteora*, 3.34–4.15: Ἡ τάξις τῆς ἀναγνώσεως ἀπ' αὐτοῦ τοῦ Ἀριστοτέλους ἐνταῦθα διδάξεται· ἓξ γὰρ οὐσῶν πραγματειῶν συνιστασῶν τὴν πᾶσαν φυσιολογίαν τρισὶ μὲν ἕπεται ἡ παροῦσα πραγματεία, τριῶν δὲ προηγεῖται. τῇ μὲν γὰρ Φυσικῇ ἀκροάσει καὶ τῇ Περὶ οὐρανοῦ καὶ τῇ Περὶ γενέσεως καὶ φθορᾶς ἕπεται· προηγεῖται δὲ τῶν περὶ ψυχῆς, τουτέστι τῆς Περὶ φυτῶν καὶ τῆς Περὶ ζῴων. καὶ οὕτω τετάξεται ἡ Περὶ ψυχῆς. αὕτη γὰρ ἀμφιβίῳ ζῴῳ ἔοικε καὶ δύναται προηγεῖσθαι καὶ ἕπεσθαι· προηγεῖσθαι μέν, ἐπειδὴ καὶ περὶ φυσικῶν διαλέγεται ἐν τῇ Περὶ ψυχῆς, ἕπεσθαι δέ, ἐπειδὴ καὶ θεολογίαι εἰσίν. τὰ δὲ φυσικὰ δεῖ πρῶτον μανθάνειν καὶ οὕτως θεολογεῖν. ὅθεν καὶ τὸ σχεδὸν δι' αὐτὴν λέγει ὁ Ἀριστοτέλης. φησὶ γάρ· 'ἐν τούτοις τοῖς εἰρημένοις σχεδὸν πληροῦται ἡ φυσιολογία'. τὸ δὲ σχεδὸν διὰ τὴν Περὶ ψυχῆς· κἀκεῖ γὰρ φυσιολογίας μέμνηται ὁ Ἀριστοτέλης. καὶ μὴ ἀπορήσῃς, πῶς ἐν τῇ Περὶ ψυχῆς φυσιολογεῖ, οὐ γὰρ ἄπορον· ὁ γὰρ ἐν τῷ ὀγδόῳ λόγῳ Περὶ φυσικῆς ἀκροάσεως περὶ νοῦ διαλεχθεὶς καὶ εἰρηκὼς πᾶσαν κατὰ φύσιν κίνησιν ἠρτῆσθαι τῆς κινήσεως τῆς ἀπλανοῦς, οὗτος καὶ ἐν θεολογικοῖς περὶ φύσεως διαλέγεται ὥσπερ ἐν φυσικοῖς περὶ νοῦ. αὕτη καὶ ἡ τάξις.

65 As Olympiodorus writes, firstly we must become acquainted with physical matters, and then we can move to divine things, which are the realm of metaphysics.

66 Olympiodorus' position seems to be confirmed by what he writes in his *Prolegomena*, for there he maintains that the treatise *De anima* belongs to natural philosophy along with *Physica*, *De generatione et corruptione*, *De caelo*, and *Meteorologica* (7.31–3).

67 For the edition of this work, see al-Fārābī, *Kitāb Iḥṣāʾ al-ʿulūm*, ʻU. Amīn ed., al-Saʿāda Press, Cairo 1931, 1949^2, 1968^3. For the edition of the Latin translation of al-Fārābī's work and its translation into German, see al-Fārābī, *Über die Wissenschaften De scientiis: Nach der lateinischen Übersetzung Gerhards von Cremona. Mit einer Einleitung und kommentierenden Anmerkungen herausgegeben und übersetzt von* Franz Schupp, Felix Meiner Verlag, Hamburg 2005. There is also a Spanish translation of the Arabic text, which is based on the ms. el-Escorial, *Derenbourg* 646, ff. 27–45: A. González Palencia, *Al-Farabi, Catálogo de las ciencias*, Consejo Superior de Investigaciones Científicas, Patronato Menéndez y Pelayo – Instituto Miguel Asín, Madrid 1932, 1953^2.

bodies and their *per se* accidents (*fa-l-ʿilm al-ṭabīʿī yanẓuru fī l-aǧsām al-ṭabīʿiyya wa-fī l-aʿrāḍ allatī qiwāmuhā fī hāḏihi l-aǧsām*)[68] (111.3–116.16), and then the eight divisions of natural philosophy are listed, which reflect the internal division of its subject, i.e. the natural bodies, and correspond to a precise Aristotelian book (117.1–120.4).[69] In introducing the investigation of the compounds of anhomeomerous parts, i.e. organic living beings, al-Fārābī mentions the investigation of plants and their species and that of animals and their species as conducted in *De plantis*, and in *De animalibus* and *De anima* respectively.

The reference to Aristotle's *De animalibus* and *De anima* in the eighth division, the last on natural philosophy, seems to imply two things. Firstly, in addition to *De animalibus*, *De anima* seems to be thought to contain a part of the inquiry into animals – in the second book. Secondly, *De anima* seems also to contain a supplement that takes the zoological investigation a little further: for, in the third book it includes the specific treatment of the human being, i.e. the highest animal species, which seems to allow the transition to the metaphysical science.[70]

This scenario seems to be confirmed in al-Fārābī's *Kitāb Taḥṣīl al-saʿāda* (*Attainment of Happiness*), where the philosopher addresses the issue of the "true philosophy" by which happiness is achieved. However, since al-Fārābī and his contemporaries have at their disposal two accounts of philosophy from the Greek tradition, i.e. that of Plato and that of Aristotle, al-Fārābī provides an overview of them in, respectively, *Falsafat Aflāṭūn* (*Philosophy of Plato*) and *Falsafat Arisṭūṭālīs* (*Philosophy of Aristotle*), in order to show the unity of their purpose and intention.[71]

---

68 That a science inquiries into a specific subject and its *per se* accidents (or attributes) has been established in Aristotle's *Posterior Analytics*, I, 28. See p. 32 above.

69 The eight divisions are the following: (i) the general investigation of the principles which all natural bodies share (*Physica*); (ii) the inquiry into (ii.i) the simple bodies, the universe, and the heavens (*De Caelo et mundo* I – first part); (ii.ii) the elements of composite bodies (*De Caelo et mundo* I – second part); (ii.iii) what simple bodies share, the heavens and their parts (*De Caelo et mundo* II – two thirds); (ii.iv) what is proper to things that are not elements, but from which elements derive (*De Caelo et mundo* II – final part, III, IV); (iii) the investigation of generation and corruption in general, and of the way in which elements are engendered (*De generatione et corruptione*); (iv) the inquiry into the principles of accidents and affections that are proper to the elements (*On Celestial Impressions* [= *Meteorologica*] I-III); (v) the investigation of the homeomerous parts, and of what all bodies composed of homeomerous parts share (*On Celestial Impressions* [= *Meteorologica*] IV); (vi) the inquiry into minerals and their species (*De mineralibus*); (vii) the investigation of the compounds of anhomeomerous parts – first part: plants and their species (*De plantis*); (viii) the investigation of the compounds of anhomeomerous parts – second part: animals and their species (*De animalibus, De anima*).

70 It is worth recalling that according to Brockelmann (1943, I, 236) the first Arabic commentary on Aristotle's *De anima* was written by al-Fārābī and is preserved in an Indian manuscript (this information is also reported by Peters (1968, 44)). However, this commentary and the manuscript containing it seem not to be extant.

71 For the edition of the *Taḥṣīl al-saʿāda*, see al-Fārābī, *Kitāb Taḥṣīl al-saʿāda*, Ǧ. Āl-Yāsīn, Dār al-Andalus, Beirut 1981. The *Philosophy of Plato* and the *Philosophy of Aristotle* occupy respectively the second and the third part of Mahdi's translation. For their edition see: *Alfarabius de Platonis phi-*

In *Taḥṣīl*, in outlining the philosophical path leading to the acquisition of happiness, al-Fārābī presents natural investigation as an inquiry into bodies and things that are in bodies (*fa-yanẓuru fī l-ağsām wa-fī l-ašyā' al-mawğūda li-l-ağsām*, 58.10) and lists the genera of bodies, qualified as sensible or possessing sensible qualities, which natural investigation is about.[72] The crucial aspect of al-Fārābī's presentation of natural investigation is the parallel that he establishes between inquiry into the heavenly bodies and that into rational animals: for, just as the inquiry into the heavenly bodies leads to a search for principles that are neither bodies nor in bodies, likewise inquiry into rational animals forces the investigator to look for principles that are neither bodies nor in bodies and that never were or ever will be in bodies, i.e. the intellect. In both cases, al-Fārābī maintains that a complete acquaintance of these two subjects demands, in addition to natural investigation, another kind of investigation, that is, metaphysical (*fa-yaḥtāğu fī ḏālika ilà faḥṣ āḫar wa-'ilm āḫar yufridu fī(bi?)-mā ba'da l-ṭabī'iyyāt min al-mawğūdāt*, 60.1–2). Inquiry into the heavenly bodies and inquiry into the rational animals stand, therefore, between two sciences: the science of nature and the science of what is *beyond* natural things in the order of investigation and instruction, and *above* them in the order of being (*fa-yaṣīru 'inda ḏālika ayḍan fī l-wasaṭ bayna 'ilmayni: 'ilm al-ṭabī'a wa-'ilm mā ba'da l-ṭabī'iyyāt fī tartīb al-faḥṣ wa-l-ta'līm wa-fawqa l-ṭabī'iyyāt fī rutbat al-wuğūd*, 60.2–4). Otherwise said, in both cases the investigation departs from the realm of the natural, sensible bodies and ascends to the realm of incorporeal principles.

That psychology (together with the investigation of the heavenly bodies) is between natural science and metaphysics is more directly and precisely stated in the *Falsafat Arisṭūṭālīs*. The divisions of Aristotle's philosophy of nature that al-Fārābī presents are those that are listed in his *Iḥṣā'*; however, here the nature of *De anima* emerges more clearly. The botanic and zoological investigation that comes after that of minerals is an inquiry into animate natural substances, i.e. plants and animals; therefore, the principles that Aristotle has introduced so far are not sufficient to account for the animation of these substances and their powers and activities, but an additional principle is required, i.e. the soul. Although it is not explicitly mentioned, it is fair enough to suppose that according to al-Fārābī the principle of

---

losophia (Falsafat Aflāṭūn), F. Rosenthal, R. Walzer eds., Warburg Institut, London 1943; *Al-Fārābī's Philosophy of Aristotle (Falsafat Arisṭūṭālīs)*. Arabic Text, Edited with an Introduction and Notes by M. Mahdi, Dār Majallat Ši'r, Beirut 1961.

72 Here al-Fārābī uses more or less the same terminology that he uses in his *Kitāb Iḥṣā' al-'ulūm* (111.4–5) in order to describe the subject of the natural investigation, i.e. the bodies and their *per se* accidents. The genera of bodies are the following: (i) the heavenly bodies (*al-ağsām al-samāwiyya*); (ii) earth, water, air, and things of this kind (fire, vapor, etc.) (*al-arḍ wa-l-mā' wa-l-hawā' wa-mā ğānasa ḏālika min nār wa-buḫār wa-ġayr ḏālika*); (iii) the stony and mineral bodies on the surface of the earth and inside it (*al-ağsām al-ḥağariyya wa-l-ma'diniyya allatī 'alà saṭḥ al-arḍ wa-fī 'amqihā*); (iv) plants (*al-nabāt*); (v) irrational animals (*al-ḥayawān ġayr al-nāṭiq*); and, (vi) rational animals (*al-ḥayawān al-nāṭiq*).

the animation of the organic bodies of plants and animals is investigated in the first two books of Aristotle's *De anima*.[73] After having introduced the treatment of the principle of plants and animals, al-Fārābī mentions a series of collateral investigations dealing with particular aspects of animal life (*Parva naturalia*).[74] After having accomplished the investigation of non-rational animals, al-Fārābī signals a transition to the investigation of human being. In particular, he introduces a new inquiry into the human being and its powers and activities, which require an additional principle, higher than the soul, in order to be accounted for. This additional principle is the intellect, which manages to render the human being as substance. Its treatment, which seems to be found in *De anima* III, brings the natural science to completion and terminates in metaphysics.

Therefore, in his *Falsafat Arisṭūṭālīs* al-Fārābī seems to split up the psychological investigation that Aristotle carried out in *De anima*, into two distinct investigations dealing with two ontologically different subjects: (a) *De anima* I-II deals with the soul insofar as it is the principle of the animation and of the psychical activities of plants and animals; (b) *De anima* III deals with the intellect insofar as it is the principle of human beings, which transcends the realm of natural philosophy and shows a crucial continuity with the metaphysical investigation.[75] Thus al-Fārābī can conclude that, with respect to the principles of the human being (as well as with that of the heavenly bodies), natural investigation terminates in incorporeal entities,[76] which belong to the realm of metaphysics.

Staying in the Middle

That *De anima* is a treatise not entirely physical nor entirely metaphysical and that psychology as a science takes a middle rank between natural philosophy and metaphysics is a position endorsed in Late Antiquity by Simplicius. In the prologue of his

---

73 Here al-Fārābī refers to the activities that are minimally constitutive of life such as nutrition, for which the soul is responsible, and which are dealt with in the second book of Aristotle's *De anima*.
74 It is noteworthy that here al-Fārābī seems to list the titles of treatises making up the bulk of *Parva naturalia* according to the list of topics supposedly treated therein and mentioned by Aristotle at the beginning of *De sensu*, 1, 436 a7–b1. See Chapter 1, n. 51.
75 It is noteworthy that, unlike the case of all the other parts of natural philosophy, in the case of the two parts into which Aristotelian psychology is split, al-Fārābī does not explicitly mention the title of *De anima* nor the internal division that he seems to assume. Within psychology, a similar distinction between an inquiry into the principle of the vital functions of the bodies, i.e. animation (= *empsychia*), and the investigation into the soul *stricto sensu*, that is, the rational soul, can be detected in Porphyry (see, for example, his *Contra Boethum*, whose fragments are preserved in Eusebius). On the notion of *empsychia* and its use in Porphyry, see G. Karamanolis, "Porphyry's notion of *empsychia*"; *Bulletin of the Institute of Classical Studies*, 50, 2007, 91–109. I owe this reference to M. Rashed.
76 With respect to psychology, here al-Fārābī explicitly refers to the Active Intellect, which is somehow the principle of the activity of the human theoretical intellect; by contrast, with respect to investigation of heavenly bodies, he refers to their mover.

commentary on Aristotle's *Physics*, he divides theoretical philosophy into three parts and assigns to both mathematics and psychology the same, intermediary position between natural philosophy and metaphysics, because their subject-matter is partly transcendent and partly not transcendent.[77] The same position is expressed in Ps.-Simplicius commentary on Aristotle's *De anima*.[78] Ps.-Simplicius maintains that study of the soul mediates between natural philosophy and metaphysics. This claim is grounded on the aforementioned passage from *De part. an.*, I, 1, where Aristotle seems to limit the task of the natural philosopher to the investigation of the soul that is the form of a natural, organic body. Thus, according to Ps.-Simplicius' interpretation, Aristotle considers the investigation of a part of soul, i.e. of νοῦς, to fall completely outside the province of natural philosophy, since it is not the form of a body and is, consequently, separable. Accordingly, its investigation is deferred to first philosophy, to which the investigation of separate substances pertains. However, Ps.-Simplicius is aware of the fact that, in the third book of *De anima*, Aristotle does deal with νοῦς and its activities. Then, given the heterogeneity of the subject of the investigation that Aristotle has undertaken in his writing, Ps.-Simplicius concludes that psychology is neither entirely physical, since it encompasses the study of the intellect which is not a properly physical entity,[79] nor entirely metaphys-

77 Simplicius, *In Aristotelis Physicorum libros quattuor priores commentaria*, ed. H. Diels, *Commentaria in Aristotelem Graeca*, vol. 9, Reimer, Berlin 1882, 1.21–2.7: τὸ δὲ περὶ τὰ πῇ μὲν χωριστὰ πῇ δὲ ἀχώριστα τῆς ὕλης εἴδη τοῦτο μαθηματικὸν καὶ περὶ ψυχῆς καλοῦσι. καὶ γὰρ τὴν μαθηματικὴν οὐσίαν μέσην λέγουσι τῷ μὲν καθόλου τὸ χωριστὸν ἔχουσαν τῆς ὕλης, τῷ δὲ διαστατῷ καὶ διακεκριμένῳ τὸ ἀχώριστον. καὶ τὴν ψυχὴν δὲ ὁμοίως κατὰ μὲν τὰς αἰσθήσεις καὶ φαντασίας καὶ κατὰ τὸν δυνάμει νοῦν πολὺ τὸ ἔνυλον ἔχουσαν νοοῦσι, κατὰ δὲ τὸν ἐνεργείᾳ νοῦν, ὃν καὶ αὐτὸν τῆς ψυχῆς ὄντα ἄκρον δείκνυσιν ὁ Ἀριστοτέλης, κἂν μὴ δοκῇ τῷ Ἀλεξάνδρῳ, τὸ χωριστὸν τῆς ὕλης ἔχειν φασίν. ἀλλὰ τὰ μὲν ἄλλα μέρη ἐν ταῖς οἰκείαις πραγματείαις ἀκριβεστέρας τεύξεται διακρίσεως. Here Simplicius criticizes Alexander's position on the epistemological status of *De anima*. I. Düring maintains that, unlike other commentators, Simplicius divided theoretical philosophy into four parts; however, it is incorrect. Actually, Simplicius divides theoretical philosophy into three parts but, unlike other commentators, includes psychology in the intermediary part, alongside mathematics. See I. Düring, *Aristotle in the Ancient Biographical Tradition*, 446. On the middle rank assigned to mathematics and psychology and to their mutual similarity, see the prologue of Proclus' commentary on Euclid's *Elements*, and the discussion of this issue in Ph. Merlan, *From Platonism to Neoplatonism*, Martinus Nijhoff, The Hague 1968, in part. Ch. 1 "Soul and Mathematicals", 8–29, and ch. 3 "The Subdivisions of Theoretical Philosophy", 53–77.

78 For the issue of the authorship of this commentary, see Chapter 1, n. 42. Consequently, due to the debated attribution of this commentary to Simplicius, I will mention its author as Ps.-Simplicius.

79 It is worth noticing that for Ps.-Simplicius *De anima* deals with the all descent soul and, therefore, the intellect investigated therein is not some transcendent intellect but the human intellect that is in us (2.33–3.2: ὅσον δὲ νοερόν, τῇ πρώτῃ φιλοσοφίᾳ, ἣ τὰ νοητὰ γινώσκουσα καὶ τὸν τῶν νοητῶν θεωρητικὸν γινώσκει νοῦν, καὶ οὐ τὸν ἐξῃρημένον μόνον, ἀλλὰ καὶ τὸν ἐν ἡμῖν). However, it is crucial to point out that this statement does not imply that the soul of mortal living beings is itself mortal, but only that the material composite in which it inheres undergoes generation and corruption (*In De anima*, 4.8–11: ἀλλ' οὐχ ὡς ἀχώριστον τοῦ σώματος τιθέμενος τὴν ψυχήν· τὴν γοῦν αἰτίαν τοῦ μὴ

ical, since it also deals with the soul insofar as it is the principle of all other activities, which are tied to the body. Psychology, therefore, holds an intermediary position between the natural and the supernatural. The fact that psychology shares in both the natural and the supernatural realm is possible – Ps.-Simplicius argues – because Aristotle has taken natural philosophy and metaphysics in a broad sense:[80] for, as been noted by other Late Ancient exegetes, the former extends upwards when it deals with the intellect, whereas the latter stretches downwards when it treats a kind of intellect, that is, the human intellect which, unlike the celestial intellects and the first unmoved mover, is not entirely separate from bodily matter (the human intellect operates with the data acquired by the external senses and elaborated by imagination).

In early Arabic philosophy a position similar to the one endorsed by Ps.-Simplicius is that of Abū Yūsuf Yaʿqūb ibn Isḥāq al-Kindī (d. 870 ca.). Al-Kindī was the first philosopher to address directly the issue of the discrete parts of philosophy, the Aristotelian books devoted to them, and their specific subject. He devoted to this reflection his *Risāla fī kammiyya kutub Arisṭāṭālīs wa-mā yuḥtāğu ilayhi fī taḥṣīl al-falsafa* (*Treatise on the Quantity of Aristotle's Books and What is Required for the Attainment of Philosophy*).[81] According to the editors of the Arabic text, this work can be divided into seven sections. The second and the seventh section offer two classifications of Aristotelian writings, from which al-Kindī's position of the epistemological status of psychology, among the other sciences, can be inferred.

μεμνῆσθαι ἡμᾶς τῆς χωριστῆς ζωῆς ἀποδίδωσιν ἐν τῷ τρίτῳ, ὡς ὄντας δηλαδὴ καὶ πρὸ τῆς εἰς σῶμα ἀφίξεως).

80 Simplicius, *In De anima*, 3.4–9: διὸ οὔτε φυσικὴ ἁπλῶς οὔτε μετὰ τὰ φυσικὰ ἡ περὶ ψυχῆς θεωρία, ἀλλ'ἀμφοῖν ἐχομένη, ὡς ἐν τούτοις ὑπὸ τοῦ Ἀριστοτέλους διώρισται. ἔοικε δὲ ἐν πλάτει ὁ Ἀριστοτέλης καὶ τὴν φυσιολογίαν καὶ τὴν μετὰ τὰ φυσικὰ τιθέμενος φιλοσοφίαν ἑκατέραν μέχρι ψυχῆς τὴν μὲν ἀνάγειν τὴν δὲ προάγειν, [...].

81 For the edition of this work, see *Rasāʾil al-Kindī al-falsafiyya*, ed. M. ʿA. Abū-Rīda, vol. I, Dār al-fikr al-ʿarabī, Cairo 1950–53, 363–384. For an introduction to, an edition of, and an annotated Italian translation of this work, see M. Guidi, R. Walzer, "Studi su al-Kindī I: Uno Scritto Introduttivo allo Studio di Aristotele", *Memorie della Reale Accademia Nazionale dei Lincei. Classe di Scienze Morali, Storiche e Filosofiche*, ser. VI, vol. VI, fasc. V, 1940, 375–419. An annotated English translation is provided by P. Adamson and P. E. Pormann in their *The Philosophical Works*, 281–296. For some insights into its content, see A. Cortabarria Beitia, "La classification des sciences chez al-Kindī", *Melanges de l'Institut Dominicain d'Etudes Orientales du Caire*, 11, 1972, 49–76; J. Jolivet, "Classifications of the sciences", in R. Rashed, J. Morelon eds., *Encyclopedia of the History of Arabic Science*, vol. 3, Routledge, London-New York 1996, 1008–1025; id., "L'*Êpître sur la quantité des livres d'Aristote*, par al-Kindī (une lecture)", in R. Morelon, A. Hasnawi eds., *De Zénon d'Elée à Poincaré. Recueil d'études en hommage à Roshdi Rashed*, Peeters, Louvain-Paris 2004, 665–683. This is the first work in Arabic philosophy to deal with Aristotle's system of science through the mediation of one (or more) Greek source(s) – in their introduction to the edition and the translation of this treatise, Guidi-Walzer claim that al-Kindī's source might have been a *prolegomenon* written by a straightforwardly Neoplatonic author around the VI century AD; see Guidi, Walzer, "Studi su al-Kindī I", 378 – and it is among the first to use the word *falsafa* in order to refer to pagan wisdom in Greek language.

The first classification of Aristotle's books begins with a preliminary distinction between the non-Aristotelian propaedeutic sciences (*ʿilm al-riyāḍa, sc.* mathematics) and the quadripartition of Aristotle's writings into logical, physical, psychological, and metaphysical. This quadripartition[82] seems to be legitimized by a concise reference to the different subject of some of these writings. In particular, with respect to the third group of writings, which includes *De anima, De sensu et sensato, De somno et vigilia,* and *De longitudine et brevitate vitae*, al-Kindī maintains that the psychological writings deal with what has no need for nature, subsists in itself, and does not require bodies, even though it exists together with bodies to which it is connected in some way (*wa-ammā l-nawʿ al-ṯāliṯ fa-fīhā kāna mustaġniyan ʿan al-ṭabīʿa qāʾiman bi-ḏātihī ġayr muḥtāǧ ilà l-aǧsām fa-innahū yūǧadu maʿa l-aǧsām muwāṣilan lahā bi-aḥad anwāʿ al-muwāṣala*, 364.15 – 365.1).[83] Thus, the subject of psychology has an ambivalent status: on the one hand, it differs from the subject of natural philosophy because it does not need a bodily substratum in order to exist; on the other hand, however, it differs from the higher subject of metaphysics because it does exist together with the body, even though it is said to have no need for it.

The second classification of Aristotle's books, by which the Kindian treatise is brought to completion, is grounded on the notion of *ġaraḍ* (goal), that is, on the intentions that Aristotle had in mind when he wrote these books.[84] It echoes the first classification but, in addition, it precisely refers to the subject dealt with in each Aristotelian book.[85] In particular, botany (*De plantis*) and zoology (*De animalibus*) conclude al-Kindī's list of Aristotle's books on natural philosophy, and psychology seems to deal with the essence of the soul, its faculties and, among them, sensation and all its species (intellectual perception included) after the books on natural philosophy. Therefore, it might well be the case that al-Kindī considered Aristotle's *De anima* not a treatise of *general psychology*, namely a theoretical introduction to the treatment of plants and animals, but as providing a specific treatment of the human soul and the perceptive faculties belonging to it, together with the account of the other, lower activities that human soul performs in and by means of the

82 It is worth recalling that an intermediate and independent position between natural philosophy and metaphysics was also assigned to psychology by the historian al-Yaʿqūbī (IX c.), and in the encyclopaedia of the Iḫwān al-Ṣafāʾ (X c.). See Guidi, Walzer, "Studi su al-Kindī I", 378 – 380.

83 A similar characterization of the subject of Aristotle's psychological writings can be found before the list of psychological writings: *fa-ammā mā qāla fīhi ʿalà l-ašyāʾ allatī lā taḥtāǧu ilà l-aǧsām fī qiwāmihā wa-ṯabātihā wa-qad yūǧadu maʿa l-aǧsām fa-hiya arbaʿa* [...] (368.12 – 13).

84 On the notion of σκοπός (goal) in the Late Ancient commentary tradition, see Simplicius, *Commentaire sur les Catégories*.

85 Aristotle's *De anima* accounts for the quiddity (*māhiyya*) of the soul, its faculties, their divisions, their common and specific features; deals with sensation (*ḥiss*); and defines its species (*taḥdīd anwāʿihī*); *De sensu et sensato* deals exhaustively with the causes of sensation and sensible things, which have been already treated in *De anima* II in a more concise manner; *De somno et vigilia* explains what sleep is, its qualities, dreams and their causes; *De longitudine et brevitate vitae* deals with the length and shortness of life.

body. Crucial in this respect are the intermediate position assigned to the science of the soul and the qualification of its subject as subsisting in itself, although it is found to exist in the body to which it is somehow related.[86]

What is more, al-Kindī qualifies the nature of the soul in a more explicit manner, i.e. as a self-subsistent substance, in his psychological writings. For, at the beginning of his *Al-Qawl fī l-nafs* (*Discourse on the Soul*), and of his *Kalām li-l-Kindī fī l-nafs muḫtaṣar waǧīz* (*Concise Statement about the Soul*), he portrays the soul, which basically corresponds to the human soul, as "simple" (*basīṭa*) and "simple substance" (*ǧawhar basīṭ*),[87] from which it is fair to infer that the Kindian soul transcends the body and is, therefore, more similar to the celestial, separate substances of metaphysics than to the terrestrial compounds of matter and form dealt with in natural philosophy. The most intriguing aspect of al-Kindī's view on the soul,[88] which can also be referred to as his view on the nature of man, is the fact that he explicitly ascribes it to Aristotle.[89] Aristotle, however, has never referred to the soul as a "simple substance".[90] The position according to which the Aristotelian soul is a "simple sub-

86 On the intermediate position that al-Kindī assigns to psychology in the *Kammiyya*, and on the fact that elsewhere he follows the traditional Aristotelian line, and identifies mathematics as the intermediate science, see P. Adamson, "The Kindian Tradition: the Structure of Philosophy in Arabic Neoplatonism", in C. D'Ancona ed., *The Libraries of the Neoplatonists*, Brill, Leiden 2007, 351–70, in part. n. 23.

87 See al-Kindī, *Fī l-qawl fī l-nafs al-muḫtaṣar min kitāb Arisṭū wa-Flāṭun wa-sā'ir al-falāsifa*, in *Rasā'il*, 273.3–5: "I (*sc.* al-Kindī) say that the soul is simple (*inna l-nafs basīṭa*) and has nobility, perfection, and great status (*ḏāt šaraf wa-kamāl ʿaẓimat al-ša'n*). Its substance originates from the substance of the Creator (*ǧawharuhā min ǧawhar al-bāri'*), the exalted One, just as the light of the Sun originates from the Sun". (English translation from Adamson-Pormann, *On the Doctrine of the Soul, Epitomised from the Book of Aristotle and Plato, and the other Philosophers*, 113); id., *Kalām li l-Kindī fī l-nafs muḫtaṣar waǧīz*, in *Rasā'il*, 281.5–6: "Al-Kindī said: Aristotle says about the soul that it is a simple substance (*innahā ǧawhar basīṭ*) which makes its acts manifest through bodies" (English translation from Adamson-Pormann, *Concise and Brief Statement About the Soul*, 120). I warmly thank M. Rashed for drawing my attention to these Kindian passages.

88 This doctrine recurs in a paraphrase of the *De anima* produced in al-Kindī's entourage, namely that published by R. Arnzen, and is found in the *Theology of Aristotle*, another work connected with his circle. See Al-Ḥasan ibn Mūsā al-Nawbaḫtī, *Commentary on Aristotle* De generatione et corruptione. *Edition, translation and commentary by* M. Rashed, Collection "Scientia Graeco-Arabica" 19, De Gruyter, Berlin-Boston 2015, 389–390.

89 See the second passage quoted at n. 87.

90 As M. Rashed has shown in his Al-Ḥasan ibn Mūsā al-Nawbaḫtī, *Commentary on Aristotle's* De generatione et corruptione, 387: "Aristotle does not mention 'simple substance', οὐσία ἁπλῆ, except in the Platonising context of his theology", that is in *Metaph.*, XII, 7, 1072 a31–2. Al-Kindī might owe it to the Late Ancient or early Byzantine doctrine of the soul as "simple substance". Iamblichus seems to have been the first to ascribe this doctrine to Aristotle; however, it is with Ammonius that "the claim becomes scholastic: the soul is a simple substance insofar as it is a form, and form is a simple substance, a part of a composite substance. This argument appears in the commentaries on the *Categories* by Ammonius, by Philoponus, and by Olympiodorus, and likewise in the commentary of Philoponus on *De anima*". See Al-Ḥasan ibn Mūsā al-Nawbaḫtī, *Commentary on Aristotle's* De generatione et corruptione, 387–389.

stance" certainly played a role in the lively debate about the soul and, notably, the nature of man in the IX-X centuries.[91] One of the actors in such a debate was Abū Muḥammad al-Ḥasan ibn Mūsā al-Nawbaḫtī (d. 912–922), a *mutakallim faylasūf* (theologian and philosopher),[92] an important Imāmī theologian of Baghdad, the author of the *Kitāb al-Ārā' wa-l-Diyānāt* (*Book of Opinions and Religions*), left unfinished and fragmentarily preserved.[93] Among his more than forty books, a treatise on the nature of man (*Al-Insān*) is listed. Unfortunately, this treatise is lost, but its outline can be inferred from the section on the essence of man (*māhiyyat al-insān*) contained in al-Šayḫ al-Mufīd (d. 1022)'s *Masā'il al-Sarawiyya*. There, al-Nawbaḫtī's doctrine of the soul as a self-subsistent, immaterial substance is said to go back to the doctrine of the soul as a simple substance (*ǧawhar basīṭ*), ascribed to some *ancient sages* (*al-ḥukamā' al-awā'il*), who might well be the same Greek philosophers to whom al-Kindī owes his doctrine of the soul. Or, alternatively, the doxographical context provided by al-Šayḫ al-Mufīd might depend directly on al-Kindī's works.

Lastly, in relation to the figure of al-Kindī, Qusṭā ibn Lūqā al-Ba'labakkī (d. 920 ca.) has to be mentioned, not only because they were active in Baghdad in the IX century, but also because of some similarities between their arrangement of the parts of philosophy and of the corresponding Aristotelian writings. However, the similarity between the two arrangements does not concern the position assigned to psychology but rather the internal subdivisions of natural philosophy. For in the classification of sciences contained in ff. 78v-81r of ms. Ayasofya 4855[94] Qusṭā ibn Lūqā divides natural philosophy, which is the first division of theoretical science to be mentioned, into three parts: (i) the science of the fundamental principles from which composition (= what is composed) derives (*al-'ilm bi-l-uṣūl allatī 'anhā kāna al-tarkīb*), which includes astronomy (*al-'ilm bi-l-falak wa-l-kawākib*), meteorology (*al-'ilm bi-l-āṯār al-kā'ina fī l-ǧaww*), and geology (*al-'ilm bi-l-āṯār al-kā'ina fī l-arḍ*); (ii) zoology (*al-'ilm bi-l-ḥayawān*), and (iii) botany (*al-'ilm bi-l-nabāt*).[95] As for the Aristotelian writings devoted to these parts of natural philosophy, Qusṭā ibn Lūqā mentions the following books: *Physics*, *On Heavens*, *On Generation and Corruption*, *On Atmospheric Phenomena*, *On the Natures of Animals*, *On Plants*, *On Sense and*

91 I will not delve into the ninth-century dispute concerning the nature of man (*Fī l-insān*). Here I am simply pointing at the connection between it and al-Kindī's philosophical treatment of the same issue.

92 On the basis of his commentary on Aristotle's *De generatione et corruptione*, M. Rashed has argued in favour of al-Nawbaḫtī's 'philosophical project', against Madelung's sharp argument in favour of his exclusively theological concern. See Al-Ḥasan ibn Mūsā al-Nawbaḫtī, *Commentary on Aristotle's* De generatione et corruptione, 365–366.

93 For a detailed profile of al-Nawbaḫtī, see Al-Ḥasan ibn Mūsā al-Nawbaḫtī, *Commentary on Aristotle's* De generatione et corruptione.

94 H. Daiber, "Qosṭā ibn Lūqā (9. Jh.) über die Einteilung der Wissenschaften", *Zeitschrift für die Geschichte der arabisch-islamischen Wissenschaften*, 6, 1990, 93–129. In this article the Arabic text, German translation, and commentary are provided.

95 See Daiber, "Qosṭā ibn Lūqā", 108–110.

What is Sensed, On the Soul, "and other books belonging to this group" (*wa-ġayrahū min al-kutub al-dāḫila fī hāḏā l-fann*).[96]

This tripartition of natural philosophy, and the titles of Aristotle's books connected with it, seem to be very similar to the articulation of natural philosophy proposed by al-Kindī in his *Risāla fī kammiyya kutub Arisṭāṭālīs*. There, the group of physical writings contains *Physics, On Heavens, On Generation and Corruption, On Atmospheric and Terrestrial Phenomena* (= *Meteorology* I-III), *On Minerals* (= *Meteorology* IV), *On Plants*, and *On Animals*. Apart from the inversion of the position of botany and zoology, the only significant difference is the fact that in Qusṭā ibn Lūqā's classification psychology does not represent another part of theoretical science, different from natural philosophy. Actually, it is not even explicitly mentioned (perhaps it is subsumed under the mention of zoology and botany, as some exegetes suggest to interpret the lack of reference to *De anima* in the prologue to Aristotle's *Meteorology*). Furthermore, *On Sense and What is Sensed* (= *De sensu et sensibilibus*) and *De anima* are mentioned as the last items of the collection of writings on natural philosophy, perhaps so as to suggest that psychology represents its culmination.

Taking a Breath

Aristotle's *De anima* can be rightly considered the first exhaustive writing devoted to sublunary soul as the formal principle of organic living beings. As emerged from this survey, the human rational soul seems to represent an exception to this global account. Though considered in some respect the form and the actuality of the human body, the human soul seems to enjoy a different status from that of its cognates: due to its capacity for performing its peculiar activity without any bodily organ, it seems to be capable of self-subsisting with no need for a body. Nonetheless, though on several occasions within and outside of the *De anima* Aristotle seems to acknowledge the peculiarity of the human soul, he never directly accounts for its specific nature which, by challenging the unity of the subject-matter of psychology, risks challenging the unity of the entire science.

The followers of Aristotle, by contrast, directly tackle the issue of the nature of the human rational soul because they are interested in preserving its exceptionality while keeping its treatment in the framework of one single science. The solutions that the exegetes of Aristotelian psychology envisaged to solve the tensions arising within it are various but, as we saw, they can be placed into three main groups. (i) The group of those who downgrade the human soul to the level of every other sublunary soul in order to make it immaterial but corruptible, like all other sublunary souls. Alexander of Aphrodisias is the main representative of this strategy (Themistius can be also included in this group). He seems to focus primarily on the way in

96 See Daiber, "Qosṭā ibn Lūqā", 110 – 113.

which Aristotle presents his project of investigation of the soul as a structured unity in *De an.*, I, 1, and his definition of the soul as the first actuality of an organic body in *De an.*, II, 1, and to deliberately ignore the difficulties raised by those passages in which Aristotle hints at the peculiarity of the human soul, and shift these to independent discussions. (ii) The group of those who believe that Aristotelian psychology is a unitary science dealing properly with every instance of sublunary souls and at the same time argue that the human rational soul is different from other souls because of its capacity for self-subsisting and its individual immortality. For this reason, they place psychology on the edge of natural philosophy, protruding into metaphysics, precisely because its treatment of a separable entity does not entirely fit in natural philosophy. Representatives of this group are, on the Greek side, Philoponus and Olympiodorus, members of the school of Alexandria, while on the Arabic side is al-Fārābī. In particular, Philoponus uses those passages of Aristotle's *De anima* (and *De partibus animalium*) in which the Stagirite seems to portray the human rational soul as different from the other sublunary souls, in order to account for its exceptionality. (iii) The group of those who claim that psychology takes a middle rank between natural philosophy and metaphysics, representing a branch of theoretical philosophy on its own (together with mathematics in the case of Simplicius/Ps.-Simplicius). In particular, they consider psychology as dealing primarily with the human rational soul, which is partly separate and partly inseparable from its bodily substratum, like the subject-matter of mathematics. Representatives of this group are Simplicius/Ps.-Simplicius and al-Kindī, whose interpretation of Aristotelian psychology, though not entirely identical (for example, unlike Simplicius/Ps.-Simplicius, al-Kindī does not believe that psychology and mathematics constitute one single branch of theoretical philosophy), rests on similar assumptions.

This survey of the exegetical vicissitudes of Aristotle's *De anima* from the III to the X century, which however is not meant to be exhaustive, represents the background requisite for understanding Avicenna's project of reworking Aristotelian psychology in the *Nafs*.

Chapter Three

Subject: *Psychologia generalis* vs. *psychologia specialis*

Introduction

The soul, particularly though not exclusively the human soul, represents the cornerstone of the philosophical system of Avicenna: for it is not only the main topic of psychology, i.e. the science of the soul, but also the subject of philosophical knowledge.[1] Throughout his philosophical pursuit Avicenna almost continuously wrote about the soul, from his first work, *Maqāla fī l-nafs ʿalà sunnat al-iḫtiṣār* (*Compendium on the Soul*), to his last writing, *Risāla fī l-kalām ʿalà l-nafs al-nāṭiqa* (*On the Rational Soul*).[2] To this topic he devoted several sorts of works, i.e. sections within expository *summae*,[3] monographic treatises, and commentaries;[4] however, Avicenna undertakes the most exhaustive inquiry into the soul in the *Nafs*, in which for the first time in Arabic philosophy an enterprise similar to the one Aristotle pursued in his *De anima* is carried out.

In his *Nafs*, as well as in the *Šifāʾ* in its entirety, Avicenna is highly dependent on Peripatetic sources.[5] This dependence results in his attempt to fit into his investigation of the soul two concerns that directly derive from Aristotle and the subsequent, Peripatetic exegesis of his *De anima*.[6] For in *Nafs*, on the one hand and in Aristotelian fashion, Avicenna investigates the soul insofar as it is responsible for the activities observable in bodies, that is, the soul *qua* principle of plant[7] and animal life,

1 The twofold aspect of the soul, the subject-matter of psychology and, at the same time, the subject of philosophical knowledge, emerges in the thought-experiment of the *Flying Man* at the end of *Nafs*, I, 1 (16.2–17 [36.49–37.68]). On this twofold aspect of the soul, see M. Rashed, "Chose, *item* et distinction: l'"homme volant" d'Avicenne avec et contre Abū Hāšim al-Ǧubbāʾī", *Arabic Sciences and Philosophy*, 28.2, 2018, 167–185, in part. 167–168. See also D. L. Black, "Avicenna on Self-Awareness and Knowing that One Knows", in S. Rahman, T. Street, H. Tahiri eds., *The Unity of Science in the Arabic Tradition. Science, Logic and Epistemology and their Interactions*, Springer, Dordrecht 2008, 63–87.

2 On these two Avicennian works see Gutas, *Avicenna and the Aristotelian Tradition*, in part. 4–8 and 80–86 on the *Compendium on the Soul*, and 67–75 on *On the Rational Soul*.

3 For a diachronic analysis of the psychological section of all Avicennian *summae*, see Chapter 6.

4 A complete list of Avicenna's psychological writings can be found in Gutas, *Avicenna and the Aristotelian Tradition*, 529–540.

5 See Chapter 1, § *Sources*.

6 See Chapter 2.

7 Although A. Tawara has recently argued that in the *Kitāb al-Nabāt* (*Book of Plants*), i.e. the botany of the *Šifāʾ*, Avicenna denies that plants have life (see A. Tawara, "Avicenna's denial of life in plants", *Arabic Sciences and Philosophy*, 24.1, 2014, 127–138), in my article "Is Nutrition a Sufficient Condition for Life? Avicenna's Position between Natural Philosophy and Medicine", in R. Lo Presti, G. Korobili eds., *Nutrition and Nutritive Soul in Aristotle and Aristotelianism*, De Gruyter – Topics in Ancient Philosophy, Berlin-Boston 2020, 221–258, I show that precisely in *Nabāt*, 1 Avicenna assigns to plants the most elementary form of life, i.e. vegetative, nutritive life.

https://doi.org/10.1515/9783110706840-005

whereas, on the other hand, he attempts to answer the question as to whether the soul corrupts or endures, a question that transcends the boundaries of Aristotle's psychology but, at the same time, seems to be conceived as urgent as the investigation of the soul *qua* principle of plant and animal life. As becomes clear to the reader of the *Nafs*, this question concerns the possibility that there might be something more to investigate than the mere phenomenal datum, that is, the soul's being the principle of activities in something else, i. e. the body. However, this question does not concern every sublunary soul but rather the human soul, the only instance of soul with respect to which it seems not senseless to investigate what it is in itself, simply because in this case there seems to be an *in itself* aspect which survives after the severance of its relation to the body.[8]

Thus, in the *Nafs* there are two investigations that run in parallel from the very beginning of the work: (a) the investigation of the soul as a *relational* entity, always considered in connection with the body, which also leads to the investigation of this entity, essential to explain the body-soul relationship, and (b) that of the human soul *in itself*, which firstly though cursorily emerges in I, 1 with the thought-experiment of the *Flying Man*, and more explicitly only in *Nafs*, V, 2 and V, 4. There Avicenna demonstrates that the human soul does not subsist as something impressed in corporeal matter, either as a form or as a faculty,[9] and answers the question as to whether the human soul corrupts (*fasada*) together with the corruption of the body, or endures

---

8 The twofold consideration of the soul, namely in relation to the body and in itself, emerges for example in *Nafs*, I, 1, 10.15–11.4 [26.24–27.36]. On this passage see p. 107 below. This idea might have come to Avicenna from Philoponus' exegesis of Aristotle's *De anima*. See Philoponus, *In De anima*, 246.27–247.7: "And besides, the intellect, insofar as it is actuality of the body (καθὸ ἐντελέχειά ἐστι τοῦ σώματος), is to that extent inseparable (ἀχώριστός). But it is actuality of the body neither in substance (οὔτε τῇ οὐσίᾳ) nor in all its activities (οὔτε πάσαις ἑαυτοῦ ταῖς ἐνεργείαις), but in the ones that it has from the relation to the body (ἐκ τῆς σχέσεως τῆς πρὸς τὸ σῶμα), among which especially the practical ones (αἱ πρακτικαί). These activities are inseparable (ἀχώριστοί) from the body. And just as the steersman (ὁ κυβερνήτης), who is the actuality of the ship, insofar as he is steersman, is inseparable from the ship (ἀχώριστός), but since he is not only steersman, but also a man (ἐπειδὴ δὲ οὐ μόνον κυβερνήτης ἐστὶν ἀλλὰ καὶ ἄνθρωπος), as a man not being actuality of the ship, he is in this way also separable (χωριστός), so also our soul (οὕτω καὶ ἡ ἡμετέρα ψυχὴ), as a soul being actuality of the body in this way would not be without a body, but since it has some activities which are also separable from the body (ἔχει τινὰς καὶ χωριστὰς σώματος ἐνεργείας), I mean those related to the intelligibles (τὰς περὶ τῶν νοητῶν φημι), which the body not only does not help, but actually hinders, it is quite clear that it will also have the substance separable (πρόδηλον ὅτι καὶ τὴν οὐσίαν ἕξει χωριστήν), and it then is and is called *intellect* (νοῦς τότε καὶ οὖσα καὶ λεγομένη), and no longer soul except in potentiality (οὐκέτι μέντοι ψυχὴ εἰ μὴ δυνάμει), just as, when it is in a body, it is also intellect in potentiality, as he also says" (English translation by W. Charlton, slightly modified). More on Philoponus' influence of Avicenna's psychology in Chapter 4. On Philoponus' influence on Avicenna, in particular with respect to the doctrine of the immateriality of the intellect, see Gutas, "Philoponos and Avicenna", and id., "Avicenna's Marginal Glosses".

9 *Nafs*, V, 2 is entitled "[*Chapter*] *on establishing that the rational soul does not subsist as something impressed in corporeal matter*".

(*baqiya*).[10] Both investigations aim to ascertain the existence and the essence of the soul *in relation to* the body, of which it is the soul, and *in itself* respectively.

In this chapter the signs of the emergence of this second investigation in Avicenna's psychology, less Aristotelian but arising as well from the opaque passages of Aristotle's writing,[11] will be scrutinized in order to assess if this could fit within the framework of a unitary, special natural science ultimately founded in metaphysics.

Grounding the Investigation of the Soul: Part 1

In the *Šifā'*, psychology as well as all the Aristotelian sciences (with the addition of mathematics) is reworked, updated, and refounded in order to conform them to the criteria of demonstrative science that Aristotle has singled out in his *Posterior Analytics*. Avicenna's purpose is therefore to render Aristotle consistent with himself, that is, to harmonize his system of science with the account of the demonstrative science expressed in his logic.[12] Thus psychology, as well as all the other particular sciences, has to deal with a specific subject, whose existence is assumed, and its *per se* attributes according to the principles proper to the science in question (and to the sciences subordinate to it, if any).[13] Avicenna's project of refounding and rearranging Aristotelian science into a hierarchical system with the metaphysics at the top is retrospectively outlined in *Ilāhiyyāt*.[14]

---

10 *Nafs*, V, 4 is entitled "[*Chapter*] *concerning the fact that human souls neither corrupt* (*lā tafsudu*), *nor transmigrate*".

11 See *De an.*, II, 1, 413 a3–5; II, 2, 413 b24–7; II, 3, 415 a11–12. On these texts, see Chapter 2, n. 23.

12 In this perspective we have to interpret Avicenna's numerous references to the logical part of the *Šifā'* in the first treatise of his *Nafs*, where the theoretical analysis on which the entire psychological inquiry is grounded seems, in turn, to be grounded on his logic. See, for instance, (i) *Nafs*, I, 1, 6.11 [19.23] (*qad 'alimta hāḏā: Maqūlāt*, III, 2; IV, 1); (ii) 8.3–4 [22.63–64] (*wa-qad bayyannā fī l-kutub al-manṭiqiyya anna ḏālika ġayr ǧayyid wa-lā ṣawāb: Ǧadal*, probably IV, 1); (iii) 10.5–6 [25.11–12] (*wa-qad bayyannā laka hāḏihi l-ašyā' fī ṣinā'at al-manṭiq: Madḫal*, I, 14; *Maqūlāt*, I, 6. Here Avicenna also refers explicitly to the writings on which these logical sections are based, namely *Īsāġūǧī*, Porphyry's *Isagoge*, and *Qāṭīġūriyās*, Aristotle's *Categories* respectively); (iv) 11.7 [27, n. 39] (*kamā awḍaḥnāhu fī l-manṭiq: Madḫal*, I, 6); 12.1 [28.53–54] (*kamā 'alimta fī ṣinā'at al-burhān: Burhān*, I, 10). In the entire *Nafs* there are only four other explicit references to logic: (v) *Nafs*, I, 5, 46.14–5 [92.83–4] (*'alà mā 'arafta fī kutub al-manṭiq*. "Logical books" are also mentioned in l. 13 [92.82] : *Burhān*, I, 4, where the same examples can be found); (vi) V, 3, 222.14 [103.18–19] (*kamā huwa mubayyin fī l-funūn al-manṭiqiyya: Burhān*, III, 5); (vii) V, 7, 259.10 [169.51–52] (*fī l-ṣinā'a al-āliyya*, here *āliyya* being the Arabic translation of the Greek ὀργανική: *Qiyās*, IX, 19, where Plato's doctrine of reminiscence is discussed. See also *Burhān*, I, 6, where Avicenna explicitly refers back to *Qiyās* (75.7)); (viii) V, 7, 260.12–13 [171.79–80] (*qad taḥaqqaqa laka fī l-manṭiq: Madḫal*, I, 9, concerning the genus as predicated of things that differ in virtue of a specific difference. Cf. *Nafs*, I, 3, 29.9–31.11 [60.62–64.12]).

13 See Chapter 2.

14 It is worth recalling that in *Burhān*, II, 7, 165, 3–7; 11–16 Avicenna maintains that the particular sciences are not parts of metaphysics but are subordinated to it, whereas metaphysics is not subor-

In *Ilāhiyyāt*, I, 1, Avicenna clearly shows that the subject of the science of divine things, i.e. metaphysics, is existent *qua* existent, whereas that of the particular sciences are the states of the existent *qua* existent, namely its specific aspects. Therefore, metaphysics deals with the subjects of the other sciences insofar as they are existent; by contrast, the particular sciences take for granted the existence of their subject, which is thus proved in another, higher discipline,[15] unless it is self-evident:[16] "For the subject-matter of each science is something whose existence (*wuǧūd*) is admitted in that science, and of which only the states (*aḥwāl*) are investigated. This has already been shown elsewhere (*fī mawāḍiʿ uḫrà, sc. Burhān*, II, 6, 155.8–9)" (*Ilāhiyyāt*, I, 1, 5.18–6.1 [4.62–64]).[17]

In addition to the investigation of the existent *qua* existent, in *Ilāhiyyāt*, I, 2 Avicenna seems to assign to metaphysics also the investigation of substance *qua* substance. The subject of natural philosophy, he says, is the body, but not *qua* existent, nor *qua* sensible substance nor *qua* compound of matter and form;[18] rather, in that it is subject to motion and rest: "We say: the subject-matter of natural science turned out to be the body, but not insofar as it is existent (*mawǧūd*), nor insofar as it is substance (*ǧawhar*), nor insofar as it is composed of its two principles, that is, of *hyle* and form, but insofar as it is subject to motion and rest" (*Ilāhiyyāt*, I, 2, 10.5–8 [9.59–62]). Avicenna formulates the same claim in general terms shortly afterwards: "Establishing [the existence] (*iṯbāt*) of the subject-matter [of a science] and verifying its quiddity (*taḥqīq māhiyyatihī*) cannot occur in the science of which it is the subject-matter, but only assuming its existence and quiddity (*taslīm inniyyatihī wa-māhiyyatihī faqaṭ*) [can occur in it]" (*Ilāhiyyāt*, I, 2, 13.11–12 [13.34–36]).[19] Therefore, every sci-

dinated to any other science. On this passage, see Bertolacci, *The Reception of Aristotle's* Metaphysics, 267.

15 Avicenna might have drawn the idea of the subalternation of the particular sciences to a common, higher science (metaphysics?) that proves the principles of the other, subordinated sciences, from Themistius' paraphrase of Aristotle's *Post. An.*, I, 9, 76 a8–17. On this topic, see A. Bertolacci, "Avicenna and Averroes on the Proof of God's Existence and the Subject-Matter of Metaphysics", *Medioevo*, 32, 2007, 61–97, in part. 72.

16 Cf. *Ilāhiyyāt*, I, 3, 20.5–6 [22.8–11]: "The doubt is hence removed. For the natural principle can either be self-evident (*bayyin bi-nafsihī*), or its clarification (*bayānuhū*) can be in first philosophy through what does not become clear later on in it (*sc.* in first philosophy) by means of it (*sc.* the natural principle)".

17 For a thorough analysis of this text, see Bertolacci, *The Reception of Aristotle's* Metaphysics, 120–121.

18 That the natural bodies are sensible substances which are composed of matter and form is investigated in *Ilāhiyyāt*, II, 1–4 (II, 1: the substance and its constituents; II, 2: the corporeal substance and its constituents; II, 3: that corporeal matter cannot be deprived of corporeal form; II, 4: the causal relationship existing between matter and form).

19 For a thorough analysis of this text, see Bertolacci, *The Reception of Aristotle's* Metaphysics, 123, and 269.

ence (metaphysics included) takes for granted both the existence and the quiddity of its own subject-matter.[20]

Furthermore, in *Ilāhiyyāt*, I, 3, Avicenna proves the foundational role that metaphysics plays with respect to the other particular sciences: although metaphysics is posterior to the other sciences in the order of knowledge because of the weakness (*ʿaǧz*, 21.6 [*infirmitas*, 24.38]) of human cognitive faculties, in itself metaphysics is prior to all of them because it ascertains the principles of the particular sciences, and validates the common notions in which they share.[21]

The question now is: does psychology in its entirety conform to this model? Or, to be precise, does psychology investigate only an aspect of the soul, while the investigation of the rest of it, notably of its existence and its quiddity, is conducted in another, higher science? This is not a trivial question about where to compartmentalize psychology. On the contrary, the suggested model would threaten the unity of psychology.

Psychology apparently conforms to this model. In the opening lines of *Nafs*, I, 1 the main purpose of this treatise is stated: "We say: the first thing we must deal with is establishing the existence of the thing (*iṯbāt wuǧūd al-šayʾ*) that is called *soul* (*nafs*)" (*Nafs*, I, 1, 4.4–5 [14.69–70]). However, shortly afterwards, the presence of two levels within Avicenna's investigation of the soul is certified and, at the same time, the preference for one over the other is attested, at least at this stage of the investigation: "This expression (*sc. nafs*, *soul*) is a name for this thing (*ism li-hāḏā l-šayʾ*) not with respect to its substance (*lā min ḥayṯu ǧawharihī*), but in virtue of a certain relation it has (*wa-lākinna min ǧiha iḍāfa mā lahū*), namely, in virtue of its being the principle for these activities (*ay min ǧiha mā huwa mabdaʾ li-hāḏihi l-afāʿīl*)" (*Nafs*, I, 1, 4.10–12 [15.78–79 (lacuna in the Latin translation)]). The entity whose existence the philosopher is going to investigate is the soul; however, this term does not designate the thing in itself, but rather the thing insofar as it is the principle of activities (operational level). Here the distinction of references of the terms *šayʾ* (thing) and *nafs* (soul) is pivotal:[22] the former refers to an entity in its totality having its own essence and being separable from the body and conceivable independently of it;[23] the latter, by contrast, designates only one characteristic of this *šayʾ*, that is, its mode of existence in relation to the body. Thus, there is the implicit recognition

---

20 As we shall see, two notable exceptions to this tenet are the investigation of God in metaphysics and the investigation of the human rational soul in psychology.

21 See *Ilāhiyyāt*, I, 3, 21.6–11 [24.38–44].

22 See pp. 70–71 below.

23 For the term *šayʾ* as a means to refer to an entity in light of its essence, see Avicenna, *Ilāhiyyāt*, I, 5. For a critical study of the concept of *šayʾ* in Avicenna and its theological background, see M. Rashed, "Chose, *item* et distinction", in part. 171, n. 10, and 183–184, A.-T. Druart, "*Shayʾ* or *Res* as Concomitant of 'Being' in Avicenna", *Documenti e studi sulla tradizione filosofica medievale*, 12, 2001, 125–42, and R. Wisnovsky, "Notes on Avicenna's concept of *thingness* (*shayʾiyya*)", *Arabic Sciences and Philosophy*, 10.2, 2000, 181–221.

that there is something behind and beside what the term *nafs/soul* designates (though this is applicable not to every kind of soul); however, its investigation is set – temporarily – aside.

At the outset of the psychological investigation, its target is thus limited to the aspect for which the *thing* is called *soul*, namely its being the principle behind the activities observable in bodies (relational entity). This phenomenal datum is crucial: direct observation (*nušāhidu*, *we see*, I, 1, 4.5, 6 [*videmus*, 14.71, 73]) is precisely the basis of the *a posteriori* proof of the soul's existence, a proof concerning all sublunary souls existing in bodies, according to which whoever sees activities in bodies cannot deny that in them there is a soul.[24]

Once the existence of this thing insofar as it has a certain characteristic – here even referred to as accident (*ʿaraḍ*, I, 1, 4.14 [*accidens*, 16.82])[25] – is established (and this is the only conclusion that can be drawn from direct observation), Avicenna twice defers the ascertainment of its essence and of the category to which it belongs to another investigation,[26] which takes place in *Nafs*, I, 3. Although the advancement of knowledge from the level of existence to that of essence is recommended, it is impossible to infer the substantiality of what is a soul from the very fact that it is a soul, in the very same way in which elsewhere the knowledge that something which is in motion has a mover does not immediately imply the knowledge of the essence of that mover.[27] The investigation of the soul belonging to natural philosophy seems to be

---

24 *Nafs*, I, 1, 4.5–10 [14.71–15.78]: "We thus say: we do sometimes see bodies that sense and move at will; indeed, we see bodies that nourish themselves, grow, and generate the like. And this does not belong to them due to their corporeality (*ǧismiyya*, *corporeitas*); therefore, it remains that in these themselves there are principles for that other than their corporeality, that is, the thing from which these activities derive. In general, whatever is a principle for the derivation of activities that are not in the same manner [as if they were] devoid of will, we call it *soul*". I note in passing that here Avicenna seems to have in mind a narrower notion of *life* that identifies with animal life. On this aspect, I take the liberty of referring to my article "Is Nutrition a Sufficient Condition for Life?".

25 It is not surprising that the characteristic with respect to which something is called *soul* is said to be an accident, at least here, when the nature of the thing in itself has not yet been ascertained. What is more, this term conforms to the term *iḍāfa* (*Nafs*, I, 1, 4.11 [a lacuna in the Latin translation]) – the term also used to designate the category of the relative – which has been used to refer to the characteristic in virtue of which something is called *soul*.

26 *Nafs*, I, 1, 4.13 (*min baʿdin* [*postea*, 16.80]); 11.4 (*baḥṯ āḫar* [*alium tractatum*, 27.35]).

27 *Nafs*, I, 1, 5.1–3 [16.82–86]: "We need to arrive, from this accident belonging to it, at an ascertaining of its essence in order to know its quiddity, just as if we had already come to know that something which is in motion has a certain mover (*anna li-šayʾ yataḥarraku muḥarrikan mā*), but we do not know from that what the essence of this mover is (*anna ḏāt hāḏā l-muḥarrik mā huwa*)". This almost neglected comparison seems to be a reference to *Samāʿ ṭabīʿī*, IV, 15, where an *a posteriori* proof of the existence of a first mover is drawn from the eternal heavenly movement without inquiring into its essence, an issue properly pertaining to metaphysics. Therefore, an analogy, at least with respect to methodological procedure, between the investigation of the soul and that of God as the First Mover seems to have been established: their existence is proved *a posteriori* through the observation of their effects, i.e. the activities of bodies and the eternal motion of heavenly substances, respectively.

then an investigation of it insofar as it has a certain relation to matter and motion, that is, insofar as it governs the body, with respect to which it is defined.[28]

Despite the limitations that Avicenna posits for his psychological investigation, the other investigation to which the ascertainment of the essence of the soul is deferred seems to take place in psychology.[29] In addition to the presence in psychology of the ontological counterpart of the investigation of the soul as operational principle, in *Nafs*, I, 1 Avicenna also acknowledges the presence of something behind and beside what the term *nafs/soul* designates. Though not identifying all sublunary souls, it raises the question as to whether the ascertainment of what soul is *in itself* pertains to psychology or to another (higher?) science. In what follows, four *loci* will be taken into account in which Avicenna seems also to ascribe this investigation to psychology and to conduct it therein, namely the prologue to *Nafs*, and chapters I, 1, I, 3, and V, 2.

Knowing the Soul from Knowing Oneself: The Prologue to *Nafs*

The prologue to the *Nafs* contains the manifesto of Avicenna's psychological investigation,[30] in which its place and its subject-matter are discussed. The primary aspect that has to be highlighted is its purpose, namely that of framing a science whose epistemological status (subject-matter, position, boundaries) seems not to be entirely

---

28 *Nafs*, I, 1, 11.1–3 [27.32–4]: "For this reason the investigation of the soul is part of natural science, because the investigation of the soul insofar as it is soul is an investigation of it insofar as it has a certain connection with matter and motion (*min ḥayṯu lahā ʿalāqa bi-l-mādda wa-l-ḥaraka* [*secundum quod habet comparationem ad materiam et ad motum*])". The same restriction of the subject of the investigation of the soul belonging to natural philosophy, namely its restriction to the soul *qua* form of the body, is confirmed in *Nafs*, V, 5, 238.3–9 [132.17–23]. More on this passage in Chapter 4.

29 Recently Olga Lizzini has interpreted Avicenna's reference in psychology to "another inquiry" to which the investigation of the soul in itself would pertain as a reference to metaphysics. See O. Lizzini, "L'âme chez Avicenne: quelques remarques autour de son statut épistémologique et de son fondament métaphysique", *Documenti e studi sulla tradizione filosofica medievale*, 21, 2010, 223–242. However, in my opinion, *min baʿdin*, and *baḥṯ āḫar* are internal references to subsequent parts of the *Nafs*, i.e. mainly to the end of I, 1, I, 3, and V, 2, where Avicenna speaks *ex professo* of the nature of the soul and the category to which it belongs. My interpretation is based on the evaluation of the different ways to which Avicenna resorts in order to refer to other places, internal and external to the *Nafs*. As a further argument in support of this interpretation, see the final sentence of *Nafs*, I, 2 where Avicenna announces the subsequent step in the investigation of the soul: "Now we must undertake the quest for the nature of the soul (*ṭalab ṭabīʿat al-nafs* [*inquirere naturam animae*])" (*Nafs*, I, 2, 27.10–11 [57.18–19]).

30 Actually, the prologue to *Nafs* contains more than that: it contains also the manifesto of Avicenna's *essentialism*, that is, of Avicenna's essentialistic approach to the study of organic forms of life. More on this in T. Alpina, "Exercising Impartiality to Favor Aristotle: Avicenna and "the accomplished anatomists" (*aṣḥāb al-tašrīḥ al-muḥaṣṣilūna*) in *Ḥayawān*, III, 1", *Arabic Sciences and Philosophy*, forthcoming.

clear. For, as already happened in the Late Ancient tradition and in the first Arabic reception of Peripatetic philosophy,[31] in the age of Avicenna there seems still to be disagreement about the epistemological status of psychology. For this reason, at the outset of his investigation of the soul Avicenna provides a sort of "global" interpretation of it.

The prologue can be divided into three parts according to the issues dealt with in them:

first part–the place of psychology within the wider context of the investigation of nature (1.4–2.1 [9.4–10.21]);

second part–the necessity of a general and unitary account of the soul (2.1–3.9 [10.21–13.58]);

third part–the summary of the conclusive sections of natural philosophy, i.e. botany and zoology, and of the third and fourth parts, i.e. the mathematics and the metaphysics, of the *Šifāʾ* (3.9–13 [13.59–65]).

A thorough analysis of the structure and the contents of this prologue together with the evaluation of its uniqueness within the *Šifāʾ* has already been dealt with at length elsewhere;[32] here, by contrast, the focus will be on its central part, which is more relevant than the others for our purposes.

If in the first part of the prologue, after providing an overview of the contents of the five previous sections on natural philosophy in the *Šifāʾ*, Avicenna assigns priority to investigation of the soul over that of issues specifically concerning plants and animals,[33] in the second part he expounds in detail the nature of such an investigation and accounts for the methodology he follows in it.

The investigation that he is about to start is general and unitary. It is *general* because it deals with the soul *qua* formal principle of any kind of sublunary living being in general terms; and it is *unitary* because the inquiry into the soul is approached in a comprehensive rather than piecemeal way, investigations of the various instances of sublunary soul not being severed from one another. At the end of

---

31 See Chapter 2.

32 See T. Alpina, "Knowing the Soul from Knowing Oneself: A Reading of the Prologue to Avicenna's *Kitāb al-Nafs* (*Book of the Soul*)", *Atti e Memorie dell'Accademia Toscana di Scienze e Lettere 'La Colombaria'*, 82 (68), 2018, 443–458.

33 On the fact that in the investigation of organic life Avicenna seems to assign priority to form over matter, see Alpina, "Knowing the Soul from Knowing Oneself", in part. 449–50. On the fact that this represents a break with the tradition with respect to the place of the *De anima* and the kind of investigation conducted therein, see M. Rashed, "De Cordoue à Byzance. Sur une prothéorie inédite de la *Physique* d'Aristote", *Arabic Sciences and Philosophy*, 6.2, 1996, 210–262, in part. 484–485, and A. Hasnaoui, *Aspects de la synthèse avicennienne*, in *Penser avec Aristote*. Études réunies sous la direction de M. A. Sinaceur, Toulouse, Erès 1991, 227–244, in part. 230, n. 4. However, it should be noted – as Rashed and Hasnaoui did – that in the outline of natural philosophy that Avicenna provides in two early works, i.e. *Maqāla fī l-nafs ʿalà sunnat al-iḫtiṣār* (*Compendium on the Soul*, 8, 361.19–362.1, ed. Landauer), and *Maqāla fī Aqsām al-ʿulūm al-ʿaqliyya* (*Treatise on the Divisions of the Intellectual Sciences*, 108.12–110.6, ed. Cairo^2), the investigation of the soul follows those of plants and animals.

the first part of the prologue Avicenna accounts briefly for the priority of inquiry into the soul,[34] whereas he devotes most of the second part of the prologue to arguing for the necessity of a general and unitary account of it (2.1–17).

There are two reasons for preferring a general and unitary account of the soul: the first reason is *a parte obiecti*, while the second reason is *a parte subiecti*. Firstly, severing the subject-matter of this inquiry, i.e. the soul, on the basis of its various sublunary instances (vegetative, animal, or human) would jeopardize the possibility of grasping the science of the soul as a whole (*ḍabṭ ʿilm al-nafs*, 2.4–5 [*apprehendere scientiam de anima*, 11.26]), where every part of the soul is related to another. This idea can be traced back to Aristotle's concept of the several instances of soul as items arranged in an ordered series, where a lower soul can be found potentially in a higher one. This concept, which Aristotle explains by using the analogy between souls and rectilinear figures, is grounded on the assumption that there is no genus *soul* internally subdivided into species, i.e. into its specific instances, just as there is no genus *figure* besides triangle, square, etc.[35] Knowledge of the soul is therefore the knowledge of all its instances. In this connection, dealing separately with each of its instances would break up the unity of the subject-matter of the science of the soul and, consequently, dissolve the science itself.[36]

If the first reason for an investigation conceived in this way is related to the nature of what is investigated, namely to the soul and, in particular, to the intrinsic correlation between its different instances, the second reason concerns the one who investigates, i.e. the human being and, ultimately, us, i.e. the human being engaged in psychology. In particular, because of our difficulty in grasping the specific differences of each instance of soul (and of its bearer) which fall outside our cognitive capacities due to their extreme specificity, we have to deal only with what is shared.

---

34 *Nafs*, prologue, 1.11–2.3 [10.16–11.24]: "What remained to us of [natural] science is to investigate the matters concerning plants and animals (*fī umūr al-nabātāt wa-l-ḥayawānāt* [*de rebus vegetabilibus et animalibus*]). Since plants and animals are rendered subsistent as to [their] essences through a form, that is the soul (*mutaǧawhirat al-ḏawāt ʿan ṣūra hiya l-nafs* [*ea quorum essentiae constituuntur ex forma quae est anima*]), and a matter, that is body and limbs, and [since] it is more appropriate (*awlà* [*melior*]) that what is science of something is [science] with respect to its form, it seemed to us [more convenient] to deal firstly with the soul. It did not seem [convenient] to us to sever the science of the soul, so as to deal firstly with vegetative soul and plants, then with animal soul and animals, [and] then with human soul and human being". It is noteworthy that the Farabian term *mutaǧawhir* is a *hapax* in Avicenna's *Nafs*.

35 Aristotle, *De an.*, II, 3, 414 b28–33. More on this aspect in Chapter 2. In *Nafs* Avicenna seems to hold the same position, see *Nafs*, I, 5, 40.4–13 [80.17–81.28] On this passage see n. 119 below. This text will be crucial for our analysis of Avicenna's psychological enterprise in Chapter 4. Here, however, the term *genus* has not to be taken in the technical sense so as to imply that for Avicenna souls can be arranged according to genera and species. On this aspect, see Chapter 4, n. 81, where the passage is quoted in full.

36 *Nafs*, prologue, 2.3–5 [10.21–11.27]: "And we did not do that for two reasons: the first [reason] is that this severing is among the things that render difficult grasping the science of the soul which relates one of its parts to another".

That being the case, the investigation of the soul has to be an investigation of the common features that all instances of sublunary souls (and their bearers) share.[37] The specific features of each of them, though essential *per se*, have to be left aside because it is extremely difficult for us to grasp them: "We are little engaged in the essential *differentiae* of each soul, of each plant, and of each animal because that is difficult for us" (2.16–7 [12.41–3]).[38] These two things account for the general and unitary character of Avicenna's investigation of the soul, which pertains to one single science and is contained in one single work (*fī kitāb wāḥid*, 2.18 [*in uno libro*, 12.44]).

However, a remark is in order. Evaluation of the common features shared by all souls, which represent the topic of this investigation, is made by the one who investigates, that is, by a human being, having himself as a touchstone in this evaluation. Consequently, the investigation does deal with what is shared, but is made from a human perspective, that is, through the mediation of the investigator's direct acquaintance with his own soul, i.e. the human soul, which is at the same time what investigates by means of the intellectual activity, and part of the subject-matter under investigation, i.e. an instance of sublunary soul.

Therefore, on the one hand, Avicenna's science of the soul evinces a *general approach* which aims at providing the most comprehensive account of the soul insofar as it is the vital principle of all sublunary living beings (plants, animals, and human beings), and thus at guaranteeing that the investigation of the soul has a unitary subject-matter. However, on the other hand, it shows a *specific orientation* by focusing on the human soul and on what it shares with plants and animals (and not the other way round), due to the investigator's privileged and direct access to it. As we shall see, examples of this specific orientation are the thought-experiment of the *Flying*

---

37 *Nafs*, prologue, 2.5–18 [11.27–12.44]: "The second [reason] is that plants share with animals the soul to which the activity of growth, nutrition, and reproduction belongs. It is unquestionably necessary that [animals] be separated from plants with respect to the psychic faculties that are proper to their genus and, then, proper to their species. And what we can deal with as regards the soul of plants is what is shared by animals, but we are not much aware of the *differentiae* that render this generic notion in plants specific. If this is the case, the relation of this part of the investigation to the fact of its being a discourse on plants has no greater claim than [its relation] to the fact of its being a discourse on animals, since the relation of animals to this (*sc.* vegetative) soul is the [same] relation as that of plants to it. And the state of the animal soul stands in similar relation to the human being and to other animals. And since we want to deal with the vegetative and the animal soul only insofar as it is shared – for there is no science of what is particular except [that which comes] after the science of what is shared – and [since] we are little engaged in the essential *differentiae* of each soul, of each plant, and of each animal because that is difficult for us, it is better that we deal with the soul in one single book".

38 In *Ilāhiyyāt*, V, 4, 220.13–18 [255.70–256.78], in dealing with the *differentia* that specifies the genus, Avicenna says that we cannot grasp what is proper to the specific difference of every genus with respect to every species, nor what is proper to the specific differences of the species of a single genus, because this knowledge escapes our cognitive capacities; rather, we can grasp the rule in virtue of which a *differentia* enters a genus and specifies it.

Man at the end of *Nafs*, I, 1, which aims at hinting at the incorporeal nature of the human soul, and the lengthy discussion on the human rational soul in *Nafs*, V, 1–7.

The Transition to the Essence-Inquiry: The *Flying Man* Argument

The transition from inquiry into the existence of the soul as a *relational* entity to inquiry into its essence is marked by the *Flying Man* argument at the end of I, 1.[39] The thought-experiment of the *Flying Man*, or *Man in the Void*, is probably the most famous passage of Avicenna's *Nafs*, and one to which many scholars have directed their attention,[40] especially for its alleged similarity with Descartes' *Cogito ergo sum*.[41] Moreover, here the thought-experiment occurs twice, in *Nafs*, I, 1 and V, 7

39 The thought-experiment of the *Flying Man* also occurs in other works, namely *Ḥikma mašriqiyya*, 135.13–21 (ed. Özcan); *Išārāt wa-tanbīhāt*, 119.1–10 (ed. Forget); and *Risāla Aḍḥawiyya*, IV, 140–151 (ed. Lucchetta).

40 On this topic, see T. Alpina, "The *Soul of*, the Soul *in itself*, and the *Flying Man* Experiment", *Arabic Sciences and Philosophy*, 28.2, 2018, 187–224; P. Adamson, F. Benevich, "The Thought Experimental Method: Avicenna's *Flying Man* Argument", *Journal of the American Philosophical Association*, 4.2, 2018, 147–164; M. Rashed, "Chose, item et distinction"; P. Adamson, *Into Thin Air–Avicenna on the Soul*, in *Philosophy in The Islamic World. A History of Philosophy without Any Gaps*, Volume 3, Oxford University Press, Oxford 2016, 133–139; J. Kaukua, *Self-Awareness in Islamic Philosophy. Avicenna and Beyond*, Cambridge University Press, Cambridge 2015, in part. chapters 2 and 3; M. Sebti, "Avicenna's "Flying Man" Argument as a Proof of the Immateriality of the Soul", in E. Coda, C. Martini-Bonadeo eds., *De l'Antiquité Tardive au Moyen Âge. Études de logique aristotélicienne et de philosophie grecque, syriaque, arabe et latine offertes à Henri Hugonnard-Roche*, Vrin, Paris 2014, 531–543; A. Alwishah, "Ibn Sīnā on Floating Man Arguments", *Journal of Islamic Philosophy*, 9, 2013, 32–53; L. Muehlethaler, "Ibn Kammūna (d. 683/1284) on the argument of the Flying Man in Avicenna's *Ishārāt* and in al-Suhrawardī's *Talwīḥāt*" in Y. T. Langermann ed., *Avicenna and his Legacy. A Golden Age of Science and Philosophy*, Brepols, Turnhout 2009, 179–203; D. L. Black, "Avicenna on Self-Awareness and Knowing that One Knows"; A. Bertolacci, "Il pensiero filosofico di Avicenna", in C. D'Ancona ed., *Storia della filosofia nell'Islam medievale*, 2 vols., Einaudi, Torino 2005, 522–626, in part. 552–554; 616–618; Hasse, *Avicenna's* De Anima, in part. 80–92; M. E. Marmura, "Avicenna's "Flying Man" in Context", *The Monist*, 69, 1986, 383–395; L. E. Goodman, "A Note on Avicenna's Theory of the Substantiality of the Soul", *The Philosophical Forum*, 1, 1969, 547–562; S. Pines, "La conception de la conscience de soi chez Avicenne et chez Abu' l-Barakat al-Baghdadi", *Archives d'histoire doctrinale et littéraire du Moyen Age*, 1954, 21–98; E. Gilson, "Les sources gréco-arabes de l'augustinisme avicennisant", *Archives d'Histoire Doctrinale et Littéraire du Moyen Age*, 5, 1930, 1–107 (Gilson has been claimed to be responsible for the name of this thought-experiment). For the version of the *Flying Man* in Avicenna's *al-Išārāt wa-l-tanbīhāt*, see M. E. Marmura, "Fakhr al-Dīn ar-Rāzī's Critique of an Avicennan *Tanbīh*", in B. Mojsisch, O. Pluta eds., *Historia Philosophiae Medii Aevi*, Amsterdam 1991, 627–637.

41 For the connection between Avicenna's *Flying Man* and Descartes' *Cogito ergo sum*, see H. Eichner, "*Endoxa* and the *Theology of Aristotle* in Avicenna's "Flying Man": Contexts for Similarities with Sceptical and Cartesian Arguments in Avicenna" in G. Veltri, R. Haliva, S. Schmid, E. Spinelli eds., *Sceptical Paths. Enquiry and Doubt from Antiquity to the Present*, De Gruyter, Berlin-Boston 2019, 67–82; A. Hasnawi, "La conscience de soi chez Avicenne et Descartes", in J. Biard, R. Rashed eds., *Descartes et le Moyen Âge*, Vrin, Paris 1997, 283–291; T.-A. Druart, "The Soul and Body Problem: Avi-

(255.6 – 15 [162.51 – 163.64]). In this section I will focus on its first and more complete formulation.

The first version of the thought-experiment, which occurs at the end of *Nafs*, I, 1 (16.2 – 17 [36.49 – 37.68]),[42] consists of two moves.[43] In the first place, Avicenna invites the reader to imagine (*tawahhama, putare debet*)[44] himself in the state of a mature human being (*ḫuliqa duf'atan wa-ḫuliqa kāmilan, quasi subito creatus esset et perfectus*) and as floating in the air or in the void (*ḫuliqa yahwī fī hawā' aw ḫalā' huwiyyan, creatus esset sic quasi moveretur in aere aut in inani*) in a condition of complete sensory deprivation, both external and internal, and of lack of memory. In the second move, the reader has to consider whether, in the aforementioned state, he will affirm the existence of anything. According to Avicenna, he will be prompted to affirm the existence of himself, i.e. of his essence (*kāna yuṯbitu ḏātahū, affirmabit se esse*), although he will not affirm the existence of anything corporeal, either of his external body or of his internal organs, like the heart or the brain, which are generally considered a human being's most basic organs.[45] Furthermore, even if he were to imag-

---

cenna and Descartes", in T.-A. Druart ed., *Arabic Philosophy and the West. Continuity and Interaction*, Georgetown University, Washington 1988, 27 – 49; T. McTighe, "Further Remarks on Avicenna and Descartes", *ibidem*, 51 – 54. See also P. Adamson, F. Benevich, "The Thought Experimental Method".

42 *Nafs*, I, 1, 16.2 – 14 [36.49 – 37.64]: "We say: one of us must imagine himself as if he is created all at once and perfect, but his sight has been impeded from observing external things, and [as if] he is created floating in the air or in the void in such a way that the air resistance does not hit him in a manner that compels [him] to sense [it], and with his limbs separated from each other so that they neither meet nor touch. Then, he considers whether he will affirm that he exists (*hal yuṯbitu wuǧūd ḏātihī*). He will not have doubts about whether or not to do so. However, he will not affirm [the existence of] any of his limbs, any of his internal organs, [his] heart, [his] brain, or any external thing. Rather, he affirms [the existence of] himself (*bal kāna yuṯbitu ḏātahū*), though he does not affirm his having height, breadth, and depth. If, in that [aforementioned] state, he were able to imagine a hand or some other limb, he would imagine it neither as part of himself nor as condition for [the existence of] himself.

You know that what is affirmed is different from what is not affirmed, and what is acknowledged (reading: *wa-l-muqarr bihī* instead of *wa-l-maqraba*) is different from what is not acknowledged (reading: *lam yuqarri bihī* instead of *lam yuqarribhu*).

Hence, the self (*ḏāt*), whose existence [this human being] has affirmed as something proper to him because this [self] is [identical to] himself, is different from his body and his limbs whose existence has not been affirmed".

43 Lukas Muehlethaler singles out these two moves in the formulation of the *Flying Man* argument occurring in Avicenna's *K. al-Išārāt wa-l-tanbīhāt*, see L. Muehlethaler, "Ibn Kammūna", 185.

44 Here *tawahhama* is translated as "to imagine"; however, this verb is related to the noun *wahm* that, in Avicenna, designates the faculty of estimation, that is, the faculty responsible for perceiving the non-sensible attributes of what is perceived by the external senses. For this consideration, see Muehlethaler, "Ibn Kammūna", 185, n. 18. On a brief but effective description of this faculty see, for example, *Nafs*, I, 5, 45.6 – 11 [89.48 – 53]. On Avicenna's internal senses, see T. Alpina, "Retaining, Remembering, Recollecting".

45 See, among other places, *Nafs*, V, 8, where Avicenna refers to the brain and the heart as seats of different psychic faculties and discusses philosophers' and physicians' positions on this issue. More on this in T. Alpina, "Exercising Impartiality to Favor Aristotle".

ine any other organ, he would imagine it neither as part of his essence, nor as condition for its existence.

Generally speaking, the outcome of this experiment is affirming the existence of the essence of the human soul as something different from the body, i.e. as being immaterial. However, its brief introduction (I, 1, 15.17–16.2 [36.43–48]) and its concise conclusion (I, 1, 16.14–17 [37.65–68]) can help us to understand more precisely the purpose of this experiment.

This thought-experiment occurs at the end of the investigation of the traditional definition of the soul in *Nafs*, I, 1, and seems to be intended to connect this investigation with that of the essence of the soul in I, 3 (I, 2 has a doxographical character).[46] That the thought-experiment marks a change of direction with respect to the investigation that Avicenna has conducted so far is clearly stated in the introduction to the experiment (15.17–19 [36.43–45]): "We have now come to know the meaning of the term (*maʿnà l-ism, intellectus nominis*) that applies to the thing called *soul* in virtue of a relation belonging to it (*bi-iḍāfa lahū, ex relatione quam habet*). We ought, then, to engage ourselves in grasping the quiddity of this thing (*māhiyya hāḏā l-šayʾ, quid sit haec res*) which, through the aforementioned consideration (*bi-l-iʿtibār al-maqūl, ex respectu praedicto*), has become soul (*ṣāra* [...] *nafsan, est anima*)".[47] Avicenna aims to move from the traditional definition of the soul to the ascertainment of its quiddity: in virtue of the possession of a certain accident, namely an *iḍāfa* to the body, a certain thing (*šayʾ*) has become soul (*ṣāra...nafsan*); however,

46 On the fact that the *Flying Man* serves as a bridge to the discussion of the substantiality of the soul in I, 3, see Hasse, *Avicenna's* De anima, 86. *Nafs*, I, 2 seems to pave the way to the investigation of the essence of the *soul of* plants and animals, since it provides a preliminary survey of the opinions of the predecessors on the soul and its essence, and their refutation (chapter title: [*Chapter*] *on what the ancients said about the soul and its substance, and its refutation*).

47 That the thought-experiment of the *Flying Man* marks the transition from the investigation of the existence of the soul to that of its essence is also clear in the *Ḥikma mašriqiyya:* "We have to undertake another inquiry (*baḥṯ āḫar*) to know the essence of the soul, and to verify its quiddity (*li-taʿarruf ḏāt al-nafs wa-taḥaqquq māhiyyatihī* [*sic*]). Before we begin with it, we must point out (*fa-yaǧibu an nušīra*) a manner of establishing the existence of the soul belonging to us by way of pointing" (135.11–14). Here the *Flying Man* argument plays the same role it has in the *Nafs*, namely that of serving as a bridge to the discussion of the substantiality of the sublunary souls while existing in bodies. In the *Ḥikma mašriqiyya* this transition is even more evident since there there is no doxographical digression ("We say: there have already been reported in the *First Teaching* in the *Book of the Cure* (*fī l-taʿlīm al-awwal fī Kitāb al-Šifāʾ*, *sc. Kitāb al-Nafs*) the opinions of the ancients about the quiddity of the soul and their difference concerning it (*ārāʾ al-qudamāʾ fī māhiyyat al-nafs wa-iḫtilāfuhum fīhā*), and there have been presented their contradictions in two places altogether (*fī l-mawḍiʿayni ǧamīʿan* (*sc.* in all likelihood in *Nafs*, I, 2 and V, 7) *munāqaḍātuhum*). Those who wish to know that shall consult these two places (*fa-man aḥabba maʿrifa ḏālika fal-yarǧiʿ ilayhimā*). Here, by contrast, we shall limit ourselves to clarify the true opinion (*fa-innā muqtaṣirūna hāhunā ʿalà bayān al-raʾy al-ḥaqq*)", 135.22–136.2). On this passage, see Hasse, *Avicenna's* De anima, 84–85. Avicenna expresses a similar position in another doxographical context, i.e. in the section of the *Ḥikma mašriqiyya* corresponding to *Nafs*, V, 7. On this passage, see Chapter 6, n. 26.

the quiddity of the thing bearing that name waits to be ascertained. The distinction of references of the terms *šay'* (thing) and *nafs* (soul), which has been hinted at at the beginning of I, 1, is thus confirmed.[48]

Then, there comes a key sentence for understanding the purpose, the method, and the recipient of the experiment: "Here we must point out a manner of [(a)] establishing the existence of the soul belonging to us [(b)] by way of pointing and reminding, [(c)] giving an indication that is adequate for someone who has the capacity for noticing the truth itself, with no need of being educated, constantly prodded, and diverted from errors" (15.19 – 16.2 [36.45 – 48]). As for the purpose of the experiment, there is disagreement in the scholarship.[49] Avicenna explicitly claims that here he is going to establish the existence of the soul belonging to us (*iṯbāt wuǧūd al-nafs allatī lanā*, *affirmetur esse animae quam habemus*). However, that the *soul of* any sublunary living being (human being included) exists has already been shown in the opening lines of chapter I, 1 by means of direct observation;[50] therefore, establishing again the existence of one of its instances would be at the same time redundant and point-

48 See n. 23 above. That the human being considered *in itself* identifies with a *šay'* (*thing*), which is his individual essence (*anniyya*) or true essence (*ḏāt bi-l-ḥaqīqa*), is clearly stated in the *Risāla Aḍḥawiyya*, IV, 140 – 145, in the same context as in the *Nafs*, namely when Avicenna hints at the essence of the human being by means of the *Flying Man* argument.

49 In the rich bibliography on this subject, three major interpretations of Avicenna's purpose in providing this thought-experiment can be singled out:

1) Goodman's interpretation (1969), according to which Avicenna resorts to the *Flying Man* in order to indicate the substantiality of the (human) soul by means of the notion of consciousness, and leaving aside the thorny issues of body-mind dualism and of the individual immortality of the soul (548). However, there are two major problems with Goodman's interpretation: i) he seems to equate the kinds of substance coming out from *Nafs*, I, 1 and I, 3, respectively (548); ii) the first version of the experiment seems to be reduced to the second version, which is, however, slightly different (552).

2) Marmura's interpretation (1986), according to which the *Flying Man* is used to account for the immateriality of the human soul and, by implication, for its immortality (384 – 85). In particular, Marmura refers to the experimental knowledge of the immaterial self through which it is possible to acquire the experimental knowledge of this immaterial existence (387).

3) Hasse's interpretation (2000), according to which, by means of the thought-experiment Avicenna aims to affirm the independence of the human soul from the body, although the incorporeality and the existence of the human soul are implied (85). The *Flying Man*, therefore, affirms the existence of his core entity, his essence, while not affirming the existence of his body (86).

I would be inclined to agree with Marmura's interpretation without, however, pushing the discussion into the issue of the immortality of the soul, even if only by implication, because this issue is irrelevant here, and Avicenna seems not even to be interested in this possibility. As for Hasse's interpretation, I see his concern about keeping distinct the two versions of the experiment occurring in the *Nafs*; however, I think that here Avicenna is primarily concerned with the immateriality of the rational soul, namely with its being distinct from the body. The notion of independence, on the basis of which the substantiality of the human rational soul is argued, will be referred to in the opening lines of *Nafs* I, 3 and directly tackled only in *Nafs*, V, 2. For an exhaustive survey of the critics on this subject, see Hasse, *Avicenna's* De anima, 80 – 87.

50 See § Grounding the Investigation of the Soul: Part 1 above.

less. The conclusion of the experiment, however, might cast some light on this. There Avicenna says: "the recipient of the pointing has a way to be alerted to the existence of the soul as something other than the body, indeed other than body (*al-mutanabbih lahū sabīl ilà an yatanabbaha ʿalà wuǧūd al-nafs šayʾan ġayr al-ǧism bal ġayr ǧism*)" (16.14–15 [37.65–66]). Therefore, by means of the thought-experiment of the *Flying Man* Avicenna seems to aim to establish not that the *soul of* human beings exists without qualification, but, rather, that it is *in itself* something different from all body, i.e. something incorporeal. The conclusion of the *Flying Man* argument can be defined as "negative":[51] it allows us to establish what the soul belonging to us is not, i.e. body – incorporeality meaning "*not being body*". The positive conclusion, by contrast, which is based on the notion of *independence/independent existence*, represents a step forward in ascertaining what the human soul *in itself* is, and will be offered in the opening lines of *Nafs*, I, 3 and demonstratively displayed only in *Nafs*, V, 2 (*Nafs* I, 2 is coherent with this perspective: it deals with what the soul is *not* according to Avicenna).

The outcome of this experiment is thus restricted to the human rational soul, the only instance of sublunary soul in which there is a *šayʾ* behind and beside what *nafs* designates, and which is consequently capable of existing in a condition of isolation from the body, as will emerge in the course of the treatise.[52] What is more, this restriction echoes the prologue to the *Nafs*, where Avicenna states that it is difficult to grasp the specific differences of each instance of soul, and therefore we should limit ourselves to what is common to all (sublunary) souls.[53] In the case of the human rational soul, however, this difficulty is overcome, because we are our soul (in the experiment the human being's *ḏāt* is identified with the human being's soul) and hence perfectly able to account for its peculiar nature due to our privileged and direct access to it: the knower, i.e. his core being taken in isolation as happens in the thought-experiment, and the object of knowledge are one and the same thing.[54]

As for the method of the experiment, Avicenna presents this mode of establishing the qualified existence of the human soul as a pointer and a reminder (*al-tanbīh wa-l-taḏkīr*),[55] which immediately recall the title of and the method used in Avicenna's latest *summa*, i.e. *Kitāb al-Išārāt wa-l-tanbīhāt*.[56] Such a "pointer-and-reminder" represents a temporary suspension of the demonstrative method that Avicenna gen-

---

51 I disagree with A. Alwishah, who maintains that the *Flying Man* argument has a positive conclusion (40).

52 It is evident in the parallel passage from the *Risāla Aḍḥawiyya* quoted in n. 48 above.

53 Cf. *Nafs*, prologue, 2.16–7 [12.41–3] quoted above.

54 See Rashed, "Chose, item et distinction", 167.

55 As we have seen, in the *Ḥikma mašriqiyya* the argument is presented as a pointer (*tanbīh*). The same happens in the *K. al-Išārāt wa-l-tanbīhāt*, where the entire argument is introduced by the word *tanbīh*. In the *Risāla Aḍḥawiyya* the thought-experiment does not have a proper introduction, but begins – so to speak – *in medias res*.

56 I am inclined to agree with Hasse on this point: *pace* Marmura, here Avicenna cannot be accused of "using a hypothetical example for categorical ends" (87).

erally follows in the *Šifā'* in order to attain universal, demonstrative knowledge in the Aristotelian fashion.[57] However, the different status of the *Flying Man* does not have to invalidate its conclusion: as Lukas Muehlethaler brilliantly notices, "the term *reminder* describes not an alternative form of argument, but an alternative way of *presenting* an argument. In a reminder, Avicenna merely hints at an argument and leaves it to the perspicacious reader to work out its exact form".[58] With respect to the *Flying Man*, what has to be spelled out is precisely the relationship existing between the knowledge coming from it and the recipient of that knowledge. In this connection, a passage from Avicenna's *Mubāḥaṯāt* (*Discussions*) helps us, as L. Muehlethaler and M. Sebti have noticed.[59] There, in answering questions posed by his disciple Bahmanyār about the *Flying Man*, Avicenna maintains that for people whose mind stops short of understanding it, "this argument (*hāḏā l-ḥuğğa*) is not useful, or rather, it is wasted (*ḍā'i'*) – I mean the argument that is discovered from the reflection of the person upon the state of his soul – and they need an argument that is based on species and genus such as 'because the bodies have such and such animal actions, they have a principle that is such and such which is the soul'[60] and similar [arguments]. With regard to the perspicacious, however, [this argument] is decisive (*qāṭi'*)".[61] Following Avicenna's explanation, the *Flying Man* has to be considered as an argument whose conclusion can be attained by the perspicacious person ("someone who has the capacity for noticing the truth itself, with no need of being educated, constantly prodded, and diverted from errors"), who makes this experiment and achieves the knowledge it conveys, namely the immateriality of the soul, that is, of the soul of the one making the experiment. As for others, the same conclusion has to be attained by means of an argument presented in another, perhaps demonstrative, way. Although two arguments presented in two different ways can reach the same conclusion, it is hard to see, *contra* Ibn Kammūna, how the very same formulation of the *Flying Man* argument can be turned into a proper demonstration syllogistically arranged.

The role that the *Flying Man* plays within the context of *Nafs*, I, 1 is, therefore, to mark a transition from the inquiry into the existence of the soul as the operational principle of activities observable in bodies, to the essence-inquiry. However, at the level of the *Flying Man* the essence-inquiry is not inquiry into the quiddity of the *soul of* the body, that is, the counterpart of the investigation of the sublunary soul

---

57 For the non-Aristotelian character of this argument, see Hasnawi, "La conscience de soi", 286; and Black, "Avicenna on Self-Awareness", 63.

58 See Muehlethaler, "Ibn Kammūna", 181, n. 9. For a reflection on the strength of the *Flying Man* argument, see also P. Adamson, F. Benevich, "The Thought Experimental Method".

59 See Muehlethaler, "Ibn Kammūna", 195–197; and Sebti, "Avicenna's "Flying Man" Argument", 535.

60 I just notice that this is precisely the way in which Avicenna proves that the soul exists in *Nafs*, I, 1, namely what I have called the *a posteriori* demonstration of the existence of the soul.

61 *Mubāḥaṯāt*, 56–59. For the English translation, see Muehlethaler, "Ibn Kammūna", 195–196.

qua operational principle conducted in chapter I, 1, to which *Nafs*, I, 3 will be devoted (we shall see in the following section what kind of inquiry it is). Rather, this first step of the essence-inquiry provides a means by which the person who is perspicacious enough can immediately acknowledge the incorporeality of his/her soul, i.e. what his/her soul – his/her human soul – *in itself* is.

The aforementioned passage from the *Mubāḥaṯāt*, however, leaves open the possibility of formulating, besides the exclusive *Flying Man* argument, another argument bearing the same conclusion, but understandable by those who are not sufficiently perspicacious. We have therefore to check whether in the *Nafs* there can be found a proper demonstration ("an argument that is based on species and genus") of the fact that the human soul is an immaterial substance.[62]

The Soul is Substance insofar as it is the Form of the Body: the Ascertainment of the Essence of Sublunary Soul

That the transition to the essence-inquiry is accomplished is marked by the title of *Nafs*, I, 3: "[Chapter] on the fact that the soul falls under the category of substance (*Fī anna l-nafs dāḫila fī maqūlat al-ğawhar*)". The introductory lines of this chapter are crucial to understanding the kind of investigation upon which Avicenna is embarking: "We ourselves say: [(a)] you know from what has preceded (*mimmā taqaddama*) that the soul is not body (*al-nafs laysat bi-ğism*). [(b)] And if it is established for you that it rightly occurs for some soul to be isolated [from the body] because of its self-subsistence (*sc.* its isolated self-subsistence) (*fa-in ṯubita laka anna nafsan mā yaṣiḥḥu lahā l-infirād bi-qiwām ḏātihā*), you will not doubt that it is a substance. [(c)] This, however, is established for you only (*innamā*) in the case of something that is said to be soul (*fī baʿḍ mā yuqālu lahū nafs*). In the case of other things, such as the vegetative and the animal soul (*miṯla l-nafs al-nabātiyya wa-l-nafs al-ḥayawāniyya*), that has not been established for you [yet]" (*Nafs*, I, 3, 27.15–19 [58.23–28]).

Here three elements are noteworthy. By referring to *what has preceded,* Avicenna resumes [(a)] the general conclusion emerging from the investigation conducted in I, 1, namely that the soul is other than body (see, for instance, *Nafs*, I, 1, 5.3–6.1), and [(b)] the specific conclusion of the *Flying Man* experiment. However, here Avicenna goes a bit further than the proper conclusion of the *Flying Man:* there it has been – negatively, I would say – concluded that the human soul is incorporeal, here – positively – that it is something independent of the body and, for this very reason, substance.[63]

62 I speak of a demonstration of the fact that the human soul is an immaterial substance because, given the primitiveness of the notion of *immateriality*, there cannot be provided a demonstration of it but, rather, of a substance of that kind, i.e. qualified as immaterial.

63 Hasse has considered this as the conclusion of the *Flying Man* experiment; see n. 49 above.

Therefore, the demonstration of the substantiality of the human soul *in itself*, that is, in the condition of complete isolation from the body, a condition that it is the only kind of sublunary soul to enjoy, is considered unnecessary. Avicenna can therefore focus on [(c)] the proper demonstration of the quiddity of the *soul of* plants and animals (human beings included) that, while existing in the sublunary world, is always connected with matter and motion, a connection that might raise some doubts about its substantiality, which thus needs to be demonstrated. However, in spite of its bodily existence, the soul of a plant or an animal is a substance, not an accident, because it exists in the body not like an accident in a subject, but like a form in a receptacle (*maḥall*): "Therefore, the existence of the soul in the body is not like the existence of the accident in the subject. Then, the soul is a substance because it is a form not in a subject (*ǧawhar li-annahā ṣūra lā fī mawḍūʿ*) (*Nafs*, I, 3, 29.6–8 [60.59–61])".

In order to account for the substantiality of vegetative and animal souls, Avicenna revives his standard criterion of substantiality derived from Aristotle's *Categories*, together with Aristotelian hylomorphism: what is not in a subject at all is said to be a substance, and since the form is not in matter as in a ὑποκείμενον, i.e. in a subject, the form is (or can be) a substance.[64] Thus, in *Nafs*, I, 1 the sublunary soul has been investigated on the operational level, namely insofar as it is principle of activities in bodies, whereas in *Nafs*, I, 3 it is proved to be a substance insofar as it is form. The investigations conducted in *Nafs*, I, 1 and I, 3, respectively, are thus complementary: the latter ascertains the quiddity of the thing of which the former ascertains the existence on the basis of its relation to the body.

However, this cannot be the end of the story. For we are left with the conclusion of the *Flying Man* argument about the human soul considered *in itself* and its refinement at the beginning of I, 3 (where Avicenna goes from incorporeality to independence in existence), which are not universal, i.e. available to everyone: the *Flying Man* is addressed to the perspicacious reader; and, the not further specified soul (*nafs mā*), whose substantiality is immediately acknowledged in virtue of the kind of existence it enjoys, in all likelihood and in the very same vein of the *Flying Man* experiment, refers not to the human soul in general, but to the particular soul belonging to a particular man. Thus, only the man reflecting on himself will not doubt that he (and not whatever human soul!) is a self-subsistent substance, since the knowledge

64 See Aristotelis *Categoriae et Liber de interpretatione* recognivit brevique adnotatione critica instruxit L. Minio-Paluello, Oxford Classical Texts, Oxford University Press, Oxford 1949, 5, 2 a11–3 a15. For Avicenna's endorsement of this as his standard criterion of substantiality, see *Maqūlāt*, III, 1, 92.5: "Our discourse is that substance exists not in a subject" (the same sentence is repeated at 93.10, and in III, 3); and in *Ilāhiyyāt*, II, 1, 57.10–11 [65.12–13]: "The second (*sc.* of the two divisions of the existent, the first being accident) is what exists without being in another thing in this manner (*sc.* as accident does). Hence it would not be in a subject at all. This is substance".

he attains by means of this reflection is not based on demonstration and, consequently, is not universal.[65]

That this is an individual, intuitive, non-demonstrative conclusion seems to be confirmed by a sort of exception that Avicenna makes to his standard criterion of substantiality – *not being in a subject at all* – in pointing at the substantiality of *that* soul. By speaking of *al-infirād bi-qiwām ḏātihā, its isolated self-subsistence*, Avicenna does not aim to introduce an alternative criterion of substantiality with the same status of his standard one; he simply hints at a way to get immediate, subjective (non-demonstrative) access to the substantiality of a particular human soul (the soul of a human being reflecting on himself): this human soul is a substance because it is a self-subsistent entity, and therefore it makes no sense to wonder whether it is in a subject or not, because what enjoys a condition of independent existence is *a fortiori* not in a subject at all.

However, in spite of its immediate acknowledgement, the substantiality of the human soul, considered *in itself* and on a universal level, seems to await a proper demonstration. A confirmation of the necessity of a demonstration of that kind can be found in all the writings in which the *Flying Man* argument occurs (*Ḥikma mašriqiyya*, *Kitāb al-Išārāt wa-l-tanbīhāt*, and *Risāla Aḍḥawiyya fī l-maʿād*): for there it is always followed by a demonstration of the quiddity of the human soul as a sort of complement.[66] In my reconstruction, this demonstration is provided in *Nafs*, V, 2, which contains exactly the same demonstration attested in all the aforementioned writings.[67]

---

65 In this perspective – I think – the references to a hypothetical reader at the beginning of I, 3 (*laka, for you*, I, 3, 27.16², 17 [*dubitabis, tibi*, 58.25, 26; the first occurrence of *laka* is omitted in Latin) should be read.

66 In the *Risāla Aḍḥawiyya* Avicenna moves from the *Flying Man* argument (chapter 4) to the proof of the self-subsistence of the human rational soul (chapter 5), which is an abridged formulation of the demonstration provided in *Nafs*, V, 2. The opening lines of chapter 5, which contains a possible prospective reference to *Nafs*, V, 2, might help us to understand the general purpose of this demonstration in the contexts in which it occurs after the *Flying Man* argument. See *Risāla Aḍḥawiyya*, V, 153.1–5: "*Fifth chapter on establishing that in order to subsist the soul does not need the body.* In many of our books there is the clarification of the substantiality of the soul (*fī ʿidda min kutubinā bayān ǧawhariyyat al-nafs*), especially in our commentary on Aristotle's *Book on the Soul* (*wa-ḫāṣṣatan fī šarḥinā li-kitāb Arisṭūṭālīs fī l-nafs*). As for that to which we will limit ourselves concerning this [topic] in this book, it is that we will demonstrate that the human soul (*fa-huwa an nubarhina anna l-nafs al-insāniyya*), which is called rational (*bi-l-nāṭiqa*), is not impressed in matter (*laysat munṭabiʿa fī l-mādda*), nor subsists in the body in any respect (*wa-lā qāʾima bi-l-ǧism min wuǧūhin*)". From these lines we get the impression that Avicenna considers this demonstration, which is the same as the one provided in *Nafs*, V, 2, the standard demonstration of the substantiality of the human rational soul, which he says to provide in many of his writings.

67 Here I disagree with Adamson-Benevich, who maintain that through the *Flying Man* experiment Avicenna rules out that the connection to body is part of the soul's essence, whereas in *Nafs*, V, 2 Avicenna proves that the connection to body is not a necessary accident of soul (n. 14). As I will argue, in *Nafs*, V, 2 Avicenna provides an *a posteriori* proof of the incorporeal essence of the human rational

The *a posteriori* Proof of the Essence of the Human Rational Soul

Avicenna's purpose in *Nafs*, V, 2 is immediately pointed out in the chapter title: "[Chapter] on establishing that the rational soul does not subsist as something impressed in corporeal matter (*Fī iṯbāt qiwām al-nafs al-nāṭiqa ġayr munṭabiʿa fī mādda ǧusmāniyya*)". Here, Avicenna aims to demonstrate that the human rational soul is an incorporeal substance, capable of self-subsistence. In the chapter title the meaningful word *iṯbāt* occurs, which is the very same word occurring in the title of *Nafs*, I, 1, though with a significant difference. There, it refers to the ascertainment of the existence of the soul insofar as it is soul, namely to the *a posteriori* proof of the existence of the sublunary soul insofar as it is related to the body as its operational principle. Here, by contrast, it cannot have the same meaning, and refer to the same purpose. If it were so, it would be redundant and useless, because a proof of the existence of the soul has been already provided and, what is more, on a general level, not limited to the rational soul. Thus, here *iṯbāt* refers to the ascertainment of the qualified existence of the human rational soul, that is, its existence as an incorporeal substance.

It is noteworthy that here, with respect to the human rational soul *in itself*, we are in the presence of the very same transition from the level of existence to that of essence that in *Nafs*, I, 1 is marked by the *Flying Man* experiment. There, however, Avicenna passes from the demonstration of the existence of the sublunary soul in general (*Nafs*, I, 1) to the allusion to the essence of one of them, namely of the human soul considered in itself (*Flying Man* experiment) and, lastly, to the demonstration of the essence of all sublunary souls (*Nafs*, I, 3). Here, by contrast, he provides a proper demonstration of what has just been hinted at by means of the *Flying Man* experiment. In this manner Avicenna brings to a proper completion also the second investigation conducted in *Nafs*, that of the human rational soul *in itself*, whereas in *Nafs*, I, 1–3 he has already accomplished the investigation of the existence and the essence of the sublunary *soul of* plants and animals, that is, as a relational entity.

Let us turn back to the word *iṯbāt*. In spite of their different purpose, the *iṯbāt* of I, 1 and that of V, 2 share the same status and the same method: they designate an *a posteriori* proof, starting from the observation of some activities for which the soul is responsible, i.e. general psychic activities, and the specific activity of the human rational soul, respectively.[68]

---

soul considered *in itself*, while through the *Flying Man* he provides an argument for that which is valid only for the soul of a human being reflecting on himself, i.e. on his own essence. For this demonstration in the *Risāla Aḍḥawiyya*, see the note above. As for the passage containing this demonstration in the *Ḥikma mašriqiyya*, see 185.20 – 192.7; as for the passage containing the same demonstration in the *Kitāb al-Išārāt wa-l-tanbīhāt*, see 130.4 – 15; 131.13 – 132.6; 176.9 – 178.8.

68 For the intellectual activity as the most specific operation of the human rational soul, see *Nafs*, V, 1, 206.11 – 13 [76.4 – 7]: "The most specific property of the human being (*wa-aḫaṣṣ al-ḫawāṣṣ bi-l-insān*) is the conceptualization of the universal, intellectual notions, which are completely abstracted from

The fact that *Nafs*, V, 2 contains something different from the investigation generally accomplished in *Nafs*, I, 1–3, and reconnects with what is alluded to in the *Flying Man* experiment, though providing something more, especially with respect to the logical status of the argument[69] and, consequently, to the universality of its conclusion, emerges from its introductory lines: "One thing about which there is no doubt is that [(a)] in the human being there is a thing (*šay'*), that is, a certain substance (*ǧawhar mā*) that obtains intelligibles by receiving [them]. [(b)] We say that the substance which is the receptacle of intelligibles is in no way a body (*al-ǧawhar allaḏī huwa maḥall al-maʿqūlāt laysa bi-ǧism*), [(c)] nor subsists in a body (*wa-lā qāʾim fī ǧism*), either as a faculty in it or as a form belonging to it (*ʿalà annahū quwwa fīhi aw ṣūra lahū bi-waǧhin*) (V, 2, 209.16–210.1 [81.89–82.93])".

The quidditative focus of the investigation on which Avicenna is embarking is immediately revealed: [(a)] it concerns a *thing*, considered in its totality and having its essence (we have already become familiar with this use of *šay'*), that is, a *substance*, whose nature has to be demonstrated (here *substance* specifies what *thing* means). This thing is the intellecting substance, which Avicenna has hinted at in the *Flying Man* experiment, and cursorily at the beginning of *Nafs*, I, 3. This intellecting substance, that is, the receptacle of intelligibles in human beings – basically the human rational soul – is said to be by no means a body [(b)]. That the human soul is not body chimes with the general conclusion of *Nafs*, I, 1, and echoes the incorporeality of the human soul, which emerged from the *Flying Man* experiment. However, here the *demonstrandum* is the fact that the human rational soul *in itself* is an immaterial substance. By contrast, that the *soul of* plants and animals, human beings included, existing in bodies, is incorporeal and a substance has been demonstrated in *Nafs*, I, 3, where Avicenna argues for this on the basis of its being a form inhering in a receptacle.[70]

That the scenario and the purpose of this investigation are different from those of *Nafs*, I is confirmed by Avicenna himself: [(c)] what will be demonstrated is that this substance, which is not body, does not subsist in a body, either as a faculty or as a form. The fact that Avicenna rules out the possibility that the human rational soul is a *form* in a body, by means of which the substantiality of the *soul of* plants and animals has been accounted for in *Nafs*, I, 3, testifies to the change of focus of the in-

matter, as we have reported and shown, and the attainment of the knowledge of unknown things from intellectual things [already] known through assent and conceptualization". See also V, 2, 216.16–18 [93.56–59]: "Let us cite as evidence of what we have shown the discourse investigating the substance of the rational soul, and its most specific activity (*bi-l-kalām al-nāẓir fī ǧawhar al-nafs al-nāṭiqa wa-fī aḫaṣṣ fiʿl lahū*) by [providing] indications [taken] from the states of the other activities belonging to it, which relate to what we mentioned".

69 The logical status of this *iṯbāt* seems uncontroversial: the terminology used therein suggests that it is a proper demonstration. See the terms *barhana* (*to demonstrate*, 214.6 [*probare*, 89.96]; 216.6 [*probare*, 92.45]), and *burhān* (*demonstration*, 214.6 [*demonstratio*, 89.96]; 218.8 [*probatio*, 96.1]).

70 See § The Soul is Substance insofar as it is the Form of the Body: the Ascertainment of the Essence of Sublunary Soul.

quiry and the transition from the investigation of the *soul of* to that of the soul *in itself* (in *Nafs*, I, 1 Avicenna has already pointed out that *form* is not capable of encompassing all instances of soul, because it excludes what is separable).[71] Together with the possibility that the human rational soul is a form, Avicenna also excludes that it is a *faculty* in a body. This aspect needs to be spelled out, because negating that the human rational soul is a faculty represents another, stronger confirmation of the aforementioned change of focus. For here the rational soul is not investigated insofar as it is a faculty belonging to the *soul of* a human being, but rather insofar as it is the essence of that soul, what a certain soul is *in itself*, what remains when its relation to the body is severed, and it is in the condition of being in complete isolation from the body.[72]

Although I believe that in *Nafs*, V, 2 Avicenna aims to demonstrate that the human soul in its entirety is an immaterial substance,[73] the reference to the *rational soul* (*al-nafs al-nāṭiqa, anima rationalis*) in the chapter title might be interpreted as a limitation of this demonstration to the rational soul, that is, to that part of the soul that is responsible for theoretical activity, i.e. the theoretical intellect.[74] In particular, the major difficulty that some scholars have found in this interpretation is that in the *Nafs* Avicenna distinguishes between the human soul and its two faculties, i.e. the practical and the theoretical intellect,[75] and argues against the possibility that the human soul identifies with the intellectual forms by identifying with the intellect.[76]

However, it should be preliminarily noted that in the *Nafs*, when Avicenna refers to the rational soul, he has in mind the human soul in its entirety, as emerges – for

71 More on this in Chapter 4.

72 See n. 66 and the second passage quoted in n. 68 above. It is noteworthy that the characterization of the human rational soul as something not impressed in a body, either as a form or as a faculty, echoes the characterization of the *ʿaql muǧarrad*, the abstracted (in the sense of "separated from matter") intellect belonging to the celestial sphere in *Ilāhiyyāt*, IX, 4, 408.13–14 [486.48–51].

73 See, for instance, the way in which Avicenna summarizes the conclusions of *Nafs*, V, 2 at the end of the chapter: "It has already become evident from the fundamental principles that we have established that the [human] soul is not impressed in the body, nor subsists through it (*min uṣūlinā llatī qarrarnā anna l-nafs laysat munṭabiʿa fī l-badan wa-lā qāʾima bihī*)" (V, 2, 221.9–10 [101.87–88]).

74 For example, Sebti holds this position in her "Avicenna's "Flying Man" Argument", esp. 534–35.

75 See, for instance, I, 5, and V, 1, where the human soul is referred to as *one, isolated substance*, having two faculties. For these passages, see n. 81 below. In general in *Nafs*, I, 5 Avicenna makes a distinction between soul and psychic faculties ensuing from it.

76 See *Nafs*, V, 6, 239.10–241.4 [134.50–138.89], where Avicenna maintains this position because the human intellect does not ceaselessly think, this being God's prerogative (*Ilāhiyyāt*, VIII, 6), and therefore, if the human soul identifies with the intellect, its essence would be identical with something that is sometimes in potentiality, and sometimes in actuality. Nonetheless, in *Ilāhiyyāt*, IX, 7, 426.9–10 [511.93–4] Avicenna maintains that in human intellection the intellect, the intellecting thing and the intellected thing are "one thing or almost one thing" (*wāḥid aw qarīb min al-wāḥid* [*unum vel paene unum*]); and in *Ilāhiyyāt*, X, 1, 435.13–14 [523.21–22] he claims that in the case of the prophet the soul becomes identical with the intellect in actuality in this life.

instance – in *Nafs*, I, 5.[77] Moreover, in several passages Avicenna prospectively refers to V, 2 as the chapter in which it is shown that the human soul (not a part of it) is not related to the body like form to matter.[78] All these references cannot be dismissed as a sort of sloppiness in style on Avicenna's part.[79]

What is more, from the outset of his investigation Avicenna clearly states that the thing whose immaterial substantiality he is going to prove is not a faculty in a body.[80]

---

77 *Nafs*, I, 5, 40.7–9 [81.21–24]: "You will learn the difference between the animal soul and the faculty of perception and of setting in motion, and the difference between the rational soul (*al-nafs al-nāṭiqa*) and the faculty concerning the aforementioned things with respect to discernment, etc."; and, I, 5, 45.17–18 [90.61–62]: "As to the human rational soul (*wa-ammā l-nafs al-nāṭiqa al-insāniyya*), its faculties are divided into a practical faculty and a cognitive faculty".

78 Apart from the important text quoted in n. 80 below, see, for instance, *Nafs*, II, 1, 57.11–12 [113.44–47]: "As for the human soul, it is not connected to the body by a formal connection (*taʿalluq ṣūrī*), as we shall show (*kamā nubayyinu, sc.* in V, 2). Then, it does not need that an organ is prepared for it"; and IV, 4, 200.14–15 [65.41–42]: "For, as we shall show (*sanubayyinu, sc.* in V, 2), the human soul is not impressed (*ġayr munṭabiʿa*) in the matter belonging to it, but it directs its endeavour towards it". *ġayr munṭabiʿa* are precisely the same words that Avicenna uses in the title of V, 2. See also *Nafs*, I, 4, 39.3–5 [78.91–93]: "As for the human faculty (*wa-ammā l-quwwa al-insāniyya*), we shall show (*sanubayyinu, sc.* in V, 2) regarding it that it is free in itself from being impressed in matter, and we shall show (*sanubayyinu, sc.* in V, 8) that all the activities ascribed to the animals need an organ" (with respect to this passage, two elements are noteworthy: (1) Avicenna contrasts the human faculty, which is in itself free from matter, with all the other psychic faculties which require a bodily organ; (2) Avicenna seems to identify the human soul with one of its faculties, namely the theoretical faculty).

79 M. Sebti, "La distinction entre intellect pratique et intellect théorique dans la doctrine de l'âme humaine d'Avicenne", *Philosophie*, 77, 2003, 23–44, esp. 26: "Cependant, dans divers passages consacrés à l'âme rationnelle – comme ceux du cinquième livre du *T.S.A.*, une imprécision dans le vocabulaire peut laisser croire qu'Avicenne identifie l'âme rationnelle à l'intellect". This position, however, is potentially dangerous because it implies a certain amount of arbitrariness in judging the Avicennian text. In the psychological section of other *summae* Avicenna assigns two faculties to the human soul and, at the same time, he quotes almost verbatim the contents of chapter V, 2: following Sebti's suggestion we have to consider all these texts to be sloppy.

80 At the end of *Nafs*, V, 1, in the very same chapter in which he makes a distinction between the human soul and its faculties, Avicenna announces the subject of the subsequent chapter (V, 2) by saying: "First of all, we must show that this soul (*sc.* the human rational soul), which is disposed to receive the intelligibles through the material intellect, is neither a body nor subsists as a form in a body" (209.12–13). Then, at the beginning of V, 2 as well as in the course of the chapter, Avicenna also excludes the possibility that the human rational soul is a faculty in a body. See *Nafs*, V, 2, 214.1–5 [88.87–89.95]: "If the intellectual form cannot be divided, nor can it inhere in an indivisible extremity of magnitudes, but [it] must have a recipient in us, then we must judge that the receptacle of the intelligibles is a substance that is not body, and also that what is within us which obtains them is not a faculty in a body. For then what attaches to the body in terms of divisions would attach to it, and the rest of the absurdities would follow. Rather, what is within us which obtains the intellectual form must be an incorporeal substance (*ǧawhar ġayr ǧusmānī*)."; and 216.3–7 [92.41–45]: "Similarly, it has already turned out to be true for us that the assumed intelligibles, which the rational faculty is capable of thinking one by one in actuality, are infinite in potentiality. And it has already turned out to be true for us that the thing that is able to manage infinite things in potentiality cannot be a

For, if the human rational soul were a faculty in a body, Avicenna would be in the difficult situation of explaining the way in which the human soul, which is said to be a substance, relates to its theoretical faculty, which is in turn another substance.

Certainly, we cannot ignore the passages in which Avicenna says that the human soul is a substance having two faculties;[81] however, it is crucial to evaluate the context in which this statement is made. In those passages Avicenna deals specifically with human faculties that, like all other faculties, are observable in bodies, and for which the soul is responsible. However, in the course of the treatise the respect in which the human soul is treated changes and, in this different respect, the distinction between soul and faculties fades.[82] In particular, the distinction holds true when Avicenna investigates the *soul of* plants and animals and distinguishes the soul from the activities of which it is the principle. However, when he turns to the soul *in itself*,

body, or a faculty in a body. This has already been demonstrated in the previous sections (*fī l-funūn al-māḍiya, sc. Samāʿ ṭabīʿī*, III, 10, see n. 95 below)".

81 See, for example, *Nafs*, I, 5, 47.7–10 [93.99–3]: "The characters that are in us are ascribed only to this (*sc.* practical) faculty because the human soul, as will become evident later on (*kamā yaẓharu min baʿdin, sc.* V, 1), is one substance (*ǧawhar wāḥid*), but it has a relation and a reference to two sides, a side below it and a side above it, and in accordance with each side it has a faculty by means of which the connection between it and that side is regulated." And, V, 1, 208.10–13 [80.58–60]: "Neither of the two (*sc.* the practical and the theoretical intellect) is the human soul; rather, the [human] soul is the thing that has these faculties, this [soul] being, as has become clear (*kamā tabayyana*), an isolated substance (*ǧawhar munfarid*) which has a disposition towards some activities."

82 See, apart from *Nafs*, V, 1, 206.11–13 [76.4–7] quoted in n. 68 above, V, 1, 207.12–13 [78.32–34], where the practical faculty is said to depend on the theoretical faculty ("This faculty (*sc.* the practical intellect) takes support from the faculty that concerns universals (*wa-takūnu hāḏihi l-quwwa istimdāduhā min al-quwwa allatī ʿalà l-kulliyyāt*): from here it grasps the major premises in what it deliberates upon, and it infers concerning particular [matters]"). On these faculties as two sides of one and the same cognitive power, see *Nafs*, I, 5 quoted in n. 77 above. Furthermore, with the exception of V, 1, which is an introductory chapter, and a cursory reference to the ethical dimension at the end of V, 2, in the rest of the fifth treatise, which is devoted to the activities of the human, rational soul, there is no further reference to the practical faculty. Avicenna defers to *Ilāhiyyāt*, IX, 7 the treatment of the way in which the human soul curbs the body and its faculties through the practical faculty in order to obtain the celestial beatitude (cf. V, 1, 208.18–19 [80.69–70]). It is noteworthy that in *Ilāhiyyāt*, IX, 7, 429.16 [517.00] Avicenna refers to the practical faculty of the soul by naming it *al-ǧuzʾ al-ʿamalī* [*partis animae quae est practica*], practical part, not *al-ʿaql al-ʿamalī*, practical intellect. On this terminological issue, and on the fact that in Avicenna the treatment of the practical intellect fits with the ethical and eschatological dimension of metaphysics more than with the epistemological dimension of psychology, see Lizzini, *Avicenna*, 282, n. 136 and 283, n. 138. The reason might be that in the *Nafs* Avicenna does not develop a "véritable antropologie de l'action", as Sebti argues (cf. Sebti, "La distinction entre intellect pratique et intellect théorique", 37). Or, perhaps, in psychology Avicenna reproduces Aristotle's treatment of νοῦς in his *De an.*, III, 4–8, where the distinction between the theoretical and the practical intellect is just assumed (it is properly spelled out only in *Nicomachean Ethics* VI, 1, 1139 a3–15), and the νοῦς is presented as "a general intellectual capacity with a general object, perhaps *logos*, differentiated according to various specific kinds of object". On this suggestion, see Johansen, *The Powers of Aristotle's Soul*, esp. 221–226.

that is, the human soul, the only instance of soul for which it is not senseless to investigate what it is *in itself*, the distinction between soul and activities collapses because the essence of the soul considered in itself is identical with its intellectual activity, since it is what remains after the separation from the body, and that by means of which it is primarily defined: "However, we say that the substance of the soul has two activities (*ǧawhar al-nafs lahū fiʿlāni*): an activity belonging to it in relation to the body, which is the guidance [of the body] (*bi-l-qiyās ilà l-badan wa-huwa l-siyāsa*), and an activity belonging to it in relation to itself and its principles, which is perception by means of the intellect (*bi-l-qiyās ilà ḏātihī wa-ilà mabādiʾihī wa-huwa l-idrāk bi-l-ʿaql*)" (*Nafs*, V, 2, 220.5–7 [9.55–58]). Even when Avicenna maintains that the human soul is a substance having two activities, the essence of the human soul is tied only to one of these activities, i.e. intellectual conceptualization. Certainly, the *soul of* human beings is responsible, among other activities, for the intellective processes occurring in the concrete human being while existing in the sublunary world. However, the human soul *in itself* is the rational soul, namely it identifies with its theoretical part, the one that endures eternally.[83] The perspective of *Nafs*, V, 2 chimes with Avicenna's rejection of *quwwa* in the sense of *faculty*, and of *ṣūra*/*form* as terms to refer to the soul in *Nafs*, I, 1: they are not broad enough to encompass all instances of soul and, therefore, prevent one from grasping what the human rational soul is.[84]

---

83 In the *Letter to Kiyā* Avicenna demonstrates that the thing in which universal intelligibles are conceived is indivisible and, therefore, incorporeal (120.14–15). There Avicenna apparently considers the intellect a sort of concomitant of the substance of the human soul ("The truth is that this [material] intellect is a disposition of the substance of the soul, not of any body, and that it accompanies the substance of the soul in every state", 121.1–2; English translation in Gutas, *Avicenna and the Aristotelian Tradition*, 56). However, in what precedes (120.17–20) Avicenna says that in the last book of *De anima* Aristotle deals with "the faculties which accompany the soul in its survival only" (*al-quwà l-murāfiqa li-l-nafs fī l-baqāʾ*, 120.18), namely the intellectual faculties. Consequently, it seems that the substance of the human soul actually identifies with the intellectual faculties that in the human soul's sublunary existence exist together with the other perishable faculties. For a similar argument and a sort of summary of the contents of *Nafs*, V, 2–4, see *Risāla fī l-kalām ʿalà l-nafs al-nāṭiqa*, in A. F. al-Ahwānī ed., *Aḥwāl al-nafs*, Dār iḥyāʾ al-kutub al-ʿarabiyya, Cairo 1371/1952, 196.9–14. The identification of the human soul with the intellect (*ʿaql*) might have been suggested by Philoponus, who maintains that *soul* always designates an entity related to a bodily substratum, whereas the human soul in itself is (and is called) *intellect* (it is the only case in which a soul has a proper name). See Philoponus, *In De anima*, 241.5–9: εἶτα ἐπειδὴ δοκεῖ αὐτῷ χωριστὸν εἶναι τὸν νοῦν, αὐτὸ τοῦτο ἐπήγαγε· ταὐτὸν δέ φησι νοῦν καὶ τὴν θεωρητικὴν αὐτοῦ δύναμιν. τοῦ γὰρ νοῦ τὸ μέν ἐστι θεωρητικόν, τὸ δὲ πρακτικόν. τὸ μὲν οὖν πρακτικὸν ἐκ τῆς σχέσεως αὐτῷ γίνεται τῆς πρὸς τὸ σῶμα· διὸ μετὰ τὸ ἀπολυθῆναι σώματος μόνος ἔσται θεωρητικός, οὐκέτι δὲ καὶ πρακτικός (emphasis mine). See also the passage quoted in n. 8 above.

84 In the case of *quwwa*, Avicenna explains that it is not appropriate to define the soul because it is equivocal. For it might refer either to the active capacity of performing a motion/activity, or to the passive capacity of receiving something, but these two meanings are irreducible to each other. See *Nafs*, I, 1, 7.10–8.8 [21.49–22.69].

The global argument, in which in *Nafs*, V, 2 Avicenna demonstrates that the human rational soul does not subsist in a body either as a form or as a faculty in it, consists of three consecutive demonstrations.[85]

1. The first demonstration is a *reductio ad absurdum a parte subiecti*, i.e. with respect to the nature of the intellecting substance. Avicenna assumes the opposite of what he aims to demonstrate, that is, that the substance receiving intellectual forms in the human beings is a body, and then he verifies whether that assumption is tenable.

The assumption is immediately split into two alternatives: the body can be either (i) indivisible or (ii) divisible.

(i) Examples of indivisible body are (i.i) the geometrical point (indivisible, unextended entity), and (i.ii) the atom (indivisible, yet extended magnitude). (i.i) Since the geometrical point cannot be actually distinguished with respect to position from the magnitude (e.g. a line) of which it is the limit (*ṭaraf*, *terminus*), the refutation of this possibility is deferred to the discussion of the second alternative (ii).[86] (i.ii) As for the atom (here Avicenna is arguing against the atomism of the *mutakallimūn*), Avicenna refutes its existence by using an argument already presented in *Samāʿ ṭabīʿī*, III, 4: the atom cannot exist because its existence would conflict with Atomists' assumption that an atom is an indivisible entity. Take, for instance, three atoms (x, y, z) in a row. The middle atom y has to hinder the contact between the two atoms x and z, otherwise they would interpenetrate one another and form one single atom (the sum of atoms is an atom), and it would then come under case (i.i). However, in order for atom y to hinder contact between x and z, x and z must be in contact with a different "side" of atom y, which would then be conceptually divided into two sides, one in contact with x, which is not in contact with z, and another in contact with z, which is not in contact with x.[87] The refutation of atomism, which can be also found in *Samāʿ ṭabīʿī*, III, 3–4, is metaphysically founded in *Ilāhiyyāt*, II, 2, and III, 9.[88]

(ii) As for the second alternative, assuming that the body receiving the intelligibles is divisible would entail that the intellectual form inhering in it is divisible. Consequently, the parts in which the intellectual form would be divisible as a conse-

85 On this argument, see P. Adamson, "From Known to Knower: Affinity Arguments for the Mind's Incorporeality in the Islamic World", forthcoming.

86 *Nafs*, V, 2, 210.6–15 [82.98–83.10].

87 *Nafs*, V, 2, 210.15–211.15 [83.10–85.34].

88 For a reconstruction of Avicenna's arguments against atomism, see A. Dhanani, "The Impact of Ibn Sīnā's Critique of Atomism on Subsequent Kalām Discussions of Atomism", *Arabic Sciences and Philosophy*, 25, 2015, 79–104, in part. 79–85. See also J. McGinnis, "Avicenna's natural philosophy", in P. Adamson ed., *Interpreting Avicenna. Critical Essays*, Cambridge University Press, Cambridge 2013, 71–90, in part. 78–81.

quence of the division of its bodily receptacle would be either (ii.i) similar or (ii.ii) dissimilar.[89]

Case (ii.i) is easily ruled out. Given that the whole must be different from its parts, it is hard to explain how similar parts can bring about something different from them. Furthermore, one cannot say that the whole, i.e. the intellectual form, is something resulting from its similar parts in virtue of an increase in magnitude or in number, because in that case the intellectual form would be characterized by a certain quantity or a certain number, which are appurtenances of matter. Intellectual forms are intelligible precisely because they are immaterial.[90]

(ii.ii) If, by contrast, the receptacle of the intellectual forms is a body divisible into dissimilar parts, the intellectual form must also have dissimilar parts. The only dissimilar parts detectable in the intellectual forms are the parts of the definition, namely genera and *differentiae*. However, if these are posited as the dissimilar parts of the intellectual form, several absurdities will follow. For instance, the parts of the body as well as those of the form, i.e. genus and *differentia*, will be potentially infinite. However, in *Burhān*, III, 6 Avicenna claims that the essential genus and *differentia* of something are not potentially infinite. Furthermore, since merely imagining the division would not set apart the genus from the *differentia* of the intellectual form, all genera and *differentiae* would need to be actually distinct in their bodily receptacle. Consequently, genera and *differentiae*, which are the dissimilar parts of the intellectual form, would also actually be infinite. Another absurdity would be that the actual division of the body might not precisely reflect the division of genus and *differentia* of the intellectual form, but it might halve the genus, or the *differentia*. Moreover, there is the problematic case of intellectual forms that are simple, do not have genus nor *differentia*, and therefore cannot be divided.[91]

After having discussed all the possible alternatives, Avicenna has to rule completely out that the substance which acts as the receptacle of the intellectual forms in the human being is a body (*anna maḥall al-maʿqūlāt ǧawhar laysa bi-ǧism* [*quod subiectum intelligibilium substantia est quae not est corpus*]), be it indivisible or divisible, or a faculty in a body (*wa-lā* [...] *quwwa fī ǧism* [*nec est virtus quae sit in corpore*]). It remains that the receptacle of the intellectual forms in us is an incorporeal substance (*ǧawhar ġayr ǧusmānī* [*substantia...non corporalis*]).[92]

2. The second demonstration is *a parte obiecti*, i.e. with respect to the object of the intellecting substance. Avicenna shows that the object of the intellecting substance is the intellectual form abstracted from quantity, place, position, and any material appurtenance that renders it particular. However, this form exists as separate from any material appurtenance only in mental existence; therefore, the intellecting

---

89 *Nafs*, V, 2, 211.15–19 [85.35–39].

90 *Nafs*, V, 2, 211.19–212.8 [85.40–86.50]. In *Ilāhiyyāt*, IV, 3 Avicenna maintains that the whole is constituted by mutually different parts.

91 *Nafs*, V, 2, 212.9–213.18 [86.51–88.86].

92 *Nafs*, V, 2, 214.1–5 [88.87–89.95].

substance cannot be a body, otherwise the intellectual form inhering in it would receive material attributes and would then cease to be universal. Consequently, the intellecting substance must be immaterial.[93]

3. The third demonstration is grounded on the activity of the intellecting substance. The intellecting substance can think of potentially infinite intellectual forms, Avicenna says.[94] Thus, since a thing having power over potentially infinite things cannot be a body or a faculty in a body,[95] the substance that thinks of potentially infinite intellectual forms cannot be in a body, nor perform its activity in it or by means of it. Furthermore, if the intellecting substance thought by means of a bodily organ, it would not think of itself nor would it be aware of having thought (here Avicenna clearly distinguishes the specific activity of the human, rational soul from the other psychic activities performed by means of a bodily organ, for which it, being higher than the other souls, is responsible in the body).[96] However, that the intellecting substance thinks of itself and is aware of having performed its intellective activity has been shown by the thought-experiment of the *Flying Man*.[97]

That the intellecting substance must be immaterial is further argued in two corollaries to the third demonstration, both derived from Aristotle's discussion in *De anima*, III.

3.1. *First corollary.* Unlike the other perceptive faculties, which are weakened, and even corrupted, by an intense sensible object, by thinking of the most intense intellectual object, the intellectual faculty is not weakened; rather, it acquires the capacity for receiving more easily the objects of thought weaker than it.[98] If it experiences weariness, it is only due to its use of perceptive bodily faculties like imagery.

3.2. *Second corollary.* Unlike the other perceptive faculties, which begin to weaken with the aging of the body (around forty years of age), the intellectual faculty is strengthened as time goes by. In other words, unlike the other perceptive faculties, the strengthening of the intellectual faculty is directly proportional to the aging of the body.[99]

Therefore, the intellectual faculty with which the human rational soul considered in itself identifies must be different from the other perceptive bodily faculties; namely, it must be incorporeal.

---

93 *Nafs*, V, 2, 214.6–216.2 [89.96–91.40]. For the discussion of the universal and its mental existence, see *Madḫal*, I, 12, and *Ilāhiyyāt*, V, 1–2.

94 Cf. *De an.*, III, 4, 429 a18, 27–29.

95 Here Avicenna seems to refer to *Samāʿ ṭabīʿī*, III, 10 ("This has already been demonstrated in the previous sections (*fī l-funūn al-māḍiya* [*in praecedentibus libris*])", 216.6–7 [92.45]), for there Avicenna argued that in the body, which is finite, there cannot be an infinite power.

96 *Nafs*, V, 2, 216.16–18 [93.56–59]. The passage is quoted in n. 68.

97 *Nafs*, V, 2, 216.3–218.14 [92.41–97.11].

98 *Nafs*, V, 2, 218.15–219.9 [97.12–98.32].

99 *Nafs*, V, 2, 219.10–220.5 [98.32–99.54].

Grounding the Investigation of the Soul: Part 2

After providing a survey of the enterprise accomplished by Avicenna in his *Nafs*, we can attempt to answer the opening question, that is, as to whether psychology conforms to the model of demonstrative science outlined in *Ilāhiyyāt*, I, 1–3 or not.

If, as part of natural philosophy *de facto*, psychology had limited itself to investigating the soul in connection with matter and motion, Avicenna's model of science would have worked perfectly in the case of psychology also. For psychology would have investigated the soul as the formal principle of the body, which accounts for its functional organization, and the activities observable therein, and only hinted at its ontological status, i.e. its being substance insofar as it is a form. Then, in *Ilāhiyyāt*, II, 1 Avicenna provides a classification of the different kinds of substance that are going to be dealt with in this writing, and form is one of them. Therefore, the use of this notion in natural philosophy (*sc.* in *Nafs*, I, 3, to refer to the ontological status of sublunary souls and, before that, in *Samāʿ ṭabīʿī*, I, 2, in dealing with the principle of natural things) turns out to be metaphysically founded.[100]

However, a part of psychology inquires into the existence and the quiddity of what is more similar to the celestial substances of metaphysics than to the generable and corruptible bodies of natural philosophy, i.e. the human rational soul.[101] What is

---

100 In *Ilāhiyyāt*, II, 1, 60.9–14 [68.76–69.83], in classifying the different kinds of substance, Avicenna distinguishes those which are parts of the body, i.e. form and matter, from those which are not parts of the body, i.e. soul and intellect, the former being tied to the body by a certain relation (*ʿalāqa*, the soul is said to be the moving principle of the body, not to be impressed in it like a form), whereas the latter is completely abstracted from the bodily matter. That the human soul is neither impressed (*lā...munṭabiʿa fī l-badan*) nor immerged in the body (*aw munġamisa fīhi*), but has a certain relation (*ʿalāqa*) to it is also stated in *Ilāhiyyāt*, IX, 7, 430.12–13 [518.25–27]. The distinction between form and soul seems to imply that here Avicenna is using the term *soul* in a narrower sense to refer only to the celestial soul. This use of the term *soul* might pose some problem with respect to the soul of plants and animals, human beings included, which in *Nafs*, I, 3 is said to be substance *qua* form. However, in *Ilāhiyyāt*, IX, 2, 386.16 [454.90], Avicenna also says that the celestial soul is the perfection and form of the celestial body; and in *Ilāhiyyāt*, IX, 4, 407.18–408.5 [485.24–34], Avicenna distinguishes the sensible forms that are not souls from those that are souls, namely celestial souls. Therefore, at least in *Ilāhiyyāt*, *soul* seems to be a sub-category of *form*. More on this in T. Alpina, "Is the Heaven an Animal? Avicenna's Celestial Psychology at the Intersection between Cosmology and Biology", in R. Salles ed., *Biology and Cosmology in Ancient Philosophy: from Thales to Avicenna*, Cambridge University Press, Cambridge forthcoming.

101 See *Nafs*, IV, 2, 178.17–8 [28.87–29.89]: "Human souls are more similar to these angelic substances than they are to the sensible bodies". These angelic substances might be the celestial intellects, since in principle they are separated from the celestial souls, which are, by contrast, the perfection and the form of the celestial body, although, in his Italian translation of the *Ilāhiyyāt*, A. Bertolacci argues that for Avicenna the celestial intellect and the celestial soul are not absolutely distinguished. See Avicenna (Ibn Sīnā), *Libro della Guarigione. Le cose divine*, Utet, Torino 2007, 710, n. 72. In *Ilāhiyyāt*, IX, 4 Avicenna describes the forms that are souls, namely the celestial souls, as self-subsistent forms (*ṣuwar qiwāmuhā bi-ḏātihā lā bi-mawādd al-ağsām ka-l-anfus*, 408.3), which is very similar to the description of human soul at the beginning of *Nafs*, I, 3 (*al-infirād bi-qiwām ḏātihā*, 27.16). More-

more, no metaphysical foundation of such an inquiry is provided; conversely, metaphysics seems to assume the conclusion of this investigation, or to merely supplement it, without providing further validation. Examples of this are the metaphysical treatment of the celestial souls (*Ilāhiyyāt,* IX, 2–5) and of eschatology (*Ilāhiyyāt,* IX, 7).[102]

As for the treatment of celestial souls, in *Ilāhiyyāt,* IX, 2 Avicenna actually maintains that a soul is the proximate mover of the celestial sphere, endowed with imagination and volition by means of which it can impart motion to the body of the sphere. This soul is defined as the perfection (*kamāl*) and the form (*ṣūra*) of the body of the celestial sphere[103] and, by being corporeal and subject to change, its relation to the celestial sphere is said to be similar to the relation of *our* animal soul to us, with minor differences concerning the degree of truth of the outcome of their perceptual activity.[104] Avicenna seems, therefore, to establish a sort of *continuity* between sublunary and celestial souls, since both are defined by using the same terminology (perfection, form, etc.) and share in some of the psychic faculties (imagination, estimation, voluntary motion).[105] All these souls seem, thus, to fall under a single category of "soul" and, consequently, one might be tempted to consider the treatment of a higher soul in metaphysics sufficient to found the treatment of lower souls (sublunary souls) in psychology. However, in *Nafs,* I, 1, Avicenna denies that the very same notion *soul* can be univocally applied to both sublunary and celestial souls. The reason of this denial has to be looked for in the hiatus between

over, that everything that apprehends something intellectually (*sc.* the human and the celestial intellect, and God) is in itself separated from matter, is clearly established in *Ilāhiyyāt,* IX, 3, 401.7: "You have already known that everything that conceives (*ya'qilu*) [something] is separate in itself". This represents an interesting parallel with the human soul, which *in itself* is not impressed in the body and identifies with the intellectual activity, but nonetheless, in this world, is tied to the body, being its principle of activity.

102 A different case is that of prophecy (*Ilāhiyyāt,* X, 1–2). In metaphysics the three types of prophecy dealt with in psychology ("imaginative", *Nafs,* IV, 2; "operative", *Nafs,* IV, 4; "intellectual", *Nafs,* V, 6) are brought to unity, and the demonstration of the prophet-legislator's necessary existence provides the metaphysical foundation of the psychological doctrine of prophecy. However, the metaphysical foundation of prophecy is not enough to provide the metaphysical foundation of all psychology. For the discourse on the prophet's exceptional cognitive capacities can be considered as a particular case of the general discourse on psychic faculties. On Avicenna's doctrine of prophecy and its metaphysical foundation, see A. Bertolacci, "The Metaphysical Proof of Prophecy in Avicenna", in A. Palazzo, A. Rodolfi eds., *Il profeta e la profezia tra XI e XIV secolo,* forthcoming.

103 See n. 100 above.

104 See *Ilāhiyyāt,* IX, 2, 386.14–387.8 [454.86–455.5]. More on this in T. Alpina, "Is the Heaven an Animal?".

105 It has to be noted, however, that in distinguishing the forms that are not souls from those that are souls (see nn. 100–101 above), Avicenna seems to consider *soul* in the proper sense only the celestial soul, whereas the soul of plants and animals seems to be considered simply a form (in *Nafs,* I, 3 Avicenna demonstrates that the soul of plants and animals is substance insofar as it is form), in the same way as all the sensible forms that are not soul, as has emerged also from the classification of substance in *Ilāhiyyāt,* II, 1.

the terrestrial and the celestial realm that Avicenna posits:[106] they do not share in the same notion of *life*, or even in the same notions of *rationality* and *sensation.*[107] The discontinuity between the two realms, the treatment of one of which Avicenna explicitly defers to *Ilāhiyyāt*, IX, 2,[108] prevents the very same notion *soul* from being genuinely, that is, univocally, predicated together of sublunary and of celestial souls. Therefore, the treatment of celestial souls in metaphysics can hardly act as a foundation of the treatment of the sublunary souls in psychology. The use of the same terminology to refer to both celestial and sublunary entities might simply point to the isomorphism between the two realms (see n. 114 below).

As for the case of the soul's afterlife, metaphysics is said to ascertain the state (*ḥāl*) of the human soul once its relation to the bodily nature is severed.[109] The use of the term *ḥāl* is crucial. In *Ilāhiyyāt*, I, 2 Avicenna has maintained that the ascertainment of the states of the particular existents pertains to the particular scien-

---

106 For the Aristotelian background of this hiatus, see Chapter 2, § How It All Began, in part. n. 29. For the hiatus between sublunary and celestial realm in Avicenna's cosmology, see M. Rashed, "Imagination astrale et physique supralunaire selon Avicenne", in G. Federici-Vescovini, V. Sorge, C. Vinti eds., *Corpo e anima, sensi interni e intelletto dai secoli XIII-XV ai post-cartesiani e spinoziani*, Brepols, Turnhout 2005, 103–117, in part. 103 and 109.

107 See *Nafs*, I, 1, 13.10–14.8 [32.87–33.5], where Avicenna reports an opinion about the celestial bodies that he seems to endorse: "These must believe that the term *soul*, when it is applied to the celestial soul and to the vegetative soul, is applied [to these entities] only by equivocation (*bi-l-ištirāk*), that this definition pertains only to the soul existing in what is composed, and that, when a stratagem is used so that animals and the celestial sphere share in the meaning of the term *soul*, the notion of plant is excluded from that group. Even so this stratagem is difficult. For animals and the celestial sphere do not share in the meaning of the term *life* nor, likewise, the meaning of the term *rationality*, because rationality here applies to the existence of a soul that has the two material intellects, and this is among the things that it is not correct [to apply] there, as you will see. For the intellect there is an intellect in actuality, and the intellect in actuality is not a constituent of the soul that is part of the definition of *rational*. Similarly, *sensation* here applies to the faculty by means of which sensible things are perceived by way of receiving what is similar to them and being affected by them. And this also is not among the things that it is correct [to apply] there, as you will see. Moreover, if by making an effort one renders the soul a first perfection for what moves by will and perceives among the bodies, so that animals and the celestial soul are included in this [definition], plants would be excluded from this group. And this is the statement validated (*wa-hāḏā huwa l-qawl al-muḥaṣṣal* [*Et haec dictio est rata*]) [through this investigation]". More on this passage in T. Alpina, "Is the Heaven an Animal?".

108 See *Nafs*, I, 1, 14.1 [32.96] (*'alà mā tarà*, as you will see), and 5 [33.1] (*'alà mā tarà*, as you will see). Both passages refer to *Ilāhiyyāt*, IX, 2.

109 See *Ilāhiyyāt*, IX, 7, 423.3–4 [506.90–91]: "Here we ought to ascertain (*an nuḥaqqiqa*) the states (*aḥwāl*) of the human souls when they separate from their bodies, and to what state (*ilà ayya ḥāl*) they will come to be [in the afterlife]". We find almost the same formulation in *Ilāhiyyāt*, I, 4, which contains a detailed table of contents of the *Ilāhiyyāt* ("[We shall discuss] what the state (*ḥāl*) of the human soul is when the relation between it and the [bodily] nature is severed, and what [then] its rank in existence (*martaba wuǧūdihā*) is", 28.1–2 [31.90–92]).

ces,[110] and to metaphysics the general investigation of the existent *qua* existent. By contrast, in *Ilāhiyyāt*, IX, 7 (and I, 4) Avicenna assigns to metaphysics the ascertainment of the state of the human soul, whose quiddity, however, has been ascertained elsewhere, i.e. in psychology (in metaphysics there is no trace of a discussion of the quiddity of such an entity). Metaphysics, then, is forced to assume the conclusions of psychology on this subject. Furthermore, before properly dealing with the destiny of eternal bliss or eternal perdition of the human soul in the afterlife, Avicenna provides five fundamental principles (*uṣūl*, sg. *aṣl* [*radices*, sg. *radix*], IX, 7, 423.13–425.14 [507.9–510.70]) of this investigation.[111] Upon closer scrutiny, however, these "metaphysical" principles turn out to be based on some psychological assumptions, i.e. that every psychic faculty has its own perfection that brings it to actualization, and that psychic faculties can obstruct each other (see *Nafs*, I, 5 and V, 2). Consequently, the metaphysical investigation of the human soul's afterlife turns out to be grounded on the psychological discourse.[112] By following Avicenna's claim in *Ilāhiyyāt*, I, 3, that the soul exists can be considered an axiom on which psychology is grounded,[113] while the ascertainment of its quiddity is the question (*mas'ala*) of psychology, which is in turn assumed by metaphysics.

Lastly, the emanative scheme outlined in *Ilāhiyyāt*, X, 1, where the human soul is listed among the other substances deriving from the First Principle can be hardly considered as a sufficient foundation of psychology.[114]

However, Avicenna seems not to be bothered by this disciplinary trespassing, which seems to be an exception to the scientific model he has outlined in *Ilāhiyyāt*, I, 1; rather, on at least two occasions he seems to authorize it (see *Ilāhiyyāt*, III, 1 and

---

110 See, for example, *Ilāhiyyāt*, I, 2, 15.2–3 [15.77–79]: "It happens that the principles of the particular sciences that investigate the *states* of the particular existents (*al-ʿulūm al-ǧuz'iyya allatī tabḥaṯu ʿan aḥwāl al-ǧuz'iyyāt al-mawǧūda*) become clear in this science (*sc.* metaphysics)".

111 The five "fundamental principles" of Avicenna's eschatological investigation are: 1) each psychic faculty has a good and a pleasure proper to it that bring its perfection to actualization; 2) the pleasure of the psychic faculty whose perfection is nobler is greater than the pleasure of the other faculties; 3) the knowledge of pleasure occurs even without its perception; 4) a state of the soul may hinder the attainment of pleasure; 5) a state, opposite to a pleasant one, may not be felt.

112 An interesting, comparable example is Avicenna's *Risāla Aḍḥawiyya*, where the metaphysical investigation of the soul's afterlife (*maʿād*) is preceded by the ascertainment of the essence (*anniyya*) of the human being through the thought-experiment of the *Flying Man* and the demonstration of its incorporeality through an argument very similar to that of *Nafs*, V, 2. See n. 66 above.

113 Either because it is self-evident or because it is proved in another, higher science.

114 For the exhaustive presentation of the emanative procession of all the kinds of substance (celestial intellects, celestial souls, celestial bodies, human beings, animals, plants, inorganic bodies, elements, prime matter) from the First Principle, with the human being as the most perfect sublunary entity, see *Ilāhiyyāt*, X, 1, 435.6–13 [522.7–523.20]. In this chapter Avicenna alludes to the isomorphism between celestial and sublunary realms: in both realms there are bodies, souls, and intellects (X, 1, 436.1–3 [523.30–33]). The distinction between soul and intellect in the sublunary world must be intended in the strongest sense, because the reference to the intellect as a mere faculty belonging to the human soul would have made no sense in a list of instances of substance.

IX, 4).[115] In psychology, by contrast, Avicenna seems to be worried by the possibility that psychology might transcend the boundaries of natural philosophy in which it is placed, and protrude into metaphysics. For this reason, the investigation of the immateriality of the human soul (V, 2), and of its individual immortality (V, 4) is somehow counterbalanced by reaffirming the necessity of the human soul's relationship with its body (V, 3),[116] and by reiterating the main purpose of the investigation conducted in the *Nafs* (V, 5).

In *Nafs*, V, 5 Avicenna seems to distinguish what is conceived as a *real possibility*, i.e. the human soul's independent existence (V, 2), from its *fulfilment*, and reiterates the focus of the *Nafs* in the very same manner as he did at the beginning of the work (cf. *Nafs*, I, 1, 11.1–3):[117] "Thus, when this immersion [in the body] and this impediment [caused by the body] cease in our soul, the soul's intellection of these [things] is the most excellent of the soul's intellections, its clearest and its most pleasant. However, since our discourse here concerns only the state of the soul insofar as it is soul, namely insofar as it is associated with this matter, we ought not to deal with the matter of the return of the soul [to the celestial realm] while we are dealing with nature until we move to the sapiential discipline (*ilà l-ṣināʿa al-ḥikmiyya*) and there investigate the separate entities (*wa-nanẓuru fīhā fī l-umūr al-mufāriqa*). As for the investigation in the natural discipline, it is peculiarly concerned with what is appropriate to natural things, namely the things having a relation to matter and motion (*al-umūr allatī lahā nisba ilà l-mādda wa-l-ḥaraka*)" (*Nafs*, V, 5, 238.1–9 [132.14–23]).

Although in *Nafs*, V, 2 it has been demonstrated that the human soul is capable of self-subsisting, the fulfilment of this possibility is deferred to the metaphysical dimension, that is, to the condition of actual separation from the body that the soul enjoys in the afterlife, to which *Ilāhiyyāt*, IX, 7 is devoted.[118] The investigation con-

115 See *Ilāhiyyāt*, III, 1, 93.5–10 [104.5–13]: "We say: we have already clarified the quiddity (*māhiyya*) of the substance and that it is predicated of what is separate, of body, of matter, and of form (*sc.* II, 1). As for the body, proving its existence (*iṯbātuhū*) is superfluous. As for matter and form, we have already proved their existence (*qad aṯbatnāhumā*) (*sc.* II, 3–4). As for what is separate, we have already proved its existence (*qad aṯbatnāhu*) by means of the potency that is close to act (*sc.* II, 4, and *Samāʿ ṭabīʿī*, IV, 15), and we will prove its existence (*wa-naḥnu nuṯbituhū*) again (*sc.* VIII-IX). However, if you remember what we have said about the soul, it appears as true to you [even now] that there exists (lit.: the existence, *wuǧūd*) a substance separate and incorporeal (*ǧawhar mufāriq ġayr ǧism*). It is convenient to pass now to verifying the [quiddities of] accidents and proving their existence". And *Ilāhiyyāt*, IX, 4, 408.16–18 [486.56–60]: "There is no doubt that here there are simple (*basīṭa*), separate (*mufāriqa*) intellects that come into being together with the coming into being of the bodies of human beings (*taḥduṯu maʿa ḥudūṯ abdān al-nās*), but do not corrupt (*lā tafsudu*) [together with the corruption of bodies], but rather endure (*tabqà*) [after the corruption of bodies]. This has already become clear in the natural sciences (*fī l-ʿulūm al-ṭabīʿiyya*) (*sc. Nafs*, V, 2 and 4)".

116 More on *Nafs*, V, 3 and V, 4 in Chapter 4.

117 See n. 28 above.

118 As we have shown, in *Ilāhiyyāt*, IX, 7 Avicenna ascertains the state of the same human soul whose quiddity has been ascertained in *Nafs*. It is noteworthy that, in IX, 7, 431.12–432.12 [519.57–520.87] Avicenna recalls the position of some scholars (*baʿḍ al-ʿulamāʾ* [*quidam ex sapientibus*]) ac-

ducted in *Nafs* is part of the investigation of nature (*wa-naḥnu mutakallimūn fī l-ṭabīʿa, we are dealing with nature*); consequently, there the soul has to be investigated insofar as it is associated with matter and motion, that is, with the body, not insofar as it is an entity capable of separate existence, whose investigation pertains to metaphysics. Avicenna's statement sounds counterfactual: in *Nafs* he does demonstrate that the human soul is a separate substance. Nonetheless, he prefers to reconnect directly the last part of his investigation of the soul, i.e. noetics, with *Nafs*, I, 1, and, more precisely, with the investigation of the *soul of* plants and animals, in order to conform the investigation of every instance of sublunary soul to the model provided at the beginning of his writing, according to which psychology perfectly fits with its being placed in natural philosophy. This model, which is essentially Aristotelian, grants primacy to the investigation of the faculties and their activities over that of the essence of the soul from which they stem.[119]

Avicenna's attempt to integrate his investigation of the soul into the boundaries of natural philosophy culminates in *Nafs*, V, 7,[120] which seals Avicenna's investigation[121] by reaffirming a principle that has been provided in the prologue, and on which the unity of psychology is grounded: the unity of the notion of *soul*. In particular, in V, 7 Avicenna provides a survey of the opinions of his predecessors about the soul and its activities in order to ascertain whether the soul is one or many. His opinion is that, in spite of the multiplicity of its activities, the soul is one essence (*ḏāt wāḥida*), performing several activities by means of the faculties that issue from it,[122] and confers unity upon those activities.[123] In refuting the possibility that the whole body, or a part of it, is the bond (*ribāṭ, vinculum*) that confers unity upon all the psychic faculties, the second version of the thought-experiment of the *Flying*

---

cording to which in the afterlife, the disembodied souls of ordinary people may still exercise their imaginative faculty to conceive rewards and punishments by connecting with the bodies of celestial beings.

119 In *Nafs*, I, 5 Avicenna seems to acknowledge two models of investigating the soul, starting from its activities and from the soul itself respectively. See *Nafs*, I, 5, 40.4–13 [80.17–81.28] quoted in n. 35 above. On the investigation of the soul pertaining to natural philosophy, and the strategy used by Avicenna to keep a unitary science of the soul within the province of natural philosophy, see Chapter 4.

120 For the theological debate on the nature of the human being acting as the polemic background of the second version of Avicenna's *Flying Man* argument, see the enlightening article by Rashed, "Chose, item et distinction".

121 The concluding chapter of the *Nafs* is actually V, 8, where Avicenna deals with the pneuma, i.e. the vehicle of the soul, and it serves as a bridge to the subsequent treatment of animals. Here, indeed, he refers four times to *Ḥayawān*: 264.5 [176.71] (*Ḥayawān*, XIII, 3); 265.1 [177.95] (*Ḥayawān*, XII, 8); 266.4 [179.27] (*Ḥayawān*, III, 1); 269.14–5 [185.26] (*Ḥayawān*, XV, 1).

122 That the variety of the soul's activities derives from the variety of its faculties has been established in *Nafs*, I, 4 ([*Chapter*] *on showing that the difference among the activities of the soul is due to the difference among its faculties*).

123 This position is presented in V, 7, 251.1–3 [155.38–41], among other passages, while its validity is affirmed in V, 7, 252.13–15 [157.83–86].

Man occurs.[124] The second occurrence of the *Flying Man* in this context is extremely peculiar and cannot be reduced to a mere repetition of what Avicenna has already affirmed at the end of *Nafs*, I, 1. Its purpose is therefore not to establish the incorporeal existence of the (rational) soul; rather, it aims to prove that the binding entity that bestows unity upon all the psychic faculties in human beings is his essence (*anniyya*),[125] i.e. his soul, not his body. Nevertheless, the immateriality of the (rational) soul is inevitably brought into play: indeed, in *Nafs*, I, 1 Avicenna has shown that the constituents of the living substance are two, namely body and soul,[126] and here he has ruled out the possibility that the binding entity is the body; consequently, the soul remains the only candidate for the role of *binding entity* which Avicenna is looking for and, therefore, it has to be different from the body, i.e. incorporeal.

The general context in which the second version of the thought-experiment is situated might suggest that, at the end of his investigation, Avicenna uses the same argument as the one he uses in *Nafs*, I, 1, but with a different purpose, namely in order to reaffirm the unity of the soul, which guarantees his investigation a unitary subject, i.e. sublunary soul. This might be the reason why in V, 7 the immateriality of the (rational) soul is just implied: Avicenna's major concern here is the unity of the soul insofar as it is the bond that gathers all the psychic faculties, which seem to be the pri-

---

124 *Nafs*, V, 7, 255.6–15 [162.51–163.64]: "Let us, then, repeat what we have previously mentioned (*sc.* I, 1, 16.2–14), and say: if a human being was created all at once, and created with his limbs separated from each other, and did not see his limbs, and [if] it were to happen that he did not touch them, and they did not touch each other, and he did not hear any sound, then he would not know the existence of all his organs, but *he would know the existence of his [individual] essence* (*wuǧūd anniyyatihī*) as one single thing, while not knowing all those [limbs].

What is by itself unknown is not what is known.

These organs do not actually belong to us, like the garments which due to their constant adherence (*li-dawām luzūmihā*) to us have become for us as parts of ourselves. And when we imagine ourselves, we do not imagine [ourselves] naked, but we imagine [ourselves] as possessing clothed bodies. The reason for this is [their] constant adherence [to us], except that in the case of clothes we are accustomed to stripping and putting them aside, thing to which we are not accustomed in the case of organs. Thus, our belief that organs are parts of us is more reliable than our belief that garments are parts of us".

125 That the term *anniyya* should be translated here as *individual essence*, instead of *existence*, as happens, for instance, in the *Ilāhiyyāt*, has been shown by Amos Bertolacci in his "A Hidden Hapax Legomenon in Avicenna's *Metaphysics:* Considerations on the Use of *Anniyya* and *Ayyiyya* in the *Ilāhiyyāt* of the *Kitāb al-Šifā*'", in A. M. I. van Oppenraay ed., with the collaboration of R. Fontaine, *The Letter before the Spirit. The Importance of Text Editions for the Study of the Reception of Aristotle*, Brill (Aristoteles Semitico-Latinus 22), Leiden-Boston 2012, 289–309. The occurrence of the term *anniyya* in psychology has been discussed at 304–305, n. 40 and n. 41.

126 See *Nafs*, I, 1, 5.6–13 [16.90–17.00]: "The parts of the subsistence [of something], as you have learned elsewhere (*sc. Samāʿ ṭabīʿī*, I, 2), are two: [(a)] a part through which the thing is what it is in actuality, and [(b)] a part through which the thing is what it is in potentiality, which is equivalent to the subject. [...] Indeed, the soul ought to be that by which plants and animals are plants and animals in actuality. And if [the principle belonging to the second division] is a body, then the form of the body is what we said".

mary subject-matter of the psychological investigation belonging to natural philosophy.[127] The two versions of the thought-experiment of the *Flying Man* serve, then, two distinct purposes: establishing the immateriality of the human rational soul, and the unity of sublunary soul, respectively.

Conclusion

In spite of their complementarity, two investigations have to be distinguished in the *Nafs:* (a) the investigation of the soul as a *relational* entity, always considered in connection with the body, and (b) the investigation of the human soul *in itself*, which identifies with the theoretical faculty, the only faculty surviving the severance of the body-soul relationship. The first, more Aristotelian investigation focuses on the *soul of* the body, as the principle that is responsible for the activities observable in natural, organic bodies, with which it does not identify. Avicenna infers the existence of this soul from the direct observation of the natural world, and then proves its substantiality by arguing that it is a form, that is, the principle that informs the bodily substratum, and enables it to perform a set of activities. The second investigation is less Aristotelian because, unlike the general approach to all sublunary souls that Aristotle exhibits in the *De anima*,[128] it is limited to the human soul, and transcends the boundaries of Aristotelian psychology. This second investigation is about the human soul *in itself*, that is, the human soul insofar as it is capable of subsisting in a condition of isolation from the body, which falls outside the province of natural philosophy, where Aristotelian psychology is officially placed, and protrudes into metaphysics, to which the investigation of what is separate, namely capable of self-subsisting, pertains.[129] Avicenna proves the immaterial essence of the human soul through the notion of *al-infirād bi-qiwām al-ḏāt, isolated self-subsistence*, namely, by referring to its peculiar mode of existence, i.e. to its separate, incorporeal existence.

The first investigation, which is properly physical and exhibits a general approach to the sublunary soul as a whole without particular restrictions, can be called *psychologia generalis*, whereas the second investigation, which is *trans*-physical (or *proto*-metaphysical) and shows a specific orientation towards the human rational soul, can be called *psychologia specialis*.

The first investigation is on the whole unproblematic in Avicenna's system of science, as it is outlined in *Ilāhiyyāt*, I, 1–3: like all the other particular sciences, psychology investigates the soul not insofar as it is a substance (the investigation of substance and its divisions pertaining to metaphysics), but insofar as it has a certain

---

127 See n. 123 above. More on this in Chapter 4.

128 See *De an.*, I, 1, 402 b1–5. On this text, see Chapter 2, n. 3.

129 That also Aristotle seems to distinguish the human, rational soul from all the other sublunary souls, emerges at least three times in the *De anima:* II, 1, 413 a3–5; II, 2, 413 b24–7; II, 3, 415 a11–12. On these passages, see Chapter 2, n. 23.

characteristic, i.e. insofar as it is the principle of activities in bodies.[130] As for the ascertainment of its quiddity in *Nafs*, I, 3, it can be considered a mere anticipation for propaedeutic reasons of the more general treatment of the substantiality of form in *Ilāhiyyāt*, II, 1; consequently, no real conflict between a lower (psychology) and a higher science (metaphysics) is detectable.[131]

By contrast, the second investigation raises the biggest problem: for in a particular science Avicenna investigates the substance of something, i.e. of the human soul, but this investigation is not metaphysically founded; rather, it founds the metaphysical discourse on the soul's afterlife, and also on the prophet's cognitive capacities.[132] In this discourse, metaphysics, like any other particular science, deals with the states (*aḥwāl*)[133] of something, whose quiddity has been ascertained elsewhere, here in psychology. The different attitude that Avicenna exhibits concerning this disciplinary trespassing in psychology and metaphysics respectively has been already pointed out.

To conclude, we are in the presence of a *shadowy area* of Avicenna's psychology and, in general, of his epistemology, which seems to suffer from a *structural* tension.[134] The psychological treatment of the existence and the quiddity of the

---

130 See n. 17 above.

131 On the possibility that treatment of an issue properly pertaining to metaphysics is anticipated in another lower science, but is ultimately founded in metaphysics, see Bertolacci, *The Reception of Aristotle's* Metaphysics, 265.

132 The treatment of the nature of the human soul in psychology cannot be assimilated to any of the three cases of relationship between metaphysics and the other specific sciences, when both deal with the same subject, which have been singled out by A. Bertolacci in his *The Reception of Aristotle's* Metaphysics, 265. On this, it can be added that all the references to metaphysics in psychology recall precise aspects of doctrines properly dealt with in metaphysics (the soul of celestial spheres, the rebuttal of the opinion according to which number is the principle of everything, the influence of the supernal intelligences on dreams, the human being's need for social life, universality and particularity, the soul's afterlife, the characteristics of the intellectual forms), and not the investigation of the quiddity of the human rational soul (see Bertolacci, *The Reception of Aristotle's* Metaphysics, 290–292). By contrast, all the references to psychology in the metaphysics seem to presuppose in the latter what has been ascertained in the former, as has been previously noted.

133 See n. 109 above.

134 In *The 'Ontologization' of Logic: Metaphysical Themes in Avicenna's Reworking of the Organon*, in M. Cameron, J. Marenbon eds., *Methods and Methodologies: Aristotelian Logic East and West 500–1500*, Brill, Leiden-Boston 2011, 27–51, A. Bertolacci has shown that, with respect to the relationship between logic and metaphysics, it is possible to find the same issues dealt with independently by both sciences, without a metaphysical foundation of their treatment in logic (e.g. the case of the difference between metaphysics and dialectic and sophistic in *Burhān*, II, 7 and *Ilāhiyyāt*, I, 2; and the predication of existence in *Maqūlāt*, I, 2 and *Ilāhiyyāt*, I, 5). According to Bertolacci, the reasons for this independence of logic from metaphysics seem to rely on both the relative chronology of the different parts of the *Šifāʾ* and the nature of logic, which Avicenna considers at the same time an instrument of philosophy (the alternative towards which he seems to incline) and a part of it (49–51). The case of logic, however, seems to be different from that of natural philosophy, and notably of psychology: with respect to logic the same doctrines are independently treated in metaphysics with minor or

human soul seems to enjoy the same exceptional status of the metaphysical treatment of God, with which the psychological treatment of the soul shares some similarities: in both sciences Avicenna deals with the existence and the quiddity of a part of their respective subjects by contravening the rule that he posited in *Ilāhiyyāt*, I, 2.[135] From this perspective one might wonder whether, according to Avicenna, the fact that a science ascertains the existence and the quiddity, not of its subject in its entirety, but only of a part of it, is acceptable. However, if the case of the treatment of God in metaphysics is not particularly surprising, since there is no other science above metaphysics to which the ascertainment of the Necessary Existent could have pertained, the case of the treatment of the existence and the quiddity of the human soul in psychology is different, since it is a subordinate, special science, and one would have expected to find in metaphysics something more fundamental concerning the entire soul than what is in psychology.

Nonetheless, Avicenna has a conceptual tool that can stem the dissolutive drives of psychology: the notion of *perfection*, together with the reworking of the Aristotelian definition of the soul. This definition, far from being Avicenna's own definition of the soul, is a tool – more or less effective, as we shall see in Chapter 4 – to restrict the focus of psychology belonging to natural philosophy, to the investigation of the soul *qua* operational principle of faculties and their activities for which it is causally responsible.

---

major differences, while with respect to psychology, metaphysics assumes its conclusions, and consequently its treatment of psychological issues (e. g. eschatology) seems to be subordinated to it, not independent of it.

135 See 61–62 above.

Chapter Four

Definition: An Attempt at Unification

Introduction, or Dialectic is the Way

Besides the *general approach* to the *soul of* sublunary living beings, which is in line with Aristotle's *De anima*, Avicenna's *Nafs* also exhibits a *specific orientation* towards the *soul in itself*, i.e. the human rational soul which, considered in isolation from the body, is a self-subistent substance, identical with the theoretical intellect, and capable of surviving its severance from the body. These two investigations result in the coexistence in psychology of a more specific science (*psychologia specialis*) within a more general one (*psychologia generalis*). Though Avicenna is not as explicit about it as he might be, the attentive reader can easily detect the twofold consideration of the soul in the *Nafs*. Therefore, though acknowledging their distinctiveness, Avicenna has to single out a common ground for both investigations within a unitary science. Singling out this common ground means finding a way of considering (*iʿtibār, respectus*)[1] the soul that captures an aspect shared by all its instances.

The common consideration in virtue of which all instances of soul (*of* and *in itself* respectively) can be accounted for is that of being a principle of activities in bodies. In order to outline this common consideration, Avicenna firstly provides a survey of the theoretical achievements of his predecessors concerning the soul; and, secondly, he expounds his own position.

The survey of his predecessors' major theoretical achievements is provided in *Nafs*, I, 1. This chapter is on the whole dialectical: here Avicenna does not present his own position, but introduces theoretical tools relevant to his purpose.[2] In the first part, Avicenna opts for the term *kamāl* (*perfection*) over other candidates as the best way to refer to the soul since it encompasses both inseparable and separable entities (this is essential to including the soul *in itself* in his account). This term, however, designates the soul insofar as it is somehow connected with matter and motion, i.e. the body, through (or in) which it performs its activities, but is not informative about its quiddity. The second part of the chapter is devoted to the reworking of Aristotle's standard definition of the soul as the *first perfection* (*kamāl awwal*) of a natural, organic body. As we shall see, this is neither an essential definition of the soul nor Avicenna's own definition. The standard definition of the soul is carefully re-

1 This term occurs three times in *Nafs*, I, 1 (7.7 [20.44]; 9.14 [25.00]; 15.19 [36.44]), and all these occurrences indicate the different respects in which something can be considered: in relation to something (like the form or the perfection), or in itself (like substance). There is also a fourth occurrence of *iʿtibār* in the expression *bi-l-iʿtibār* (*with regard to*, I, 1, 7.6 [20.42]).

2 On the usefulness of dialectic and its heuristic value, see *Ǧadal*, I, 5. See also the interesting though concise remark in *Samāʿ ṭabīʿī*, I, 2, 18.1-4 [27.76-79].

https://doi.org/10.1515/9783110706840-006

worked in order to avoid any reference to the essence of the soul (though it implies that it is more similar to a formal principle) but, at the same time, to narrow down the focus of psychological investigation to the soul as the principle and cause of a set of (unexercised) capacities. In *Nafs*, I, 1 (with the exclusion of the thought-experiment of the *Flying Man*) Avicenna deliberately avoids making any explicit reference to the soul's quiddity, which will be the subject of another investigation.[3] Consequently, though preliminarily useful, *Nafs*, I, 1 alone is not sufficient to provide a strong basis for psychology.

Since a science cannot be based on a nonessential characteristic of its subject-matter (in this case, the soul being an operational principle), Avicenna devotes *Nafs*, I, 3 to founding the application of the term *kamāl* to refer to the soul on the quidditative level. Once he has demonstrated that the soul is a substance independently of its being an instance of perfection, the term *kamāl* passes from designating the soul insofar as it has a relation to the body (operational level) to designate it inasmuch as it is a substance (ontological level). This could be considered Avicenna's own definition of the soul: the soul is not a substance because it is a perfection; rather, the soul is a perfection as substance. Its being perfection as substance results in its being the causal principle of activities observable in bodies, regardless of the kind of substance the soul is.

Nafs, I, 3 represents, then, Avicenna's positive account of the soul, which frames the investigation of the soul's faculties in the rest of the writing. However, focusing, in the Aristotelian fashion, on the soul's faculties inevitably points out the distinctiveness of the human rational soul with respect to all other instances of soul (the *specific orientation* of Avicenna's psychology). As we shall see, this distinctiveness, which concerns the peculiar relation of the human rational soul to its own body, emerges in *Nafs*, V, 2–4, where Avicenna supplements the theoretical framework provided in *Nafs*, I, 3 in view of the inquiry into the functioning of intellection.

3 In this respect, my interpretation of *Nafs*, I, 1, and of the first treatise in general partially contrasts with that expounded by M. Sebti in the article "La signification de la définition avicennienne de l'âme comme 'perfection première d'un corps naturel organique' dans le livre I du Traité de l'âme du *Šifa*'", *Bulletin d'Études Orientales*, 51, 1999, 299–312. For, in *Nafs*, I, 1 Sebti detects the same *aporiai* as raised by Aristotle at the beginning of his *De anima* (I, 1, 402 a23–b16); however, she maintains that "l'ordre des réponses à ces questions est inversé. Cette inversion, loin d'être fortuite, est en elle-même un élément important de la lecture avicennienne d'Aristote" (301). In my opinion, however, there is no such inversion in Avicenna (an inversion for which Sebti does not convincingly argue): Avicenna's argumentation is not exactly the same as Aristotle's; the fundamental questions might be the same, but their answers and, what is more, their purposes are clearly not the same. Therefore, it may only be noted that in *Nafs*, I Avicenna seems to distinguish two levels of investigation that Aristotle, by contrast, combines, namely that of definition and that of quiddity. This represents the theoretical framework on which Avicenna bases the four following treatises.

Giving a Name or Pointing at the Quiddity? Form (*ṣūra*) vs. Perfection (*kamāl*)

After having ascertained that in bodies there must be a principle other than corporeality which is responsible for their activities, namely the soul (4.4–6.1 [14.69–18.10]), which should be in Avicenna's mind the primary focus of psychological investigation as belonging to natural philosophy, he devotes the first part of *Nafs*, I, 1, (6.1–8.8 [18.11–22.69]) to a careful inspection of several terms by which his Peripatetic predecessors have referred to the soul in different respects. The soul has been referred to as *power* (*quwwa*, *vis*), with respect to both the activities ensuing from it (*quwwa* as faculty) and its reception of sensible and intellectual forms (*quwwa* as receptivity/potentiality); as *form* (*ṣūra*, *forma*), with respect to matter; and as *perfection* (*kamāl*, *perfectio*), with respect to the whole, i.e. to the complete thing, in which it inheres in order to make the incomplete genus realized into a (higher or lower) species.[4] The term *quwwa* seems to have been included in the list only for the sake of completeness since it can be considered the opposite of the term *perfection*, which will be the one preferred by Avicenna. For it has already been ascertained by means of two arguments that the soul is the part of a thing's subsistence through which that thing is what it is in actuality, that is, "the form, like the form, or like the perfection".[5] Further arguments will be provided in support of this claim. In particular, Avicenna will rule out that *quwwa* is an appropriate term to name the soul because it is equivocal: for it encompasses both the meaning of *power* as principle of activity (*quwwa* as faculty) and the meaning of *power* as prin-

4 *Nafs*, I, 1, 6.1–13 [18.11–19.26], and 6.18–7.6 [20.34–42].

5 *Nafs*, I, 1, 5.3–6.1 [16.87–18.10]: "We say: if the things to which we believe the soul belongs are bodies, and their existence insofar as they are plants or animals is completed only through the existence of this thing for them, this thing is, then, part of their subsistence (*ǧuzʾ min qiwāmihā* [*pars...in constitutione eorum*]). The parts of the subsistence [of something], as you have learned elsewhere (*sc. Samāʿ ṭabīʿī*, I, 2), are two: [(a)] a part through which the thing is what it is in actuality, and [(b)] a part through which the thing is what it is in potentiality, which is equivalent to the subject. [(First argument)] If the soul belongs to the second division – and there is no doubt that the body belongs to that division – animals and plants, then, are not completed as animals and plants either by the body or by the soul. Therefore, they need another perfection, which is the principle in actuality for what we said. But that would be the soul, and it is [the topic] on which our discourse is. Indeed, the soul ought to be that by which plants and animals are plants and animals in actuality. And if [the principle belonging to the second division] is a body, then the form of the body is what we said. [(Second argument)] If it is a body with a certain form, then it would not be that principle insofar as it is a body, but its being a principle is in virtue of that form, and the derivation of those states would be from that form itself, even though it happens through the mediation of this body. Therefore, the first principle would be that form and its first actuality would be by means of this body. And this body would be part of the body of the animal, but it is the first part to which the principle is connected. However, inasmuch as it is body, it is but [part] of the whole subject. It is, therefore, clear that the soul itself is not a body, but is a part of the animal and the plant: it is a form, or like the form, or like the perfection (*hiya ṣūra aw ka-l-ṣūra aw ka-l-kamāl* [*quae est ei forma aut quasi forma aut quasi perfectio*])". For the outlines of the two arguments, see nn. 18 and 20 to my translation.

ciple of receptivity (*quwwa* as potentiality). Soul can be referred to as *quwwa* in both senses: insofar as it is principle of motion, soul is *quwwa* as principle of activity, whereas insofar as it is principle of perception at various degrees, soul is *quwwa* as principle of receptivity. However, these two meanings are irreducible to each other, and the term *quwwa* cannot be used in both senses at the same time to refer to the soul except by equivocation. If, by contrast, one meaning is preferred to the other, something of the essence of the soul will inevitably escape.[6] *Form* and *perfection* remain the only valid alternatives.[7]

Avicenna opts for the term *perfection* because it is the most indicative of the meaning of the soul[8] and includes both the separable soul and the soul that does not separate.[9] It seems evident that Avicenna's primary concern here is to include within his account of the soul also the human soul, which, unlike the other sublunary souls, is separable from the body, and possibly the celestial soul, to which the human soul is said to be similar.[10]

---

6 *Nafs*, I, 1, 7.10 – 8.8 [21.49 – 22.69]. See § 4.6.2 of my translation.

7 *Nafs*, I, 1, 6.4 – 13 [18.14 – 19.26]: "It would also be correct to call it "form" in relation to the matter in which it inheres so that a material substance, be it vegetative or animal, is made of them. It would also be correct to call it "perfection" in relation to the perfection of the genus through it as a realized species in the higher or lower species. For the nature of the genus is incomplete and undefined unless the nature of the simple or non-simple *differentia* is added to it; once it is added to it, the species becomes perfect. For the *differentia* is the perfection of the species inasmuch as it is species. However, not every species has a simple *differentia* – you have already learned that – but it belongs only to the species that are themselves compound of matter and form, and of these the form is the simple *differentia* of that for which it is the perfection". The simple *differentia* is the form or nature of the essence, whereas the non-simple (or logical) *differentia* is the predicate, which is derived by paronymy from the form (or nature) and is predicated of the species. For instance, "rationality" is a simple *differentia*, whereas "rational" is a non-simple *differentia*. For the distinction between simple and non-simple *differentia*, see *Maqūlāt*, III, 2, 101.12 – 102.9. In *Maqūlāt*, IV, 1, 133.18 – 134.12, Avicenna says that the discrete quantity and the continuous quantity are examples of species having only a non-simple *differentia*.

8 *Nafs*, I, 1, 7.8 – 10 [20.44 – 21.48]: "From this it is clear that, if in determining the soul (*fī taʿrīf al-nafs, in doctrina de anima*) we say that it is perfection, it is the most indicative (*adall, hoc plus significat*) of its meaning. It would also include all the species of soul in all their respects, the soul separable from matter not being an exception to this".

9 *Nafs*, I, 1, 8.4 – 8 [22.64 – 69]: "Moreover, if we say perfection, [it] would include both meanings. For the soul with respect to the power by means of which the perception of the animal is perfected is perfection and, with respect to the power from which the activities of the animal derive, is also perfection. And both the separable soul and the soul that does not separate are perfection (*wa-l-nafs al-mufāriqa kamāl wa-l-nafs allatī lā tufāriqu kamāl* [*anima etiam separata est perfectio, et anima quae nondum est separata est perfectio*])".

10 *Nafs*, IV, 2, 178.17 – 8 [28.87 – 29.89]. For the fact that Avicenna names the celestial souls *kamāl*, see Chapter 3, n. 100. On the similarities and dissimilarities between the human and the celestial soul, see Chapter 3. See also T. Alpina, "Is the Heaven an Animal?".

Avicenna's solution should not be considered a break with Aristotle. Rather, it puts Aristotle's doctrine of the soul *qua* form into a broader Peripatetic perspective.[11]

Firstly, the notion of *perfection* is primarily defined with respect to the species, i.e. to what is already complete: "Perfection requires a relation to the complete thing from which activities derive (*nisba ilà l-šay' al-tāmm allaḏī ʿanhu taṣduru l-afāʿīl*), since it is perfection in accordance with its consideration in terms of the species" (*Nafs*, I, 1, 7.6–8 [20.42–44]). In this respect, Avicenna's notion of *perfection* can be considered as an example of or a variant on Alexander of Aphrodisias' second-order form, which supervenes on a thing already formed, like an activity. Alexander introduced the notion of *perfection* (τελειότης in Greek) in order to gloss the Aristotelian notion of ἐντελέχεια in his own *De anima*, when he recalls Aristotle's definition of the soul.[12] By this gloss, Alexander means that the soul is the ἐντελέχεια of a natural, organic body, having life in potentiality, not in the sense of ἐνέργεια (actuality), but in the sense that such a body, when it possesses it, achieves its τελειότης (perfection).[13] Alexander distinguishes two fundamental senses of τελειότης: (i) one external to the thing of which it is the τελειότης (οὗ ἕνεκά τινος), that is, a perfection the thing yearns for (for example, the first Unmoved Mover, the assimilation to which the living being longs for); and (ii) one internal to the thing (οὗ ἕνεκά τινι), that is, a sort of self-perfection. Internal perfection is the *proper perfection* (ἡ οἰκεία τελειότης) of the composite substance in which the form inhering in it is properly realized. The second type of τελειότης is, therefore, always the realization of the form (or "l'état d'achèvement de la forme", to use Rashed's words), that is, a second-order form, the ultimate (formal) perfection of something already holding a determined formal nature (εἶδος).[14] Alexander's distinction between two degrees of formality, i.e. that of the εἶδος and that of the τελειότης, can be interpreted – as Rashed does – as the distinction between εἶναι and εὖ εἶναι: the εἶδος corresponds to εἶναι, namely to a composite substance deriving its being (εἶναι) from its form (εἶδος), whereas τελειότης corresponds to εὖ εἶναι, namely to the composite substance's *well-being*, i.e. to the composite substance existing in accordance with its own *differentia*, as a human being living in accordance with (or by exercising) his rationality. Alexander's τελειότης is, then, related to the specific difference and to the activities ensuing from

11 For the notion of *perfection* Avicenna is heavily indebted to the Late Ancient exegesis of Aristotle. I do not intend to recall here all the phases of this exegesis, which has been exhaustively outlined in the first part of R. Wisnovsky's monograph *Avicenna's Metaphysics*. Rather, here I would briefly recall some elements that might be useful to reconstruct Avicenna's theoretical background.

12 See Alexander, *De anima*, 16.1; 16.5–6; 17.12–13; 24.1; 52.2–3; *Mantissa*, 103.4–5. On these passages, see M. Rashed, *Alexandre d'Aphrodise. Commentaire perdu à la* Physique *d'Aristote (livres IV-VIII). Les scholies byzantines: édition, traduction et commentaire*, Commentaria in Aristotelem Graeca et Byzantina 1, De Gruyter, Berlin 2011, 164, n. 325

13 See Simplicius, *In Physicorum*, 414.25–28. On this passage, see Rashed, *Alexandre d'Aphrodise*, 164, n. 327.

14 For the doctrinal and historical reason for this terminological choice, which is related to the exegesis of Aristotle's *Physics*, I, 9, 192 a16–19, see Rashed, *Alexandre d'Aphrodise*, 136–137; 146–147.

it. This perspective might have influenced Avicenna's conception of perfection, and its application to the soul, though in Alexander's view perfection is never separable from its subject.[15]

However, separability (at least of some of its instances) is the characteristic that distinguishes the notion of *perfection* from that of *form*, and makes it broader than *form*, and consequently more appropriate than it to refer to the soul: "Moreover, every form is a perfection, but not every perfection is a form: for the king is the perfection of the city, and the steersman is the perfection of the ship, but each is not the form [respectively] of the city and of the ship (*fa-inna l-malik kamāl al-madīna wa-l-rubbān kamāl al-safīna wa-laysā bi-ṣūratayni li-l-madīna wa-l-safīna*). Therefore, whatever perfection is itself separate is not in reality a form for matter, nor in matter. For the form which exists in matter is the form impressed in it and subsisting through it,[16] unless it is agreed to call the perfection of the species the form of the species" (*Nafs*, I, 1, 6.13–18 [19.27–20.33]).

The simile of the steersman of the ship – I will return to the simile of the king of the city in due course – traces back to the end of *De anima*, II, 1, where Aristotle wonders whether the soul, which has been defined as actuality of the body, can be also considered like the boatman of the boat (πλωτὴρ πλοίου),[17] probably alluding to the possibility that the soul can also act as the moving/efficient cause of the body.[18]

---

15 However, Avicenna's idea of the supervenience of a separable perfection, like the rational soul, upon an already composite substance and, consequently, of its actual separation from the body, might rest on a passage from Alexander's *De anima*, where Alexander distinguishes what contributes to a thing's εἶναι and, because of that, is inseparable from it, and what contributes to a thing's εὖ εἶναι and supervenes (προσγίνεται) on a thing already formed. See Alexander of Aphrodisias, *De anima*, 81.13–20: γίνεται δὲ ὁ ἄνθρωπος οὐκ εὐθὺς ἔχων τήνδε τὴν ἕξιν, ἀλλ' ἔχων μὲν δύναμιν καὶ ἐπιτηδειότητα τοῦ δέξασθαι αὐτήν, ὕστερον μέντοι λαμβάνων αὐτήν. ὃ καὶ σημεῖον ἐναργέστατον **τοῦ μὴ πρὸς τὸ εἶναι τήνδε τὴν δύναμιν συντελεῖν τοῖς ἔχουσιν αὐτήν, ἀλλὰ πρὸς τὸ εὖ εἶναι. ὅσα μὲν γὰρ πρὸς τὸ εἶναι συντελεῖ, ταῦτα ἀχώριστα τοῦ ἔχοντος**, ὡς ἡ θρεπτικὴ δύναμις καὶ τῆς αἰσθητικῆς ἡ ἁπτική, **ὅσα δὲ πρὸς τὸ εὖ εἶναι, ταῦτα τελειουμένοις προσγίνεται**, ὅτε τοῦ κυρίως εὖ εἶναί ἐστιν ἐπιδεκτικά. **ἐν γὰρ τῷ τελείῳ τὸ εὖ** (emphasis mine).
16 This is precisely what Avicenna excludes in *Nafs*, V, 2, and repeatedly maintains in V, 3–4, as we have shown in Chapter 3.
17 Here I translate πλωτήρ as "boatman", that is, a generic sailor travelling on a ship and performing no specific activity. The Arabic cognate for πλωτήρ can be *mallāḥ* (*rākib* is also attested as a translation of πλωτήρ in the Arabic version of Aristotle's *De anima* edited by ʿA. Badawī). I use "steersman" to translate κυβερνήτης, that is, the term by which the Late Ancient commentators interpreted Aristotle's generic reference to πλωτήρ. The Arabic cognate for κυβερνήτης is *rubbān*, which can be also translated as "captain" (see, for instance, the Arabic translation of Themistius' paraphrase of Aristotle's *De anima*, 54.1 (ed. Lyons)). However, *mallāḥ* as a translation for κυβερνήτης is also attested, though not in writings belonging to the Aristotelian tradition.
18 *De an.*, II, 1, 413 a8–9: ἔτι δὲ ἄδηλον εἰ οὕτως ἐντελέχεια τοῦ σώματος ἡ ψυχὴ <ἢ> ὥσπερ πλωτὴρ πλοίου. In presenting the Aristotelian simile and its purpose I rely on the interpretation advanced by G. R. Giardina in "Se l'anima sia entelechia del corpo alla maniera di un nocchiero rispetto alla nave". According to Giardina, this simile has to be interpreted as an allusion to the fact that the soul, besides being the actuality of the body, can be accounted for as the moving cause of the body. Giardina's

However, unlike Aristotle, Avicenna seems to use it to argue for the separability of the soul (or of a part of it) from the body. Avicenna's use of this simile is in line with the interpretation advanced in the Late Ancient exegetical tradition by Philoponus. In particular, Philoponus connects the simile with the passage that immediately precedes it, where Aristotle maintains that nothing prevents some parts of the soul from being separable from the body on account of their not being actualities of any body,[19] and concludes that this has to refer to the human rational soul, which is separable because it is actuality of no body (or part of the body).[20] The separability of the human rational soul is then compared with that of the steersman (κυβερνήτης, not πλωτήρ)[21] of the ship, who perfects the form of the ship to which, inasmuch as steersman, he is essentially related, while being separable (τελειοῖ γὰρ τὸ εἶδος τοῦ πλοίου ὁ κυβερνήτης χωριστὸς ὤν, 224.18–19).[22]

Philoponus' exegesis of the Aristotelian simile depends on his understanding of the notion of τελειότης, which sensibly diverges from Alexander's since it encompasses both inseparable and separable entities. At the beginning of his commentary on the second book of the *De anima*, in introducing Aristotle's definition of the soul, and the homonymous term ἐντελέχεια through which the soul is defined, Philoponus distinguishes two entities which that term encompasses, namely the inseparable form, and something separable. Both – he says – are perfection (τελειότης); however, the former, like the form of the flesh, or the non-rational (i.e. animal), and the vegetative soul, perfects the subject in which it inheres with its *substance* (τῇ οὐσίᾳ), whereas the latter, like the steersman of the ship, or the rational soul,

reading of this passage echoes one of the interpretations of it that Plotinus gives in *Enn.* IV 3, 21. There Plotinus suggests that the simile of the boatman can be interpreted as an (unsatisfactory) explanation of how the soul is in the body according to Aristotle, that is, as a moving principle. It should be noted that Giardina's reading is based on the following emendation of the Greek text printed in the Ross edition, which is suggested by Th. Tracy: ἔτι δὲ ἄδηλον [ἐστι] εἰ, οὕτως [οὖσα] ἐντελέχεια τοῦ σώματος, ἡ ψυχὴ [ἐστι] ὥσπερ πλωτὴρ πλοίου. See Th. Tracy, "The soul/boatman analogy in Aristotle's *De anima*", *Classical Philology*, 77/2, 1982, 97–112.

19 *De an.*, II, 1, 413 a6–7: οὐ μὴν ἀλλ' ἔνιά γε οὐθὲν κωλύει, διὰ τὸ μηθενὸς εἶναι σώματος ἐντελεχείας. See also Philoponus, *In De anima*, 223.21–224.9.

20 See Philoponus, *In De anima*, 223.37–224.4: ἀλλ' εἰ καὶ ταῦτα, φησί, τὰ μόρια τῆς ψυχῆς ἀχώριστα εἶναι ἀνάγκη τοῦ σώματος, <ἔνιά γε οὐδὲν κωλύει> εἶναι χωριστὰ <διὰ τὸ μηδενὸς εἶναι σώματος ἐντελεχείας>. ἐναργῶς ἄρα οὐ βούλεται ἐντελέχειαν εἶναι τοῦ σώματος τὴν λογικὴν ψυχήν, καὶ διὰ τοῦτο χωριστὴν εἶναι τοῦ σώματος ἀποφαίνεται.

21 Unlike a generic πλωτήρ, the κυβερνήτης exercises a specific perfecting activity on the ship.

22 For Philoponus' commentary on *De an.*, II, 1, 413 a8–9, see Philoponus, *In De anima*, 224.14–225.30. The fact that Philoponus assigns a different ontological status to the human rational soul derives from those shadowy passages within and outside of the *De anima*, where Aristotle seems to waver about the nature of the human intellect. On these Aristotelian passages, see Chapter 2, n. 23. As for the dependence of Philoponus' doctrine of the human rational soul on these passages, see Chapter 2, n. 62.

being separable, perfects the subject to which it is related by its *activity* alone (τῇ ἐνεργείᾳ μόνῃ).[23]

Philoponus' distinction of two kinds of perfection seems to be precisely what Avicenna has in mind when he distinguishes inseparable and separable *kamāl*.[24] However, here a clarification is in order. As we have already said, bio-bibliographers do not attest any Arabic translation of Philoponus' commentary on the *De anima*.[25] Nonetheless, the similarity between Avicenna's and Philoponus' account of *perfection* can be explained by referring to the anonymous paraphrase of Aristotle's *De anima* attributed to Ibn al-Biṭrīq, which is based on Philoponian materials.[26] There, in correspondence to the beginning of the second book of the *De anima*, the author provides four divisions of the notion of *tamām* (*perfection*), which renders the Greek ἐντελέχεια.[27] The second and the third divisions are relevant for Avicenna's account of the soul *qua* perfection, since both point at the way in which the human soul is a separable perfection of its subject. According to the second division, perfection can be either separable (*mufāriq*), like the boatman (*mallāḥ*) of the boat, or inseparable (*ġayr mufāriq*), like the heat of fire. In the first case, the corruption of the subject to which perfection is related does not entail its own corruption, whereas in the second case, the corruption of the composite substance entails the corruption of the perfection that inheres in it like a form.[28] According to the third division, perfec-

---

23 Philoponus, *In De anima*, 206.18–28: ἡ γὰρ ἐντελέχεια λέγεται καὶ ἐπὶ τοῦ εἴδους τοῦ ἀχωρίστου τοῦ σώματος καὶ ἐπὶ τοῦ χωριστοῦ. ἔστι γὰρ τελειότης καὶ ὁ κυβερνήτης τοῦ πλοίου καὶ τὸ τῆς σαρκὸς εἶδος τοῦ τῆς σαρκὸς σώματος· ἀλλ' ὁ μὲν χωριστὸς ὢν τοῦ πλοίου μόνην τὴν ἑαυτοῦ ἐνέργειαν τελειωτικὴν ἔχει τοῦ πλοίου, τὸ δὲ τῆς σαρκὸς εἶδος καὶ καθόλου τὰ ἔνυλα εἴδη αὐτῇ τῇ οὐσίᾳ ἑαυτῶν τελειωτικά ἐστι τῶν ὑποκειμένων. οὕτως οὖν καὶ ἐπὶ τῶν ψυχῶν ἡ μὲν ἄλογος ψυχὴ καὶ ἡ φυτικὴ ἀχώριστον ἔχουσα τὴν οὐσίαν τοῦ ὑποκειμένου καὶ μηδὲ ἐνεργῆσαι χωρὶς τοῦ ὑποκειμένου δυναμένη, αὐτὴν τὴν οὐσίαν ἔχει τελειωτικὴν αὐτοῦ· **ἡ μέντοι λογικὴ ψυχὴ οὐ τῇ οὐσίᾳ, ἀλλὰ τῇ ἐνεργείᾳ μόνῃ τελειοῖ τὸ ζῷον**· τῇ βουλήσει γὰρ ἑαυτῆς κινεῖ αὐτὸ τοιῶσδε ἢ τοιῶσδε ὡς ὀργάνῳ τῇ ἀλόγῳ ψυχῇ χρωμένη (emphasis mine).

24 The Philoponian echo is more striking in Avicenna's *Risāla fī l-kalām ʿalà l-nafs al-nāṭiqa*. There in the Philoponian vein Avicenna argues that the human soul can be called *form* only if by *form* the "activity" of the human soul is meant, for the body is not the receptacle of the soul, but only of its activity, with respect to which it can be called "receiver of the soul". See *Risāla fī l-kalām ʿalà l-nafs al-nāṭiqa*, 198.9–12: "For the appellation 'form' may be applied to the soul and the appellation 'the receiver of the soul' may be applied to the body, even if the meaning of this 'receiving' is unlike that of a receptacle 'receiving' what occupies it, but is rather like that of a place where an activity occurs 'receiving' the activity (*bal ka-qubūl maḥall al-taṣarruf li-l-taṣarruf*): the body 'receives' the activity of the soul (*fa-l-badan yaqbalu taṣarruf al-nafs*), and from this point of view it is possible to call the body 'receiver of the soul', to call the soul 'form', and to designate the severance of the association between the two with the expression 'separation of the form from the receivers'" (the English translation is that provided in Gutas, *Avicenna and the Aristotelian Tradition*, 73–74).

25 See Chapter 1, nn. 46–48.

26 See R. Arnzen, *Aristoteles'* De anima. More information on this paraphrase in Chapter 1, n. 45.

27 For an insightful analysis of the Graeco-Arabic translations of the term ἐντελέχεια, see Wisnovsky, *Avicenna's Metaphysics*, in part. Chapter 5, 99–112.

28 See R. Arnzen, *Aristoteles'* De anima, 217.3–8.

tion can be either the perfection in itself (*al-tamām bi-ʿaynihī*), like the heat of fire, or that which enacts perfection (*fāʿil li-l-tamām*), like the boatman of the boat or the builder of the building. In both divisions, the (human rational) soul is associated with the separable perfection, since it enacts the perfection of the subject to which it is related but, not inhering in the subject, it survives its severance from it.[29]

Alexander's neo-Aristotelian doctrine of τελειότης, and Philoponus' later reworking of it in accordance with new agendas – mainly the necessity of granting some kind of ontological independence to the human soul, which was not Alexander's concern at all – shape Avicenna's notion of *perfection*, which is broad enough to encompass both separable and inseparable entities, similar to Aristotelian forms.[30] Thus, though going beyond Aristotle's notion of form, Avicenna manages to include it in his account of the soul. Here insistence on the activities for which perfection is responsible in order to define perfection and to distinguish it from form[31] seems to be crucial. As emerged in Chapter 3, the soul's being the *perfection of* the body points at a relation existing between soul and body by means of which the former perfects the latter, enabling it to perform a set of activities. However, the soul's being the perfection of the body does not render explicit the modality through which the perfection of the body occurs, i.e. either through the soul's entire substance, that is, through the reception of the soul into the body as a form in matter (inseparable perfection, i.e. substantial form), or through the soul's activity alone, like a separable substance that perfects an entity to which is somehow related, while remaining independent, as the king or the steersman are perfection of the city and the ship respectively, by exercising their governing, i.e. perfective, activity on them, without depending on them (separable perfection).[32]

For this very reason, after singling out *perfection* as the most adequate term with which to name the soul, Avicenna firmly rejects the equation of perfection with substance,[33] precisely because it is impossible to infer the substantiality of what is a perfection from the very fact that it is a perfection. For, if saying that the soul is substance insofar as it is form, as some (e.g. Aristotle) did, is completely uncontroversial,[34] because the form is unquestionably a substance inasmuch as it

---

29 See R. Arnzen, *Aristoteles'* De anima, 217.9–16.

30 This is Avicenna's broad notion of *perfection*, encompassing the final and efficient causality together with the formal causality, to which Wisnovsky refers in his *Avicenna's Metaphysics*, 127–141.

31 See *Nafs*, I, 1, 7.6–8 quoted above.

32 For the passages from *Nafs*, V, 3–4 where Avicenna refers to *qubūl* and *nisba* as two different kinds of relation existing between a thing and its matter, see *infra*.

33 *Nafs*, I, 1, 8.8–10.14 [22.70–26.23].

34 *Nafs*, I, 1, 8.14–9.1 [23.77–85]: "If someone says: "I call the soul substance, and I mean by it the form, and I do not mean by it a meaning more general than form, but the meaning that it is substance is the meaning that it is form" – and this is what some people have said, then *there would be no room for discussion and disagreement with them at all.* The meaning of their saying that the soul is substance is that the soul is form. Rather, their saying that the form is substance is like their saying

is not in a subject at all,[35] saying that it is substance insofar as it is perfection raises some difficulties. Perfection can be either substance or accident (e.g. a human being's capacity for laughter is a perfection of the human being, but it is an inseparable, necessary accident, or concomitant (*lāzim*), not a substance), because its being a part of the composite does not entail its being not in a subject at all and, consequently, it is not sufficient to account for its being a substance.[36] What is more, by supplementing the account of substance and accident that Aristotle provides in the *Categories* with Porphyry's discussion of substantial and accidental in the *Isagoge*, Avicenna carefully distinguishes "being a substance (*ǧawhar*)" from "being substantial (*ǧawharī*)", i.e. being a part of a substance, as well as "being an accident (*ʿaraḍ*)" from "being accidental (*ʿaraḍī*)", i.e. not being a part of a substance.[37] According to this distinction, the fact that something is a substance (or an accident) is not *relational*, that is, it cannot be determined with respect to something else (the body, in this case), but is a consideration belonging to that something in itself. This distinction is

that the form is form or configuration (*ṣūra aw hayʾa* [*forma vel affectio*]), or that man is man or human being, which is a senseless discourse" (emphasis mine).

35 Avicenna's criterion for being a substance, i.e. "being not in a subject at all" (*laysa fī mawḍūʿ al-battata*, *Nafs*, I, 1, 9.1 [24.86]), is obviously derived from the Aristotelian "not being in any subject" (ἐν ὑποκειμένῳ δὲ οὐδενί ἐστιν, *Cat.*, 1, 1 a22, 1 b3). Cf. *Maqūlāt*, I, 3, and *Ilāhiyyāt*, II, 1. According to Avicenna, the form is in the matter not as an accident in a subject because, unlike the subject, matter needs the form in order to exist. See the text quoted in n. 5.

36 Avicenna lists three instances of perfection, two of which are substances and one of which is an accident, precisely to show that the notion of *perfection* does not univocally refer to what is in itself substance. See *Nafs*, I, 1, 10.8–14 [26.15–23]: "[(a)] If every soul exists not in a subject, then every soul is substance. [(b)] If some soul is self-subsisting, while each of the remaining souls is in the *hyle*, not in a subject, then, every soul is a substance. [(c)] If some soul subsists in a subject and, nevertheless, is part of the composite, it is an accident. All these [aforementioned entities] are perfection. However, by our positing that the soul is a perfection, it has not become clear yet for us whether the soul is a substance or not a substance. Thus, those who thought that this was sufficient for them to render the soul a substance like the form made a mistake".

37 See *Nafs*, I, 1, 9.18–10.6 [25.5–12]: "It is not the case that, if [something] is not an accident in a thing, then it is a substance in it. For the thing can be neither an accident in the thing nor a substance in it, just as the thing can be neither one nor many in a thing, but it is in itself either one or many. Substantial and substance are not one [thing]; nor is the accident in the sense of accidental that is in the *Isagoge* the accident that is in the *Categories*. We have already shown to you these matters in the discipline of logic (*fī ṣināʿat al-manṭiq* [*in doctrina artis logicae*], *sc. Madḫal*, I, 14, but also *Maqūlāt*, I, 6)". On this reference to logic in *Nafs*, I, 1, see Chapter 3, n. 12. For the fact that here Avicenna is arguing against the position of unnamed opponents (in all likelihood the representatives of Baghdad Peripatetic School, such as Ibn Suwār and Ibn al-Ṭayyib), according to which the parts of substance are *ipso facto* substance, see F. Benevich, "Fire and Heat: Yaḥyâ B. ʿAdī and Avicenna on the Essentiality of Being Substance or Accident", *Arabic Sciences and Philosophy*, 27, 2017, 237–67. For the Aristotelian background of this controversy, see *Cat.*, 5, 3 a29–32: μὴ ταραττέτω δὲ ἡμᾶς τὰ μέρη τῶν οὐσιῶν ὡς ἐν ὑποκειμένοις ὄντα τοῖς ὅλοις, μή ποτε ἀναγκασθῶμεν οὐκ οὐσίας αὐτὰ φάσκειν εἶναι· οὐ γὰρ οὕτω τὰ ἐν ὑποκειμένῳ ἐλέγετο τὰ ὡς μέρη ὑπάρχοντα ἔν τινι, where Aristotle seems to distinguish the way in which the parts are in the composite from the way in which the accidents are in a subject and, consequently, to assign to the former the status of substance.

crucial for the case of the soul, for the fact that it is part of the composite substance's subsistence (*ǧuzʾ min qiwāmihā*)[38] does not exclude *ipso facto* the possibility that the soul is in itself an accident: "It is, therefore, clear that the soul's being in the composite like a part does not remove its accidentality. Rather, it must be in itself not in a subject at all (*fī nafsihā lā fī mawḍūʿ al-battata* [*in se sit ut non in subiecto ullo modo*])" (*Nafs*, I, 1, 10.6–7 [25.12–26.14]).

In order for the term *perfection*, which in *Nafs*, I, 1 designates the relation (*iḍāfa* [*relatio*], I, 1, 4.11; 15.18) of a certain thing (*šayʾ*) to the body, to designate the soul *qua* substance, its being substance needs to be proved by means of another, independent investigation, as we have shown in Chapter 3. Therefore, though it cannot be considered a proper advancement of knowledge of the soul because it remains at the level of *names* without grasping the quiddity, this *terminological* excursus has the merit of isolating a unitary label under which all the sublunary souls, in spite of their irreducible differences,[39] are included inasmuch as constitute principle (or cause) of activities.

Which Return to Aristotle?

In introducing the Peripatetic standard definition of the soul, Avicenna iterates the boundaries of the investigation conducted so far, which perfectly fits with its having been placed in natural philosophy, and underscores the limits of Aristotle's definition of the soul that he is about to discuss: "Then we say: when we know that the soul is perfection, by whatever clarification and distinction we designated the perfection, we would not know yet the soul and its quiddity; rather, we would know it insofar as it is soul. The term "soul" does not apply to it with respect to its substance, but insofar as it governs bodies and is related to them. For this reason the body is included in its definition, just as the building, for example, is included in the definition of the builder, even though it is not included in his definition insofar as he is a human being. For this reason the investigation of the soul is part of natural science, because the investigation of the soul insofar as it is soul is an investigation of it insofar as it has a certain connection with matter and motion. However, we must devote another inquiry (*baḥṯ āḫar, alium tractatum*) to our acquaintance with the essence of the soul. If we had come to know through this (*sc.* through the investigation conducted so far) the essence of the soul, then it would not have been obscure to us into which category it falls. For whoever knows and understands the essence of

38 See *Nafs*, I, 1, 5.6 [16.90]. See n. 5 above for the full quotation. Cf. *Nafs*, I, 3, 28.11 [59.43] where, in the context of the demonstration of the substantiality of the soul of plants and animals *qua* form, Avicenna says that the soul is a constitutive part of its proximate subject (*muqawwima li-mawḍūʿihā l-qarīb* [*constituens suum proprium subiectum*]).

39 They are all substances, but of different kind and belong to different realms and, consequently, their investigation should pertain to different sciences.

something and then presents to himself the nature of something essential belonging to it, its existence for it (*sc.* that something) would not be obscure to him, as we have explained in logic (*sc.* in *Madḫal*, I, 6)" (*Nafs*, I, 1, 10.15–11.4 [26.24–27.36]).

As has emerged in the part of the chapter devoted to the terminological excursus, the fact that the soul is referred to as perfection is not informative about its quiddity (*māhiyya*). If the soul's "being a perfection" had been an essential attribute of the soul, the preceding investigation would have contributed to our knowing its essence (*ḏāt*) because, as is suggested in *Madḫal*, I, 6, to which Avicenna in all likelihood is referring at the end of this passage, the essential, constitutive attributes of something must be grasped together with the essence of that something, otherwise they are not essential attributes of it (I, 6, 34.13–35.5).[40] But "being a perfection" does not reveal the essence of the thing which is said to be a perfection. For this reason, another inquiry should be devoted to the ascertainment of the essence (*ḏāt*) of the soul.

Nonetheless, the term *perfection* captures an aspect of soul: that is, its being a relational entity insofar as it governs the body and is related to it. It is from this perspective, that is, insofar as it is connected with matter and motion, that the soul is investigated in natural philosophy. Consequently, the body, being the other element of the relation, must be included in its definition (as the Aristotelian definition of the soul does). Therefore, the (Aristotelian) definition of the soul as perfection is not an essential definition of it on which the science of the soul can be grounded, but nevertheless it contributes to delimiting the investigation of the soul that legitimately pertains to natural philosophy.[41]

The standard Aristotelian definition of the soul as "the first actuality of a natural, organic body"[42] is rephrased as "the first perfection of a natural, organic body, having the capacity of performing the activities of life",[43] the Greek term ἐντελέχεια (actuality, fulfilment) being rendered with the Arabic term *kamāl* (perfection).[44] Avicenna's formulation of this definition is the outcome of a series of distinctions, i.e. that between first and second perfection, that between artificial and natural bodies, and, within the latter, that between simple and composite bodies, which reproduce exactly the same distinctions that led into the Aristotelian definition of the soul.[45]

The first distinction, namely that between first and second perfection, is crucial. "Perfection, however, [can] be of two ways: [(a)] first perfection, and [(b)] second per-

---

40 More on this aspect in P. Adamson, F. Benevich, "The Thought Experimental Method".

41 See Chapter 3, n. 28.

42 *De an.*, II, 1, 412 b4–6: εἰ δή τι κοινὸν ἐπὶ πάσης ψυχῆς δεῖ λέγειν, εἴη ἂν ἐντελέχεια ἡ πρώτη σώματος φυσικοῦ ὀργανικοῦ.

43 *Nafs*, I, 1, 12.7–8 [29.62–63]: *kamāl awwal li-ǧism ṭabīʿī ālī lahū an yafʿala afʿāl al-ḥayā.*

44 We are already acquainted with the notion of τελειότης/*kamāl* as an interpretation of the Aristotelian notion of ἐντελέχεια.

45 Aristotle's definition of the soul, provided in *De an.*, II, 1, 412 b4–6, is preceded by: (1) the distinction between artificial and natural bodies (412 a11–13); (2) the distinction, within natural bodies, between inorganic (i.e. simple), and organic (i.e. composite) bodies (412 a13–16); and, lastly, (3) the distinction between first and second actuality (412 a21–27).

fection. [(a)] The first perfection is that by means of which the species becomes a species in actuality, like shape for the sword (*ka-l-šakl li-l-sayf* [*sicut figura ensi*]). [(b)] The second perfection is one of the things that follow the species of the thing in terms of its activities and affections, like cutting for the sword, and like discernment, deliberation, sensation, and motion for the human being. For these are unquestionably perfections of the species, but are not first [perfections]: for, in order to become what it is in actuality, the species does not need these things to occur for it in actuality. Rather, when the principle of these things (*sc.* second perfections, that is, activities and affections) occurs for it (*sc.* for the species) in actuality so that these things become for it in potentiality after having not been in potentiality – except in a remote potentiality that needs something to occur before them so that they become in reality in potentiality – then the animal becomes animal in actuality. The soul is, therefore, a first perfection" (*Nafs*, I, 1, 11.7–17 [27.40–28.51]).

Avicenna distinguishes two ways in which *perfection* is articulated: (a) first perfection, which is like a certain shape or configuration (*šakl*) of matter; and (b) second perfection, which refers to the activities or affections ensuing from that shape, namely from the first perfection. The soul is, then, equated with first perfection.

Here a remark is in order. In distinguishing first and second perfection Avicenna seems to follow closely the Aristotelian distinction between first and second actuality and, consequently, to ascribe to the first perfection a sort of *formal* nuance. The soul is a first perfection insofar as it is the *formal principle* of the body, immanent to it,[46] which, like the shape of the sword, organizes the body in such a way that a set of activities or affections, i.e. the second perfections, derives from it. However, in introducing the standard formulation of the Aristotelian definition of the soul, Avicenna maintains that referring to it as *perfection* does not allow us to infer anything about its quiddity. Here, by contrast, if first perfection is equated with *form* (*ṣūra*) and the soul is referred to as first perfection, then the soul will automatically be substance *qua* form because saying that the form is substance is unproblematic; rather, it is

46 In a similar vein Aristotle says that the body that is potentially alive is not that which has lost the soul, but that which has one, meaning that the soul is the principle of the vital activities that the body possessing the soul, i.e. that principle, is capable of performing at will. See *De an.*, II, 1, 412 b 25–6: ἔστι δὲ οὐ τὸ ἀποβεβληκὸς τὴν ψυχὴν τὸ δυνάμει ὂν ὥστε ζῆν, ἀλλὰ τὸ ἔχον. On the fact that for Avicenna the form in the proper sense is inseparable from matter, see *Ilāhiyyāt*, IX, 4, 405.1–7: "In general, even though the material form is a cause that brings matter to actuality and perfects it, matter also has an influence on its (*sc.* of form) existence, that is, in rendering it specific and in determining it, even though [the form] is the principle of existence without matter, as you have already learned (*sc. Ilāhiyyāt*, II, 4). Then each of them (sc. form and matter) is unquestionably a cause for the other in something, but not in one single respect. Otherwise, it would be impossible for the material form to depend, in any manner whatsoever, on matter. For this reason, we have previously said that form alone is not sufficient for the existence of matter; rather, it is like a part of the cause (*sc. Ilāhiyyāt*, II, 4). If this is the case, then it is impossible to make form a cause for matter in all respects, having no need for other than itself".

a sort of tautology, as Avicenna stated earlier in this chapter.[47] What is more, the equation of perfection with form in relation to the soul has been already rejected: the former is broader than the latter, and more indicative of the meaning of soul.[48]

That the sublunary soul is substance *qua* form is not in question: Avicenna will prove that in *Nafs*, I, 3. What is more, outside *Nafs* Avicenna usually refers to sublunary soul, which is a principle of activities in the body, as *ṣūra*, because its being substance has been already proved, or is a conclusion of psychology.[49] However, in *Nafs*,

47 *Nafs*, I, 1, 8.14–9.1 [23.77–85]. For the full text, see n. 34 above.
48 See the text quoted in n. 8 above.
49 See, for instance, *Samāʿ ṭabīʿī*, III, 12, 242.15–16: "It seems, thus, that the human soul does not exist as a form (*ṣūra*), unless as belonging to a body of the sort that it performs the human movements if nothing impedes it". The context is the same as that of *Nafs:* the soul is said to be a form of the body insofar as it is the principle of certain activities in it. This is also the reason why in the passage from the *Samāʿ ṭabīʿī* as well as in *Nafs*, I, 1, among the activities ensuing from the human soul Avicenna does not mention intellectual conceptualization (*taṣawwur*), according to which the human soul *in itself* is primarily defined, but limits himself to mentioning generic *human movements* (*al-ḥarakāt al-insāniyya*) in the case of *Samāʿ ṭabīʿī*, or to listing discernment, deliberation, sensation, and motion, the latter two being common to all animals, in the case of *Nafs*. These activities are those performed by the soul insofar as it is a formal principle, immanent to the body, which is responsible for its organization. Intellection, by contrast, is an activity that the human soul performs by itself, being something more than a form, and using the body as an instrument which it gets rid of when it reaches its own perfection. In this connection, see *Nafs*, V. 3, 223.5–10 [105.33–39], where Avicenna uses the simile of the *riding animal* in order to explain the relation between the human rational soul and the corporeal faculties, after which the human rational soul is more correctly named *ʿaql* (intellect), the term designating the human soul *in itself* (it does not exist an equivalent for the other souls). Here, again, Avicenna's dependence on Philoponus' exegesis of Aristotle's *De anima* is crucial. There, Philoponus argues that the rational soul too, insofar as it is responsible for the perfection of the living being through certain activities, is inseparable from the body, and is called *soul*, which is a relative term, whereas the human rational soul considered *in itself* is separable and is (and is called) intellect. See Philoponus, *In De anima*, 224.28–225.8: δύναται γὰρ καὶ κατά τινα τρόπον, ὡς ἤδη εἶπον, **λέγεσθαι καὶ ἡ λογικὴ ψυχὴ ἀχώριστος εἶναι τοῦ σώματος, καθό ἐστιν ἐντελέχεια.** τὰς γὰρ ἐνεργείας, καθ' ἃς τελειοῖ τὸ ζῷον κινοῦσα αὐτὸ τοιῶσδε ἢ τοιῶσδε ἀχωρίστους ἔχει τοῦ σώματος· ἐξελθοῦσα γὰρ αὐτοῦ οὐκέτι ταύτας ἐνεργήσει· ἴσχει γὰρ αὐτὰς ἐκ τῆς σχέσεως τῆς πρὸς τὸ σῶμα. ὥστε ταύτῃ καθὸ ἐντελέχειά ἐστι, λέγω δὴ κατὰ τάσδε τὰς ἐνεργείας, ἀχώριστος ἂν εἴη τοῦ σώματος, ὥσπερ καὶ τοῦ κυβερνήτου αἱ ὡς κυβερνήτου ἐνέργειαι τοῦ πλοίου εἰσὶν ἀχώριστοι, καὶ χωρίζεται μὲν ὡς ἄνθρωπος, ὡς μέντοι κυβερνήτης ὢν ἐνεργείᾳ ἅμα τε κεχώρισται τῆς νεὼς καὶ ἐφθαρμένας ἔχει τὰς τοιαύτας ἐνεργείας. οὕτως οὖν καὶ ἡ λογικὴ ψυχὴ ὡς μὲν χωριστὴν ἔχουσα οὐσίαν οὐκ ἔστιν ἐντελέχεια σώματος, ὡς μέντοι τοιάνδε σχέσιν ἀναλαμβάνουσα πρὸς τὸ σῶμα, **καθὸ καὶ τὸ ψυχὴ λέγεσθαι ἔχει (ἡ γὰρ ψυχὴ πρὸς τὸ σῶμα λέγεται)** ἐντελέχειά τ' ἐστὶ τοῦ σώματος καὶ ἀχώριστος αὐτοῦ· χωρισθεῖσα γὰρ αὐτοῦ ἀπόλλυσι ταύτας τὰς ἐνεργείας, ἃς ἐκ τῆς πρὸς αὐτὸ σχέσεως ἀνειλήφει, οἷον τὸ ζῳοποιεῖν, τὸ κινεῖν αὐτὸ πάσας τὰς φυσικὰς κινήσεις, καὶ εἴ τι τοιοῦτον ἄλλο. τί γὰρ φυσικῶς κινήσει ἢ ζῳοποιήσει παντὸς οὖσα ἔξω σώματος; (emphasis mine). See also *In De anima*, 246.27–247.7, where Philoponus identifies the human rational soul with the intellect, quoted in Chapter 3, n. 8. On the distinction between the soul, which is responsible for the activities in the body, and the intellect, which is the principle of the human being, somehow transcending the physical realm, see the section on al-Fārābī, and the brief discussion of the notion of *empsychia* in Chapter 2.

I, 1 this has not been proved yet and, most importantly, it has to be proved independently of its being an instance of *perfection*. For this reason, recourse to the term *šakl* in illustrating what first perfection means is crucial. Here Avicenna illustrates this with the example of the *šakl* of the sword, not with its *ṣūra* (*form*), which would be the appropriate term by which to designate a formal principle.[50] Therefore, it might be the case that Avicenna uses the word *šakl*, which brings out the connotation of *form* as being immanent and related to the body,[51] in order to avoid using the word *ṣūra*. For *ṣūra* carries heavily ontologically connotations, and Avicenna does not want to confuse the operational level, on which he is focusing here (and on which he wants psychology belonging to natural philosophy *officially* to focus), with the ontological level, which he has sharply distinguished from the operational level at the outset of this investigation, and to which he will devote another investigation (the investigation of the quiddity of the *soul of* is contained in *Nafs*, I, 3).[52]

Consequently, as Wisnovsky convincingly argued in his analysis of the passage,[53] although Avicenna's distinction between first and second perfection depends broadly on Aristotle's distinction between first and second ἐντελέχεια in *De an.*, II, 1, it also

50 Cf. *Nafs*, I, 1, 6.4–6 [18.14–16]. It should be noted that here Avicenna describes the "first perfection" by using the same formula (*huwa llaḏī yaṣīru bihī l-nawʿ nawʿan bi-l-fiʿl*, 11.8) through which in *Nafs*, I, 1, 8.9–10 [22.71–23.73] he has referred to the notion of *perfection* without qualification, not to that of form.

51 *Pace* Wisnovsky (121), here *šakl* does not necessarily refer to an extrinsic feature, i.e. the external configuration, of something, as the Greek μορφή does. Overall, Wisnovsky's analysis of this passage is persuasive: by following the Aristotelian path, Avicenna equates the first perfection/first ἐντελέχεια with the capacity for performing a certain function but, unlike Aristotle, he does not equate it with the substantial form of a certain material composite, but with its shape (μορφή). It might be possible, however, to explore the possibility that Avicenna's first perfection is *shape* (*šakl*) not in the same sense in which the Greek word μορφή means shape. Here *šakl* may not (only) refer to the mere external configuration as μορφή does, but, rather, may render the Greek σχῆμα, which refers not only to the external appearance of something but also to the formal structure conferred upon something by means of which that something is enabled to perform a set of functions according to the level of organization of its body. For the various meanings of the word σχῆμα, see H. G. Liddell-R. Scott, *A Greek – English Lexicon*. Revised and augmented throughout by H. S. Jones with the assistance of R. McKenzie and with the cooperation of many scholars; with a revised supplement, Clarendon Press, Oxford 1996, 1745. What is more, Wisnovsky (125) argues that "in the sense that it is the springboard for future activities, the soul is more like a form as shape – the arrangement of matter structured with a view to performing some function – than it is like a form as substance". However, this seems to be a description more of an essential formal principle than of an extrinsic configuration of matter, and Wisnovsky seems to subscribe this at 126.

52 See Chapter 3.

53 See Wisnovsky, *Avicenna's Metaphysics*, 121: "Avicenna might have reasoned along the following lines: given that Aristotle says at the very beginning of L1 [*sc. De an.*, II, 1, 412 a6–28] that the soul is an *entelekheia* in the sense of substantial form; given that Aristotle goes on to say later in L1 that the soul is a first *entelekheia*; and given that in L1 and in the later passage (412 b11–413 a3) Aristotle illustrates what first *entelekheia* means by using an example that is most easily interpreted as referring to a capability to perform a function, form and capability to perform a function are therefore equivalent".

echoes Aristotle's distinction between the capacity for performing one or more functions and the actual exercise of that capacity, and the equation of the form *qua* first perfection with the capability to perform a function.[54] The soul's being first perfection would then be equated with providing a certain structure or configuration which enables a certain body to perform a set of vital activities according to its level of organization, independently of the modality by means of which it connects with the body, namely as a substantial form or as an independent substance, that is, regardless of the quiddity of the perfection. By depriving the standard formulation of the Aristotelian definition of the soul of (almost) any reference to the quiddity of the soul, Avicenna seems to shift the focus from the essence of the soul to its being the principle and cause of a set of (unexercised) capacities.

As for the other two distinctions, they concern the characteristics of the body which is included in the definition of the soul. The soul cannot be the perfection of just any body; rather, it has to be a natural body (*ǧism ṭabīʿī*), endowed with organs (*ālī*), and capable of performing vital activities, namely a body that, unlike the four elements, has a suitable structure to receive a certain configuration, and the activities ensuing from it.[55]

The standard formulation of the Aristotelian definition of the soul is then recalled.

---

54 See *De an.*, II, 1, 412 b11–413 a3: τοῦτο δὲ τὸ τί ἦν εἶναι τῷ τοιῳδὶ σώματι, καθάπερ εἴ τι τῶν ὀργάνων φυσικὸν ἦν σῶμα, οἷον πέλεκυς· ἦν μὲν γὰρ ἂν τὸ πελέκει εἶναι ἡ οὐσία αὐτοῦ, καὶ ἡ ψυχὴ τοῦτο· χωρισθείσης δὲ ταύτης οὐκ ἂν ἔτι πέλεκυς ἦν, ἀλλ' ἢ ὁμωνύμως, νῦν δ' ἔστι πέλεκυς. οὐ γὰρ τοιούτου σώματος τὸ τί ἦν εἶναι καὶ ὁ λόγος ἡ ψυχή, ἀλλὰ φυσικοῦ τοιουδί, ἔχοντος ἀρχὴν κινήσεως καὶ στάσεως ἐν ἑαυτῷ. θεωρεῖν δὲ καὶ ἐπὶ τῶν μερῶν δεῖ τὸ λεχθέν. εἰ γὰρ ἦν ὁ ὀφθαλμὸς ζῷον, ψυχὴ ἂν ἦν αὐτοῦ ἡ ὄψις· αὕτη γὰρ οὐσία ὀφθαλμοῦ ἡ κατὰ τὸν λόγον (ὁ δ' ὀφθαλμὸς ὕλη ὄψεως), ἧς ἀπολειπούσης οὐκέτ' ὀφθαλμός, πλὴν ὁμωνύμως, καθάπερ ὁ λίθινος καὶ ὁ γεγραμμένος. δεῖ δὴ λαβεῖν τὸ ἐπὶ μέρους ἐφ' ὅλου τοῦ ζῶντος σώματος· ἀνάλογον γὰρ ἔχει ὡς τὸ μέρος πρὸς τὸ μέρος, οὕτως ἡ ὅλη αἴσθησις πρὸς τὸ ὅλον σῶμα τὸ αἰσθητικόν, ᾗ τοιοῦτον. ἔστι δὲ οὐ τὸ ἀποβεβληκὸς τὴν ψυχὴν τὸ δυνάμει ὂν ὥστε ζῆν, ἀλλὰ τὸ ἔχον· τὸ δὲ σπέρμα καὶ ὁ καρπὸς τὸ δυνάμει τοιονδὶ σῶμα. ὡς μὲν οὖν ἡ τμῆσις καὶ ἡ ὅρασις, οὕτω καὶ ἡ ἐγρήγορσις ἐντελέχεια, ὡς δ' ἡ ὄψις καὶ ἡ δύναμις τοῦ ὀργάνου, ἡ ψυχή· τὸ δὲ σῶμα τὸ δυνάμει ὄν· ἀλλ' ὥσπερ ὀφθαλμὸς ἡ κόρη καὶ ἡ ὄψις, κἀκεῖ ἡ ψυχὴ καὶ τὸ σῶμα ζῷον.

55 *Nafs*, I, 1, 11.17–12.6 [28.52–29.61]: "And, since the perfection is perfection of something, the soul is the perfection of something, this something being the body. The body must be taken in the generic, not material sense, as you have learned in the discipline of demonstration (*sc. Burhān*, I, 10). And this body of which the soul is the perfection is not every body: for the soul is not the perfection of the artificial body, like the bed, the chair, etc., but the perfection of the natural body (*al-ǧism al-ṭabīʿī*). Nor [is the soul the perfection] of every natural body: for the soul is not the perfection of fire, nor of earth, but in our world it is the perfection of a natural body from which its second perfections derive by means of organs of which it makes use in the activities of life, the first of which are nutrition and growth."

Does Avicenna Formulate a Definition of the Soul?

As has emerged from the survey conducted so far, *Nafs*, I, 1 consists of two juxtaposed parts. In the first part Avicenna offers an excursus on the terms by which predecessors have referred to the soul, whereas in the second he revives the standard formulation of the Aristotelian definition of the soul. The terminological excursus ends up with *kamāl/perfection* as the most appropriate term to refer to the soul, whereas the revival of the Aristotelian definition of the soul results in a formula where the locution ἐντελέχεια ἡ πρώτη (*first actuality*) is rendered as *kamāl awwal* (*first perfection*), by determining a shift from the Aristotelian notion of *actuality* to the Late Ancient and early Arabic interpretation of it as τελειότης/*kamāl*. These two parts turn out then to be far from homogeneous: for, on the one hand, Avicenna declares that the notion of *perfection* is better than that of *form* because it is broad enough to encompass all instances of soul, including the separable soul, whereas, on the other hand, he seems to assimilate the notion of *first perfection* precisely to the notion of *form*, limiting its scope to the inseparable soul. In this connection, the definition of the soul seems to pose the biggest problem because it does not account for the essence of the *definiendum* (not even of a subset of it) and, therefore, does not provide a solid basis on which the science of the soul can be grounded. Still, scholars have never questioned whether the definition of the soul formulated in *Nafs*, I, 1 was indeed Avicenna's.[56]

56 By agreeing on the translation of *naḥuddu* (12.7) as *we define*, scholars show a certain *consensus* with respect to the way in which *Nafs*, I, 1, 12.6–8 has to be understood. In a pioneering article published in 1969 on Avicenna's theory of the substantiality of the soul, L. E. Goodman translates the aforementioned passage as follows: "Thus the soul, as we define it is: *the primary entelechy of a natural body organized so as to carry out the function of life*" ("A Note on Avicenna's Theory", 559). After three decades, in an article entirely devoted to the exegesis of Avicenna's definition of the soul, M. Sebti paraphrases the aforementioned passage as follows: "il (*sc.* Avicenne) peut alors conclure ce premier chapitre (*sc.* du *De anima*) par la définition de l'âme comme "la perfection première d'un corps naturel organique capable d'accomplir les actes de la vie"" ("La signification de la définition avicennienne de l'âme", 308). This analysis is confirmed one year later in her monograph on the human soul in Avicenna (*Avicenne, L'âme humaine*, Presses universitaires de France, Paris 2000, 16: "Il (*sc.* Avicenne) énonce au livre I une définition générique de l'âme qui s'applique aux trois espèces du vivant : 'L'âme est la perfection première d'un corps naturel organique capable d'accomplir les actes de la vie' (I, 1, p. 10 [ed. Cairo])"). In 2003, in chapter 6 of the first part of his monograph, which is devoted to Avicenna's reworking of the notion of *perfection*, R. Wisnovsky translates the passage quoted above as follows: "So the soul which we are defining is a first perfection of a natural instrumental body [which the soul uses] to perform the activities of living" (*Avicenna's Metaphysics*, 114). In their anthology of classical Arabic philosophy texts, J. McGinnis and D. C. Reisman provide the following translation of the passage in question: "Thus, the soul–the one we are defining here (note that *here* does not correspond to anything in the Arabic text)–is a first perfection of a natural body possessed of organs that performs the activities of life" (*Classical Arabic Philosophy: An Anthology of Sources.* Translated with Introduction, Notes, and Glossary by J. McGinnis and D. C. Reisman, Hackett Publishing Company, Inc., Indianapolis-Cambridge, 2007, 178). Lastly, in an article which appeared in 2010, where the position of psychology in Avicenna's system of science is investigated, O.

However, there are reasons for arguing that this is not Avicenna's own definition of the soul, but rather the standard formula through which in the Aristotelian tradition it is customary to define sublunary souls.[57] Apart from the doctrinal coherence within Avicenna's thought, the phrasing of the sentence in which the formulation of the definition of the soul is contained, is unusual: "*fa-l-nafs allatī naḥudduhā hiya* [...]" (*the soul that we are defining is* [...]). In formulating his own definition of the soul, one would have expected a more straightforward sentence rather than this convoluted formulation. At the outset of an investigation of the soul that aspires to be exhaustive, Avicenna would not have used a sentence that gives the impression of excluding some soul from the general psychological inquiry upon which he is embarking: for the sentence we read seems to imply that there is some soul that Avicenna will not define nor deal with in *Nafs*.[58]

The major obstacle to interpreting this as not being Avicenna's own definition of the soul is the use of the verb *ḥadda* (I, 1, 12.7, *to define* [*invenimus*, 29.61][59]), which echoes the infinitive *taḥdīd* (I, 1, 4.3, *defining* [*definire*, 14.68]) in the chapter title, and the noun *ḥadd* (10.19; 12.10; 13.12, *definition* [*definitio*, 27.30; 29.65; 32.89]).[60] However, نحد, the *rasm* of the word *naḥuddu* without dots and dashes, can be also read as *nağidu* (*we find*), which is explicitly attested as a variant for *naḥuddu* in some manuscripts[61] and in the Latin translation of *Nafs* (*invenimus*, *we find*, and not *definimus*, *we define*). Therefore, Avicenna might have meant to say that "the soul that we *find*"

Lizzini translates *Nafs*, I, 1, 12.6 – 8 as follows: "l'âme que l'on va ici définir est donc perfection première d'un corps naturel organique [ou instrumental ou doué d'organes] qui accomplit les actes de la vie" ("L'âme chez Avicenne", 227, n. 13). O. Lizzini refers to this formulation as Avicenna's definition of the soul in *Fluxus (fayḍ). Indagine sui fondamenti della metafisica e della fisica di Avicenna*, Edizioni di Pagina, Bari 2011, 102; and in *Avicenna*, Carocci editore, Roma 2012, 237.

57 It is noteworthy that, in their reading of Avicenna's passage, R. Wisnovsky, J. McGinnis – D. C. Reisman, and O. Lizzini seem to acknowledge the limited scope of the retrieved definition of the soul; nonetheless, they do not question whether this definition is indeed Avicenna's.

58 On the fact that Aristotle seems to introduce some limitations to his investigation of the soul in the *De anima*, see Chapter 2.

59 On the Latin translation of this passage, see n. 63 below.

60 The weight of these *contra* arguments, however, can be limited by considering that the standard formulation of the Aristotelian definition of the soul is to all intents and purposes a definition, and thus it is no surprise that Avicenna refers to it by using the term *ḥadd*.

61 See mss. (1) UK, Oxford, Bodleian Library, Pococke 125 (Uri's catalogue I, 435); (2) Turkey, Istanbul, Süleymaniye Kütüphanesi, Damad İbrahim Paşa 823; (3) Egypt, Cairo, Maktabat al-Azhar al-Šarīf, Beḫīt 331 *falsafa* (*ḫuṣūṣiyya*), 44988 (*ʿumūmiyya*); (4) The Netherlands, Leiden, Universiteitsbibliotheek, Or. 84 (Golius Collection) (Catalogue CCO, nr. 1445); (5) Turkey, Istanbul, Nuruosmaniye Kütüphanesi, 2709; (6) Iran, Tehran, Kitābḫānah-i Mağlis-i Šūrā-yi Islāmī (form.: Kitābḫānah-i Mağlis-i Šūrā-yi Millī), 5254; (7) USA, Princeton, Princeton University Library, 861; (8) UK, London, British Library, Oriental and India Office Collections (ex: British Museum), Ar. 1796 (Loth's catalogue, 476). More information on these manuscripts and, in general, on the manuscripts preserving the Arabic text of Avicenna's *Nafs*, in Alpina, "Al-Ğūzğānī's Insertion of *On Cardiac Remedies*". It should be noted that mss. (1), (3), (4), and (8) are used by Rahman, who nevertheless seems not to correctly record their readings in the critical apparatus.

– not "that we *define*" – is the first perfection of a natural, organic body, having the capacity to perform the activities of life, without committing himself to endorsing the Aristotelian definition of the soul, which carries the aforementioned disadvantages (it would be a non-quidditative definition because the equation of "perfection" with "being a substance" is not allowed). If it is agreed that in *Nafs*, I, 1 Avicenna simply revives the Aristotelian definition of the soul without endorsing it, the meaning of this retrieval and of the limitation introduced by the clause "[*the soul*] *that we find*" has to be explained. This explanation, however, cannot overlook the context in which this retrieval occurs, that is, *Nafs*, I, 1–3.

As has been pointed out at the beginning of this chapter, *Nafs*, I, 1 has to be considered on the whole dialectical, where the major theoretical achievements of predecessors concerning the soul are offered as a way of introducing Avicenna's own position on the subject. The definition of the soul is one of those achievements. Its formulation testifies Avicenna's reverence towards the Aristotelian tradition (as we saw, it even stems from the same series of distinctions that have led into the Aristotelian definition of the soul). Therefore, here Avicenna does not want to provide his own definition of the soul;[62] rather, he revives the standard definition of the soul as a catch-all formula, capable of encompassing all instances of sublunary soul (vegetative, animal, human) while they are in our world (in this perspective *naǧidu* has to be read in connection with *fī ʿālaminā, in our world,* I, 1, 12.5 [*in hoc nostro mundo*, 29.58]),[63] namely insofar as they are the principle of organization and activity in the body, not in themselves (it is therefore not an essential definition, nor a definition on which Avicenna can ground his science of the soul).[64] Here a remark is in order. I think that my explanation of the role of Avicenna's retrieval of the standard Aristotelian definition of the soul in *Nafs*, I, 1 holds true even if Avicenna had said *naḥuddu* (*we define*) instead of *naǧidu* (*we find*). In this case, however, we must interpret *naḥuddu* as "we – as Aristotelian – define" and consider the definition formu-

---

62 A further, *ex silentio* argument in favour of this interpretation is provided by parallels in other sections of the *Šifāʾ*, and in other Avicennian works. In the *Šifāʾ*, the soul is referred to as *ṣūra* (*form*) and *kamāl* (*perfection*), while in other *summae*, when the soul is referred to as *first perfection*, Avicenna never presents it as his own way to define the soul. Examples in the *Šifāʾ* are: *Nafs*, V, 7, 254.4 [160.22–3], where the soul is said to be perfection (not first perfection!) of the body; *Burhān*, II, 9, 182.11–12 (this passage is quoted in Wisnovsky, *Avicenna's Metaphysics*, 121, n. 12 as a compressed formulation of the same definition of the soul provided in *Nafs*, I, 1); *Ilāhiyyāt*, IX, 2, 386.14–387.8 [454.86–455.5]. Examples outside the *Šifāʾ* are the passages from *Qānūn*, and *al-Maʿād al-aṣġar* (*Lesser Destination*) quoted below, and the psychological section of the *Mašriqiyyūn*, where Avicenna says that the soul is *kamāl awwal* without saying that it is a/his definition of the soul.
63 In the same perspective there has to be read the addition *in animali et vegetabili* that the Latin translators add in order to explain the absolute occurrence of *invenimus* (*naǧidu*), probably by echoing precisely *in hoc nostro mundo* (*fī ʿālaminā*), which occurs a few lines before.
64 One might suggest to define the soul *qua* related to the body and consider this definition to be distinct from that of the soul in itself. However, this would not be possible because this would be like defining *white man*.

lated in I, 1 a "putative definition". The advantage of reading *naǧidu* is that Avicenna would appear less committed to a definition that, though useful to narrowing down the scope of natural psychology, cannot be the basis of a comprehensive science of the soul. This remodeling and exegesis of Aristotle's definition of the soul, functional to Avicenna's project, seems to be validated by the aforementioned passage from the *De anima.*[65] In this manner Avicenna manages to provide the science of the soul with a unique subject, i.e. the sublunary soul grasped during its existence in our world, and related to matter and motion,[66] which guarantees the possibility of placing it in natural philosophy with full rights:[67] psychology, being a particular science, should investigate attributes and properties of the *thing* insofar it is *soul*, namely insofar as it is a relational entity, without directly tackling the issue of its quiddity, which should be assumed.

As for the interpretation of Avicenna's reference to the standard definition of the soul as a means to narrow down the focus of his investigation in *Nafs* by referring to the soul in its sublunary existence, further confirmation can be found in the *Qānūn*, and in the so-called *al-Maʿād al-aṣġar* (*Lesser Destination*). In the former, by contrasting the position held by philosophers with that held by physicians about the meaning of the term *nafs* (*soul*) and the adjective *nafsānī* (*psychic*), Avicenna explicitly maintains that, when philosophers employ the term *nafs* in referring to the terrestrial soul (*al-nafs al-arḍiyya*), they have in mind the perfection of a natural, organic body, namely an operational principle in bodies, from which the faculties and the corresponding activities derive.[68] What is more, in the latter, Avicenna – if he is to be considered the author of this work[69] – argues that there are several kinds of soul, some

65 See n. 54 above.

66 See *Nafs*, I, 1, 10.15 – 11.3 [26.24 – 27.34], and V, 5, 238.3 – 9 [132.17 – 23] quoted in Chapter 3.

67 On the kind of investigation that is up to a particular science, and on the fact that every science should assume the quiddity of their subject-matter, see Chapter 3.

68 See *Qānūn*, I, i, vi, 4, 127.27 – 29: "[...] when philosophers (*falāsifa*) said *soul* (*nafs*) [referring] to the terrestrial soul (*li-l-nafs al-arḍiyya*), they meant [by it] "perfection of a natural, organic body" (*kamāl ǧism ṭabīʿī ālī*), and had in mind the principle of each faculty itself from which motions and activities derive."

69 This treatise, written for one or a number of unspecified friends "of pure heart" (*ḫullaṣ*), is known in the manuscript tradition under a wide variety of titles, though it can now be safely identified as *Al-Maʿād* (*The Destination*), which al-Ǧūzǧānī says Avicenna wrote in Rayy while in the service of the Būyid Maǧd al-Dawla, that is, approximately in 404H/1013 – 4. Its relatively early date of composition is also clear from its style and occasional use of Greek rather than Arabic terminology. For the edition of this treatise, see *Aḥwāl al-nafs*, ed. A. F. al-Ahwānī, Dār iḥyāʾ al-kutub al-ʿarabiyya, Cairo 1371H/ 1952, 43 – 142. For the debate on the authenticity of this work see Gutas, *Avicenna and the Aristotelian Tradition*, 102 – 103; 477 – 479, and J. Michot, "Avicenne. *La Définition de l'âme.* Section I de l'*Épître des états de l'âme.* Traduction critique et lexique", in A. de Libera, A. Elamrani-Jamal, A. Galonnier eds., *Langages et philosophie. Hommage à Jean Jolivet*, Vrin, Paris 1997, 239 – 256, who consider the work authentic, even though they suggest two different dates of composition; and M. Sebti, "La question de l'authenticité de l'*Épître des états de l'âme* (*Risāla fī aḥwāl al-nafs*) d'Avicenne", *Studia graeco-*

separable and immortal, some inseparable and mortal, and that the definition of the soul as *first perfection* has to be taken as a formula referring exclusively to the terrestrial (*arḍiyya*) soul, namely to the vegetative, animal, and human soul existing in our world after having been emanated from above.[70] A similar claim, though not as explicitly stated as in the *Qānūn* and the *Maʿād aṣġar*, seems to emerge also from *Nafs*, I, 1, 13.12 [32.89–90]: "This definition [of the soul] pertains only to the soul existing in what is composed (*hāḏā l-ḥadd innamā huwa li-l-nafs al-mawǧūda li-l-murakkabāt* [*haec definitio non est nisi animae quae est in compositis*])". Furthermore, in *Nafs* Avicenna qualifies the soul of those having the nutritive faculty, and of those having, in addition to this, also the sense of touch, as *terrestrial* (*arḍiyya*, *Nafs*, II, 3, 67.9; 12 [*terrena*, 130.83; 131.88]): these two faculties univocally identify the two classes to which all sublunary animated beings belong, namely those of plants and animals.

In *Nafs*, I, 1 Avicenna establishes the existence (*iṯbāt*) of the soul insofar as it is the principle of activities in bodies by means of an *a posteriori* demonstration. The soul is thus named *perfection* (*kamāl*), a notion capable of encompassing both inseparable and separable entities, and is referred to by the standard Aristotelian definition of the soul, a catch-all formula for all sublunary souls. The maximum that we get from *Nafs*, I, 1 is, therefore, the ascertainment of the existence of the soul *qua* operational principle, which represents the characteristic of the *thing* (*šayʾ*) called *soul* (*nafs*) that psychology as a special science belonging to natural philosophy is called to investigate. The ascertainment of its essence, by contrast, is deferred to another investigation. The transition from the inquiry into the existence of the soul as a *relational* entity to inquiry into its essence is marked by the *Flying Man* argument, though its conclusion about the essence of the human soul is negative.[71]

It is only in *Nafs*, I, 3 that Avicenna presents his own position. As we have seen in Chapter 3, there he hints at the substantiality of the soul *in itself*, by resuming and refining the conclusion of the *Flying Man* experiment,[72] and demonstrates that the *soul of* sublunary beings is a substance insofar as it is form.[73] Once the substantiality of the soul *in itself* has been hinted at, and that of the *soul of* has been duly ascertained, Avicenna recalls the term *kamāl* (*perfection*), which in *Nafs*, I, 1 has been used to refer to the soul with no reference to its essence, and concludes that, when it is referred to the soul, *kamāl* always designates a substance, not an accident: "Consequently, when the soul is the perfection of a subject, that subject is rendered subsistent by it, and it (*sc.* the perfection) is also what renders perfect the species and makes it. [(...)] The soul, therefore, is not among the accidents through which the spe-

arabica, 2, 2012, 331–354, who does not consider the work authentic. The passage from the *Qānūn* that I have quoted above can be considered a new datum in support of the authenticity of the work.

70 See *al-Maʿād al-aṣġar*, 1, 56.2–3.

71 We have already explained this in Chapter 3.

72 See *Nafs*, I, 3, 27.15–19 [58.23–28]. The *a posteriori* demonstration of the substantiality of the soul *in itself* will be provided in *Nafs*, V, 2. See Chapter 3.

73 See *Nafs*, I, 3, 29.6–8 [60.59–61].

cies do not differ, and which do not enter the constitution of the subject. The soul is, then, perfection as substance, not as accident,[74] but it does not necessarily follow from this that perfection is either separable or inseparable. For not every substance is separable. For neither is matter separable, nor is form, but you have already learned that things are this way (I, 3, 32.15–33.2 [66.41–67.49])".

Going beyond the dialectical detour of *Nafs*, I, 1 (and the doxographical survey of *Nafs*, I, 2),[75] in *Nafs*, I, 3 Avicenna founds the application of the term *kamāl* to the soul (*of* and also, with respect to the opening lines of the chapter, *in itself*) on the quidditative level: *kamāl* passes then from designating the soul insofar as it has a relation (*iḍāfa*) to the body (operational level) to designate it insofar as it is a substance (ontological level). This could then be considered Avicenna's own definition of the soul: the soul is not a substance because it is a perfection; rather, the soul is a perfection as substance. Its being perfection as substance results in its being the causal principle of activities. In doing so, he also succeeds in unifying the notion of *kamāl:* when applied to the soul, it always refers to a substance, regardless of its being an instance of separable or inseparable perfection or, what amounts to the same thing, of a self-subsistent substance or a substantial form. It is noteworthy that here any reference to the distinction between first and second perfection disappears: a further confirmation of the fact that the definition of the soul as first perfection provided in *Nafs*, I, 1 was not Avicenna's. Furthermore, on a more general level, Avicenna manages to provide the science of the soul with a proper, unitary place in natural philosophy: for it investigates the sublunary soul *qua* principle and cause of activities in bodies, and provides a glimpse of its essence.[76]

Which Body for which Soul? Reception (*qubūl*) vs. Relation (*nisba*)

That Avicenna shifts the focus of his investigation from the essence and the definition of the soul to the faculties ensuing from it is apparent from the last sentence of *Nafs*, I, 3: "Let us now indicate in a concise way the faculties of the soul and

74 Reading *ka-l-ǧawhar lā ka-l-ʿaraḍ* as attested in mss. ABDFG in Rahman's edition.

75 *Nafs*, I, 2 contains a doxography of what the ancients have said about the soul by classifying their opinions in four main groups: (i) the group of those who have considered the soul as the principle of movement; (ii) the group of those who have considered the soul as the principle of knowledge; (iii) the group of those who have considered the soul as the principle of both movement and knowledge; (iv) the group of those who have considered the soul as a general principle of life.

76 For Avicenna's reference to the sublunary soul as the cause (*ʿilla*, *causa*) of actual existence and organization of plants and animals, see *Nafs*, I, 3, 28.3; 6 [58.36; 59.38]. In this connection, the major difficulty with Wisnovsky's interpretation, is that Wisnovsky seems to believe that *Nafs*, I, 1 contains Avicenna's positive account and, consequently, he tries to reconcile the two parts of the chapter (notably the distinction between form and perfection, and that between first and second perfection) within an overall theoretical framework in which the essential role played by *Nafs*, I, 3 is completely disregarded.

their activities and then we will submit them to a close scrutiny (*bi-l-istiqṣā'*)" (*Nafs*, I, 3, 33.3–4 [67.49–51]). This change of focus is very similar to that of *De anima*, II, 2, where Aristotle moves with a fresh start from investigating what is clearer in itself (the soul) to investigating what is clearer and more familiar to us (the faculties of the soul and their activities) as a better way to get knowledge of what is clearer in itself.[77] Avicenna's philosophical psychology turns then out to be a faculty psychology like Aristotle's. This shift is confirmed by the subsequent chapters of the first treatise, by which the theoretical framework of Avicenna's psychology is brought to completion: I, 4 offers the criterion to distinguish the main faculties of the soul; and I, 5 provides a survey of all the psychic faculties (and their activities) that will be treated in this writing.

Starting from the differences observable in the psychic activities, in *Nafs*, I, 4 Avicenna wonders whether every activity needs a distinct faculty responsible exclusively for it. His answer is that one single faculty is in itself principle for one single activity. Besides its primary activity, a faculty can be also responsible for other activities, which derive from the primary one like branches (*ka-l-furū'*, *quasi rami*). That faculty will be then a principle also for them, but derivatively. Likewise, a faculty which is primarily responsible for a certain activity might need another faculty to perform its activity before this faculty is able to perform its own activity.[78] Three main groups of psychic activities are then singled out, for which different faculties are responsible: "We now say that the primary divisions of the activities of the soul are three: i) the activities that animals and plants share, like nutrition, nurturing, and reproduction; ii) the activities that animals, or most of them, share, but in which plants take no part, like sensation, imaginative faculty, and voluntary motion; and iii) the activities that are peculiar to human beings, like conceptualization of intelligibles, invention of arts, deliberation about generable and corruptible things, and the distinction between good and bad" (*Nafs*, I, 4, 37.13–17 [76.58–65]).

The conclusion of I, 4 chimes with the opening lines of I, 5: "Let us now enumerate the faculties of the soul by way of convention (*'alà sabīl al-waḍ'* [*quasi ponendo*]); then we shall engage in the clarification of the state of every faculty (*ṯumma li-naštaġil bi-bayān ḥāl kull quwwa* [*deinde procedemus ad declarandum unamquamque illarum* (*sc. virium*)]). We say, thus, that the psychic faculties are divided, according

77 See *De an.*, II, 2, 413 a11–13: Ἐπεὶ δ' ἐκ τῶν ἀσαφῶν μὲν φανερωτέρων δὲ γίνεται τὸ σαφὲς καὶ κατὰ τὸν λόγον γνωριμώτερον, πειρατέον πάλιν οὕτω γ'ἐπελθεῖν περὶ αὐτῆς. See also *Phys.*, I, 1, 184 a16–18: πέφυκε δὲ ἐκ τῶν γνωριμωτέρων ἡμῖν ἡ ὁδὸς καὶ σαφεστέρων ἐπὶ τὰ σαφέστερα τῇ φύσει καὶ γνωριμώτερα· οὐ γὰρ ταὐτὰ ἡμῖν τε γνώριμα καὶ ἁπλῶς.

78 See *Nafs*, I, 4, 35.18–37.12 [72.21–75.57]. An example of the first case is imaginative faculty: it primarily perceives forms abstracted from matter, but not from material appurtenances. These abstracted forms happen to be a certain color, or taste, or sound, or magnitude and, thus, the imaginative faculty is also the principle of their perception as color, taste, sound or magnitude, but only derivatively. An example of the second case is the locomotive faculty that, in order to perform its activity, needs the imaginative or intellective faculty and the desiderative faculty each to perform their own activity first.

to the primary division, into three parts" (39.13–14 [79.3–5]). The three main divisions of psychic faculties correspond to the three kinds of soul that are traditionally associated with them, namely i) vegetative soul (*nafs nabātiyya, anima vegetabilis*); ii) animal soul (*nafs ḥayawāniyya, anima vitalis vel sensibilis*);[79] iii) human soul (*nafs insāniyya, anima humana*).

Though abiding by the established tradition[80] of enumerating and then presenting the psychic faculties instead of the souls themselves, Avicenna also envisages the possibility of dealing with the souls themselves, not with the psychic faculties, by focusing on the arrangement of souls according to their degree of perfection, and by making the lower soul a genus for the higher.[81] This would result in a close scrutiny (*istiqṣā'*)[82] of what the soul, be it vegetative, animal, or human, is. This possibility, however, is not actualized, since the purpose that Avicenna explicitly assigns to psychology *qua* part of natural philosophy is to treat the soul as operational principle of activities observable in bodies by focusing on its faculties, as Aristotle did.[83] For this reason, that is, to stress the focus of the investigation in the *Nafs*, at the be-

---

79 On the double translation of *ḥayawāniyya*, see Alpina, "Is Nutrition a Sufficient Condition for Life?".

80 Here Avicenna's use of the term *'āda* (*usum, custom*, 40.4 [80.17]) to introduce the customary practice of focusing on the psychic faculties instead of on the souls themselves, echoes the beginning of the chapter where he says that the enumeration of the psychic faculties he is going to provide is "by way of convention" (*'alà sabīl al-waḍ'*, *quasi ponendo*, 39.13 [79.3]).

81 See *Nafs*, I, 5, 40.4–13 [80.17–81.28]: "If there were not [such a] custom, it would be best to make every [perfection coming] first a condition that is mentioned in the description of the following [perfection], if we want to describe the soul, not the psychic faculty belonging to the soul in accordance with the activity for which it is responsible. For *perfection* is included in the definition of the soul, not in the definition of the faculty of the soul. You will learn the difference between the animal soul and the faculty of perception and of setting in motion, and the difference between the rational soul and the faculty concerning the aforementioned things with respect to discernment, etc. If you want a close scrutiny, the right thing [to do] would be to make the vegetative [soul] a genus for the animal [soul], and the animal [soul] a genus for the human [soul], and to include the more general in the definition of the more specific. However, if you take into consideration the souls insofar as they have specific faculties in their animality and in their humanity, then you may be satisfied with what we have mentioned (*sc.* the traditional tripartition mentioned at 39.14)". As has been noted in Chapter 3, n. 35, here the term *genus* needs not be taken in the technical sense so as to imply that for Avicenna souls can be arranged according to genera and species. Here Avicenna speaks of including the lower instance of soul as a condition (*šarṭ*) in the description (*rasm*) of the higher instance of soul, implicitly excluding that this procedure can result in a definition: through it we can only describe (*rasama*) the soul, precisely because there cannot be a proper definition of what has no genus internally subdivided into species.

82 It is noteworthy that the term *istiqṣā'* has been used at the end of *Nafs*, I, 3 to refer to the subsequent investigation of the psychic faculties, not that of the instances of soul.

83 The primacy granted to faculties and their activities over the soul itself in the psychological investigation echoes *De an.*, I, 1, 402 b9–16; and II, 4, 415 a14–22, where Aristotle maintains that the investigation of the correlative objects must come first, and then that of the activities and the parts of the soul responsible for them must follow.

ginning of chapter I, 5 the vegetative, the animal, and the human soul are referred to as *first perfection* (39, 15, 18; 40, 2).

The choice of focusing on the faculties of the soul instead of on the souls undeniably provides psychology with a strong unity. At the same time, however, it unavoidably contributes to disclosing the peculiarities of the different instances of soul from which these faculties ensue and, more importantly, the distinctiveness of the human rational soul with respect to all the other instances of soul (the *specific orientation* of Avicenna's psychology). As we have seen in the previous chapter, this distinctiveness, which concerns the relation of the human rational soul to its own body, is hinted at through the whole *Nafs* (I, 1; I, 3; I, 4; II, 1; IV, 4)[84] and demonstratively shown in *Nafs*, V, 2, where the theoretical framework of *Nafs*, I is supplemented in order to ground the treatment of intellection. Nonetheless, in order to keep the investigation of the psychic faculties within a unitary theoretical framework (the soul as the operational principle of activities in bodies), in *Nafs*, V Avicenna has to account for the essential relation of the soul, especially of the human rational soul, to the body. This necessity results in the specific inquiry into the issue of the human soul's embodiment, which includes two sub-issues: (i) the issue of the individuation of the soul and of the essential unity of the human being, and (ii) the issue of its individual immortality.

Avicenna hints for the first time at the relation of the human rational soul to the body at the very end of *Nafs*, V, 2, probably in order to introduce the topic of the subsequent chapter and to stress the nature of the investigation of the soul in psychology: "It has already become evident from the fundamental principles that we have established, that the [human] soul is not impressed in the body, nor subsists through it. Therefore, the fact that the soul is peculiar to the body must be by a way that requires a particular configuration in the soul, which pulls [it] to occupy itself with guiding the particular body, due to an essential providence peculiar to it (*sc.* to the body) (*fa-yağibu an yakūna iḫtiṣāṣuhā bihī ʿalà sabīl muqtaḍà hay'a fīhā ğuz'iyya ğāḏiba ilà l-ištiġāl bi-siyāsat al-badan al-ğuz'ī li-ʿināya ḏātiyya muḫtaṣṣa bihī*). According to this [configuration] the soul becomes as it is together with the existence of its body, which is characterized by its [own] configuration and temperament" (*Nafs*, V, 2, 221.9–13 [101.87–93]).[85]

Since the fact that the human soul is not impressed in the body nor subsists through it has been demonstrated but, at the same time, that it exists together with a body is evident, Avicenna concludes that the cause of the body-soul relationship or, to be precise, of the fact that a certain soul is peculiar to a certain body (*iḫtiṣāṣ*) must be in the soul. This cause turns out to be a configuration (*hay'a*), internal to the soul, which pulls it into taking care of a particular body, thus meeting a providential order. Although here the issue of the body-soul relationship is only sketch-

84 See Chapter 3 in general and, in particular, the texts quoted in n. 78.

85 Cf. *Ilāhiyyāt*, IX, 7, 430.12–13 [518.25–27]. On this passage, see Chapter 3, n. 100.

ed,[86] the main aspect of Avicenna's position is clearly outlined: the body-soul relationship cannot be random. The configuration belonging to the soul incites it to take care *not of whatever* body, but *of its own particular* body, to which its caring and guiding activity is essentially directed in virtue of an essential providence proper to the body.

Nafs, V, 3 is mainly devoted to the issue of the human soul's need for the relationship with the body. There Avicenna argues for the human soul's two-level need for such a relationship: at the *epistemological* level, it needs *a* body, namely a body of a certain kind (a human body) as an appropriate instrument[87] to achieve intellectual knowledge (222.16 – 223.10 [104.22 – 105.39]), whereas, at the *metaphysical* level, it needs *its own* body since it is said to be its principle of individuation (223.11 – 225.10 [105.40 – 109.90]).

The first argument shows that the human soul needs the body or, to be precise, the bodily perceptive faculties in order to get the principles of its intellectual activities, i.e. conceptualization (*taṣawwur*) and assent (*taṣdīq*). However, Avicenna adds, its need for the body is temporally limited: once it acquired the principles that trigger its intellectual activities, the soul returns to itself because the body becomes a hindrance that averts it from achieving its own perfection: "The human soul makes use of the body to attain these principles for conceptualization and assent. Once it attains them, it returns to itself. [(...)] This is something that happens at the beginning [of its activity], but less often thereafter. However, when the soul becomes perfect and strong, it performs absolutely singlehandedly its activities, while the sensitive faculties, the imaginative faculties, and the rest of the bodily faculties avert it from its activity, as [for example] a man may need a riding animal and [other] instruments to reach by means of them some destination but, when he arrives there, and one of [those] means happens to impede him from setting them aside, the means that brought [him to the destination] become themselves an impediment" (*Nafs*, V, 3, 222.16 – 223.10 [104.22 – 105.39]). Avicenna seems then to consider the body-soul relationship instrumental, as the simile of the riding animal seems to suggest. For, just as a man may need a riding animal (*dābba*, *iumentum*)[88] in order to reach a certain destination but, once the destination is reached, the riding animal becomes a hindrance to get rid of in order to accomplish other activities, so the human soul needs the body in order to get the principles of its intellectual activities but, once it has acquired them, the body becomes a hindrance to get rid of in order

86 See also *Nafs*, V, 3, 226.11 – 12 [111.20 – 22]; and V, 4, 234.3 – 6 [125.17 – 19]. In both passages Avicenna seems to refer back to *Nafs*, V, 2.

87 On the fact that the soul needs an appropriate substrate in order to come into being, see *Ilāhiyyāt*, IV, 2.

88 For a presentation of *dābba* as Qur'anic term, see S. Tlili, *Animals in the Qur'an*, Cambridge University Press, Cambridge 2012, 71.

for the soul to achieve its own perfection.[89] Furthermore, the simile of the riding animal also tells us something more about the kind of body that the human soul needs: just as a man needs whatever riding animal, be it a horse, a mule, or a donkey, to reach a certain destination, the only proviso being that the animal is such that it can be ridden, so the human soul's need for a body is met not by one particular body but, rather, by whatever body belonging to the human species, which is thus capable of performing specific activities like, for instance, external and internal perception, essential for intellection.[90] The conclusion of this first argument is therefore that the relationship between the human soul and its body is instrumental and, to some extent, casual. This conclusion might also leave room for souls' transmigration, a position which Avicenna opposes at the end of *Nafs*, V, 4. As a consequence, the fact that whatever human body meets the human rational soul's epistemological need for the body challenges the essential unity of the human being.

The second argument is, therefore, precisely designed to strengthen the body-soul relationship and renders it essential by showing that the human soul has a *metaphysical* need for a specific human body in order to be individuated. The line of reasoning is the following: human souls do not exist individually separate from bodies, which afterwards they begin to animate. Souls are one in species and in notion. If they were to exist before the existence of their bodies, they would be one, because what is one in species and notion (later on Avicenna says "in quiddity and form") cannot be multiplied except by matter and material appurtenances like place, time, etc. Therefore, souls need a principle of individuation, which begins to exist together with its specific soul and is suitable for the temporal origination of that soul, that is, the body: "[Souls] do not differ from one another in quiddity and form, because their form is one. Therefore, they differ from one another only with respect to what receives the quiddity or to that to which the quiddity is properly related *(min ǧiha qābil al-māhiyya aw al-mansūb ilayhi l-māhiyya bi-l-iḫtiṣāṣ)*, and this is the body. If the soul can exist with there being no body, then one soul cannot differ in number from another soul. This is absolute in every thing: for the multiplication of things that in themselves are only [formal] notions, while their being species has been already multiplied through their individuals, is only either due to things that bear them, receive them, and are affected by them, or due to a certain relation to them and their times (*bi-l-ḥawāmil wa-l-qawābil wa-l-munfaʿilāt ʿanhā aw bi-nisba mā ilayhā wa-ilà azminatihā faqaṭ*)" (*Nafs*, V, 3, 223.18 – 224.6 [106.49 – 58]).

---

89 See *Nafs*, V, 5, 237.16 – 19 [131.7 – 12]: "The inability of the intellect to conceptualize things that are at the highest degree of intelligibility and abstraction from matter is neither due to something [that is] in those things themselves, nor to something [that is] in the natural disposition of the intellect; rather, [the inability of the intellect] is due to the fact that the soul is occupied in the body with the body and, then, it needs the body in many things; therefore, the body removes the soul from the most excellent of its perfections".

90 More on this aspect in Chapter 5.

A noteworthy aspect of the quoted passage is that, in arguing for the body as the principle that multiplies souls, which are one in species, Avicenna seems to be particularly careful in acknowledging the peculiarities of the various instances of soul. Assigning to the body the role of principle of individuation of the soul can be potentially problematic because the main conclusion of *Nafs*, V, 2 (reiterated in V, 3–4) is that the human rational soul is not impressed in bodily matter nor subsists through it.[91] Therefore, in saying that the body is the principle of individuation of the soul, Avicenna has to account for the peculiar way in which the body performs its individuating function in the case of the human rational soul, which is the main focus of the discourse of *Nafs*, V, 2–4.

For this reason, the body *qua* principle of multiplication of souls is qualified as either "what receives the quiddity" or "that to which the quiddity is properly related". Shortly afterwards Avicenna adds that the multiplicity of what is one in species can depend on either "the things that bear them, receive them, and are affected by them" or "a certain relation to them (*sc.* the bearers and recipients of what is one in species)" and "their times (*sc.* the bearers and recipients' temporal origination)". Therefore, here Avicenna seems to acknowledge two ways in which what is one in species can be multiplied by the body: i) by way of *reception* (*qubūl*), which is proper to forms inhering in matter, like vegetative and animal souls, or ii) by way of *relation* (*nisba*), which is proper to the souls that are only related to the body in order to perform their activities, like human rational souls, the steersman of the ship, and the king of the city.

Avicenna, however, needs to explain more clearly how the soul is individuated. In order to do that, he refines what he has previously said about the way in which the body acts on *its* soul. Each body is said to individuate its soul through certain states and concomitant accidents that are associated exclusively with it but are not essential to it *qua* soul (otherwise, they would be common to all souls), and in turn each soul has in itself a natural inclination to take care of that particular body with which it begins to exist: "To express it differently, we say: these souls are individuated as one soul out of the whole of their species only through some states attached to them (*bi-aḥwāl talḥaquhā*), but not necessarily following them insofar as they are soul (otherwise they would be shared by all souls), and through the concomitant accidents attached to them (*al-aʿrāḍ al-lāḥiqa*) from some beginning that is unquestionably temporal, because they follow a cause that occurs to some of them but not to others. Thus, the individuation of souls is also something that comes into being. Hence, souls are not pre-eternal, and do not perish, but their origination occurs together with a body. It is, therefore, true that souls come into being as there comes into being a bodily matter which is suitable to be used by the soul. The body coming into being is their kingdom and their instrument, whereas in the substance of the soul coming into being together with a certain body – that body re-

91 See the passages quoted in n. 86 above.

quires [its] soul's coming into being from the first principles[92] – there is the configuration of a natural inclination (*hay'a nizāʿ ṭabīʿī*) to occupy itself with it, to use it, to take care of its states, and to be attracted to it, [a configuration] which is proper to that soul and averts it from all other bodies. It is, therefore, inevitable that, when [the soul] is found individuated, the principle of its individuation attaches to it something in terms of configurations by means of which it is determined as an individual; those configurations are required in order for this body to be peculiar to that soul and [for] adequacy of suitability between one of the two to the other, even though this state and this relationship are hidden to us; and, the principles of the perfection are expected for the soul by means of it, that is, its own body" (*Nafs*, V, 3, 224.15 – 225.10 [107.70 – 109.90]).

As a result, this second argument accounts for a body-soul relationship stronger than that emerging from the first argument: the human soul is individuated by its specific body to which it is essentially related (and in which it is not received like form in matter). The body is then not a hindrance to the soul's activity; rather, through it, the soul attains the principles of its self-perfection.[93]

However, an objection might be raised against the claim that the body is the principle of the soul's individuation: what guarantees the human soul's individuation after the severance from its body? Avicenna lists three scenarios that, according to a potential opponent, might occur when souls separate from their bodies: i) souls corrupt; ii) souls become one; iii) souls remain multiplied. Avicenna favoured the last scenario, but he has to explain how the bodily matter can still act as a principle of individuation of the soul once it is separated from it.[94]

Avicenna's concise answer to this objection is "the soul's individual history". The human rational soul is individuated by means of certain states and concomitants: the specific bodily matter in which it dwells throughout its sublunary existence, the exact time of its origination, and the configuration belonging to it in virtue of its specific body. Once the soul separates from its body, it is capable of retaining those individualizing aspects that occurred to it during its sublunary history and, consequently, of retaining the individuality that depends on them: "We reply that after the souls' separation from the bodies, each soul would unquestionably exist as an isolated essence (*ḏāt munfarida*) because of the difference of their matters that had been, because of the difference of the times of their origination, and because of the difference of the configurations belonging to them in accordance with their different bodies (*bi-ḫtilāf mawāddihā llatī kānat wa-bi-ḫtilāf azmina ḥudūṯihā*

92 A parallel passage is *Nafs*, V, 4, 228.19 – 229.5 [115.77 – 116.88]. More on this passage *infra*. It is noteworthy that the simile of the body-kingdom seems to refer back to the simile of the king of the city mentioned by Avicenna in *Nafs*, I, 1 as an example of separable perfection.

93 Avicenna is probably thinking of the human soul's attainment of its first perfection, namely the intellectual contact with the supernal world, through acquisition of the principle of intellectual activity by means of the bodily faculties.

94 *Nafs*, V, 3, 225.10 – 13 [109.91 – 95].

wa-ḫtilāf hay'ātihā llatī lahā bi-ḥasab abdānihā l-muḫtalifa lā maḥālata)" (*Nafs*, V, 3, 225.14 – 17 [109.96 – 110.1]).

Avicenna's solution, however, is not completely satisfactory because it neglects to explain how the human rational soul, whose incorporeal nature has already been proved, could retain those individualizing aspects belonging to it only in virtue of its relationship with the body once the body-soul relationship is severed. What is more, it is hard to see how the human rational soul can retain the memory of its past relationship with the body after death, because memory is a bodily faculty, and consequently it can perform its activity only by means of a specific part of the brain, which however is no longer related to the soul.[95] Therefore, perhaps in order to contain the problems arising from his position, Avicenna concludes the chapter by saying that the thing through which the human soul is individuated is not its being impressed in matter; rather, its individuation depends on a certain configuration, or a certain power, or a certain immaterial accident, or the sum of them, which belong to the soul and cumulatively individuate it, even though we do not know what they are exactly: "Soul is, therefore, not one. It is many in number, while its species is one, and it comes into being, as we have shown. Then, there is no doubt that it is individuated by something, and that this something in the human soul is not its being impressed in matter (the falsehood of saying this has been known, *sc. Nafs*, V, 2); rather, that something belonging to the soul is a certain configuration, a certain power, a certain spiritual accident, or the sum of them that individuates it through their combination, even if we do not know what they are (*hay'a min al-hay'āt wa-quwwa min al-quwà wa-ʿaraḍ min al-aʿrāḍ al-rūḥāniyya aw ǧumla minhā tušaḫḫiṣuhā bi-ǧtimāʿihā wa-in ǧahilnāhā*)" (*Nafs*, V, 3, 226.9 – 14 [111.19 – 25]).

The undetermined notion of *hay'a* (*configuration*, or *disposition*) seems to be crucial to understand how the human rational soul is individualized without being impressed in bodily matter. In the concluding lines of the chapter Avicenna claims that what is certain is that, once the soul comes into being together with the coming into being of a certain bodily temperament, it acquires an individualizing *hay'a*. This *hay'a* might concern the rational activities and affections peculiar to a certain soul, but not to another; or the acquired configuration, namely the intellect in actuality, which peculiarly distinguishes one soul; or the soul's awareness of its essence, which is proper to it, and does not belong to any other soul; or the moral dispositions that a certain soul has in virtue of its bodily faculties. All these examples refer to individualizing characteristics occurring to the soul once it is created together with its disposed bodily matter. Avicenna seems to deliberately leave these characteristics undetermined: all or some of them are hidden to us; however, they undoubtedly follow the soul from the moment it comes into being onwards.[96] Avicenna's strategy in

---

95 This has been argued by Peter Adamson in his article "Correcting Plotinus", in part. 73 – 74. In this connection, see *Ilāhiyyāt*, IX, 7, 431.12 – 432.12 [519.57 – 520.87] quoted in Chapter 3, n. 118. For a thorough study of memory in Avicenna, see T. Alpina, "Retaining, Remembering, Recollecting".

96 *Nafs*, V, 3, 227.6 – 10 [112.38 – 113.43].

V, 3 seems to echo that used at the end of chapter V, 2: there, he attempted to limit the human soul's independence of the body by hinting at its essential relationship with it; here, by contrast, he attempts to limit its dependence on the body with respect to its individuation, by claiming that the soul's individuation does not depend on its being impressed in a bodily matter, but on some configuration belonging to the soul. Nonetheless, at the end of *Nafs*, V, 4, Avicenna explicitly highlights that the soul's coming into being together with a specific body is neither due to chance, nor to fortune (*wa-ẓahara min ḏālika anna hāḏā lā yakūna ʿalà sabīl al-ittifāq wa-l-baḫt*, 233.8–9 [124.99]).

It is precisely in *Nafs*, V, 4[97] that Avicenna definitely settles the question. Here, in tackling the issue of the human rational soul's individual immortality and arguing against souls' transmigration, Avicenna wonders whether some sort of dependence (*taʿalluq*) of the soul on the body is detectable. Avicenna's conclusion is that, in spite of its temporal origination (*ḥudūṯ*) with the body,[98] the human soul does not corrupt together with the corruption of the body because the human soul is not tied to it by any kind of dependence in existence, where the corruption of the latter entails the subsequent corruption of the former. "The dependence of the soul on the body is, therefore, not the dependence of what is caused on an essential cause, even though the temperament and the body are accidentally a cause for the soul. For, when the matter of a body suitable to be an instrument for the soul and a kingdom for it comes into being, the separate causes[99] bring about the particular soul (*aḥdaṯat al-ʿilal al-mufāriqa al-nafs al-ǧuzʾiyya* [*tunc causae separatae quae solent dare unamquamque animam, creant animam*]), or [the particular soul] comes into being from them in this way. For, the origination of the soul without a specific cause – namely the origination of one [soul] and not of [another] one – is impossible. Nonetheless, it (*sc.* the origination of a soul without a specific cause) would prevent the occurrence of the numerical multiplicity of souls, because of what we have already shown (*sc.* in *Nafs*, V, 3); [also] because anything that comes to be after not being must be preceded by a matter, in which there is the preparedness to receive it or the preparedness to be related to it (*tahayyuʾ qubūlihī aw tahayyuʾ nisba ilayhi* [*sit apta recipere illud aut apta comparari ad illud*]), as became clear in other sciences (*sc. Samāʿ ṭabīʿī*, I, 2–3, and *Ilāhiyyāt*, IV, 2, 178.17–179.3, where Avicenna precisely refers to the case of the soul that needs a matter in order to come into being)" (*Nafs*, V, 4, 228.19–229.5 [115.77–116.88]).

---

97 For a study of *Nafs*, V, 4 and, in particular, of the way in which Avicenna accounts for the co-origination of the soul and the body, see S. N. Mousavian, S. H. S. Mostafavi, "Avicenna on the Origination of the Human Soul", *Oxford Studies in Medieval Philosophy*, 5, 2017, 41–86.

98 See P. Adamson, "Correcting Plotinus"; and T.-A. Druart, "The Human Soul's Individuation and Its Survival after the Body's Death: Avicenna on the Causal Relation between Body and Soul", *Arabic Sciences and Philosophy*, 10, 2000, 259–273.

99 Here Avicenna must have in mind the celestial intelligences. This could be also a specific reference to the so-called *Dator formarum*.

The body and its temperament are jointly a concomitant cause of the human soul's sublunary and, consequently, individual existence, whereas the soul's individual existence is essentially due to the separate causes (*al-ʿilal al-mufāriqa*), which bring about the particular soul.[100] Nonetheless, the separate causes are a necessary, but not sufficient condition for the soul's individual existence: a body suitable for that specific soul is also needed. Therefore the individual rational soul exists only if both conditions are satisfied, namely the causal activity of the separate causes which originate a particular soul and the presence of a suitable body which, acting as a concomitant cause, provides a substrate in which the soul is received or to which it is related (as in *Nafs*, V, 3 Avicenna acknowledges the distinctiveness of the human rational soul). As a result, the soul owes its individual existence to a self-subsistent essence, abstracted from matter and magnitudes, while it owes the time of its existence, that is, the determination of its temporal origination in the sublunary world, to the body: "What bestows the existence of the soul is something which is neither a body, nor a faculty in a body; rather, it is unquestionably something self-subsisting, free from matters and magnitudes. Then, since the existence of the soul is from that thing, whereas from the body there is attained only the moment (*waqt* [*debitum horae*]) in which it deserves to exist, then the soul does not have a dependence in its own existence on the body, nor is the body a cause for it, unless accidentally" (*Nafs*, V. 4, 229.17–230.2 [118.3–8]).

In addition to that, the human soul is said to be a simple substance (*ǧawhar basīṭ*),[101] separable in essence, in which, unlike composite substances, the actuality to remain in existence is not combined with the potentiality to corrupt. In *Nafs*, V, 4 in the case of human soul we are then in the presence of the suspension of Aristotelian hylomorphism: although the human soul comes into existence together with the body, which is somehow responsible for its individuation, it does not corrupt together with the corruption of the body and does not lose its individuality after its separation from it. However, this suspension is not surprising: as we have said at the beginning, Avicenna's investigation of the human soul *in itself* in its entirety, though somehow arising from the Aristotelian text, goes far beyond the purposes of Aristotle's psychology and, consequently, there cannot be applied to it a model that was not elaborated to account for that kind of soul.

---

100 On the causal role played by the separate, celestial causes on the sublunary world in Avicenna's emanative cosmology with a specific focus on the issue of theodicy, see M. Rashed, "Théodicée et approximation: Avicenne", *Arabic Sciences and Philosophy*, 10, 2000, 223–257, in part. 226–233.
101 On the soul as a simple substance, see al-Kindī in Chapter 2.

Conclusion on a Tightrope

In the *Nafs* Avicenna, like a tightrope walker, carefully moves between two extremes variously referred to: form (*ṣūra*) and perfection (*kamāl*); reception (*qubūl*) and relation (*nisba*); being inseparable (*ġayr mufāriq*) and being separable (*mufāriq*).

These extremes, taken individually, represent the cornerstone of the main interpretations of Aristotle's *De anima* and, at the same time, of the most influential doctrines about the soul. This is not a novelty: as we have seen in Chapter 2, the difference between the aforementioned extremes is the basic difference between Aristotle, who deals with the soul in its entirety *qua* formal principle of all instances of sublunary life, and his predecessors (Plato and his followers among others), who focused almost exclusively on the human soul.

Avicenna's plan is more challenging: he wants to keep both extremes together in a unitary framework, that is, he wants to account for the soul *qua* principle of all instances of sublunary life while acknowledging the distinctiveness of the human rational soul which, unlike other souls, is a self-subsisting substance, capable of surviving severance from its body. Like a tightrope walker or a man running on a branch over an abyss[102] who has to focus firmly on his goal in order not to fall and to make his body move along the rope (or the branch), Avicenna has to concentrate on the ultimate goal of his psychological investigation, that is, making the soul a unitary subject-matter investigated within a unitary science, to bridge the gap between the two extremes.

In doing this, Avicenna critically revises the theoretical tools put in place by his predecessors to account for the soul (various terms, and a standard definition). Among others, Avicenna concentrates on Philoponus, who is an extraordinary example of a subtle exegete of the Aristotelian text in accordance with new agendas (mainly the separability of the human soul).[103] Following his legacy, in *Nafs*, I, 1 Avi-

---

102 For the passage in which Avicenna refers to a man running on a branch, see *Nafs*, IV, 4, 200.1–6 [64.25–30].

103 On the heavy impact of Philoponus *qua* commentator of Aristotle's *De anima* on Avicenna, see Wisnovsky, *Avicenna's Metaphysics*, 113–114: "What I mean is that important Neoplatonic ideas found their way to thinkers such as Avicenna on board a large number of different vehicles, particularly the Aristotle-commentaries by philosophers such as Syrianus, Ammonius, Philoponus, Simplicius and Olympiodorus (the Arabic translations of which – though only a few now appear to be extant – are attested to in the catalogues of Ibn an-Nadīm, Ibn al-Qifṭī and Ibn Abī Uṣaybiʿa); and that these Neoplatonic ideas were not all stuffed into the two or three mislabeled vehicles which we do have at hand: the Plotinian *Theology of Aristotle*, the Proclean *Liber de causis* and the works of pseudo-Alexander. The fact that Avicenna received important elements of Aristotelianism already Neoplatonized in the commentaries, is particularly important given how uncomfortable he seems to have been with many of the ideas expressed in the *Uthūlūjiyā*. This will become most apparent later on in this chapter, where I shall show that Avicenna's position on the soul and its relationship with the body owes much more to the Aristotle-commentator Philoponus than it does to Plotinus or Proclus".

cenna uses the notion of *perfection* to refer to the soul: unlike *form*, it is broad enough to encompass also separable entities, and allows him to focus on the soul only as operational principle of activities, with no reference to its quiddity. *Nafs*, I, 1, however, offers only a dialectical discussion on a nonessential characteristic of the soul (its being an operational principle *qua* perfection) that does not provide the science with a strong unity. Avicenna has to devote *Nafs*, I, 3 to founding the application of the term *perfection* to the soul on the quidditative level. Once he has demonstrated that the soul is a substance independently of its being perfection, the term *kamāl* passes from designating the soul insofar as it has a relation to the body (operational level) to unequivocally designating it insofar as it is a substance (ontological level). However, the theoretical framework provided in *Nafs*, I, 1–3 is not sufficient to account for the distinctiveness of the human rational soul and its activity, which cursorily emerged at the end of I, 1 and the beginning of I, 3 (see Chapter 3). For this reason, in *Nafs*, V, 2–4 Avicenna supplements it with a thorough inquiry into the thorny issue of human soul's embodiment.

Chapter Five

Activity: A Clue to the Twofold Nature of the Human Soul

Introduction

Avicenna devotes chapters V, 5 and 6 to his doctrine of human intellection. These are the last chapters of *Nafs* devoted to specific faculties of the soul, since V, 7 shows that the soul is the unitary bond (*ribāṭ*) of all psychic faculties, and V, 8 deals with pneuma/spirit (*rūḥ*) as the bodily vehicle of the soul and its faculties.

The theoretical faculty (*quwwa naẓariyya*), which is also called theoretical intellect (*ʿaql naẓarī*), and the activity for which it is responsible, that is, intellectual contemplation (*naẓar*), deserve particular attention for two reasons. Firstly, as we have said in Chapter 3, this faculty seems to be considered in two different though complementary respects, which justify its having a proper name, i.e. *ʿaql*: on the one hand, together with the practical intellect (*ʿaql ʿamalī*), it is one of the faculties peculiarly distinguishing the *soul of* human beings while it exists in the body (*Nafs*, I, 5; V, 1)[1] whereas, on the other hand, this faculty seems to identify with the human rational *soul in itself*, i.e. it is what survives after the severance of the soul's relation to the body, though the fulfilment of this possibility, i.e. the actual, independent, individual existence of the human rational soul considered in itself, is deferred to the afterlife (*Nafs*, V, 2; V, 5).[2] Secondly, as we have said in Chapter 4, this is the only faculty of the soul whose treatment requires a supplement to the theoretical framework provided in *Nafs*, I, 1–3. This supplement, which is provided in chapters V, 2–4 and is necessary to account for intellection, fully displays the distinctiveness of the essence of the human rational soul, which was hinted at at the end of *Nafs*, I, 1 and concisely at the beginning of I, 3: in order to perform its activity, and to survive individually the severance from its own body, the human rational soul "is in no way a body, nor subsists in a body, either as a faculty in it or as a form belonging to it" (*Nafs*, V, 2, 210.1).[3] Nonetheless, this soul is essentially related to its own body for both an epistemological need, i.e. for performing its intellectual activity, and a metaphysical need, i.e. for being individuated.

Avicenna's doctrine of human intellection is a perfect litmus test for verifying the conclusions of the previous chapters about the amphibious status of the human rational soul and, consequently, the intermediate status of psychology between natural philosophy and metaphysics. For, the process through which human beings acquire universal, intellectual forms is intrinsically related to the ontological status of the

1 For the relevant passages in chapters I, 5 and V, 1, see Chapter 3, n. 81.

2 For the relevant passages in chapters V, 2 and V, 5, see Chapter 3, § Grounding the Investigation of the Soul: Part 2.

3 See also the texts quoted in Chapter 4, n. 86, where Avicenna iterates this claim.

https://doi.org/10.1515/9783110706840-007

soul. It involves two opposite movements: a movement *downwards*, i.e. the human soul's examination of the particulars acquired through the lower perceptive faculties, which operate through the body, and its consequent abstraction of intellectual forms from those particulars; and a movement *upwards*, i.e. the contact of the human soul with the Active Intellect above it, and the consequent emanation of something[4] from it. These two movements, far from being incompatible, seem to account perfectly for, on the one hand, the soul's need for a relation to (not a reception in) the body, and on the other hand, its independence of it in performing its own activity. In *Nafs*, V, 2, Avicenna explicitly acknowledges the twofold aspect of the activity of the human soul, which is both (and primarily) active, and (only secondarily) receptive: "You will learn (*sc.* in *Nafs*, V, 5) that the rational soul's reception of many infinite things is a reception [occurring] after an active mode of acting" (216.14–15 [93.54–56]).

Abstraction & Emanation: Which One do You Side with?

Avicenna's noetics and, especially, the simultaneous presence of two (apparently) conflicting movements in the account of human intellection have consistently puzzled scholarship on Avicenna's thought. Here I will outline the more significant facets of this dilemma in the research. Generally speaking, a tendency to overcome the (apparent) conflict in Avicenna's account by *reducing* one movement to the other or by *downplaying* the role of one of them in order to understand Avicenna's model of human intellection can be detected in almost all contributions on this issue.

An article published by E. Gilson in 1929 can be considered the first contribution on this topic: although outdated, it deserves to be mentioned because it has influenced many subsequent interpreters. In his pioneering work, Gilson focuses on the Greek and Arabic antecedents (in the Latin translation) of Avicenna's doctrine of human intellection, especially on the post-Aristotelian tradition (Alexander of Aphrodisias and his teacher Aristocles) and its first reception in Arabic philosophy (al-Kindī and al-Fārābī); and on the Latin reception of Avicennism. The cornerstone of his interpretation is a form of *reductionism* of the movement of the soul *downwards* (abstraction) to its movement *upwards* (emanation). According to Gilson, *abstraction* is an activity belonging to the Active Intellect and refers in particular to the process through which it strips the material concomitants away from intellectual forms which then emanate from the Active Intellect upon the rational soul. Therefore, the rational soul is completely receptive to what flows from the Active Intellect: it has only to be prepared for this emanation through examination of imaginative particulars.[5] How-

4 I am deliberately keeping what is emanated from above vague.

5 See E. Gilson, "Les sources gréco-arabes de l'augustinisme avicennisant", *Archives d'Histoire Doctrinale et Littéraire du Moyen Age*, 5, 1930, 1–107, in part. 65: "L'oeuvre accomplie par l'Intelligence agente est précisément de dénuder la forme sensible de la matière et de tous les caractères qui en dépendent, pour l'imprimer dans l'intellect possible de l'âme raisonnable. C'est ce que l'on

ever, Gilson's interpretation is not limited to the exegesis of Avicenna's noetics; rather, it aims at proving the existence, in the Latin West, of a school of thought which he labels *augustinisme avicennisant*, which includes, for example, William of Auvergne, Roger Bacon, and John Peckham, and which conflates Augustine's doctrine of illumination as a means of achieving the truth and Avicenna's doctrine of emanation as a means of achieving universal concepts. This is done in order to solve the problem, which Aristotle left unsolved, as to how universal knowledge can be acquired if knowledge is obtained only by means of abstraction.[6] The main outcome of his interpretative effort has been to bestow on Avicenna's noetics a mystical vein that has been difficult to eradicate.[7] F. Rahman took the same interpretative line by arguing that Avicenna's language of abstraction is only a metaphor for emanation, a mere *façon de parler.*[8] H. Davidson developed Gilson's intuition about the connection between cosmology and epistemology[9] and identified the Active Intellect with the Giver of Forms and assigned to this celestial intelligence a twofold role: on the cosmological level, it is the eternal cause of the forms flowing into matter; on the epistemological level, it is the cause of human thought, with the aid of the lower fac-

---

nomme *l'abstraction.* [...] Ce qui se passe alors est simplement ceci: l'âme raisonnable considère les images qu'elle possède, elle les examine et les compare pour ainsi dire (*consideratio, cogitatio*) et ces mouvements la préparent à recevoir de l'Intelligence agente l'abstraction. Ainsi, dans la doctrine d'Avicenne, tout l'intelligible est reçu du dehors et toute abstraction est une émanation."

6 Gilson, "Les sources gréco-arabes", 102–107.

7 The mystical aspect of Avicenna's theory of knowledge is part of a more general and long-lasting tendency of a part of the scholarship on Avicenna's thought that, by misinterpreting the surviving part of Avicenna's *al-Mašriqiyyūn* or *al-Ḥikma al-mašriqiyya* (*The Easterners* or *Eastern Philosophy*) and the last sections of his *al-Išārāt wa-l-tanbīhāt* (*Pointers and Reminders*), maintains that Avicenna's true philosophy (or, better, wisdom) is a form of mysticism (A. F. Mehren) or illuminationism, i.e. an anticipation of the school of thought of which Suhrawardī may be considered the most famous representative (H. Corbin, S. H. Nasr). Dimitri Gutas has vehemently denied the mystical interpretation of Avicenna's thought; see D. Gutas, "Avicenna. Mysticism", in E. Yarshater ed., *Encyclopaedia Iranica*, vol. III, Routledge and Kegan Paul, London-Boston 1987, 79–83; id., *Avicenna and the Aristotelian Tradition*, 119–144; id., "Ibn Tufayl on Ibn Sīnā's *Eastern Philosophy*", *Oriens*, 34, 1994, 222–241; id., *"Avicenna's Eastern ("Oriental") Philosophy.* Nature, Contents, Transmission", *Arabic Sciences and Philosophy*, 10, 2000, 159–180; id., "The Study of Arabic Philosophy in the Twentieth Century. An Essay on the Historiography of Arabic Philosophy", *British Journal of Middle Eastern Studies*, 29, 2002, 5–25, in part. 9–10. For his denial of any mysticism in Avicenna's theory of knowledge, see D. Gutas, "Intellect without limits: the absence of mysticism in Avicenna", in M. C. Pacheco, J. F. Meirinhos eds., *Intellect et imagination dans la Philosophie médiévale. Actes du XIe Congrès International de Philosophie Médiévale de la Société Internationale pour l'Études de la Philosophie Médiévale (S.I.E.P.M.) – Porto, du 26 au 31 août 2002*, Brepols, Turnhout 2006, 351–372; id., "Imagination and transcendental knowledge in Avicenna", in J. E. Montgomery ed., *Arabic Theology, Arabic Philosophy. From the Many to the One: Essays in Celebration of Richard M. Frank*, Uitgeverij Peeters en Departement Oosterse Studies, Leuven-Paris-Dudley, MA 2006, 337–354.

8 See F. Rahman, *Prophecy in Islam: Philosophy and Orthodoxy*, Allen and Unwin, Chicago-London 1958, in part. 15. For another emanationist interpretation, see F. Jabre, "Le sens de l'abstraction chez Avicenne", *Mélanges de l'Université Saint-Joseph*, 50.1, 1984, 283–310.

9 Gilson, "Les sources gréco-arabes", 64.

ulties of the soul, which prepare the human intellect to receive intellectual forms from above. Therefore, by following the path traced by Gilson, Davidson reduced the human intellection to a form of emanation from an external and superior cause, i. e. the Active Intellect; accordingly, Davidson maintains that references to abstraction should not be taken literally.[10] D. Black and R. Taylor endorsed the same position.[11] Recently, however, R. Taylor, endorsing the conclusions of an article I published in 2014, whose main ideas are contained in this chapter,[12] switched from the emanationist to the abstractionist side of the debate.[13] Lastly, in an article that appeared in 2010, O. Lizzini exploited the concept of emanation in determining the epistemological status of Avicenna's psychology: in particular, by focusing on the ontological status of the human soul and transferring the concept of emanation from the epistemological level to the cosmological and metaphysical level, Lizzini tried to bring inquiry into the nature of the soul within an exclusively Neoplatonic, emanative framework.[14] But this is only one side of the scholarship on this topic.

---

10 H. A. Davidson, "Alfarabi and Avicenna on the Active Intellect", *Viator*, 3, 1972, 109 – 178; id., *Alfarabi, Avicenna and Averroes, on Intellect: Their Cosmologies, Theories of the Active Intellect, and Theories of the Human Intellect*, Oxford University Press, New York-Oxford 1992, in part. 74 – 126.

11 D. L. Black, "Avicenna on the Ontological and Epistemic Status of Fictional Beings", *Documenti e studi sulla tradizione filosofica medievale*, 8, 1997, 425 – 453, in part. 445: "Avicenna explicitly denies any causal influence of the imagination upon the intellect, that is, he denies the reality of abstraction as a cognitive process. The imagination functions at most as an occasion for the reception of an influx from the agent intellect, which is the only true cause of the possession of an intelligible form"; ead., "Psychology: soul and intellect", in *The Cambridge Companion to Arabic Philosophy*, P. Adamson, R. C. Taylor eds., Cambridge University Press, Cambridge 2005, 308 – 326, in part. 319 – 320: "The function of the agent intellect in this process is therefore not to illumine the sense images so that universals can be abstracted from them. The ultimate cause of the production of new intelligible concepts in individual minds is not an act of abstraction at all, but, rather, a direct emanation from the agent intellect". R. Taylor, "Al-Fārābī and Avicenna: Two Recent Contributions", *MESA Bulletin*, 39, 2005, 180 – 182, in part. 182: "Simply put, intelligibles in act exist in the separate Agent Intellect which is itself wholly in act and so cannot be a recipient of abstractions from the data of sense perception. Moreover, the unity of intersubjective discourse requires the unity of intelligible references in the Agent Intellect. Abstraction or *tajrīd*, then, is less a description of an idea or an intelligible than a *façon de parler* denoting a linking to intelligibles in act in the Agent Intellect so that individual human beings may in some way be called knowers." A survey of both of these interpretations is provided in D. N. Hasse, *Avicenna's epistemological optimism*, in P. Adamson ed., *Interpreting Avicenna. Critical Essays*, Cambridge University Press, Cambridge 2013, 109 – 119, in part. 110, n. 5.

12 T. Alpina, "Intellectual Knowledge, Active Intellect and Intellectual Memory in Avicenna's *Kitāb al-Nafs* and Its Aristotelian Background", *Documenti e studi sulla tradizione filosofica medievale*, 25, 2014, 131 – 183.

13 R. C. Taylor, "Avicenna and the Issue of the Intellectual Abstraction of Intelligibles", in *Philosophy of Mind in the Early and High Middle Ages*, ed. M. Cameron, Routledge, London-New York 2019, 56 – 82. In this article he also establishes a connection between Avicenna's and Themistius' positions.

14 See Lizzini, "L'âme chez Avicenne", in part. 241: "Physique et métaphysique ne vont donc pas s'opposer de façon paritaire comme si l'une était antinomique par rapport à l'autre. La métaphysique, qui contient la physique, gère le système dans son intégralité. L'âme, tout comme la vie à laquelle elle peut dans un certain sens être réduite, n'est alors pas une entité équivoquement liée aux deux cotés

The other, significant approach is doubtless represented by D. Gutas' (and his followers') contributions, whose merit is to have called attention to the process of abstraction and the crucial role it plays within Avicenna's doctrine of human intellection. The distinctive feature of all Gutas' contributions, starting from his monograph published in 1988, to his last article on this subject which appeared in 2012,[15] is to show, through a close scrutiny of the text, that the human being is entirely responsible for the process of intellection; in other words, there is no external cause for such a process that is accomplished completely within the limits of the rational soul. Therefore, Gutas interprets Avicenna's introduction of the Active Intellect as a means to solve an *ontological* problem, immediately related to human intellection, which, however, does not concern the way in which human beings acquire intellectual knowledge, but rather the depository in which they store it. Avicenna explicitly denies the possibility of intellectual memory: if intellectual forms were stored in the intellect, the intellect would ceaselessly think of them, which is patently impossible. Nonetheless, Avicenna has to admit a storage facility for these forms, namely the Active Intellect; otherwise, we could not retain knowledge of anything.[16] Consequently, Gutas rightly argues that the Active Intellect is Avicenna's answer to this problem: it is the depository of the intellectual forms already acquired, to which the human in-

---

du monde. S'il est vrai qu'il y a un regard ou un point de vue physique sur l'âme, et que la psychologie est une partie de la physique, il est d'autant plus vrai que la physique n'est a son tour qu'une partie de la métaphysique: c'est dans la métaphysique que la physique est contenu, c'est dans la métaphysique que la science de la nature retrouve ses principes. La métaphysique d'Avicenne, en reprenant les termes qu'Alain De Libera a réservés à Albert le Grand, peut être définie de "métaphysique du flux"; elle explique le monde parce qu'elle l'englobe." For a more nuanced position, see Lizzini, *Avicenna*, in part. 232. As I pointed out in Chapter 3, n. 14, in *Burhān*, II, 7, Avicenna explicitly maintains that the particular sciences are subordinated to metaphysics, not parts of it.

15 See Gutas, *Avicenna and the Aristotelian Tradition*, 179 – 201 (on the notion of *intuition*), 288 – 296 (on the so-called *Metaphysics of the Rational Soul*); id., "Avicenna, *De anima* (V 6). Über die Seele, über Intuition und Prophetie", in K. Flasch ed., *Hauptwerke der Philosophie: Mittelalter*, Reclam, Stuttgart 1998, 90 – 107; id., "Avicenna: Die Metaphysik der rationale Seele", in T. Kobusch ed., *Philosophen des Mittelalters*, Primus Verlag, Darmstadt, 2000, 27 – 41; id., "Intuition and Thinking: The Evolving Structure of Avicenna's Epistemology", in R. Wisnovsky ed., *Aspects of Avicenna*, Markus Wiener Publishers, Princeton 2001, 1 – 38; id., "Avicenna: The Metaphysics of the Rational Soul", *The Muslim World* (Special Issue: *The Ontology of the Soul in Medieval Arabic Thought*), 102/3 – 4, 2012, 417 – 425 (an English abridged and revised version of the German article), and id., "The Empiricism", 391 – 436. For a critical assessment of Gutas' last article, see J. Kaukua, "Avicenna's Outsourced Rationalism", *Journal of the History of Philosophy*, 58.2, 2020, 215 – 240 and M. S. Zarepour, "Avicenna's Notion of Fiṭrīyāt: A Comment on Dimitri Gutas' Interpretation", *Philosophy East and West*, 70.3, 2020, 819 – 833.

16 The other alternatives that Avicenna rejects are: (i) a bodily depository, because if the body were the depository of intellectual forms, they would cease to be intelligible as universal concepts; and (ii) the possibility of intellectual forms' self-subsistence, because admitting this possibility would mean acceptance of a Platonic theory of forms which Avicenna discards in *Ilāhiyyāt*, VII, 3. For the discussion of these alternatives, see *Nafs*, V, 6, 245.5 – 247.5 [146.95 – 149.43].

tellect can turn in order to make these forms present again in the mind.[17] Now, I do believe that Avicenna uses the Active Intellect in order to solve the ontological problem pointed out by Gutas; nevertheless, I doubt that he introduces it *only* for this reason. The issue of the recovery of an intellectual form already acquired and, consequently, of the intervention of the Active Intellect in this process is dealt with in *Nafs*, V, 6; nonetheless, Avicenna mentions the Active Intellect for the first time in *Nafs*, V, 5, where he deals not with the process of recovery of an intellectual form already acquired but, rather, with the process leading to the first acquisition of an intellectual form. Therefore, it seems reasonable to suppose that in this context the Active Intellect plays a different role from that which Gutas has singled out.[18]

In the work he has devoted to Avicenna's *Nafs* and its reception in the Latin West, D. N. Hasse depicts human intellection as "an abstraction mediated by the active intellect": the function of the Active Intellect is to illuminate the objects of abstraction and let the abstracted forms occur to the rational soul, whereas the human intellect plays an active role within the process of intellection and does not need to be enabled from outside (i.e. from the Active Intellect) to produce thoughts and considerations.[19] Then, in the same vein as Gutas, Hasse stresses the function the Active Intellect plays in the process of recovery of an intellectual form already acquired. A similar interpretation is confirmed in an article which appeared shortly afterwards, where Hasse suggests that an evolution is detectable in Avicenna's epistemology (in his later works the Active Intellect plays little or no role) and concludes that "the protagonist in abstraction remains the human intellect".[20]

As emerges from the brief survey provided above, the scholarship on Avicenna's noetics divides into two main branches: on the one hand, the branch of those who solve the apparent inconsistency between the two movements in Avicenna's doctrine of human intellection by downplaying the role of the abstractive process, conceived as a mere *façon de parler*; and, on the other hand, the branch of those who restore the pivotal role of abstraction within the process of acquisition of intellectual knowl-

---

17 Gutas, "The Empiricism", 411: "What has to be kept in mind is that for Avicenna the concept of the emanation of the intelligibles from the active intellect has its place in his cosmology and it serves to solve essentially an *ontological* problem, not an epistemological one, which is the *location* of the intelligibles".

18 That V, 5 is the first place where Avicenna explicitly refers to the Active Intellect clearly emerges from the list of occurrences of *ʿaql faʿʿāl* (Active Intellect) in the *Nafs*: V, 5, 234, 13; 235, 3, 8, 13, 20; 236, 1; V, 6, 243, 12; 244, 2; 247, 14, 17; 248, 7, 14; 249, 20, 21. In *Nafs*, I, 5, 50.2–9 [98.65–99.74] Avicenna simply maintains that in order to attain the degree of acquired intellect (*ʿaql mustafād*) our intellect in potentiality needs to come into a sort of contact with an intellect that is always in actuality. This intellect, however, is never called "active" (*faʿʿāl*). What is more, here Avicenna seems to refer to *Nafs*, V, 5 as the place in which this issue will be exhaustively dealt with (*it will become clear to us, sayattaḍiḥu lanā*, 50.6 [*declarabitur nobis*, 99.70]).

19 Hasse, *Avicenna's* De anima, 186.

20 See D. N. Hasse, "Avicenna on Abstraction", in R. Wisnovsky ed., *Aspects of Avicenna*, Markus Wiener Publishers, Princeton 2001, 39–72, in part. 63.

edge, and assign to the Active Intellect a unique role as a *collector* of intellectual forms. Thus, both branches seem to sacrifice an aspect of Avicenna's doctrine for the sake of internal coherence and, consequently, to tell only half of the story. The impression one gets is that further research and closer scrutiny of Avicenna's own statements is required to overcome the opposition between abstractionists and emanationists.

In a contribution that appeared in 2013, Hasse proves to be perfectly aware of the limits of both the emanationist and the abstractionist interpretations and therefore tries to overcome the difficulties they raise. He suggests that their opposition is misleading given that Avicenna never conceived abstraction and emanation as opposites.[21] After having discussed two recent interpretations of Avicenna's doctrine of human intellection,[22] Hasse argues that Avicenna has to face two problems: the epistemological problem concerning the way in which human beings acquire material forms that are not separate from matter, and the ontological problem whence these universal forms come – both those separate from matter in themselves and those that need to be abstracted from it. Hasse argues that abstraction and emanation, far from being incompatible, are precisely Avicenna's solutions to the two aforementioned problems. According to Hasse, abstraction is the way in which human beings acquire material forms. Abstraction, however, explains only the epistemological side of Avicenna's theory; the ontological part can be accounted for only by using the Active Intellect since, Hasse argues, "ontologically the forms come from the active intellect". However, when he deals with the ontological side of the story, i.e. how intellectual forms *ontologically* come from the Active Intellect, he claims that the ontological reason for maintaining that intellectual forms come from the Active Intellect is Avicenna's denial of intellectual memory: thus, the ontological question Avicenna intended to solve by using the Active Intellect no longer concerns the origin of intellectual forms but rather – as with Gutas' position – the issue of where intellectual forms are stored after having been conceived by the human intellect.[23]

---

21 Hasse, "Avicenna's epistemological", 110: "In the present chapter, I shall propose a way out of the antagonism of interpretation by arguing that the opposition between abstraction and emanation is foreign to Avicenna's philosophy and also problematic in itself".

22 The two recent interpretations involved are: C. D'Ancona, "Degrees of Abstraction in Avicenna. How to Combine Aristotle's *De Anima* and the *Enneads*", in S. Knuuttila, P. Kärkkäinen eds., *Theories of Perception in Medieval and Early Modern Philosophy*, Springer, Helsinki 2008, 47–71; and, J. McGinnis, *Avicenna*, Oxford University Press, Oxford 2010, and id., "Making Abstraction less Abstract: The Logical, Psychological, and Metaphysical Dimensions of Avicenna's Theory of Abstraction", *Proceedings of the American Catholic Philosophical Association*, 80, 2007, 169–183. These two interpretations are discussed in Hasse, *Avicenna's epistemological*, 110–114. Among the recent contributions on this topic, see also N. Germann, "Avicenna and Afterwards", in J. Marenbon ed., *The Oxford Handbook of Medieval Philosophy*, Oxford University Press, Oxford 2012, 83–105, in part. 85–88.

23 Hasse, "Avicenna's epistemological", 117: "In sum, the form (or more precisely, the material form, since the immaterial form is grasped directly without abstraction) has to be grasped by way of abstraction, but it nevertheless comes from the active intellect, as soon as the abstraction process is

I do believe that Hasse's general point has hit the mark by focusing on the two problems which Avicenna's theory of human intellection has to face, i.e. the epistemological problem concerning the first acquisition of universal forms and the ontological problem of the place in which they are stored; he therefore singles out precisely the task of Avicenna's model. Nonetheless, his interpretation fails to bridge the gap between abstraction and emanation, which are no longer two well-integrated moments of one and the same process, as Avicenna intended to show; they appear rather as two juxtaposed processes, completely unrelated, aimed at solving two distinct problems. For, in spite of the ontological correspondence between universal forms in the Active Intellect and particular forms in the sublunary world, which Hasse rightly points out, his interpretation is unable to explain the way in which Avicenna combines these two processes on the other level, i.e. the epistemological one.

I believe that Avicenna's answer to both aforementioned problems is precisely the Active Intellect, to which he assigns two different but complementary roles. At the epistemological level, the Active Intellect is the *source* of intelligibility of any intellectual form in the sublunary realm: it is a separate intellect in which there are the principles of all intellectual forms in an abstracted way; consequently, its presence in Avicenna's epistemological (and cosmological) system provides the *condition of possibility* for the human intellect's potentiality to conceive intellectual forms.[24] At the ontological level, the Active Intellect is the *collector* of intellectual forms: Avicenna's denial of intellectual memory requires a *depository* of the intellectual forms already acquired in order to avoid supposing that a new process of acquisition is initiated for every subsequent recovery of an intellectual form. I shall try to provide further grounds in support of this interpretation.

It should be mentioned that recently S. Ogden has advanced a new interpretation which is meant to overcome the opposition between emanationists and abstractionists.[25] According to Ogden's interpretation, the Active Intellect bestows upon the human rational soul not the content of intellectual knowledge, but rather the power of abstraction (*quwwat al-taǧrīd*). In doing this, Ogden claims to reconcile Avicenna's explicitly emanationist passages with the abstractionist ones and, ultimately, to make the human intellect entirely responsible for abstraction once the Active In-

completed and the perfect disposition for receiving the form is reached. This is possible since the essences of material forms exist both as universals in the active intellect and as particulars in the sublunar world. But abstraction is only needed for the first acquisition of a form. After that, the rational soul can make the form be present in the mind whenever it wishes: 'The first learning is like the cure of an eye', as Avicenna puts it."

24 In his interpretation of Alexander of Aphrodisias' noetics, Paul Moraux maintains that, in Alexander's theory, the Active Intellect is "la source de toute intelligibilité" of intellectual forms without exercising any direct role in the abstractive process performed by the human intellect. See P. Moraux, *Alexandre d'Aphrodise: Exégète de la Noétique d'Aristote*, Bibliothèque de la Faculté de Philosophie et Lettres de l'Université de Liège, Liège-Paris 1942, in part. 88–89.

25 S. R. Ogden, "Avicenna's Emanated Abstraction", *Philosophers' Imprint*, forthcoming. I am commenting upon the pre-publication draft uploaded by the author on his Academia.edu page.

tellect has conferred upon it the power of abstraction. However, though fascinating, this interpretation poses some problems. Firstly, as Ogden acknowledges, Avicenna never explicitly endorses such a position. Secondly, this interpretation seems to posit a divide between the lower perceptive faculties and the intellect, which is foreign to Avicenna's thought (see *Nafs*, I, 5, and II, 2). According to Ogden, the imperfect abstraction performed by the lower perceptive faculties would directly stem from these faculties and, ultimately, from the soul, whereas the abstraction performed by the intellect would be the result of the Active Intellect's bestowal of this power upon the human rational soul. However, if this were the case, given that the Active Intellect performs a role in the first acquisition of an intellectual form (Ogden and I agree on this point), then either the Active Intellect would bestow the power of abstraction in every act of cognition of an intellectual form, or the Active Intellect would confer this power upon the human rational soul only once, and then the soul would keep it. This second alternative, however, would *de facto* exclude any role on the part of the Active Intellect in the first acquisition of an intellectual form, except for the very first one. The first alternative seems also untenable, for it would imply that every act of intellectual cognition requires the bestowal of the abstractive power from above. However, Avicenna clearly argues that all the faculties/powers of the soul, intellective power included, stem from the soul.[26] What is more, by commenting upon the Aristotelian metaphor of light used by Avicenna to explain intellection, Ogden equates the Active Intellect's bestowal of the abstractive power upon the soul, which is only potentially capable of intellecting, with the Sun's bestowal of the power of vision upon our eyes, which are only potentially capable of seeing. However, as we shall see, in *Nafs*, V, 5 Avicenna clearly maintains that the light of the Active Intellect shines primarily on imaginative particulars, i.e. on what is potentially intelligible, and only derivatively on our intellect, in the very same way in which the light of the Sun illuminates primarily what is potentially visible, and only derivatively our eyes.[27]

---

26 In this connection, see the occurrences of the verb *ṣadara* to refer to the derivation of faculties from the soul (and of activities from faculties) in the first treatise of *Nafs:* I, 1, 4, 8; 6, 2; 7, 7; 8, 6; 12, 5; 13, 1; 14, 13, 16; 15, 1², 2, 5; I, 3, 30, 13; I, 4, 33, 16; 37, 7, 18; 38, 1.

27 I will address direct and more specific criticisms to Ogden's interpretation when I analyze *Nafs*, V, 5. What I can add here is that the passages that Ogden uses to corroborate his claim, namely that the Active Intellect bestows on the sublunary world not only forms but also powers and, notably, the abstractive power, are either too general (like *Afʿāl wa-Infiʿālāt*, II, 1, 256.9 – 11 [79.78 – 81] where Avicenna also mentions the attractive power conferred upon the iron from above. However, iron is inanimate, and consequently does not have a soul from which this power can stem), or can be interpreted differently (like *Nafs*, V, 6, where Avicenna seems to say not that the Active Intellect bestows the intellect, i.e. the intellective faculty responsible for abstraction, but rather that it bestows something upon the intellect (*al-mabdaʾ al-wāhib li-l-ʿaql*, 247.8 [149.48]). To be fair, before ruling it out, Ogden discusses this alternative translation of the passage). Lastly, Ogden is right in pointing at some dubious passages from the *Compendium on the Soul*, where Avicenna seems to maintain that the Active Intellect bestows the power of perception upon the human rational soul. However,

Immaterial Forms, Abstracted Forms, and Recovered Forms

By following the Aristotelian path, inquiry into the way in which intellectual knowledge is achieved and through which forms are acquired by means of the process outlined in Avicenna's *Nafs*, V, 5 is preceded by an inquiry into what kind of forms are the object of human intellection. For Avicenna, the intellectual forms that the human intellect can acquire fall into two main classes: (i) the class of immaterial forms and (ii) the class of material forms, the latter being further subdivided into (ii.i) material forms acquired for the first time by way of abstraction, and (ii.ii) material forms recovered after having been already conceived once. These classes are not meant to be mutually exclusive: for example, immaterial forms too can be recovered after their first acquisition. However, a notable difference between material and immaterial forms can be detected: as to the former, the process by means of which they are firstly acquired (abstraction) differs from the process by means of which they are further recollected (emanation); as to the latter, instead, the distinction between the two processes is hazy. Therefore, the classification of intellectual forms that I have provided mirrors Avicenna's selective approach to the forms in psychology and delineates the scope of his inquiry into intellectual knowledge in the *Nafs*. It shows that there is no one single form of intellectual knowledge, but rather there are at least two, namely intellectual knowledge of immaterial forms acquired from above with no need for abstraction, and intellectual knowledge of material forms abstracted from the imaginative forms of the particulars of the sublunary world and stored in the Active Intellect. However, only the intellectual knowledge of the latter, which the human intellect abstracts from matter and recovers after having conceived them once, is achieved through the intellectual process expounded in *Nafs:* it is the intellectual process that the human soul performs with the help of the body while it exists in the latter. As we have seen, the study of the enmattered soul, responsible of the activities observable in bodies, is precisely the official focus of psychology.[28]

Nafs, II, 2, 58.1–61.17 [114.50–120.41] is the main text by Avicenna on the two kinds of intellectual forms that human beings can conceive. However, before focusing on this portion of *Nafs*, II, 2, the general framework of the first half of the chapter deserves particular attention, since it contains Avicenna's most comprehensive exposition of his theory of abstraction and its kinds (*aṣnāf*), or degrees (*marātib*), belonging to all the perceptive faculties (external and internal senses, intellect).[29] Firstly, Avicenna shows how the abstractive process is related to perception (*idrāk*), by which he means the perceptive activity of every cognitive faculty: perception consists

also in this case, Avicenna does not explicitly mention the power of abstraction. What is more, the *Compendium on the Soul* is Avicenna's first writing; therefore, it can hardly be used as an exegetical tool to interpret his later and more mature texts.

28 On the official focus of Avicenna's psychology, see Chapter 4.

29 This chapter is entitled "[*Chapter*] *on the verification of the kinds of perceptions belonging to us*" (*Fī taḥqīq aṣnāf al-idrākāt allatī lanā*, 58.2 [114.48–49]).

in grasping the form of what is perceived (*ṣūrat al-mudrak*), namely the formal core (*maʿnan*)[30] of the object perceived, through a process of abstraction (*taǧrīd*) that allows the perceiver to divest it of matter and material appurtenances. Avicenna singles out two main kinds of abstraction (which will be further specified) depending on the degree of completeness of the abstractive process itself: there is an incomplete abstraction due to which the formal core is abstracted with some or all of its material appurtenances (*ʿalāʾiq*); and a complete one (*kāmil*), which succeeds in freeing the formal core from all its material attributes (*lawāḥiq*). This second kind of abstraction is essential for universal knowledge and hence for predication, since this operation allows us to distinguish the essential features of something from its accidental aspects (such as being multiplied or possessing some physical properties), which belong to something only insofar as it inheres in a certain matter. These kinds of abstraction (and their intermediate degrees) are related cumulatively to all perceptive faculties, from the five external senses (taken as a whole), through imaginative faculty and estimation (the two internal senses to which Avicenna assigns an active role),[31] to the intellect. The external senses have an elementary abstractive capacity: in order to perceive the form, the senses have to be ceaselessly related to the material substratum in which the form inheres. The fact is that the perception of the form lasts as long as the sense remains in contact with the bearer of that form. Thus, the objects of sense perception are particular, sensible forms, completely submerged in their material properties. Internal senses have a stronger abstractive capacity: imaginative faculty disentangles the form from the matter to a higher degree, for it is capable of breaking off its connection with matter. Nevertheless, it extracts the form from matter together with all its material concomitants; thus the imaginative form is still a particular thing with a certain quality, quantity and position, and cannot be predicated of all individuals of the species to which that form belongs.[32] Estimation,

---

30 It is worth noticing that here *maʿnan* does not seem to refer to the specific object of the estimative faculty (*wahm*), namely the non-sensible attributes of perceptible objects. Rather, it seems to refer in general to the formal core of every perceptible object which could be partially or completely divested of its material attributes. Thus, we might say that here *maʿnan* refers to the essence of a perceptible object considered in itself.

31 For a presentation of Avicenna's internal senses, see Alpina, "Retaining, Remembering, Recollecting".

32 See *Nafs*, II, 2, 59.14–60.10 [117.88–118.5]: "As for imagery and the imaginative faculty, it frees the form extracted (*al-ṣūra al-manzūʿa*) from matter in a stronger way. For it grasps the form from matter in such a way that the form does not need, in order to exist in it, the existence of its matter, because even though matter disappears or ceases [to exist], the form remains firmly existent in imagery. Then, its grasping (*sc.* the grasping of imagery) of it breaks the connection between it and [its] matter in a complete way, even though imagery has not yet abstracted it from the material attributes. Therefore, the sense did not abstract it from matter in a complete way, nor abstracted it from the attributes of matter. Imagery has already abstracted it from matter in a complete way, but it has not abstracted it from the attributes of matter at all, because the form that is in imagery depends on the sensible form and is according to a certain measure, a certain qualification and a certain position. It is by no means possible that a form is imagined in imagery in such a state that all the individuals of that species can

by contrast, perceives the so-called *meanings* (*maʿānin*),[33] the non-sensible attributes of material, perceptible objects, which are not in themselves material, since their being enmattered is entirely accidental.[34] Then there is the intellectual faculty, to which there is assigned the highest degree of abstraction, namely the complete or perfect abstraction.[35]

---

share in it. For the imagined man is like one of the men, and there might exist and be imagined men who are not as imagery imagined that man". Though being two distinct faculties, here imagery (*ḫayāl*) and the imaginative faculty (*quwwa mutaḫayyila*) are treated together because their objects share the same level of abstraction from matter.

33 The correct translation of the word *maʿnan* when it is referring to the proper object of the internal sense has puzzled many scholars. Several translations have been proposed (*intention*, *notion*, *connotational attribute*, *meaning*). I use *meaning* because, though not entirely satisfactory, this translation points to a crucial aspect of *maʿnan*, namely its relational nature: for in this context *maʿnan* expresses the meaning that a certain form has for a certain perceiver. On this is Alpina, "Retaining, Remembering, Recollecting", n. 14.

34 See *Nafs*, II, 2, 60.10–61.5 [118.6–119.25]: "As for estimation, it sometimes goes a little beyond this degree of abstraction, since it acquires the meanings that in themselves are not material, even though they happened to be in matter. For shape, color, position and what is alike are things that cannot be except in bodily matters. As for good and evil, appropriate and [its] contrary, and what is alike, they are things in themselves immaterial, but they sometimes happen to be material. The sign of these things' being immaterial is that, if these things were material in their own right, good and evil, appropriate and [its] contrary would not be intellected, unless they happen to be in a body. But these things (*lit.* that) are sometimes intellected; indeed, they are found [not in matter]. It is, therefore, clear that these things in themselves are immaterial, but they happened to be material. Then, estimation acquires and perceives only what is similar to these things; consequently, estimation perceives immaterial things and grasps them from matter just as it also perceives non-sensible meanings, even though they were material. This extraction (*fa-hāḏā l-nazʿ*) is, therefore, stronger in investigation and nearer to simplicity than the first two extractions (*min al-nazʿayni l-awwalayni*, *sc.* those of external senses and of imagery and the imaginative faculty), except that it (*sc.* the extraction performed by estimation) nevertheless does not abstract this form from the attributes of matter. For it grasps this form as particular, according to a certain matter after another, in relation to it, depending on a sensible form, which is surrounded by the attributes of matter, and with the participation of imagery in it". It is noteworthy that at the end of this passage Avicenna refers twice to the object of the abstraction performed by estimation by using *ṣūra* not *maʿnan*.

35 See *Nafs*, II, 2, 61.5–14 [120.26–37]: "As to the faculty in which forms are stable (*sc.* the intellect), either the forms existing [in this faculty] are not at all material, nor have they happened to be material, or the forms existing [in it] are material, but freed (*mubarraʾa*) from the appurtenances of matter in every respect; then, it is clear that it perceives the forms since it grasps them in the way of abstraction (*bi-an taʾḫuḏahā aḫḏan muǧarradan*) from matter in every respect. As to what is in itself separate (*mutaǧarrad*) from matter, the issue (*amr*) is evident (*ẓāhir*). As to what exists in matter, either because its existence is material, or [because] it happens to be [material], [the intellective faculty] extracts it (*tanziʿuhū*) from matter and material attributes at the same time, and grasps it in the manner of abstraction (*taʾḫuḏuhū aḫḏan muǧarradan*) so that it is like "man" which is predicated of many and the many is grasped as a single nature, and [the intellective faculty] separates it from all material quantity, quality, place and position. If [the intellective faculty] did not abstract it from that, it would not be predicated of all [men]".

Among the objects of the intellective faculty, Avicenna distinguishes immaterial forms, namely forms that are not at all material, nor happened to be material, like God or the celestial intelligences,[36] from the material forms that are completely disentangled from matter and its appurtenances (or attributes) by way of abstraction (*immā... aw...*, 61.5–9 [120.26–30]). In this framework, "it (*sc.* the theoretical faculty) grasps them in the way of abstraction" (*taʾḫuḏuhā aḫḏan muǧarradan*, 61.8 [120.28–29]) seems to directly refer to what immediately precedes, namely to material forms and the way in which they are acquired, as Avicenna shows immediately afterwards, and not to the *abstract manner* through which the human intellect *grasps* immaterial forms.[37] The distinction between immaterial and material forms is further specified in the subsequent lines (*ammā... wa-ammā...*, 61.9–12 [120.30–33]): the immaterial forms are in themselves separate (*mutaǧarrad*) from matter and with respect to them, namely to their condition and acquisition, there is no need for explanations since the issue is evident (*ẓāhir*); by contrast, the material forms, i.e. either those whose existence is material[38] or those that happen to be in matter but whose existence is not in itself material,[39] are extracted from matter and all the material attributes and grasped by way of abstraction (*taʾḫuḏuhū aḫḏan muǧarradan*), i.e. as abstracted. Given the content of this passage, it seems fair to conclude that: (i) there are two objects of human intellection, namely immaterial and material forms; (ii) the way in which material forms are acquired requires a process of abstraction; by contrast, (iii) the way in which intellect acquires immaterial forms is not specified since Avicenna considers the issue evident. It is not clear why Avicenna states that with respect to immaterial forms the issue is evident without giving further information; nonetheless, we might speculate that the reason is that the acquisition of immaterial forms is somehow immediate, since they do not need to be stripped away from matter, and therefore it does not involve abstraction which, by contrast, is a process articulated in precise steps that need to be singled out and explained. Moreover, the context in which the reference to immaterial forms is made is *Nafs*, II, 2, a chapter entirely devoted to the different degrees of abstraction that are related to each perceptive faculty. Thus, it is reasonable to suppose that Avicenna focuses on those forms that are the object of that process, disregarding those that are acquired otherwise. What is more, the official focus of Avicenna's *Nafs* is to deal with the soul while

---

36 Hasse, "Avicenna's epistemological", 115, n. 28. On this identification, see *Madḫal*, I, 2, 12.12–13 (quoted by Hasse), and *Ilāhiyyāt*, I, 2, 15.18–16.1 [16.2–4].

37 For this different translation, see Hasse, "Avicenna's epistemological", 115.

38 Examples of material forms whose existence is material are physical and mathematical entities, the former being inseparable from matter and motion in both external and mental existence; the latter being inseparable from matter in external existence, but separable in mental existence. See *Madḫal*, I, 2, 12.15–13.4.

39 Examples of material forms that happen to be in matter, even though their existence is not in itself material can be being, unity, multiplicity, causality. On these examples, see *Madḫal*, I, 2, 13.4–5, and *Ilāhiyyāt*, I, 2, 16.2–3 [16.6–17.7].

it is related to matter and motion, namely to the body: material forms are the only objects of intellectual knowledge that are acquired through the help of the bodily faculties; therefore, it is again reasonable that in *Nafs* Avicenna mainly focuses on material forms and the process through which the intellect acquires those forms, while immaterial forms (and the way in which they are acquired) remain in the background, because they fall outside the official boundaries of natural philosophy.[40] It is no coincidence that in *Nafs* Avicenna deals only with the process through which human intellect acquires material forms with scanty reference to the other object of intellectual knowledge, i.e. immaterial forms.

As I have indicated, *Nafs*, II, 2 contains the most exhaustive classification of the objects of intellectual knowledge. However, there are other passages in *Nafs* in which Avicenna brings forward or recalls this general classification. For instance, in *Nafs*, I, 5 Avicenna briefly refers to the main distinction between immaterial and material forms: "As for the theoretical faculty, it is a faculty such that it is impressed with the universal forms abstracted from matter. If they are abstracted in themselves (*muǧarrada bi-ḏātihā*), the faculty's grasping of their form in itself is easier (*ashal*). If, by contrast, they are not [in themselves abstracted from matter], they become abstracted by the faculty's abstraction of them so that nothing of the material appurtenances remain in them. We will explain how this [happens] later on (*sc.* in *Nafs*, II, 2 or V, 5)" (*Nafs*, I, 5, 48.1–5 [94.15–95.20]).

After having indicated in a preliminary fashion that the theoretical faculty is imprinted with the universal forms abstracted from matter, Avicenna distinguishes the kinds of forms whose impression is received by the theoretical faculty. These forms are either those in themselves abstract (or separate) from matter and, therefore, the theoretical faculty's grasping of them is *easier*, or those that are not in themselves abstracted from matter and, therefore, need to be abstracted by the theoretical faculty. At first glance this distinction seems to echo exactly the distinction between immaterial and material forms provided in *Nafs*, II, 2. Nonetheless, Avicenna's qualification of the theoretical faculty's grasping of forms in themselves abstract from matter as *easier* in comparison with the faculty's grasping of the forms that have not yet been abstracted, needs be spelled out, especially because in the final part of *Nafs*, V, 5 Avicenna refers to the inability (*ʿaǧz*) of the intellect to conceptualize the things that are at the highest degree of intelligibility and abstraction from matter (*al-ašyāʾ allatī hiya fī ġāyat al-maʿqūliyya wa-l-taǧrīd ʿan al-mādda*), i.e. the immaterial forms.[41] However, the (apparent) disagreement between I, 5 and V, 5 concerning the qualification of the intellection of immaterial forms might be solved by arguing that here Avicenna does not want to suggest that it is easier to grasp immaterial

40 See Chapter 3.
41 *Nafs*, V, 5, 237.16–19 [131.7–12]. See also V, 5, 238.1–3 [132.14–16]; 238.9–10 [132.24–133.1].

forms (which seems false) but, rather, that it is easier to see how they could be grasped when they are grasped, because they do not need to be separated from matter.[42]

In sum, according to Avicenna there are two objects of intellectual knowledge, i.e. immaterial and material forms, and two different ways of apprehending them, i.e. emanation from above with no need for abstraction, and abstraction from imaginative particulars. Nonetheless, in *Nafs* Avicenna deals only with material forms and the processes related, respectively, to their first acquisition (abstraction) and their subsequent recovery (emanation, i.e. contact with the Active Intellect). As we have already suggested, the fact that Avicenna disregards the process by which immaterial forms are acquired and further recollected can be explained by referring to the boundaries of psychology: being part of natural philosophy, the inquiry into the soul has to be restricted to the study of the soul while it exists in the body; consequently, in *Nafs* Avicenna deals only with those psychic activities that are performed with the help (or mediation) of the body, and material forms are precisely that sole object of intellectual knowledge that is acquired through the mediation of the bodily faculties, although the process of abstraction of material forms from the imaginative particulars is combined with the intervention of the Active Intellect, as will clearly emerge from examination of the model of intellectual knowledge given in *Nafs*, V, 5.

How do We Intellect Material Forms? *Nafs*, V, 5

In *Nafs*, V, 5 Avicenna speaks *ex professo* of his doctrine of intellectual knowledge of material forms and makes reference to the Active Intellect for the first time;[43] therefore, in order to understand what Avicenna means by "intellection" and what role the Active Intellect plays in the process leading to the acquisition of intellectual knowledge, a close scrutiny of this text is essential.

Avicenna begins his treatment with a general consideration: the human soul is potentially capable of intellection, but at some point it begins actually to exercise that capacity. As Avicenna argues, the transition from potentiality to actuality can be accounted for only by referring to a cause in actuality that brings the process about.[44] Likewise, in the case of human intellection, there must be a cause that brings our souls from potentiality to actuality with regard to intellectual forms; and since it is the cause of giving (*iʿṭāʾ*) intellectual forms to the human intellect,

---

42 A similar, concise formulation of the distinction between immaterial and material forms can be found in *Nafs*, V, 6, 239.3–6 [134.41–44]: "We say that the soul thinks because it pulls into itself the form of the intelligibles abstracted from matter. The form's being abstracted is either by the intellect's abstraction of it, or because that form is in itself abstract from matter; thus, the soul is saved the effort of abstracting it (*fa-takūnu l-nafs qad kufiyat al-maʾūna fī taǧrīdihā*)".

43 See n. 18 above.

44 For the Aristotelian background of this claim, that is, the priority of actuality over potentiality, see *Metaph.*, IX, 8, 1049 b4–1050 b6, and XII, 6, 1071 b12–1072 a18.

that cause must be an actual intellect in which exist the principles of intellectual forms in an abstracted way (*ʿindahū mabādiʾ al-ṣuwar al-ʿaqliyya muǧarradatan*), that is, the Active Intellect.[45] After having laid down this sort of general rule, Avicenna explains that human intellection occurs when two conditions are satisfied:

1. the intellectual faculty's looking at the particulars stored in the imagery (*iṭṭalaʿat ʿalà l-ǧuzʾiyyāt allatī fī l-ḫayāl*, 235.2–3 [127. 39–40]);
2. the Active Intellect's shining light upon the imaginative particulars (*ašraqa ʿalayhā nūr al-ʿaql al-faʿʿāl*, 235.3–4 [127. 40–41]).

When these two conditions are satisfied, the imaginative particulars turn into things that are abstracted (*istaḥālat muǧarrada*, 235.4 [127. 41]) from matter and its appurtenances and are impressed (*inṭabaʿat*, 235.4 [127.42]) onto the rational soul. However, the transformation of imaginative particulars implies neither their transfer from imagery to the intellect nor their reduplication in the intellect; rather, their inspection prepares the rational soul, so that what is abstracted flows upon it from the Active Intellect (*muṭālaʿatuhā tuʿiddu l-nafs li-an yafīḍa ʿalayhā l-muǧarrad min al-ʿaql al-faʿʿāl* , 235.7–8 [127.45–47]). In the final part of the first section of this chapter (235.8–236.2 [127.48–128.63]), Avicenna summarizes the foregoing considerations in order to outline his own account of intellection of material forms: the intellectual process occurs when the rational soul establishes a certain relation (*nisba*) with imaginative particulars through the mediation of the illumination of the Active Intellect (*bi-tawassuṭ išrāq al-ʿaql al-faʿʿāl*, 235.12–3 [128. 52–53]) and the counterparts of those particulars, abstracted from their imperfections, come to be in it ([...] *li-an taḥduṯa fīhā min ḍawʾ al-ʿaql al-faʿʿāl muǧarradāt tilka l-ṣuwar ʿan al-šawāʾib*, 236.1–2 [128.62–63]). Therefore, the intellectual forms that come about in the rational soul are, in one way, of a kind with the imaginative particulars but, in another, they are not. The reason for the twofold nature of the relationship between imaginative particulars and intellectual forms is that imaginative particulars, which trigger the process of the acquisition of intellectual forms, are only potentially intelligible; however, what becomes actually intelligible are not the imaginative particulars themselves, but what is collected from them (*mā yultaqaṭu ʿanhā*, 235. 16 [128.58]), namely their essence divested of all material appurtenances.

What has to be clarified is, in general, how Avicenna manages to combine the human intellect's inspection of imaginative particulars with the Active Intellect's intervention and, in particular, what is the role that he assigns to the Active Intellect's shining light in the intellective process: Avicenna always refers to it by using the met-

---

45 The fact that in the Active Intellect there are the principles of intellectual forms in an abstracted way, namely the essences in themselves, goes against McGinnis' interpretation according to which what flows from the Active Intellect upon the human intellect are *intelligible accidents* or *intellectualizing forms*, that is, the accidents that determine the abstract essence when it is being conceptualized. On the reference to McGinnis' interpretation, see n. 22 above.

aphorical language of the well-known analogy of light with no further reference to the Intellect's function.

The Epistemological Role of the Active Intellect in First Acquisition of an Intellectual Form

In order to evaluate the respective roles of human and Active intellect in the acquisition of intellectual knowledge, in the table below the functions assigned to them in *Nafs*, V, 5 are listed.[46]

	Human intellect	Active intellect
1.	(A) The intellectual faculty **looks at** the imaginative particulars...	...and (B) the luminosity of the Active Intellect **shines** on the imaginative particulars
2.	(A) The **inspection** of the imaginative particulars prepares the soul...	...so that (B) what is abstracted **flows** onto the soul from the Active Intellect
3.	(A) Thoughts and reflections are motions that **prepare** the soul...	...for (B) the reception of the **effluence**
4.	(A) When to the rational soul **there occurs a certain relation** to an imaginative particular...	...(B) **through the mediation of the illumination** of the Active Intellect...
5.	...(C) from it there **comes to be** in the rational soul something that on the one hand is of its genus, while on the other hand is not of its genus	
6.	(A) The rational soul **inspects** the imaginative particulars...	...and (B) the luminosity of the Active Intellect **comes into a mode of contact** with the imaginative particulars
7.	(A) The rational soul **is prepared** so that in it...	...(B) **from the light** of the Active Intellect...
8.	...(C) **come to be** the counterparts of the imaginative particulars, abstracted from their imperfections	

Four considerations can be made at the outset:

a) the activity of *inspection* on the part of the human intellect seems to be prior to the activity of *illumination* or *emanation* on the part of the Active Intellect, and to trigger it off;

46 A similar analysis can be found in Hasse, "Avicenna on Abstraction", in part. 55–57 in which, however, the author endorses a slightly different position concerning Avicenna's description of the activity of the human intellect.

b) the contents of the imagery somehow correspond to the objects of thought;
c) the activity of the human intellect is characterized using terms like "to look at" (*iṭṭalaʿa*) and "inspection" (*muṭālaʿa*), whereas the activity[47] of the Active Intellect is metaphorically hidden behind the verb "to shine" (*ašraqa*), or circumlocutions like "through the mediation of the illumination of the Active Intellect" (*bi-tawassuṭ išrāq al-ʿaql al-faʿʿāl*);
d) both the human and the Active intellect have an active role in the intellective process (all the verbs that indicate their roles are in the active voice), and neither is, strictly speaking, affected by the other.

Consequently, a correct interpretation of Avicenna's theory of intellection must take into account four elements: the *primacy* of the human intellect's inspection of imaginative particulars over the Active Intellect's illumination; the *correspondence* between imaginative particulars and intellectual forms; the *assimilation* of the role of the Active Intellect to that of the illumination or radiation of light; and, the *absence* of any affection or alteration in the human intellect.

It is clear from the table above that for Avicenna intellection is a process composed of two movements: (A) the human intellect's voluntary inspection of imaginative particulars, and (B) the Active Intellect's shining light on those particulars. Together, these two movements lead to (C) the human intellect's achievement of the intellectual, universal counterparts of those particulars, which both are and are not of the same genus as those particulars.

The intimate correspondence between imaginative particulars and intellectual forms[48] is grounded on Avicenna's metaphysical doctrine of the distinction (or mutual connection) of essence and existence.[49] An accurate analysis of this doctrine

---

47 Here I improperly use the term "activity", since *strictly speaking* the Active Intellect does not perform any activity in the intellective process, but is simply *perpetually active*, as I will show. For this reason, I prefer to refer to this intellect by using the term "Active", rather than "Agent".

48 On the correspondence between imaginative particulars and intellectual forms with respect to the common nature they share, see McGinnis, "Making Abstraction less Abstract"; and M. Sebti, "Le statut ontologique de l'image dans la doctrine avicenniene de la perception", *Arabic Sciences and Philosophy*, 15, 2005, 109–140, in part. 133–135.

49 In *Ilāhiyyāt*, I, 5, the *locus classicus* where the primary concepts *existent/existence* and *thing/essence* are exhaustively dealt with, Avicenna focuses on their distinction as well as on their mutual connection. They are distinct since they have different intensions: *existence* refers to the fact of being established in reality, whereas *essence* is that by means of which something is what it is (the latter is sometimes called "proper existence" which, however, does not mean *existence* in the proper sense, namely "the fact of being established in reality", but is a synonym of quiddity or essence). Avicenna argues for the distinction between these notions by means of the analysis of propositions: since statements connecting essence (as subject) with real existence (as predicate) are informative, these two entities must be distinct from one another. However, in spite of their distinction, Avicenna maintains that existence is an inseparable concomitant (*lāzim*) of essence, since essences always exist in some way or another. Therefore, in order faithfully to reconstruct Avicenna's doctrine, it is essential to highlight both aspects of the relationship between these concepts. For a thorough

is beyond the scope of the present chapter; therefore, I will limit myself to the partial account of this doctrine provided in *Ilāhiyyāt*, V, 1–2 where, within the framework of his doctrine of universals, Avicenna approaches the issue by stressing the external character of existence with respect to essence and, consequently, the distinction of these concepts. This doctrine,[50] which stands against Platonic realism,[51] distinguishes the absolute consideration of an essence from what applies to the same essence in the subject in which it exists. In other words, Avicenna distinguishes the essence as such (e.g. horseness) from its existence as a particular, concrete object in external reality (e.g. Bucephalus, the horse of Alexander the Great), or as a universal concept in the soul (i.e. the intellectual form "horseness", conceptualized in the mind as its object, considered in abstraction from the individuating conditions it has in its particular instances). The common essence, considered in itself, is nothing other than itself: horseness, for example, points out a determinate essence, namely being a four-legged solid-hoofed animal with flowing mane and tail, regardless of its existence in external reality or in the human mind (even though essences always exist in one way or another).[52] *Universals*, by contrast, exist only in the mind, namely when the essence is conceived as a *universal concept* by the abstractive mind or, what amounts to the same thing, when universality attaches to essence in mental existence. Thus Avicenna insists on the separation of essence and existence and contends that existence in external objects or in the mind, together with other extrinsic features like oneness and multiplicity, does not enter into the notion of an essence as

---

reconstruction of the doctrinal and historical context of Avicenna's position, see A. Bertolacci, "The Distinction of Essence and Existence in Avicenna's *Metaphysics:* The Text and Its Context", in F. Opwis, D. C. Reisman eds., *Islamic Philosophy, Science, Culture, and Religion. Studies in Honor of Dimitri Gutas*, Brill, Leiden 2012, 257–288.

50 The same doctrine is hinted in *Madḫal*, I, 2, 15.1–17, and more systematically expounded in *Madḫal*, I, 12, 65.1–70.7, which is entirely devoted to the analysis of the concept *universal*.

51 On this aspect of Avicenna's doctrine of universals, see M. Rashed, "Ibn ʿAdī et Avicenne: sur les types d'existants", in V. Celluprica, C. D'Ancona, R. Chiaradonna eds., *Aristotele e i suoi esegeti neoplatonici. Logica e ontologia nelle interpretazioni greche e arabe. Atti del convegno internazionale, Roma, 19–20 ottobre 2001*, Bibliopolis, Napoli 2004, 107–171, in part. 116–119.

52 Even though Avicenna maintains that the essence or common nature, absolutely considered, is existent neither in external reality nor in the soul, it is worth noticing that in *Ilāhiyyāt*, V, 1, 205.1–2 [237.24–25] he assigns to the essence as such a divine existence (*al-wuǧūd al-ilāhī*). In particular, in dealing with the essence as such, like "animal-as-such", whose existence is prior to its existence in concrete individuals, Avicenna qualifies its existence as divine. As a consequence, Avicenna seems to assimilate essences (or common natures) to the intellectual forms that exist before multiplicity in the mind of God and angels and are the cause of the existence of the forms in concrete objects (see *Ilāhiyyāt*, VIII, 7, 363.5–10 [423.88–424.98]). What is more, assigning a divine existence to the essences might lead one to reconsider the relationship between the essence as such and the universal existing before multiplicity, which is referred to in *Madḫal*, I, 12, 65.4–10 within the well-known tripartition of universals into universals existing before, during, and after multiplicity, whose identification M.E. Marmura has firmly rejected in his "Avicenna's Chapter on Universals in the *Isagoge* of his *Shifā*'", in A. T. Welch, P. Cachia eds., *Islam: Past Influence and Present Challenge*, Edinburgh University Press, Edinburgh 1979, 34–56.

it is expressed in its definition, i.e. is not constitutive of this latter. That said, the relationship between essence in external reality and essence in the human mind is the same relationship as exists between imaginative particulars and intellectual forms. In this connection, imaginative particulars are the likeness, the counterpart of sensible particulars in the internal senses and, like the essences in external reality, are particularized by the material appurtenances they retain after having been perceived by the soul. Intellectual forms, by contrast, correspond to the essences in conceptualization: for they are universal. Thus, the imaginative particulars and the intelligible forms, even though they differ with respect to their way of existence, are not unrelated; rather, they share the same, common nature which is in itself neither particular nor universal.

The *correspondence* between imaginative particulars and intellectual forms, and the *continuity* between internal senses (imagery, in particular) and intellect are crucial in order to explain how intellection takes place, and to put the entire process in the right perspective. At the first stage of the intellective process, the soul is not only provided with a mere disposition to acquire intellectual forms, but is also somehow, i.e. potentially, acquainted with the very object of thought. For, when Avicenna claims that the intelligible is what is collected from imaginative particulars, namely the common nature shared by both imaginative particulars and intellectual forms, which the intellect succeeds in freeing from material appurtenances, he certifies the aforementioned correspondence. Ultimately, imaginative particulars and intellectual forms can be said to be the same with respect to their essence, namely with respect to the formal core they share, while they differ according to their way of existence, which is connected with particularity in one case and with universality in the other.

Avicenna highlights the continuity between intellect and lower perceptive faculties several times.[53] More precisely, he shows that intellection is not a self-contained cognitive process, completely unrelated to the lower level of perception (external and internal senses); on the contrary, it is the peak of a complex but unique "perceptive chain",[54] whose extremes are respectively the external senses and the intellect. In this model the results of the lower faculties are acquired and further reworked by the highest ones, as Aristotle himself points out at the beginning of his *De anima*

53 See, for example, (a) *Nafs*, I, 5, 45.2–6 [89.44–48], where Avicenna briefly accounts for the intellect's use of the compositive imagination, which is called cogitative faculty (*quwwa mufakkira*); and (b) the first part of *Nafs*, V, 3, which is entitled "[*Chapter*] *including two issues: (i) how the human soul makes use of the senses, and (ii) establishing the temporal origination of the soul* (*yaštamilu 'alà mas'alatayni iḥdāhumā kayfiyya intifā' al-nafs al-insāniyya bi-l-ḥawāss wa-l-ṯāniya iṯbāt ḥudūṯihā*)." On the cogitative faculty in Avicenna's epistemology, see D. L. Black, "Rational Imagination: Avicenna on the Cogitative Power", in L. X. Lopéz-Farjeat, J. A. Tellkamplack eds., *Philosophical Psychology in Arabic Thought and the Latin Aristotelianism of the 13th Century*, Vrin, Paris 2013, 59–81, and the bibliography presented therein.

54 By the expression "perceptive chain" I refer to the continuous relationship existing, according to Avicenna, among all the perceptive faculties of the soul.

with regard to the relationship between intellect and imagination (φαντασία) which, for Aristotle, importantly proves the dependence of the intellect on the body.[55]

Avicenna presents what I have called "perceptive chain" at the end of *Nafs*, I, 5,[56] after a general classification of the faculties of the soul. In this passage, Avicenna suggests that the different faculties are arranged like a chain, from the highest faculty, namely the intellect, down to the four elementary qualities (cold, hot, dry, wet). This chain is continuous, without gaps: each faculty *rules* (*raʾusa*) the faculty which follows and *serves* (*ḫadama*) that which precedes.[57] This arrangement of the faculties provides further insight into the way in which Avicenna thinks about the relationship between imagery and intellect. This is not particularly surprising, since his overarching aim is to explain the unity of a living being by recourse to the unity of its faculties. Here, it is particularly interesting that Avicenna explains the intellective process as the result not only of the intellect's efforts, but also of the activities of the lower, servile faculties which provide the intellect with the potential intellectual forms.

However, the *primacy* of the human intellect's activity of inspecting the imaginative particulars and their *correspondence* with the intellectual forms in actuality do not sufficiently account for Avicenna's well-constructed intellective process. Indeed, in *Nafs*, V, 5, in outlining the process leading to the first acquisition of an intellectual form, Avicenna explicitly refers to the Active Intellect. Therefore, it is essential not to underestimate the role of the Active Intellect and to inquire into the purpose of Avicenna's *assimilation* of its role to that of the illumination (or radiation) of light.

Avicenna refers to the Active Intellect by using the analogy of light. A preliminary sketch of his account of vision, to which he devotes the third treatise in *Nafs*, will provide a helpful background to this theory of human intellection. He begins by distinguishing three terms which usually refer to light indiscriminately in Arabic: *ḍawʾ*, *nūr*, and *šuʿāʿ*. Avicenna gives each of these terms a precise, technical meaning. The term *ḍawʾ*, which I translate as "light",[58] refers to the light that belongs to the Sun and fire alone and does not involve the distinction of any color. The term *nūr*, which I translate as "luminosity",[59] refers to the light that radiates from things having light and is imagined to fall upon bodies, so that colors are actually visible. Finally, the term *šuʿāʿ* can be translated as "glare" if it is found in a body that has ac-

55 *De an.*, I, 1, 403 a8–10.

56 *Nafs*, I, 5, 50.13–51.16 [99.79–102.15].

57 On this Galenic terminology in Avicenna's arrangement of psychic faculties in *Nafs*, I, 5, see Chapter 1, n. 55.

58 Hasse translates *ḍawʾ* as "natural light"; see Hasse, *Avicenna's* De anima, 109, n. 154. J. McGinnis, by contrast, translates it as "luminous light"; see J. McGinnis, "New Light on Avicenna: Optics and Its Role in Avicennian Theories of Vision, Cognition and Emanation", in L. X. Lopéz-Farjeat, J. A. Tellkamplack eds., *Philosophical Psychology in Arabic Thought and the Latin Aristotelianism of the 13th Century*, Vrin, Paris 2013, 41–57, in part. 45–52.

59 McGinnis translates *nūr* as "radiant light"; see McGinnis, "New Light", 45–52. On the contrary, Hasse translates it as "light" or "acquired light"; see Hasse, *Avicenna's* De anima, 108–114.

quired it from another body, or "ray" if it is found in a body by itself. Avicenna, then, maintains that light is visible by itself if there is a transparent medium between a potential perceiver and the body having light; luminosity, in turn, also requires a body possessing light in order to be seen, since luminosity is precisely the light radiating from a body having light which is acquired (*mustafād*) by a non-transparent body. Accordingly, Avicenna singles out two classes of body: (a) the class of transparent bodies, like air or water, and (b) the class of non-transparent bodies. The class of non-transparent bodies is further subdivided into two subclasses, namely (ba) the subclass of non-transparent bodies, luminous by themselves, which require only a transparent medium in order to be visible and hinder the perception of what is behind them; and (bb) the subclass of non-transparent bodies that, besides the transparent medium, require a body having light, which causes them to be a certain color and, consequently, visible;[60] otherwise, these bodies are only potentially colored and, consequently, visible.[61]

In sum, in Avicenna's account, the visual process requires: (a) the light of the Sun, fire or the like, (b) the luminosity that, by being acquired by a non-transparent body and mingling with its potential color, makes it actually visible, and (c) a transparent medium that enables light to cause a movement (or alteration) in the non-transparent body, potentially colored. When all the aforementioned conditions are satisfied, the actual color emanates from the illuminated body as a ray and projects a form, similar to the form of the visible object, behind the crystalline humor in the perceiver's eye; then vision occurs.[62] For our purpose, one should keep in mind that for Avicenna light (of the Sun, or the like) is the cause (*sabab*) of the manifestation of color because light, always shining from above and acquired by a visible object and mingling with its potential color, makes the potential color actually visible to the potential perceiver.[63]

---

60 For all these distinctions, see *Nafs*, III, 1, 91.5–92.21 [169.4–173.50].

61 As Hasse (in Hasse, *Avicenna's* De anima, 109–119) and McGinnis (in McGinnis, "New Light", 47–48) have noticed, Avicenna's reference to the potential state of color when there is no light marks a significant difference between Aristotle's and Avicenna's accounts of vision: for, according to Aristotle, colors are always in actuality, while the medium can be either potentially or actually transparent; according to Avicenna, however, the medium is always transparent in actuality, while the color might be in a state of potentiality or actuality. Consequently, according to Avicenna's account, "darkness" does not mean that the medium is dark and prevents vision; rather, darkness refers to the privation of light in a non-transparent body. Nevertheless, Avicenna sometimes follows Aristotle and refers to the potential state of the transparent, although he argues that its actualization does not involve any alteration or movement on the part of the medium; rather, it involves an alteration or movement on the part of the body potentially colored that is brought into actuality by the light's falling upon it. Therefore, "color" strictly speaking only refers to color in actuality (or phenomenal color), and its manifestation is the result of the mixture of potential color and luminosity. See *Nafs*, III, 1, 92.21–95.4 [173.50–177.5].

62 *Nafs*, III, 7, 141.11–142.1 [253.88–254.00].

63 *Nafs*, III, 3, 103.14–19 [192.23–30]: "For even if we say that light is not the manifestation of the color, we do not deny that light is a cause for the manifestation of the color and a cause for its transfer

In a similar vein, Avicenna claims that, in order for actual intellection to occur, the *light* of the Active Intellect must radiate upon the imaginative particulars and mingle, so to speak, with their potential intelligibility.[64] The Active Intellect's *shining light* points metaphorically at the Active Intellect's proper activity of *perpetually intelligizing* the principles of intellectual forms, i.e. the essences themselves. This illumination is accordingly the cause (*sabab*, V, 5, 234.15, 16, 17 [*causa*, 126.31, 32, 33]) of the bestowal of intellectual forms on the human intellect: the light of its perpetual intellection of intellectual forms shines upon the imaginative particulars, which are potentially intelligible, and makes them actually intelligible to the human intellect and, consequently, establishes a connection between them and the human intellect, which results in intellection. Therefore, the Active Intellect acts in no way upon the human intellect; rather, it acts on imaginative particulars and brings their potential intelligibility into actuality.

As the comparison with the Sun's light indicates, no wilful agency is admitted on the part of the Active Intellect: for, as the Sun does not decide to make living beings see (or feel the warmth emanating from it), but emanates light (and warmth) simply by its being, likewise the Active Intellect does not arbitrarily make intellectual forms flow upon human intellect, but by its being alone it perpetually thinks the forms and, thus, provides the context wherein human beings can actually practice intellection. The intellective process is triggered by the human intellect's inspection of imaginative particulars, just as visual perception is triggered by the perceiver's turning to visible objects. The voluntary act of inspection of those particulars puts the human intellect on the right path to acquiring intellectual forms; nevertheless, the perfection of that act of inspection is the Active Intellect's shining light upon those particulars. Both conditions are necessary, but – alone – not sufficient to bring about intellection. Strictly speaking, the Active Intellect does nothing in this process other than being what it is, namely providing the *condition of possibility* for an imaginative particular's actual intelligibility. As a result of the combination of the human intellect's inspection of imaginative particulars and the Active Intellect's shining light on them, the human intellect can actually conceive intellectual forms since it is brought to the stage of the acquired (*mustafād*) intellect, i.e. the disposition of the intellect in (first)

[in something else]. And we say that light is part of the whole of this visible thing which we call color and, when it mixes with color in potentiality, there comes to be from both [light and potential color] the thing which is color in actuality through admixture. If that disposition was not there, there would then be illumination and pure glare".

64 It is worth noticing that when, in dealing with the relationship between the imaginative particulars and the light of the Active Intellect that shines on them and makes them actually intelligible, Avicenna refers to the light of the Active Intellect by using the term *nūr* (V, 5, 235.1, 3, 20 [127.38, 41]), which is precisely the term that, in his account of vision, indicates the light which radiates from the Sun and makes potentially colored visible objects actually colored. Avicenna, however, also makes use of the term *ḍaw'* in order to refer to the light of the Active Intellect (V, 5, 236.1 [128.62]); therefore, it is fair to conclude that Avicenna's use of the terms *nūr* and *ḍaw'* in *Nafs*, V, 5 is not entirely coherent with his terminological analysis in *Nafs*, III, 1.

actuality to think of intellectual forms is brought to the second actuality.[65] This is, however, a *basic* reading of Avicenna's cryptic text: the formula *condition of possibility*, which I have used, is not completely satisfactory and demands a further interpretative effort in order to be clarified. What exactly does it mean that the Active Intellect's shining light provides the condition of possibility for the imaginative particulars' actual intelligibility? Perhaps the answer should be sought in Avicenna's attempt to provide universal knowledge with a more solid ground than induction (*istiqrā'*) or, even, experience (*tağriba*). For if the knowledge that pre-exists universal knowledge is experience, a problem arises as to how the knowledge acquired on that basis can be universal or, better, as to how the knower can be certain that the knowledge acquired on an empirical basis is universal.[66] Avicenna's solution to this problem, namely to the certainty issue, involves the Active Intellect and, in general, his structure of the world. It has become clear that in Avicenna's epistemology, the Active Intellect is an intellect engaged in perpetually intelligizing the principles of intellectual forms that it possesses in itself and then in making those forms actually intelligible to the human intellect. Similarly, in his cosmological system, the *Dator formarum* (or *Giver of Forms*, *wāhib al-ṣuwar*), i.e. the last celestial intelligence, possesses all forms and is responsible for infusing them in the sublunary matter that is prepared to receive them.[67] Although the identification of the *Dator formarum* with the Active Intellect seems to be reasonable, at least for the sake of economy, Avicenna has never argued in favour of their identification and has kept distinct the cosmological (and ontological) domain from the epistemological domain, to which the *Dator formarum* and the Active Intellect respectively belong.[68] Nevertheless, identifi-

---

65 Naming the human intellect which is exercising its disposition to think "acquired intellect" might mislead Avicenna's interpreters, since it might seem that the human intellect receives its capacity for thinking as well as its contents from above, that is, from the Active Intellect. On the contrary, the Active Intellect only provides the condition of possibility of the human intellect's actual intellection of imaginative particulars, which are potentially intelligible, by radiating its light on them. It is not coincidence that, outside *Nafs*, I, 5, Avicenna only mentions the "acquired intellect" in *Nafs*, V, 6, that is, when he deals with the recollection of an intellectual form already acquired which is, then, directly emanated upon (or acquired by) the human intellect whenever it comes into contact with the Active Intellect. This note of caution can, therefore, prevent confusion in approaching these two texts: *Nafs*, V, 5 and V, 6.

66 The epistemological problem related to a strong empiricist position echoes the problem raised by Aristotle's in *An. Post.*, II, 19 with regard to the knowledge that must pre-exist the acquisition of the principles of demonstration: according to Aristotle, pre-existing knowledge must be perception, which provides an inferential, inductive basis to demonstrative knowledge, and thus avoids an infinite regress of cognitive faculties. In a similar vein, Avicenna elaborates his model of scientific knowledge.

67 See *Ilāhiyyāt*, IX, 3–5.

68 I shall not discuss the arguments *pro* and *contra* the identification of the *Dator formarum* with the Active Intellect. For this debate, see J. Janssens, "The Notions of *Wāhib al-ṣuwar (Giver of Forms)* and *Wāhib al-ʿaql (Bestower of intelligence)* in Ibn Sīnā", in M. C. Pacheco, J. F. Meirinhos eds., *Intellect et imagination dans la Philosophie médiévale. Actes du XIe Congrès International de Philosophie Médié-*

cation of these two entities is crucial for Avicenna's theory of intellectual knowledge because it entails the identification of the forms that the *Dator formarum* infuses in sublunary matter with the forms whose actual intelligibility is guaranteed by the Active Intellect's perpetually intelligizing their principles. If the relation of the epistemological level of the Active Intellect to the onto-cosmological level of the *Dator formarum* is assumed, the sense in which the Active Intellect provides the *condition of possibility* for the imaginative particulars' actual intelligibility becomes clearer: the Active Intellect's shining light guarantees that the human intellect has correctly abstracted from matter the very forms that the *Dator formarum* has previously infused in it.

Consequently, the Active Intellect's presence in Avicenna's model of human intellection provides *certainty* that the human intellect has correctly acquired universal, intellectual forms. This interpretation can be considered a more comprehensive reading of Avicenna's text, a reading that further research is called to refine and, hopefully, to consolidate. Here I will limit myself to pointing to a passage from *Burhān*, I, 9, which seems to support my interpretation. There, Avicenna seems to distinguish the level of certainty resulting from experience (*taǧriba*), which is based on repeated observations at stipulated conditions,[69] from universal certainty (*yaqīn kullī*). The latter is said not to derive from experience, "but rather from the separate cause that provides the principles of certainty, whose account is contained in sciences other than logic (*bal ʿan al-sabab al-mubāyin allaḏī yufīdu awāʾil al-yaqīn wa-ḫabaruhū fī ʿulūm ġayr al-manṭiq*)" (*Burhān*, I, 9, 98.1–2). In all likelihood, in this passage Avicenna refers to the Active Intellect as what is responsible for universal certainty, namely to the certainty connected with universal knowledge. Here the expression "the separate cause that provides the principle of certainty" can be compared with the characterization of the Active Intellect as "a cause that brings our souls from potentiality to actuality with respect to intelligibles" and "an intellect in actuality in which are the principles of intellectual forms in an abstracted way [from matter]" in *Nafs*, V, 5, 234.16–18. Indeed, the account of the Active Intellect is provided out-

vale de la Société Internationale pour l'Études de la Philosophie Médiévale (S.I.E.P.M.) – Porto, du 26 au 31 août 2002, Brepols, Turnhout 2006, 551–562; D. N. Hasse, "Avicenna's 'Giver of Forms' in Latin Philosophy, Especially in the Works of Albertus Magnus", in D. N. Hasse, A. Bertolacci eds., *The Arabic, Hebrew and Latin Reception of Avicenna's Metaphysics*, "Scientia Graeco-Arabica", 7, De Gruyter, Berlin 2012, 225–249. For a new contribution to the history of the *Dator formarum*, see C. D'Ancona, "Aux origines du *dator formarum*. Plotin, l'*Épître sur la science divine* et al-Farabi", in E. Coda, C. Martini Bonadeo eds., *De l'Antiquité tardive au Moyen Age. Études de logique aristotélicienne et de philosophie grecque, syriaque, arabe et latine offertes à Henri Hugonnard-Roche*, J. Vrin, Paris 2014, 381–414.

69 On the notion of "experience", its difference from induction, and its role in Avicenna's epistemology, see J. McGinnis, "Avicenna's Naturalized Epistemology and Scientific Method", in S. Rahman, T. Street, H. Tahiri eds., *The Unity of Science in the Arabic Tradition. Science, Logic and Epistemology and their Interactions*, Springer, Berlin 2008, 129–152; and J. Janssens, ""Experience" *(tajriba)* in Classical Arabic Philosophy (al-Fārābī – Avicenna)", *Quaestio*, 4, 2004, 45–62.

side logic, that is, to be precise, in psychology (V, 5) and, *qua Dator formarum*, in metaphysics.

The analogy of light does not, therefore, represent a genuine endorsement of an illuminationist position on Avicenna's part, but is part of Avicenna's more structured answer to the epistemological problem related to the first acquisition of an intellectual form, which explains the passage from the inductive level of the experience (*taǧriba*) to the level of universal, demonstrative knowledge. As we have seen, Avicenna's epistemology has an empirical basis;[70] his empiricism, however, might be problematic with regard to intellectual knowledge, which is by nature universal and demonstrative. In order not to break away from his fundamental empiricism, Avicenna elaborates a model in which, on the one hand, the *starting point* of intellectual knowledge is the sensible data, and the human intellect is not enabled by an external cause to start to think of intellectual forms,[71] whereas, on the other hand, the correct *conclusion* of the intellective process is guaranteed by his reference to the Active Intellect, that is, to what makes the imaginative particulars actually *visible* to the human intellect.

The Ontological Role of the Active Intellect in Recovering an Intellectual Form already Acquired

As I pointed out at the end of the introduction to this chapter, Avicenna makes use of the Active Intellect also to solve the ontological problem related to the recollection of an intellectual form already acquired.[72] In particular, this problem arises from Avicenna's denial of intellectual memory in *Nafs*, V, 6,[73] which encountered severe criticism in the Latin West. According to Avicenna, after the first acquisition of an intellectual form, the soul's disposition to acquire this form is perfect. Thus, whenever it wishes, the soul can establish a contact with the Active Intellect and let the form be present in the mind. But this presence only lasts as long as the intellect actually thinks of the form since there is no intellectual memory. Here Avicenna refers once again to the analogy between intellection and vision: the first acquisition (*al-*

70 On Avicenna's empiricism, see Gutas, "The Empiricism".

71 This interpretation seems to be confirmed by the reference to "the intellect that is affected through our souls" (*wa-l-ʿaql al-munfaʿil ʿan anfusinā*, 234.13 [*de (sc. intelligentia) patiente ex nostris animabus*, 126.28]) in the second part of the title of *Nafs*, V, 5. The mention of "the intellect that is affected through our souls" seems to suggest that, according to Avicenna, the human, passive (i.e. material) intellect is affected not by the Active Intellect but, rather, through the human soul itself, that is, through the intellective process initiated by the human intellect's inspection of the particulars that leads to the acquisition of intellectual forms.

72 Several contemporary scholars maintain that the ontological problem related to the recollection of an intellectual form already acquired is sufficient to account for Avicenna's introduction of the Active Intellect in his model of human intellection, as I have shown in the introduction of this chapter.

73 On this chapter, see Gutas, "Avicenna, *De anima* (V 6)".

taʿallum al-awwal) of a certain intellectual form is like the cure of an eye disease, says Avicenna. When the eye is cured, it is in a state in which it can grasp the form of a certain visible object whenever it wishes; and if it turns away from that visible object, it becomes potentially visible in a way that is very close to actuality.[74]

The denial of intellectual memory and, consequently, the claim that the intellect has no intellectual forms in itself when it is not actually thinking, are not surprising since Aristotle himself may be taken to endorse this position. In *Nafs*, V, 6 Avicenna seems to hold the same position as Aristotle and to consider memory as a part of the animal soul. Indeed, he draws a distinction between imaginative and intellectual forms:[75] the former are stored in two storage faculties of the animal soul, namely in imagery (*ḫayāl*) or the form-bearing faculty (*quwwa muṣawwira*), and in the faculty of memory (*quwwa ḥāfiẓa* or *quwwa mutaḏakkira*), which are the depositories (*ḫizāna*) of these forms,[76] whereas the latter are present in the rational soul only as long as it thinks, but cannot be stored in it. The claim according to which imaginative forms are stored in two faculties of the animal soul is not problematic:[77] the imaginative forms are particular, so their being stored in a faculty located in a body does not corrupt or adulterate their nature. The case of intellectual forms is different: they do not exist completely in actuality in the intellect, which cannot be their depository. For if they were in a body, and thus endowed with a location, they would lose their universality and, consequently, would not be intelligible at all. Therefore, the existence of intellectual forms in the intellect lasts only as long as it thinks of them, and their intellection depends on the Active Intellect's shining light upon the imaginative particulars according to the human intellect's request (*ṭalab*),[78] namely as a result of the human intellect's act of inspection of those particulars, but is interrupted when the human intellect turns away from them.

After the specific status of imaginative and intellectual forms is clarified, Avicenna explicitly faces the question of the further recollection of an intellectual form already acquired. Does it require a new process of acquisition? According to Avicenna a new process of acquisition of that intellectual form is not needed: it is sufficient for the human intellect to reconsider the form already acquired that it establishes a contact with the Active Intellect where intellectual forms are stored. In this connection, first acquisition of a specific, intellectual form implies that, whenever one wishes, one will be able to bring that form back to one's mind, by coming into contact (*ittaṣala ittiṣāl*) with the Active Intellect, from which that specific form flows again upon

74 *Nafs*, V, 6, 247.11–13 [149.51–53]. For the reconstruction of Avicenna's denial of the intellectual memory, see Hasse, *Avicenna's* De anima, in part. 186–189.

75 *Nafs*, V, 6, 244.10–245.5 [144.74–146.94]; 246.13–247.2 [148.30–40].

76 It should be noted here that, according to Avicenna, in the faculty of memory *maʿānin* (*meanings*), i.e. the object of estimation, are stored. For a discussion of these faculties, see Alpina, "Retaining, Remembering, Recollecting".

77 With the caveat expressed in the previous footnote.

78 On the notion of *ṭalab*, see Gutas, "Intuition and Thinking", 30, n. 59.

the human intellect.[79] Therefore, the ontological role that the Active Intellect plays in the process of recollection of an intellectual form already acquired is as a *collector* of intellectual forms since, insofar as it is a separate intellect, it is an immaterial entity and, consequently, can preserve immaterial forms.

The distinction between first acquisition of a form and its further recollection at will explains why in some passages about the Active Intellect one reads about abstraction and emanation, whereas others deal only with emanation: the latter are about the re-acquisition of intellectual forms already acquired, for which abstraction is not needed. As D. N. Hasse has maintained, it seems that "Avicenna makes fuller use of the emanation terminology in passages about retrieving an already known form than in those about the first acquisition of it".[80]

Conclusion

Avicenna's theory of human intellection has to be considered as an attempt to solve two problems within a single, coherent paradigm. The cornerstone of this paradigm, namely the element that guarantees its fundamental unity, is the Active Intellect, to which Avicenna assigns two different but complementary roles at two different levels. In particular, at the epistemological level, the Active Intellect acts as the *source of intelligibility* of any intellectual form in the sublunary realm: its active presence throughout the intellective process provides the *condition of possibility* for the actualization of the human intellect's potentiality to conceive intellectual forms, and the *certainty* that the human intellect has correctly acquired those forms. At the ontological level, by contrast, the Active Intellect acts as the *collector* of intellectual forms: Avicenna's denial of intellectual memory requires a *depository* of the intellectual forms already acquired in order to avoid a new process of acquisition in the case of any subsequent recovery of them.

On a more general level, Avicenna's theory of human intellection is a perfect litmus test for verifying the conclusions of the previous chapters about the amphibious status of the human rational soul, since the process through which human beings acquire universal, intellectual forms is intrinsically related to the ontological status of the soul. It involves two movements that, far from being incompatible, seem to account perfectly for, on the one hand, the soul's need for a relation to the body, and on the other hand, its independence of it in performing its own activity.

---

79 *Nafs*, V, 6, 245.5–246.13 [146.95–148.30]; 247.2–248.8 [148.41–150.66].
80 See n. 74 above.

Chapter Six

Avicenna's Psychology: A Diachronic Perspective

Introduction

As was pointed out at the beginning of Chapter 3, throughout his long philosophical career Avicenna almost continuously wrote about the soul, to which he has devoted different kinds of works, i.e. sections within expository *summae*, monographic treatises, commentaries. However, in presenting Avicenna's science of the soul in diachronic perspective, the psychological sections of his other *summae* besides the *Šifāʾ* will be preferred for three reasons: (a) the name of Avicenna is particularly related to the philosophical *summa*, since he can be rightly considered the pioneer of this literary genre; (b) within the *summae* reflection on a specific scientific field can be evaluated within the wider context of the relations among different sciences, which is crucial for the present study; and, lastly, (c) Avicenna's *summae* cover the whole period of his philosophical activity and, therefore, close scrutiny and comparison might make it possible to evaluate the development of his thought (if any), in particular with respect to the three issues singled out in the preceding chapters, i.e. the subject and consequently the epistemological status of the science of the soul, the traditional formulation of the definition of the soul (and its implications for the unity of the science of the soul), and the human being's first acquisition of an intellectual form.

The psychological sections that will be taken into account are those belonging to the following *summae: K. al-Maǧmūʿ* or *al-Ḥikma al-ʿArūḍiyya* (*The Compilation* or *Philosophy for ʿArūḍī*), *ʿUyūn al-Ḥikma* (*Elements of Philosophy*), *K. al-Hidāya* (*The Guidance*), *K. al-Naǧāt* (*The Salvation*), *Dānešnāme-ye ʿAlāʾī* (*Philosophy for ʿAlāʾ al-Dawla*), *al-Mašriqiyyūn* or *al-Ḥikma al-Mašriqiyya* (*The Easterners* or *Eastern Philosophy*), and *K. al-Išārāt wa-l-tanbīhāt* (*Pointers and Reminders*).[1] In what follows, a survey of their content with a brief presentation of the work will be provided, whereas a comprehensive, comparative evaluation between them and the *Nafs* will be made at the end of the chapter. In addition to the psychological sections of Avicenna's other *summae*, two other texts will be taken into account: the section on the intellectual knowledge leading the human soul from inception to perfection in the eighth chapter of the *Maqāla fī l-nafs ʿalà sunnat al-iḫtiṣār* (*Compendium on the Soul*), Avicenna's earliest philosophical treatise, and the section on the fundamental (as opposed to the derivative) divisions of natural philosophy in the *Maqāla fī Aqsām*

1 As will be explicitly highlighted at the beginning of and within each section dealing with each one of the Avicennian *summae*, all the pieces of information concerning the date and the occasion (if any) of their composition, together with further general details, are drawn from Gutas, *Avicenna and the Aristotelian Tradition.*

https://doi.org/10.1515/9783110706840-008

al-ʿulūm al-ʿaqliyya (*Treatise on the Divisions of the Intellectual Sciences*), a writing specifically devoted to the classification of the sciences. These texts, which are presented at the end of this chapter, can cast some light on Avicenna's position about the place and the subject of psychology also in contexts independent of the Peripatetic character of the *Šifāʾ*.

K. al-Maǧmūʿ or al-Ḥikma al-ʿArūḍiyya (The Compilation or Philosophy for ʿArūḍī)[2]

The *K. al-Maǧmūʿ* or *al-Ḥikma al-ʿArūḍiyya* (*The Compilation* or *Philosophy for ʿArūḍī*) seems to be the first medieval philosophical *summa*, and "a precedent for all subsequent philosophical *summae*, both by Avicenna and by his successors, both in the East and in the West". In Avicenna's *Biography* we read: "In my neighborhood there was a man called Abū l-Ḥasan al-ʿArūḍī (*sc.* the Prosodist) who asked me to compose for him a comprehensive book on this science (*sc.* the science that Avicenna has attained). I composed for him *The Compilation* (*al-Maǧmūʿ*), and I gave it his name (i.e. *al-Ḥikma al-ʿArūḍiyya*). In it I included all the sciences except mathematics" (38.3–5). As Gutas has noticed, "the work was Avicenna's first attempt to treat in a systematic way and within the confines of a single book all the branches of theoretical philosophy according to the Aristotelian classification", with the exception of mathematics and practical philosophy. In Gutas' opinion, Avicenna wrote the *K. al-Maǧmūʿ* in 391H/1000–1, a date calculated on the basis of Avicenna's statement in the *Biography* that he was twenty-one years old when he completed it.

In the following table the *divisio textus* of the psychological section of *K. al-Maǧmūʿ* is provided, which covers 155.5–160.10 in Ṣāliḥ edition, and folios 78^{r}- 81^{v} of the manuscript preserving it,[3] together with the corresponding chapters of the *Nafs*.

Ṣāliḥ ed.	*al-Maǧmūʿ*	*Nafs*
155.5–7	General introduction	-
155.7–19	Plants and vegetative soul: faculties of nutrition, growth, and reproduction	I, 5, 40.14–41.3
155.20–157.20	Animals and animal soul:	I, 5, 41.4–45.16

2 It is extant in a unique, though incomplete, independent manuscript, Uppsala 364, and in various excerpts in later works by Avicenna (for instance, *al-Maǧmūʿ*, 155 (Ṣāliḥ ed.) corresponds to *Naǧāt*, 318.2–319.8 (Dānišpažūh ed.)). The text of the manuscript was printed, though not accurately and without any annotation and consultation of previous partial editions, by Ṣāliḥ (2007). All this information is derived from Gutas, *Avicenna and the Aristotelian Tradition*, 86–93, 417.

3 The edition seems to include in the psychological section also 160.11–5 which, according to Gutas, belongs to the metaphysical treatment of natural theology. See Gutas, *Avicenna and the Aristotelian Tradition*, 89–90.

Continued

Ṣāliḥ ed.	al-Maǧmūʿ		Nafs
	five external senses (taste, touch, smell, hearing, sight); internal senses (common sense, imagination/cogitation, estimation); locomotion; concupiscible and irascible faculty		
157.21–160.10	157.21–4	Human beings and human soul. General introduction, distinction between theoretical and practical intellect	I, 5, 45.17–19; 46.7–8; V, 1, 207.13–15
	157.24–158.6	Four degrees of the theoretical intellect	I, 5, 48.18–50.12
	158.6–10	Brief mention of the first acquisition of intellectual forms	V, 5, 234.14–19
	158.10–20	Demonstration of the incorporeality of the theoretical intellect	V, 2, 212.9–214.5
	158.20–159.20	Difference between the bodily faculties and the theoretical intellect with respect to their activity	V, 2, 216.16–220.5
	159.20–160.10	Difference between the intellectual pleasure in this life and the pleasure in the afterlife; intermediate position of the soul	V, 5, 237.16–238.9

ʿUyūn al-Ḥikma (Elements of Philosophy)[4]

This *summa* contains a concise treatment of philosophy, encompassing logic, natural philosophy, and metaphysics, and was subjected to a massive commentary by Faḫr al-Dīn al-Rāzī. As Gutas has noticed, "the work itself appears to have been generated by splicing together two independent parts, one on logic, which was originally composed independently and circulated under the title *al-Mūǧaz al-ṣaġīr fī l-manṭiq* (*Short Epitome on Logic*), and the other on natural philosophy and metaphysics". The original independence of these two parts "is further corroborated by the fact that Avicenna opens the part on natural philosophy by giving a definition of philosophy (*ḥikma*) which is then followed by a classification of the philosophical sciences, something normally provided at the very beginning of a work".[5] The dating is uncer-

4 For the edition of this work, see *ʿUyūn al-Ḥikma*, ed. ʿA. Badawī, Cairo, Publications de l'Institut Français d'Archeologie Orientale, 1954; Dār al-Qalam, Beirut, Wakālat al-Maṭbūʿāt, Kuwait, 1980². The general information about this work is drawn from Gutas, *Avicenna and the Aristotelian Tradition*, 417–419.

5 For the proem to the second part of the work, see *ʿUyūn al-Ḥikma*, 63.1–64.7.

tain: according to Gutas, the work might be tentatively placed during what he has called "Avicenna's Transition Period"; however, in order to be proved, this conjecture requires further investigation into the doctrinal relationship of the contents of this work with those of other Avicennian works.

In the following table the *divisio textus* of the psychological section of *'Uyūn al-Ḥikma* is provided together with the corresponding chapters of the *Nafs*.

Badawī ed.	***'Uyūn al-Ḥikma***	***Nafs***
76.12–18	Brief introduction on plants Faculties of nutrition, growth, and reproduction	I, 5, 40.14–41.3
76.19–20	Introduction on animals and their two main faculties, i.e. perception and locomotion	I, 5, 41.4–45.16
76.21–22	External and internal senses	
76.23–25	The sense of touch	
77.1–3	The sense of taste, smell, and hearing	
77.4–78.7	The sense of sight and the theory of vision	III, 5–7
78.8–13	The common sense	
78.14–16	The form-bearing faculty	
78.17–21	Estimation and memory	
78.22–24	Imagination/cogitation	
78.25–79.5	Conclusion on animal perception	
79.6–13	Locomotion and its faculties: the concupiscible and irascible faculty; the faculties of repulsion and attraction	
79.14–80.1	General remarks on animal faculties	
80.2–11	Brief presentation of the rational soul and its faculties	[V, 1][6]
80.12–14	The practical intellect	I, 5, 45.17–20
80.15–16	The dispositions specific to the human being	I, 5, 46.5; V, 1, 204.13–15; 205.9–11
80.17–18	Brief introduction on the activity of the theoretical intellect	V, 1, 206.11
80.18–81.13	*Excursus* on the kinds of abstraction of the perceptive faculties (external senses, imagination, estimation, intellect)	II, 2, 58.1–61.14
81.14–21	The two faculties of the rational soul: the practical and the theoretical faculty	I, 5, 47.8–18; V, 1, 207.4–6

6 Square brackets indicate general, thematic similarity.

Continued

Badawī ed.	*ʿUyūn al-Ḥikma*	*Nafs*
81.22–82.6	The degrees of the theoretical intellect and the process of human intellection (the intervention of the Active Intellect and the analogy of the Sun)	I, 5, 48.18–50.12 V, 5, 234.14–19
82.7–84.3	Demonstration of the incorporeality of the soul by referring to the fact that theoretical intellect does not perform its activity by means of a bodily organ	V, 2, 217.4–218.14

K. al-Hidāya (The Guidance)[7]

According to al-Ǧūzǧānī's biography of his master, Avicenna wrote the *K. al-Hidāya* (*The Guidance*) while imprisoned in the castle of Fardaǧān outside of Hamadān in 414H/1023–4, probably at the same time as he wrote the first section of logic, the first six sections of natural philosophy, and the metaphysics of the *Šifāʾ*, according to Gutas' chronology (412–414H/1021–1024). The comparison between the psychological section of the *K. al-Hidāya* and that of the *Šifāʾ*, provided in the table at the end of this section, will provide further ground in support of the plausibility of their simultaneous composition. In a brief introduction, Avicenna addresses a "dear brother" (*al-aḫ al-ʿazīz*), "who may be his real brother, ʿAlī, and says that he will include in the book 'synopses (*ǧawāmiʿ*) of the philosophical sciences expressed as concisely and clearly as possible' ". The philosophical sciences he treats are logic, natural philosophy, and metaphysics, concluding with the so-called "metaphysics of the rational soul".

As Gutas noticed, "the style, in addition to its brevity, is literary and distinguished by the avoidance of technical terminology". Gutas formulates three hypotheses to explain the reason why Avicenna adopted a more literary style in this *summa:* either (a) "he may not have had access to his philosophical books and notes while imprisoned, and was writing from memory; or (b) he expected his "brother" to appreciate and understand philosophy better if it were put in less technical terms which he would find more appealing [...]; or, as Michot suggested, (c) Avicenna employed an extremely concise style as an exercise intended to distract and amuse him during his imprisonment. Perhaps all of these factors were operative".[8]

In the following table the *divisio textus* of the psychological section of *K. al-Hidāya* is provided together with the corresponding chapters of the *Nafs*.

---

7 For the edition of this work, see *Kitāb al-Hidāya*, ed. M. ʿAbduh, Maktaba al-Qāhira al-ḥadīṯa, Cairo 1974. The general information about this work is drawn from Gutas, *Avicenna and the Aristotelian Tradition*, 419–420.

8 Gutas, *Avicenna and the Aristotelian Tradition*, 420.

ʿAbduh ed.	*al-Hidāya*	*Nafs*
204.1–205.3	The vegetative soul and its faculties	I, 5, 40.14–41.3
206.1–7	The animal soul and its faculties	I, 5, 41.4–45.16
206.8–208.4	External senses Sense of touch and its objects Sense of taste and its objects Sense of smell and its objects Sense of hearing and its objects	
208.5–209.2	Sense of sight. Three theories of vision The theory of the supporters of mathematics	III, 5–7
209.3–210.2	The theory of physicians	III, 5–7
210.3–211.3	The theory of natural philosophers	III, 5–7
211.4–6	Summary of the exposition on the external senses	
211.7–213.8	Internal senses Common sense and imagery	
213.9–214.3	Estimation, memory, and the [faculty] that organizes [the data collected by other internal senses]	
215.1–6	Locations of the internal, perceptive faculties	
215.7–9	Summary of the exposition on the animal soul	
216.1–6	The human rational soul	II, 2, 60.2–10; 61.5–14 I, 5, 46.7–8; [V, 1]
216.7–217.10	Faculties of the human rational soul	
217.11–220.6	Independence (*istiqlāl*) of the rational soul from matter	V, 2, 210.6–214.5
221.1–6	Demonstration of the rational soul's self-perception	V, 2, 216.2–217.8
222.1–223.2	Demonstration of the fact that the rational soul does not perform its activity by means of a bodily organ	V, 2, 218.15–220.5
223.3–226.1	Eternity of the rational soul. Demonstration of the separation of the rational soul from the body	V, 4, 227.13–16; 229.12–231.2
227.1–228.2	Demonstration of the simplicity of the rational soul	V, 4, 232.7–233.5
229.1–230.2	The contact between the rational soul and the Active Intellect	V, 5, 234.14–235.2
230.3	Conclusion of the second part (*sc.* that on natural philosophy) of *The Guidance*	-

K. al-Naǧāt (The Salvation)[9]

In the Avicenna's biography al-Ǧūzǧānī says that his master wrote the *K. al-Naǧāt* en route to Šābūr-Ḫwāst immediately after having completed the last books of the *Šifāʾ*. According to the chronology established by Gutas, the *K. al-Naǧāt* was written in 417H/1026–7 or 418H/1027–8.

"This work was a commissioned piece. In his brief introduction Avicenna refers to a group of unspecified friends who asked him to compile a book that would include the indispensable philosophical knowledge that a person has to acquire in order to be counted among the educated elite. In particular, they asked him to include only the fundamental principles of logic and natural philosophy, as much information from geometry and arithmetic as is necessary for one to deal with mathematical proofs, practical information from astronomy related to calendars and *ziǧes,*[10] music and metaphysics".[11]

As al-Ǧūzǧānī informs us, Avicenna compiled the *K. al-Naǧāt* practically without composing a single line anew. As to the part on natural philosophy, the most interesting for the purpose of the present study, Avicenna copied the corresponding chapters from the *K. al-Maǧmūʿ*, except for the psychological section, for which he resorted to the chapter from the *al-Maʿād al-aṣġar*, or *Ḥāl al-nafs al-insāniyya* (*Lesser Destination* or *State of the Human Soul*).[12] It is, therefore, worth recalling that the *K. al-Naǧāt* "is not a summary or an abridgment of the *Šifāʾ*, as frequently stated,

9 For the two more recent editions of this work, see *Al-Naǧāt min al-ġaraq fī baḥr al-ḍalālāt*, ed. M. T. Dānišpažūh, Dānišgah-i Tehran, Tehran 1985 (which is the edition I refer to in the present study); *Kitāb al-Naǧāt*, ed. M. Faḫrī, Dār al-afāq al-ǧadīda, Beirut 1985. For the translation of the psychology section, see F. Rahman, *Avicenna's Psychology* (English translation of Book 2, Chapter 6), Oxford University Press, London 1952. For the general information provided in this section, see Gutas, *Avicenna and the Aristotelian Tradition*, 115–117.

10 This generic name refers to Islamic astronomical books that tabulate parameters used for astronomical calculations of the positions of the Sun, Moon, stars, and planets. The name is derived from the Middle Persian (or Sassanian) term *zih* or *zīg*, meaning *cord*. The term is believed to refer to the arrangement of threads in weaving, which was transferred to the arrangement of rows and columns in tabulated data. In addition to the term *zīǧ*, some were called by the name *qānūn*, derived from the equivalent Greek word κανών. See K. E. Stewart, *Islamic Astronomical Tables*, American Philosophical Society, Philadelphia 1956.

11 Gutas, *Avicenna and the Aristotelian Tradition*, 115. It is worth noting that, as he openly says, al-Ǧūzǧānī completed the work by adding "the chapters on geometry, astronomy, and music from earlier works by Avicenna found in his own possession and, since he could find nothing appropriate for arithmetic, he took it upon himself to abridge from Avicenna's larger work on arithmetic in *Šifāʾ* those passages that are especially pertinent to music, and to include them in *K. al-Naǧāt*. He also wrote a very brief prologue to the part on mathematics from which the aforementioned information is derived". For al-Ǧūzǧānī's explanation of Avicenna's omission of the mathematical part, see Gutas, *Avicenna and the Aristotelian Tradition*, 116–117.

12 On the first chapter of this work, see Chapter 4, n. 69. It should be noted that the beginning of the psychological section of the *Naǧāt* reproduces verbatim the beginning of the psychological section of the *K. al-Maǧmūʿ* ("*wa-qad yatakawwanu...al-maḏkūra*", 318.2–4).

but rather both it and the *Šifā'* contain passages taken from earlier works by Avicenna".

In the table below the contents of the psychological section of the *K. al-Naǧāt* are provided alongside the corresponding chapters of the *Nafs*.

Dānišpažūh ed.	***Naǧāt***	***Nafs***
318.1–320.14	Brief introduction The vegetative soul and its faculties	I, 5, 39.13–41.3
321.1–330.5	The animal soul Locomotion and its faculties: the concupiscible and irascible faculty External senses: sight; hearing; smell; taste; touch; Theories of vision Internal senses: Distinction between form and meaning; Distinction between perception with activity and perception without activity; Distinction between first and second perception; *Phantasia*, or common sense; imagery, or form-bearing faculty; imagination, or cogitation; estimation; memory; relationship between internal senses; Conclusion on the animal faculties	I, 5, 41.4–45.16 III, 5–7
330.6–332.13	The rational soul	I, 5, 45.17–47.17
333.1–336.10	The theoretical faculty and its degrees	I, 5, 48.1–50.12
339.1–341.9	The rational soul's acquisition of knowledge	V, 6, 248.9–250.4
341.10–343.9	Hierarchy of the psychic faculties	I, 5, 50, 13–51.16
344.1–349.8	Distinction between the perception of the external senses, the perception of imagination, the perception of estimation, and the perception of intellect	II, 2, 58.4–61.17
349.9–356.7	The particular is not perceived by what is separated from matter, and the universal is not perceived by what is material	IV, 3, 188.2–194.2
356.8–364.13	The receptacle of the intelligibles is an incorporeal substance	V, 2, 209.17–216.8
364.14–371. 11	The intellective faculty does not perform its activity by means of a bodily organ	V, 2, 216.18–221. 17
371.12–374.14	The assistance of the animal faculties to the rational soul	V, 3, 221.17–223.10
375.1–378.2	The temporal origination of the soul	V, 4, 223.15–225–17

Continued

Dānišpažūh ed.	*Naǧāt*	*Nafs*
378.3–386.11	The immortality of the rational soul	V, 4, 227.13–233.5
386.12–387.17	Refutation of the doctrine of transmigration	V, 4, 233.6–234.11
388.1–394.6	Unity of the soul	V, 7, 261.9–262.15
394.7–396.7	Evidence for the existence of the Active Intellect	[V, 5, 234.14–236.2]

Dānešnāme-ye ʿAlāʾī (Philosophy for ʿAlāʾ al-Dawla)[13]

"This work was written in Persian at the express request of the Kākūyid ʿAlāʾ al-Dawla during Avicenna's stay in Iṣfahān. Since Avicenna lived in Iṣfahān from 414H/1023–4 until his death in 428H/1037, it could have been written any time during this long period". Since it closely resembles the *K. al-Naǧāt* both in scope and in execution, Gutas suggests placing it around 418H/1027–8; however, it may be possible to arrive at a more precise relative date after a thorough doctrinal study and a comparison of its major doctrinal points "with those in other works in order to detect shifts in emphasis".

In the introduction Avicenna says "that ʿAlāʾ al-Dawla specifically asked him to set down in an abridged manner the fundamental principles and major points of five sciences, i.e. logic, natural philosophy, astronomy, music, and metaphysics. Avicenna, in fact, actually wrote only three, omitting the two parts on mathematics", which were added by al-Ǧūzǧānī (who included "not only astronomy and music, as Avicenna was asked and intended to do, but also arithmetic and geometry", as happened in the *K. al-Naǧāt*),[14] and "changed the order of presentation of the rest into logic, met-

13 For the edition of the logic and natural philosophy part, see *Manṭiq-Ṭabīʿiyyāt. Dānešnāme-ye ʿAlāʾī*, ed. M. Meškāt, Anǧoman-e Āṯār-e Mellī, Tehran 1951; for the edition of the metaphysics part, see *Ilāhiyyāt. Dānešnāme-ye ʿAlāʾī*, ed. M. Muʿīn, Anǧoman-e Āṯār-e Mellī, Tehran 1951; for the edition of the mathematics part, see *Riyāḍiyyāt. Dānešnāme-ye ʿAlāʾī*, ed. M. Mīnovī, Anǧoman-e Āṯār-e Mellī, Tehran 1951. For the translation, see Avicenne, *Le Livre de science*, eds. M. Achena, H. Massé, Les Belles Lettres/UNESCO, Paris 1955, 1958², 1986³. The general information about this work is drawn from Gutas, *Avicenna and the Aristotelian Tradition*, 118–119.

14 The entire mathematical part "is largely a Persian translation of the corresponding parts that al-Ǧūzǧānī added to *K. al-Naǧāt:* geometry, astronomy, and music from earlier works by Avicenna, and arithmetic from his own selection of issues pertinent to music from the arithmetical part of the *Šifāʾ*", see Gutas, *Avicenna and the Aristotelian Tradition*, 119.

aphysics, and natural philosophy, a new arrangement Avicenna was later to follow in *al-Mašriqiyyūn*".

In the following table the content of the psychological section of this work is provided together with the reference to the corresponding chapters of the *Nafs*.

Meškāt ed.	*Dānešnāme-ye 'Alā'ī*	*Nafs*
78.4–80.8	The vegetative soul	I, 5
80.9–83.5	The animal soul	
83.6–86.9	External senses except sight	
87.1–95.1	Refutation of previous opinions on vision On the exposition of Aristotle's opinion on vision	III, 5–7
95.2–7	On the common sensibles	[I, 4/III, 8][15]
95.8–99.5	Internal senses	I, 5
99.6–100.10	Animal soul and its faculties	
101.1–102.5	The human soul	I, 5
102.6–108.2	The theoretical intellect and intellectual forms	II, 2; V, 1
108.3–109.12	Degrees of the theoretical intellect	I, 5
110.1–113.7	Pointing out (*nišān dādan*) that the intellectual activity does not occur by means of a bodily organ	V, 2
113.8–119.6	Demonstration (*burhān*) of the fact that the receptacle of the intelligibles is not a body	
119.7–122.2	Supplement to the demonstration of the independence of the intellectual activity from the body	
122.3–123.6	The eternity (*baqā'*) of the soul, and the faculty that survives the severance from the body	V, 4
123.7–129.8	The Active Intellect	V, 5
129.9–131.5	The cause of sleep	[IV, 2]
131.6–135.1	The cause of dream and its truthfulness	

15 A reference to common sensibles can be found in *Nafs*, I, 4, 34.15–35.1; and III, 8, 159.15–162.8. For Aristotle's list of common sensibles, i.e. movement, rest, figure, number, and magnitude, see *De an.*, II, 6, 418 a17–9.

Continued

Meškāt ed.	***Dānešnāme-ye ʿAlāʾī***	***Nafs***
135.2–136.6	The cause of the connection of the human soul with the invisible world	
136.7–139.4	The cause of the non-existing forms that are perceived by the senses	
139.5–141.9	The origin of miracles (*muʿǧizāt wa-karāmāt*)	[IV, 4]
141.10–145.3	The powerful souls	V, 6
145.4–146.4	The holy soul belonging to prophets (*payġām-bar*)	

Al-Mašriqiyyūn or al-Ḥikma al-Mašriqiyya (The Easterners or Eastern Philosophy)[16]

The Prologue to the *Šifāʾ* plays a pivotal role in dating *al-Mašriqiyyūn*. Since there Avicenna refers to *al-Mašriqiyyūn*, it might well be the case that he had written the Prologue to the *Šifāʾ* shortly after he had written the *Šifāʾ* and the *al-Mašriqiyyūn*, which must have been written around 418–420H/1027–1029. According to Gutas, Avicenna intended to include in this *summa* the following parts, in this order: 1) logic; 2) metaphysics: 2a) universal science, and 2b) theology; 3) natural philosophy; 4) ethics.[17] Unfortunately, this *summa* is only partially extant, since it was lost in 425H/1033–4. The parts that survive today are the part on logic from the beginning to the section corresponding to Aristotle's *Prior Analytics*, and the part on natural philosophy. As for the logic part, Avicenna apparently wrote the text anew, whereas the entire part on natural philosophy is copied verbatim from the *Šifāʾ* with some alterations in and abridgement of the text. In particular, "the part of *al-Ḥikma al-mašriqiyya* devoted to the theory of the soul is the most extensive in the extant portions of the book, something which well illustrates the significance Avicenna attached to the subject. It occupies 37 fols. in the III. Ahmet MS (fols. 658b-695a), while everything

16 The logic part was published in *Manṭiq al-mašriqiyyīn*, ed. M. al-Ḫaṭīb, ʿA. al-Qatlā, al-Maktaba al-Salafiyya, Cairo 1328H/1910, 1–83, which is based on the Cairo ms. Ḥikma 6 Muṣṭafā Fāḍil, ff. 116^{v}-138^{r}. The natural philosophy part was made available in a doctoral dissertation by Ahmet Özcan, *İbn Sīna'nın el-Hikmetu' l-meşrikiyye adlı eseri ve tabiat felsefesi*, Marmara Üniversitesi Sosyal Bilimler Enstitüsü, İslam Felsefesi Bilim Dalı, Istanbul 1993. Only the introduction has been translated into English, see Gutas, *Avicenna and the Aristotelian Tradition*, 34–41. For the general information about this work, I rely on Gutas, *Avicenna and the Aristotelian Tradition*, 119–144.

17 See Gutas, *Avicenna and the Aristotelian Tradition*, 137.

that preceded it in Physics occupies only 61 fols. (597b-658b). It is also the part that follows the text of the *Šifāʾ* very closely; it is, in essence, a verbatim transcript with numerous omissions and rephrasings".[18] It should be added that, although the psychological section of *al-Mašriqiyyūn* follows the text of the *Šifāʾ*, in some cases it provides a simplified version of it, as in the case of the passage containing the traditional definition of the soul.[19]

In the following table the content of the psychological section of this work is provided according to Özcan edition, together with the reference to the corresponding chapters of the *Nafs*.

Özcan ed.	***Nafs***
130.9–21	Prologue
130.21–136.2[20]	I, 1
136.3–137.11	I, 3
137.12–140.17	I, 4
140.17–146.10	I, 5
146.11–147.17	II, 1[21]
147.18–150.15	II, 2[22]
150.16–153.23	II, 3
154.1–155.2	II, 4
155.3–157.9	II, 5
157.10–165.21	III, 1–3; 5; 8
166.1–173.11	IV, 1–2[23]
173.12–178.6	IV, 3
178.7–182.22	IV, 4[24]
183.1–185.19[25]	V, 1
185.20–191.8	V, 2
191.8–194.8	V, 3

18 See Gutas, "Avicenna's *Eastern* ("*Oriental*") *Philosophy*", 172.
19 See Chapter 4, n. 62.
20 On the fact that at 135.22–136.2 Avicenna clearly says that in *al-Mašriqiyyūn* he will omit the doxographical discussion that can be read in *Nafs*, I, 2, see Chapter 3, n. 47.
21 Up to II, 1, 55.4 with the addition of 55.19–56.4.
22 Up to II, 2, 61.18 with the addition of 66.6–67.5.
23 With a lacuna from IV, 1, 167.18 to IV, 2, 172.6.
24 Up to IV, 4, 201.13, that is, omitting the passage in which Avicenna refers to his "medical books".
25 This chapter is a patchwork of *Nafs*, V, 1: it starts with 206.16 and ends at 209.11 with the insertion of sentences from 203–204.

Continued

Özcan ed.	*Nafs*
194.9 – 198.20	V, 4
198.21 – 200.15	V, 5
200.16 – 205.14	V, 6
205.15 – 209.3[26]	V, 7
209.4 – 212.17	V, 8

K. al-Išārāt wa-l-tanbīhāt (Pointers and Reminders)[27]

K. al-Išārāt wa-l-tanbīhāt is Avicenna's last philosophical *summa*, which, according to Gutas' chronology, was written sometime between 421–425H/1030–1034.[28] "This work marks the culmination of Avicenna's philosophical career because it achieves the greatest possible extrapolation from Aristotelian models of presentation, surpassing the stage reached during his period of Eastern philosophy, and it provides a concrete and magnificent example of his concept of the philosophical praxis which proceeds by deriving corollaries on the basis of fundamental principles through the help of the syllogistic procedures highlighted by guessing correctly the middle terms (*ḥads*)".[29] As to the style of this *summa*, Avicenna chose to write the entire work by using the indicative method of *pointers*. "This method of teaching depends on providing hints and guidelines, rather than ready-made arguments to the student, who is then expected to work out the entire theory on his own, as emerges from the prologue to the second part of the *summa*. This is what the two words of the title, *pointers* and *reminders*, refer to. Because of its succinctness, the work was apparently felt to be in need of oral exposition, and hard to understand even during

---

26 This chapter covers only the positive content of *Nafs*, V, 7, that is, an abridgement of 252.15–262.15. Avicenna does not engage in the exposition and consequent refutation of the doctrines of his predecessors that he deems incorrect. For that exposition he explicitly refers the reader to the *Nafs* of the *Šifāʾ*: "The falsehood (*buṭlān*) of each of these doctrines (I read *al-maḏāhib* instead of *al-marātib*) has been already shown in the *Kitāb al-Šifāʾ* (*sc.* in *Nafs*, V, 7)" (205.20).

27 For the editions of this *summa*, see Ibn Sīnā, *Le livre des théorèmes et des avertissements*, ed. J. Forget, Brill, Leiden 1892 (which is the edition I refer to in the present study); *Al-Išārāt wa-t-tanbīhāt maʿa Šarḥ Naṣīr al-Dīn al-Ṭūsī*, ed. S. Dunyā, 4 parts in 3 vols., Dār al-maʿārif, Cairo 1960–68. For the translation, see Ibn Sīnā (Avicenne), *Livre des Directives et Remarques* (*Kitāb al-Išārāt wa-l-tanbīhāt*), traduction avec introduction et notes par A.-M. Goichon, Commission internationale pour la traduction des chefs-d'oeuvre, Vrin, Beirut-Paris 1951, repr. 1999.

28 For the discussion of other dating proposals, see Gutas, *Avicenna and the Aristotelian Tradition*, 155–157.

29 See Gutas, *Avicenna and the Aristotelian Tradition*, 157.

Avicenna's lifetime; in the subsequent philosophical tradition it was subjected to repeated commentaries".[30]

"The arrangement of the contents of the work still follows the traditional order of logic, natural philosophy, and metaphysics, although natural philosophy and metaphysics are interwoven to form the second part", which can be then simply referred to as "philosophy". "Each part contains ten chapters: those of the logical part are called *nahǧ* (method, path), while those of the physical and metaphysical part are called *namaṭ* (form, i.e. kind of subject-matter or exposition)".[31]

In the following table, the contents of the third *namaṭ* (on psychology), and of the psychological part of the seventh *namaṭ* are provided together with the corresponding chapters of Avicenna's *Nafs*.

Forget ed.	***Išārāt wa-l-tanbīhāt***[32]	***Nafs***
Third *namaṭ*		
119.2–10	*Reminder.* On the proof of the existence of the human soul	I, 1, 16.2–14 V, 7, 255.1–15
119.11–17	*Reminder.* On the soul's self-awareness	-
119.18–120.10	*Reminder.* On the fact that the soul does not perceive itself by means of the senses	-
120.11–18	*Belief and reminder.* On the fact that the soul is not perceived only by means of its actions	-
120.19–121.10	*Pointer.* On the fact that the soul is neither corporeality nor temperament	I, 1, 4.4–10
121.11–122.4	*Pointer.* On the fact that the soul is one	I, 3, 31.11–32.19 V, 7, 251.1–3; 252.13–254.20
122.5–11	*Pointer.* On the perceptible object	II, 2, 58.3–8
122.12–14	*Reminder.* On the different kinds of perception	II, 2, 58.9–61.14
122.15–125.15	*Pointer.* On the internal senses	I, 5, 44–3–45.16

30 See Gutas, *Avicenna and the Aristotelian Tradition*, 158–159. For the commentary tradition on the *Išārāt*, see R. Wisnovsky, *Avicenna's Islamic reception*, in P. Adamson ed., *Interpreting Avicenna. Critical Essays*, Cambridge University Press, Cambridge 2013, 190–213, in part. 194; and A. Shihadeh. *Doubts on Avicenna: A Study and Edition of Sharaf al-Dīn al-Mas'ūdī's* Commentary *on the* Ishārāt, Islamic Philosophy, Theology and Science. Texts and Studies 95, Brill, Leiden-Boston 2015.

31 See Gutas, *Avicenna and the Aristotelian Tradition*, 159.

32 The words "pointer" (*išāra*), "reminder" (*tanbīh*), "belief" (*wahm*), "surplus" (*ziyāda*), "supplement" (*takmila*), "promise" (*maw'id*), "clarification" (*tabṣira*), and "tale" (*ḥikāya*) are Avicenna's, whereas what comes after are editorial titles.

Continued

Forget ed.	*Išārāt wa-l-tanbīhāt*[32]	*Nafs*
125.16–127.1	*Pointer.* On the faculties of the rational soul.	I, 5, 45.17–19 V, 1, 207.13–15
	On the Qur'anic allegory of the oil lamp	-
127.2–9	*Reminder.* On the difference between intuition and reflection	V, 6, 243.7–244.9
127.10–18	*Pointer.* On the holy faculty	V, 6, 248.9–250.4
128.1–129.11	*Pointer.* On the role of the Active Intellect in the recovery of intellectual forms	V, 6, 244.10–248.8
129.12–15	*Pointer.* On the cause of the contact between the human and the Active Intellect	-
129.16–130.3	*Pointer.* On the preparation of the rational soul for the reception of intellectual forms	V, 5, 235.7–11
130.4–15	*Pointer.* On the incorporeality of the substance of the rational soul	V, 2, 211.14–214.5
130.16–131.12	*Belief and reminder.* On the division of the content of the imagination	-
131.13–132.6	*Belief and reminder.* On the division of the intelligible	V, 2, 214.6–216.2
132.7–16	*Pointer.* On the fact that every intelligizing thing is intelligible	-
132.17–133.5	*Belief and reminder.* On the fact that the abstracted form does not think of itself	-
133.6–19	*Belief and reminder.* On the fact that individual accidents do not hinder the knowledge of quiddity	-
134.1–6	*Reminder.* Conclusion	-
	Supplement to the third *namaṭ*. On the movements caused by the souls	
134.8–10	*Reminder.* Introduction	-
134.11–135.3	*Pointer.* On the movements related to the vegetative soul	I, 5, 40.14–41.3
135.4–8	*Pointer.* On the movements related to the animal soul	I, 5, 41.5–16; 45.19–46.2
135.9–15	*Pointer.* On the movements related to the celestial soul	[*Ilāhiyyāt,* IX, 2]
135.16–19	*Premise.* On the demonstration of the existence of the celestial soul	
135.20–136.4	*Pointer.* On the fact that the celestial soul has an intellectual will	

Continued

Forget ed.	*Išārāt wa-l-tanbīhāt*[32]	*Nafs*
136.5–137.4	*Reminder.* On the particular will belonging to the celestial soul	
137.5–18	*Promise and reminder*	-
Seventh *namaṭ*		
176.9–177.4	*Clarification.* On the fact that the state of the soul in the intellective process does not depend on the state of the body	V, 2, 218.15–219–9
177.5–8	*Surplus of clarification.* On the effects of the exertion	V, 2, 219.10–19
177.9–13	*Surplus of clarification.* On the comparison between the perception of the sensitive faculties and that of the intellectual faculties	
177.14–178.8	*Surplus of clarification. Reductio ad absurdum:* the rational soul does not think by means of a bodily organ	V, 2, 217.4–21
178.9–16	*Supplement to these pointers.* On the essential perfections of the soul	V, 4, 232.7–233.5
178.17–179.9	*Belief and reminder.* On the fact that the soul does not become the intelligibles in the intellective process	V, 6, 239.10–240.3; 240.6–241.4
179.10–12	*Surplus of reminder.*	-
179.13–180.4	*Belief and reminder.* On the refutation of the opinion according to which the acquired intellect is the Active Intellect	-
180.5–9	*Tale.* Against Porphyry	V, 6, 240.3–6

Conclusive Considerations

The comparison of the content of the psychological sections of Avicenna's other *summae* with the *Nafs*, which is visually summarised in the synoptic table provided at the end of this chapter, allows us to make a conclusive evaluation of Avicenna's science of the soul in a diachronic perspective.

First of all, we have to assess the epistemological status assigned to psychology, if it is possible. However, in the psychological sections of the *summae* other than the *Šifāʾ* it does not immediately emerge, because there Avicenna's investigation of the soul starts *in medias res* with the investigation of the psychic faculties. Generally, in these *summae* Avicenna passes from the treatment of inorganic bodies to that of organic bodies by simply referring to the balanced proportion of elements firstly detectable in plants, which are the most basic organic beings and, at the same time, the first capable of receiving life from heavenly entities. However, two exceptions to this model are the psychological sections of *al-Mašriqiyyūn* and *K. al-Išārāt wa-l-tanbīhāt* for two different reasons. The former contains a prologue (130.9–21), comparable with that to the *Nafs* (though shorter), in which, in a vein similar to the *Nafs*, psychology seems to be considered introductory to botany and zoology. It should be noted, however, that the surviving part on natural philosophy of *al-Mašriqiyyūn* ends with psychology, and no attestation of a botanical or a zoological section can be found. The latter, by contrast, begins directly with the human rational soul and the proof of its existence, confining the treatment of the lower souls and their faculties to a supplement (*takmila*) to the third *namaṭ*. Actually, this supplement seems to be primarily devoted to the celestial soul as the psychic principle of celestial motion. However, also in the psychological section of this *summa* there is a reference to the proportion of the elements as essential to receive life from above. For at the end of the preceding *namaṭ*, the temperament of the human body is described as the most balanced, and thus the most suitable to serve as a nest (*istawkara*, 118.17–20) for the human soul.

That being said, however, some indirect pieces of evidence about the epistemological status of psychology can be gathered from the position, the content, and the extent of the psychological sections of the other *summae*. As for the position of psychology, in all the *summae* neither botany nor zoology is attested and psychology is the last section of natural philosophy before metaphysics.[33] Notable exceptions are *K. al-Išārāt wa-l-tanbīhāt*, where a part of the psychological discussion is interestingly intermingled with the properly metaphysical part of the *summa*, and the *Dānešnāme* and *al-Mašriqiyyūn* (according to Gutas' reconstruction), where natural philosophy is not followed by metaphysics. As for the content and the extent of psychology, from a quick glance at the psychological section of each *summa* it clearly emerges that Avicenna usually devotes to the treatment of the human rational soul and its activity half of the entire psychological section, in some cases even more (see the *Naǧāt*). The only exception is *al-Mašriqiyyūn*, which however closely follows the contents of the *Nafs* (more on the content of the *summae* will be said below). In general, it seems that in the other *summae* (except *al-Mašriqiyyūn*) Avicenna's focus is not the sublunary soul *tout court*, but rather what can be referred to as *noetics*, that is, everything that pertains to the human soul and its peculiar activity. What is

33 Some examples: 1) the psychological section of the *K. al-Maǧmūʿ* is followed by the metaphysical treatment of the Necessary Existent ([*faṣl*] *fī wāǧib al-wuǧūd* [*mā baʿda l-ṭabīʿa*], 160.16 (the words in square brackets are editor's integrations); 2) in *ʿUyūn al-Ḥikma*, *K. al-Hidāya*, and *Dānešnāme* the conclusion of the natural philosophy after psychology is explicitly stated. See, respectively, 84.4: "Be this the last thing of what we say about natural things" (*wal-yakun hāḏā āḫir mā naqūluhū fī l-ṭabīʿiyyāt*); 230.3: "[This is] the end of the second section of the *Book of the Guidance*" (*āḫir al-fann al-ṯānī min Kitāb al-Hidāya*); 146.4: "Hitherto, we have sufficiently dealt with the natural science (*andar ʿilm ṭabīʿī*)"; 3) in the *K. al-Naǧāt* the formula "The part on natural philosophy of the *Book of the Salvation* ended" (*tammat al-ṭabīʿiyyāt min Kitāb al-Naǧāt*) is attested after the psychological section by some manuscripts on which the edition is based (see 396, n. 8).

more, the human rational soul is the only instance of soul whose nature is explicitly accounted for, in terms that highlight its distinctiveness from other souls. For instance, in the *K. al-Maǧmūʿ* the human rational soul is said to be "a self-subsistent substance (*ǧawhar qāʾim bi-ḏātihī*, 158.10)". In the *ʿUyūn al-Ḥikma* the human soul is called *rational* (*nāṭiqa*), which is considered a nickname for its essence (*laqab li-ḏātihā*, 80.4), and is said to be the receptacle of the intellectual forms in virtue of its being an isolated substance (*fa-yakūnu ǧawhar al-nafs bi-infirādihī maḥall li-tilka l-ṣūra*, 83.4). Likewise, in the *K. al-Hidāya* Avicenna ascribes to the human rational soul an isolated essence (*fa-yakūnu lahū infirād ḏāt*..., 219.8–220.1). In the *Dānešnāme* the human rational soul is referred to simply as substance (*gohar*, 101.3), whereas in the *K. al-Išārāt wa-l-tanbīhāt* it is said to be "not impressed" (*ġayr munṭabiʿa*, 176.5) in the body.

The conclusion that can therefore be drawn from these preliminary remarks about the epistemological status of psychology is that in all the *summae* the science of the soul is placed within the part on natural philosophy as its culmination, showing in most cases a strong continuity with metaphysics, to which the treatment of the human rational soul seems to pertain *de iure*, even not *de facto*.[34] The only exception is *K. al-Išārāt wa-l-tanbīhāt:* it offers a complex and more interesting scenario where part of psychology is placed within the metaphysical discourse, thus showing a clear-cut disciplinary divide and splitting psychology between two distinct sciences. The reasons for this should, however, be further investigated.

Secondly, the subject-matter of the psychological sections of the *summae* has to be taken into consideration. In this respect, with the exclusion of *al-Mašriqiyyūn*, whose content – as has been said – closely follows that of the *Šifāʾ* (though simplifying its most difficult passages), the psychological sections of all other *summae* do not show the *general approach* detectable in the *Nafs*, either in structure or in content. Rather, they exhibit right from the beginning a *specific orientation* towards the essence and the activity of the human rational soul, which are exhaustively dealt with, somehow disregarding the lower sublunary souls and their faculties. The only exceptions to this *specific orientation* are the following. Firstly, at the outset of the psychological sections all the *summae* contain a treatment of the faculties for which the vegetative and animal soul are responsible (*K. al-Išārāt wa-l-tanbīhāt* offers it in the supplement to the third *namaṭ*). However, this treatment is no more than a quick survey, comparable with the classification of the psychic faculties provided in *Nafs*, I, 5, which is placed at the beginning of the psychological section probably because the human rational soul also performs vital activities such as self-nutrition, growth, reproduction, etc. on behalf of the lower kinds of soul. Secondly, most *summae* provide a lengthy discussion of sight and of the opinions of

34 The intermediate position (*tawassuṭ*) of psychology between natural philosophy and metaphysics or, to be precise, of the human rational soul as its main subject, is explicitly pointed out, for example, at the end of the psychological section of the *K. al-Maǧmūʿ* (see 160.7–10).

the predecessors on vision. This discussion seems to reflect Avicenna's increasing interest in vision and in the ancients' opinions on it, which is peculiar to the *summae* belonging to the so-called "Middle Period" (414–418H/1023–1028).[35] Thirdly, in the *K. al-Maǧmūʿ*, the *Dānešnāme*, and *al-Mašriqiyyūn* there is a specific treatment of the connection between the imaginative faculty and the supernal world with respect to veridical dreams and the capacity to perform miracles, that is, with respect to the influence of the supernal world on the sublunary soul. It must be recalled that the treatment of vision and the doctrine of internal senses represent Avicenna's most original expansions of Aristotle's *De anima* also in the case of the *Nafs*.[36]

These three exceptions, however, are not enough to alter our general outline of the psychological sections of Avicenna's *summae:* their specific orientation towards the human rational soul is evident.

Lastly, the way in which the human being's first acquisition of an intellectual form is accounted for in Avicenna's other *summae* should be taken into account. Some scholars maintain that an actual development is detectable with respect to the role that Avicenna assigns to the Active Intellect in the process of the first acquisition of intellectual forms. In particular, they claim that he moves from assigning to it a decisive role in the entire process to relegating it to the function – negligible with respect to the process of the first acquisition of a form – of *collector* of the intellectual forms once they have been acquired by means of the activity of the human intellect alone. Actually, Avicenna seems to remain consistent with his metaphorical explanation of the process of human intellection. Starting from the *K. al-Maǧmūʿ* he always makes use of the analogy of the Sun in order to explain the way in which the Active Intellect is present throughout the process.[37] What is more, from *K. al-Hidāya* onwards, he progressively clarifies all the elements of the analogy. Thus, in Avicenna's *summae*, the process of human intellection can be regarded as a litmus test for assessing the amphibious status of the human soul, which seems to be *in confinio* between natural philosophy and metaphysics.

In conclusion, as for the epistemological status of psychology and its subject-matter, the survey of Avicenna's other *summae* shows that the *Nafs* of the *Šifāʾ* is a *unicum*, a fact that explains the tensions and the fluctuations observable in it, which emerged in the previous chapters of this study. As for the doctrine of human intellection, by contrast, a *noetic tension* between abstraction and emanation, which is rendered through the analogy of the Sun, seems to be a *basso continuo*, common to all Avicenna's *summae*.

---

35 Gutas, *Avicenna and the Aristotelian Tradition*, 165. On the reasons for Avicenna's lengthy treatment of sight in *Nafs*, III, see Chapter 1.

36 See Chapter 1.

37 In this respect *al-Išārāt wa-l-tanbīhāt* represents only a partial exception since there Avicenna makes use of the Qurʾanic allegory of the oil lamp, see 125.16–127.1. For a developmental approach to Avicenna's epistemology, see Chapter 5, n. 20.

Synoptic table[38]

38

Legenda:
Chapter(s) [or section(s)] providing a list of all psychic faculties with the addition, in some cases, of the discussion of the opinions of the predecessors on vision
Chapter(s) concerning Avicenna's doctrine of the degrees of abstraction belonging to the perceptive faculties as a whole
Chapter(s) hinting at the transcendence of the soul with respect to a type of prophecy
Chapter(s) concerning the human rational soul: its nature and its activity(ies)
"[partially]" in the column of the *summae* refers to a less precise correspondence between the content of the chapter(s) of the *summa* in question and that of the chapter of the *Nafs*

Nafs	***Kitāb al-Maǧmūʿ***	***ʿUyūn al-Ḥikma***	***Kitāb al-Hidāya***	***Kitāb al-Naǧāt***	***Dānešnāme-ye ʿAlāʾī***	***al-Mašriqiyyūn***	***Kitāb al-Išārāt wa-l-tanbīhāt***
Prologue	-	-	-	-	-	130.9–21	-
I, 1	-	-	-	-	-	130.21–136.2	119.2–10; 120.19–121.10
I, 2	-	-	-	-	-	-	-
I, 3	-	-	-	-	-	136.3–137.11	121.11–122.4
I, 4	-	-	-	-	95.2–7 [partially]	137.12–140.17	-
I, 5	155.5–158.6	76.12–77.4; 78.8–80.1; 80.12–16; 81.14–24	204.1–208.4; 211.4–216.6; 217.5–6	318.1–323.10; 327.4–336.10; 341.10–343.9	78.4–86.9; 95.8–102.5; 108.3–109.12	140.17–146.10	122.15–127.1; 134.11–135.8
II, 1	-	-	-	-	-	146.11–147.17	-
II, 2	-	80.18–81.13	216.7–217.4	344.1–349.8	102.6–106.6	147.18–150.15	122.5–14
II, 3	-	-	-	-	-	150.16–153.23	-
II, 4	-	-	-	-	-	154.1–155.2	-
II, 5	-	-	-	-	-	155.3–157.9	-

Continued

Nafs	*Kitāb al-Maǧmūʿ*	*ʿUyūn al-Ḥikma*	*Kitāb al-Hidāya*	*Kitāb al-Naǧāt*	*Dānešnāme-ye ʿAlāʾī*	*al-Mašriqiyyūn*	*Kitāb al-Išārāt wa-l-tanbīhāt*
III, 1	-	-	-	-	-	157.10–165.21	-
III, 2	-	-	-	-	-		-
III, 3	-	-	-	-	-		-
III, 4	-	-	-	-	-		-
III, 5	-	-	208.5–211.3	323.11–327.3	87.1–95.1		-
III, 6	-	77.5–78.7					-
III, 7	-						-
III, 8	-	-	-	-	-		-
IV, 1	-	-	-	-	-	166.1–173.11	-
IV, 2	159.15–20	-	-	-	129.9–139.4		-
IV, 3	-	-	-	349.9–356.7	-	173.12–178.6	-
IV, 4	-	-	-	-	139.5–141.9	178.7–182.22	-
V, 1	157.21–24	80.2–11; 15–18; 81.14–21	217.7–10 [partially]	-	106.7–108.2	183.1–185.19	125.16–127.1
V, 2	158.10–159.20	82.7–84.3	217.11–223.2	356.8–371.11	110.1–122.2; 128.1–129.6	185.20–191.8	130.4–15; 131.13–132.6; 176.9–178.8

Continued

Nafs	***Kitāb al-Maǧmūʿ***	***ʿUyūn al-Ḥikma***	***Kitāb al-Hidāya***	***Kitāb al-Naǧāt***	***Dānešnāme-ye ʿAlāʾī***	***al-Mašriqiyyūn***	***Kitāb al-Išārāt wa-l-tanbīhāt***
V, 3	-	-	-	371.12 – 374.14	125.6 – 126.1	191.8 – 194.8	-
V, 4	-	-	223.3 – 228.2	375.1 – 387.17	122.3 – 123.6; 129.6 – 8	194.9 – 198.20	178.9 – 16
V, 5	158.6 – 10; 159.20 – 160.10	81.25 – 82.6	229.1 – 230.2	394.7 – 396.7 [partially]	123.7 – 125.6; 126.2 – 127.9	198.21 – 200.15	129.16 – 130.3 [partially]
V, 6	-	-	-	339.1 – 341.9	141.10 – 146.4	200.16 – 205.14	127.2 – 129.11; 178.17 – 179.12; 180.5 – 9
V, 7	-	-	-	392.3 – 394.4	-	205.15 – 209.3	119.2 – 10; 121.11 – 122.4
V, 8	-	-	-	-	-	209.4 – 212.7	-

Psychology in Classificatory Writings

As a complement to the discourse about the psychological sections of Avicenna's other *summae*, in this appendix two other texts will be taken into account as a means to assess the status of science of the soul in Avicenna's thought. These texts are the eighth chapter of the *Maqāla fī l-nafs ʿalà sunnat al-iḫtiṣār* (*Compendium on the Soul*),[39] and the section on the fundamental (*aṣlī*, as opposed to the derivative, *farʿī*) divisions of natural philosophy in the *Maqāla fī Aqsām al-ʿulūm al-ʿaqliyya* (*Treatise on the Divisions of the Intellectual Sciences*).[40] In these texts, Avicenna provides two outlines of natural philosophy that can be compared with the one provided in the prologue to the *Nafs*.[41] As has been said in the introduction to this chapter, this comparison can shed some light on Avicenna's position about the place and the subject-matter of psychology also in contexts different from the *Šifāʾ*.

***Nafs*, prologue, 1.4–2.1 [9.4–10.21]**	***M. fī l-nafs ʿalà sunnat al-iḫtiṣār*, chap. 8, 361.19–362.1 (ed. Landauer)**	***M. fī Aqsām al-ʿulūm al-ʿaqliyya*, 108.12–110.6 (ed. Cairo²)[42]**
The *communia naturalia* [*al-samāʿ al-ṭabīʿī*, corresp. to the *Physics*];	Matter, form, privation, nature, place, time, rest and motion [*Physics*];	The *communia naturalia*, matter, form, motion, nature, causes, finitude, infinity, what connects motions to the movers, and their result in a first, unmoved mover [*Physics*];
the heavens, the world, the celestial bodies, and the primary motions [*al-samāʾ wa-l-ʿālam*, corr. to the *De Caelo et mundo*];	celestial bodies and bodies composed of the elements [*De Caelo et mundo*];	the heavens, the celestial bodies, the four elements, and their nature, motion and position [*De Caelo et mundo*];

39 For the edition of this work, see *M. fī l-nafs ʿalà sunnat al-iḫtiṣār* (*Compendium on the Soul*), in S. Landauer, "Die Psychologie des Ibn Sīnā", *Zeitschrift der Deutschen Morgenländischen Gesellschaft*, 29, 1875, 339–372.
40 For the edition of this work, see *Rasāʾil fī l-ḥikma wa-l-ṭabīʿiyyāt*, 2 vols., Dār al-ʿarab, Cairo 1980², 104–118. For its presentation, see Gutas, *Avicenna and the Aristotelian Tradition*, 416. For a study of the passages on psychology and prophetology of this work, see O. Lizzini, "L'*Epistola sulle divisioni delle scienze intellettuali* di Avicenna: alcune note sulla definizione e la collocazione della profetologia e della psicologia", in S. Caroti, R. Imbach, Z. Kaluza, G. Stabile, L. Sturlese eds., *Ad Ingenii Acuitionem. Studies in Honour of Alfonso Maierù*, Brepols, Turnhout 2006, 221–248.
41 Some considerations concerning the classification of natural science provided in the *Nafs* and those provided in the *M. fī l-nafs ʿalà sunnat al-iḫtiṣār*, and in the *M. fī Aqsām al-ʿulūm al-ʿaqliyya* have been provided in Chapter 3, n. 33.
42 In translating this passage I take into account the textual improvements suggested by J. Michot in his "Les sciences physiques et metaphysiques selon la Risālah fī Aqsām al-ʻulūm d'Avicenne. Essai de traduction critique", *Bulletin de philosophie médiévale*, 22, 1980, 62–73.

Continued

Nafs, prologue, 1.4–2.1 [9.4–10.21]	***M. fī l-nafs ʿalà sunnat al-iḫtiṣār*, chap. 8, 361.19–362.1 (ed. Landauer)**	***M. fī Aqsām al-ʿulūm al-ʿaqliyya*, 108.12–110.6 (ed. Cairo²)[42]**
generation and corruption, and the nature of elements [*al-kawn wa-l-fasād*, corr. to the *De gener. et corr.*];	the principles of generation and corruption [*De generatione et corruptione*];	the state of generation and corruption, and the primary bodies [*De generatione et corruptione*];
the activities and affections of the primary qualities and the mixtures resulting from these qualities [*al-afʿāl wa-l-infiʿālāt*, corr. to *Meteorologica* IV];	generation of phenomena in the atmosphere [*Meteorologica* IV];	the four elements, and their mixture, the impression of the celestial bodies on them, and phenomena in the atmosphere (i.e. shooting stars, rains, thunders, thunderbolts, etc.) [*Meteorologica* I-III];
mineralogy and geology, i.e. the study of the inorganic bodies [*al-maʿādin wa-l-āṯār al-ʿulwiyya*, corr. to *Meteorologica* I-III];	in the mines [*Meteorologica* I-III];	the inorganic bodies and the minerals [*De mineralibus*, i.e. *Meteorologica* IV];
psychology. i.e. the study of the essence *qua* form of plants and animals [*al-nafs*, corr. to *De anima*];		
botany [*al-nabāt*, corr. to ps.-Aristotle, *De plantis*];	and on the surface of the earth: plants [ps.-Aristotle, *De plantis*];	plants [ps.-Aristotle, *De plantis*];
zoology [*al-ḥayawān*, corr. to the *Historia*, *De partibus*, and *De generatione animalium*]	and animals [*Historia*, *De partibus*, and *De generatione animalium*];	animals [*Historia*, *De partibus*, and *De generatione animalium*];
	the real nature of the human being and the real nature of the self-conceptualization of the soul (*ḥaqīqat al-insān wa-ḥaqīqa taṣawwur al-nafs li-nafsihā*) [*De anima*]	the knowledge of the soul and of the perceptive and motive faculties that are in the animals and, especially, those that are in the human being (*maʿrifat al-nafs wa-l-quwà l-darrāka wa-l-muḥarrika allatī fī l-ḥayawānāt wa-ḫuṣūṣan allatī fī l-insān*). It has been also shown there that the soul belonging to the human being does not die when the body dies, and that it is an im-

Continued

***Nafs*, prologue, 1.4–2.1 [9.4–10.21]**	***M. fī l-nafs ʿalà sunnat al-iḫtiṣār*, chap. 8, 361.19–362.1 (ed. Landauer)**	***M. fī Aqsām al-ʿulūm al-ʿaqliyya*, 108.12–110.6 (ed. Cairo²)[42]**
		material, divine substance (*wa-yubayyanu fīhi anna l-nafs allatī li-l-insān lā tamūtu bi-mawt al-badan wa-annahā ǧawhar rūḥānī ilāhī*) [*De anima, De sensu et sensato*]

At a quick glance, it is immediately evident that in these two other classifications Avicenna assigns to psychology the place that was assigned to zoology in the prologue to the *Nafs*. There, psychology seems to be the peak of natural philosophy, and not a general investigation of the principle of sublunary life, preliminary to the specific inquiry into plants and animals. Avicenna seems, therefore, to chart an ascending course, starting from the simplest organic beings, i. e. plants, and arriving at the most complex (and most perfect) organic being, i. e. man. In the case of the *M. fī l-nafs ʿalà sunnat al-iḫtiṣār* this *specific orientation* is particularly explicit: the subject of psychology is unequivocally the real nature (*ḥaqīqa*) of the human being and its activity of self-conceptualization. In the case of the *M. fī Aqsām al-ʿulūm al-ʿaqliyya*, by contrast, this position is softened: there, a *general approach* to the sublunary soul in its entirety, and to the perceptive and motive faculties of animals, is combined with a *specific orientation* towards the faculties of the human soul.[43] Then, Avicenna refers to the peculiar kind of substance the human soul is: it is an immaterial, divine substance, that does not corrupt together with the corruption of the body. Consequently, although psychology seems to deal with the soul of all perishable living beings, it has to encompass two different kinds of substance, i. e. the human soul, and the souls of plants and animals which, unlike the human soul, are not divine and immortal. Furthermore, it is noteworthy that both in the *M. fī l-nafs ʿalà sunnat al-iḫtiṣār* and in the *M. fī Aqsām al-ʿulūm al-ʿaqliyya* the treatment of the states of the human soul in the afterlife, which in the *Šifāʾ* Avicenna assigns to metaphysics, depends on psychology with respect to the preliminary ascertainment of the nature of the human soul.[44]

43 Here the use of the adverb *ḫuṣūṣan* (*especially*) is particularly telling.
44 For the metaphysical section dealing with the human soul's afterlife in these two writings, see *M. fī l-nafs ʿalà sunnat al-iḫtiṣār*, 362.12–16, and *M. fī Aqsām al-ʿulūm al-ʿaqliyya*, 114.17–116.2.

Conclusion, or Explaining Avicenna by Way of Avicenna

In this study I have analyzed Avicenna's reworking of Peripatetic psychology in the *Nafs* of the *Šifā'*, where he gives the most detailed and exhaustive exposition of his *'ilm al-nafs* (*scientia de anima*). I have supplemented the treatment of the soul provided in this writing by referring to the psychological sections of his other *summae* in order to contextualize the *Nafs* and assess its distinctiveness from Avicenna's other works. Preliminarily, I have provided a general outline of Avicenna's *Nafs* by presenting its contents and main sources (Chapter 1) and have outlined both the remote and the proximate background of Avicenna's philosophical enterprise (Chapter 2). This background includes Aristotle, late Ancient commentators such as Alexander of Aphrodisias, Philoponus, and Simplicius, and early Arabic philosophers such as al-Kindī, and al-Fārābī. In this manner, all the elements of Avicenna's original synthesis of the tremendous exegetical labour on Aristotle's *De anima* can be identified and appreciated.

The main purpose of this study was to reconstruct the theoretical framework of Avicenna's psychology on which the treatment of specific aspects of the soul depends. In particular, this study aimed to establish the epistemological status of psychology, to determine its subject-matter, and to evaluate how the epistemological status of psychology and its subject-matter influence one another. To address these three questions two different but complementary approaches to Avicenna's *Nafs* have been taken: an external approach, and an internal approach. The external approach seemed to lead to a division of the science of the soul, whereas the internal approach seemed to preserve its unity. The final purpose of this study was to show Avicenna's effort to integrate these two approaches in a coherent treatment of the soul.

In Chapter 3 we took the external approach and became acquainted with a **division** of psychology into two parts. In *Ilāhiyyāt*, I, 1–3 Avicenna clearly distinguishes the prerogatives of metaphysics from those of particular sciences: to the science of divine things, i.e. metaphysics, pertains the investigation of the existent *qua* existent, whereas to the particular sciences the investigation of the states of the existent *qua* existent, namely its specific aspects. Furthermore, every science (metaphysics included) – Avicenna adds – takes for granted both the existence and the quiddity of its own subject-matter. Apparently psychology seems to conform to this model: in *Nafs*, I, 1 the existence of the soul is assumed on the basis of direct observation, and Avicenna seems to concentrate on the activities observable in bodies, for which the soul is responsible. However, in *Nafs*, I, 1, I, 3, and V, 2 Avicenna does deal with the *quiddity* of the soul. All sublunary souls are substance because they are not in a subject. The soul of plants and animals is not in a subject because it is a form, and forms inhere in a receptacle, not in a subject; moreover, form is a constitutive part of its proximate subject. The human, rational soul is not in a subject

https://doi.org/10.1515/9783110706840-009

because it is a self-subsistent substance, and what enjoys a condition of independent existence does not need a subject. The ascertainment of the quiddity of the human soul is, thus, achieved by referring to the notion of *existence*. Thus psychology deals with existence and quiddity of its subject-matter: it goes therefore beyond the prerogatives of a particular science. However, the demonstration of the substantiality of the soul of plants and animals is grounded on the notion of *form*, treated *ex professo* in *Ilāhiyyāt*, II, 1. By contrast, the demonstration of the substantiality of the human soul not only is not founded in metaphysics, but rather founds the metaphysical discourse on the soul's afterlife in *Ilāhiyyāt*, IX, 7, unless we consider *Ilāhiyyāt*, IX, 7 to provide an *ex post* demonstration of the existence of the human soul as a self-subsistent substance. In psychology, Avicenna seems to be worried by the possibility that psychology might transcend the boundaries of natural philosophy in which it is placed, and therefore at the beginning and then almost at the end of the *Nafs* (I, 1; V, 5) he limits the investigation of the soul conducted in natural philosophy to what has a relation to matter and motion. In metaphysics, by contrast, Avicenna does not seem to be bothered by this disciplinary trespassing; rather, he seems to authorize it, since on two occasions (*Ilāhiyyāt*, III, 1; IX, 4) he seems to suggest that metaphysics has to assume the conclusions of psychology concerning the existence of a separate, incorporeal substance, i. e. the human rational soul, without providing further grounds for it. Thus, psychology not only is close to metaphysics, since it demonstrates the existence and the quiddity of a part of its subject, just as metaphysics proves the existence and the quiddity of God, which is a part of its subject (also metaphysics contravenes the tenet established in *Ilāhiyyāt*, I, 1–3), but is also, to some extent, above metaphysics, to which it gives premises (Avicenna takes from the *Nafs* the premises not only for his eschatological doctrine but also for his argument that God is an intellect!). By standing at the crossroads between natural philosophy and metaphysics, psychology seems to be properly subordinate to none of the aforementioned theoretical sciences, and not to be fully founded by the latter. At this point one might wonder whether it is the consequence of a fault of psychology, or of a deficiency of metaphysics. This remains an open question.

In Avicenna's psychology two different but complementary aspects are then detectable: (i) a *general approach* to the *soul of* sublunary living beings (plants, animals, human beings) which, in line with Aristotle's *De anima*, is the *formal principle* of the body, immanent to it. This approach guarantees the science of the soul a strong focal unity, unquestionably places it within natural philosophy, and accounts for the anticipation in it of the demonstration of the substantiality of the soul insofar as it is form; and (ii) a *specific orientation* towards the *soul in itself*, i. e. the human rational soul that, considered in isolation from the body, is a *self-subsistent substance*, identical with the theoretical intellect and capable of surviving severance from the body. These two aspects result in the coexistence in Avicenna's psychology of two investigations, that is, a more specific and less physical science (*psychologia specialis*) within a more general and overall physical one (*psychologia generalis*). This coexistence seems to cause an epistemological tension between an overall physical, and then a *trans*-physical (or *proto*-metaphysical) account of the soul. However, by taking an internal approach to psychology, we pointed at Avicenna's way to soften this tension and provide the science with sufficient unity.

In Chapter 4 we showed the **unification** of Avicenna's psychology. Avicenna achieves the unification of psychology through the definition of its subject-matter. In order for the unity of the subject-matter of psychology to be preserved, Avicenna assigns priority to a catch-all formula for the definition of all sublunary souls over the investigation of their quiddity. In unifying the subject-matter of psychology Avicenna's strategy is articulated into three fundamental phases: (i) the individuation of *kamāl* (*perfection*) as a notion that can be predicated of all sublunary souls (*Nafs*, I, 1 – first part); (ii) the reworking of Aristotle's standard definition of the soul, by depriving it of (almost) any reference to the quiddity of the soul (*Nafs*, I, 1 – second part); (iii) the independent demonstration of the substantiality of the soul, and the consequent application of the term *kamāl* to the soul on the quidditative level (*Nafs*, I, 3).

In the first part of *Nafs*, I, 1 Avicenna opts for the term *kamāl* to refer to the soul because it is the most indicative of its meaning and includes both the separable soul and the soul that does not separate. This term, when it is referred to the soul, indicates an *iḍāfa* (relation) existing between soul and body, in virtue of which the former is responsible for the activities observable in the latter. Although it is said to indicate an *iḍāfa*, which in principle should be placed among the accidents, the term *kamāl* refers to a characteristic belonging to the soul from which the accidentality (or non-accidentality) of the soul cannot be inferred.

In the second part of *Nafs*, I, 1 Avicenna retrieves and reworks Aristotle's standard definition of the soul as the *first perfection* (*kamāl awwal*) of an organic body. This definition has to be interpreted not so much within the framework of the Aristotelian distinction between first and second perfection, according to which the first perfection is the *formal principle* of the body but, rather, within the broader framework of the distinction between the capacity for performing one or more functions and the actual exercise of that capacity, and the equation of the form *qua* first perfection with the capability to perform a function, which is suggested by Aristotle himself in *De an.*, II, 1. Although Avicenna does not consider it his own definition of the soul, its adoption represents a further step toward the unification of the science of the soul: in the *Nafs* the soul has to be investigated on the operational level, namely insofar as it is the principle responsible for the activities in the body.

That being said, the process of the unification of the subject-matter of psychology is not accomplished yet. Although the sense in which the term *kamāl* refers to the soul has been explained, the notion of *kamāl* is not sufficiently unitary: when applied to the soul, it can refer to an accident as well as to a substance. Therefore, in *Nafs*, I, 3 Avicenna demonstrates the substantiality of the soul independently of its being perfection, and then founds the application of the term *kamāl* to the soul on the quidditative level: *kamāl* passes then from designating the soul insofar as it has a relation (*iḍāfa*) to the body (operational level) to designate it insofar as it is a substance (ontological level). This could be then considered Avicenna's own definition of the soul: the soul is not a substance because it is a perfection; rather, the soul is a perfection as substance. Its being perfection as substance results in its being the causal principle of activities. In doing so, Avicenna also succeeds in unifying the notion of *kamāl*: when applied to the soul, it always refers to a substance, regardless of its being an instance of separable or inseparable perfection or, what is the same, of a self-subsistent substance or a substantial form. It is noteworthy that here any reference to the distinction between first and second perfection disappears. Furthermore, on a more general level, Avicenna manages to provide the science of the soul with a proper, unitary place in natural philosophy: for it investigates the sublunary soul *qua* principle and cause of activities in bodies and provides a glimpse of its essence. This is what I have labelled internal approach to the *Nafs*.

In Chapter 5 we confronted with the crucial instance of **integration** of Avicenna's account of human intellection, that is, the proper activity of the human, rational soul, within the theoretical framework outlined above. From the end of *Nafs*, I, 3 onwards Avicenna shifts the focus of his investigation from the essence and the definition of the soul to its faculties as part of his plan to render psychology unitary: his philosophical psychology turns out to be a faculty psychology like Aristotle's. However, though providing psychology with a strong unity, focusing on the faculties of the soul unavoidably contributes to disclosing the peculiarities of the different instances of soul from which these faculties ensue and, more importantly, the distinctiveness of the human rational soul with respect to all the other instances of soul (the *specific orientation* of Avicenna's psychology). Avicenna's doctrine of human intellection is, therefore, a perfect litmus test for evaluating the amphibious status of the human rational soul and, consequently, the intermediate status of psychology between natural philosophy and metaphysics. For, the process through which human beings acquire universal, intellectual forms is intrinsically related to the ontological status of the soul. It involves two opposite movements: a movement *downwards*, i.e. the human soul's examination of the particulars acquired through the lower perceptive faculties, which operate through the body, and its consequent abstraction of intellectual forms from those particulars; and a movement *upwards*, i.e. the contact of the human soul with the Active Intellect above it and the consequent emanation of something from it. These two movements, far from being incompatible, seem to account perfectly for, on the one hand, the soul's need for a relation to (not a reception in) its body and, on the other hand, its independence of it in performing its own activity.

In Chapter 6 we provided the **evaluation** of the *Nafs* with respect to the psychological sections of the other Avicennian *summae*. The evaluation has been conducted on three main points emerging from the investigation conducted on the *Nafs:* (i) the epistemological status of psychology; (ii) the subject-matter of psychology; and (iii) the account of human intellection. With respect to the third point, all the *summae* outline the process of human intellection in the same way, that is, as a combination of abstraction and emanation. The *noetic* tension generated by this combination can be therefore considered as a *basso continuo*, present in the psychological section of all Avicenna's *summae.* By contrast, with respect to the epistemological status of psychology and its subject-matter, the *Nafs* seems to be a *unicum.* As for the epistemological status of psychology, in all the other *summae* psychology is placed at the end of natural philosophy as its pinnacle, with the notable exception of *K. al-Išārāt wa-l-tanbīhāt*, where a part of the psychological section is intermingled with the properly metaphysical part of the *summa.* In the *Nafs,* by contrast, it precedes botany and zoology. As for the subject-matter of psychology, with the exclusion of *al-Mašriqiyyūn,* the psychological section of all the other *summae* does not show the *general approach* detectable in the *Nafs*, either in structure or in content; rather, it exhibits right from the beginning a *specific orientation* towards the essence and the activity of the human rational soul. Therefore, the psychological section of the other *summae* amounts to a *noetics*, primarily focused on the human rational soul, whereas the psychology of the *Šifāʾ* seems to be intended to provide the theoretical framework for the study of sublunary life in its entirety, together with a specific focus on the human rational soul, a fact that explains the epistemological tension observable therein.

In the introduction to the present study *subject*, *definition*, *activity*, i. e. the three concepts on which this research is based, are said to correspond to *soul*, *perfection*, *intellection*, i. e. the concepts on which Avicenna's psychology is grounded. However, these three concepts are not only the cornerstone of Avicenna's *Nafs*, but also contain in themselves the interpretative tools of this writing. For, *soul*, *perfection*, *intellection* stand for the three key moments of the Avicennian reflection on the soul in the *Nafs*, that is, *division*, *unification*, *integration.* Thus, in a manner similar to the exegetical practice of "explaining Homer by way of Homer" (Ὅμηρον ἐξ Ὁμήρου σαφηνίζειν), Avicenna's own concepts can be used as exegetical tools to intepret his writing (it is an exegetical approach similar to the one Late Ancient commentators on Aristotle used, as we saw, for instance, in Philoponus' commentary on the *De anima*).

Soul represents the entire subject-matter of psychology. However, it is hard to encapsulate a global investigation of the soul within one single science, which is in turn subordinate to one single branch of theoretical philosophy, because soul is too broad: it encompasses the lowest, vegetative soul as well as the loftiest, celestial soul. Treating the soul without qualification can therefore cause a *division* within psychology.

Perfection, when applied to the *soul*, delimits the respect in which the soul can be successfully investigated within the auspices of one single science: the sublunary soul *qua* operational principle and cause of the activities observable in bodies, regardless of its being an instance of separable or inseparable perfection. Thus, the *unification* of psychology is grounded on the concept of perfection.

Intellection is the last psychic activity accounted for in Avicenna's *Nafs* and, at the same time, the outermost limit of a physical investigation of the soul. For, though being one of the activities of an instance of sublunary soul, by performing it the human rational soul lifts itself up to the celestial realm, comes into contact with the tenth (and last) celestial intelligence, and "resembles the first principles of all existence" (I, 5, 50.11–12). Thus, within Avicenna's faculty psychology, the treatment of human intellection marks the *integration* of a divine spark within natural science: the human rational soul *qua* self-subsistent substance which, on the one hand, needs a relation to (not a reception in) its body but, on the other hand, is capable of performing its own activity independently of it.

In conclusion, Avicenna's *Nafs* can be considered in all respects the masterful synthesis of a long-running debate on the science of the soul. There, on the one hand, Avicenna acknowledges the distinctiveness of the human rational soul, whereas, on the other hand, he constantly refers to the relation of all sublunary souls to their bodies. In doing this, he succeeds in unifying the account of the soul provided in the *Nafs* and avoiding the dissolution of psychology.

Appendix

Translation of Avicenna's *Kitāb al-Nafs*

Note on the Text

The following translation is based on the text of Avicenna's *Kitāb al-Nafs* edited by Fazlur Rahman in 1959.

I have refrained from interpreting pronouns when their meaning is clear from context. All expressions that needed to be added in order for the translation to be understandable are in square brackets, as are references to the pagination of Rahman's edition (= [**R**]).

In general, I have privileged homogeneity and adherence to the Arabic text in the translation as often as possible so that one can grasp at least some of the structural features of the original. This is done on several occasions at the cost of some awkwardness. Whenever a literal translation would have affected one's ability to understand the sense of a passage in English, I have opted for less literal solutions to secure intelligibility. I shall not note the numerous cases in which I refrained from translating *wa* at the beginning of a sentence or other particles that do not affect the sense.

The division of the text into sections and subsections is entirely mine.

https://doi.org/10.1515/9783110706840-010

[(**Prologue**)]

[**R1**] In the name of God the Compassionate, the Merciful

The sixth section of [the second part on] natural philosophy, that is, the *Book of the Soul*

[1. Summary of the previous sections and subject of the present inquiry]

[1.1 Summary of the previous five sections of the natural philosophy][1]
We have already completed the discourse on the *communia naturalia*[2] in the first section;[3] then, we followed it with the second section on the knowledge of the heaven, the world, the celestial bodies, the forms and the primary motions in the world of nature, and we ascertained the states of the bodies which do not corrupt and of those which corrupt.[4] Then, we followed this with the discourse on generation and corruption, and their elements,[5] and then we followed this with the discourse on the activities of primary qualities, their affections, and the mixtures resulting from them.[6] It remained for us to deal with generated things, whereas the inanimate bodies and what has neither sensation nor voluntary motion are prior to them and closer

1 The investigation of nature begins with a general inquiry into the principles common to all natural bodies, and proceeds to deal singularly with all the varieties of natural bodies, organized according to their distinctive characteristics, and arranged from the top downwards (emanative scheme) and, in the case of sublunary bodies, from the simplest ones to the most complex ones (ascending scale). For an exhaustive presentation of the emanative procession of all kinds of substance (celestial intellects, celestial souls, celestial bodies, human beings, animals, plants, inorganic bodies, elements, prime matter) from the First Principle, with the human being being the highest sublunary entity in the ascending scale of being, see *Ilāhiyyāt*, X, 1, 435.6–13 [522.7–523.20]. A similar outline of the investigation of nature can be found in the third and the fourth sections of the natural philosophy of the *Šifā'*, i.e. *Kawn wa-Fasād* (*De generatione et corruptione*), and *Af'āl wa-Infi'ālāt* (*De actionibus et passionibus qualitatum primarum*). In the third section there is not a real, separate prologue; rather, at the beginning of the first chapter Avicenna briefly recalls the topic of the two previous natural investigations (1, 77.7–10 [1.3–2.8]), as he does, for example, also at the beginning of the *Ilāhiyyāt* (I, 1, 3.8–10 [1.4–6]). In the fourth section, by contrast, there is a real, separate prologue, like the one in the corresponding Aristotelian writing, i.e. *Meteorology* (*Meteor.*, I, 1, 338 a20–339 a94); however, it is shorter than the prologue to the *Nafs* (201.4–10 [1.2–2.4]), and merely lists the topics of the previous three sections of natural philosophy (201.4–6 [1.2–5]), presents the topic of the investigation that Avicenna is about to start (201.6–7 [1.6–8]), and hints at the topic of the subsequent four sections of natural philosophy (201.7–10 [1.9–2.14]).

2 By *al-kalām 'alà l-umūr al-'āmma* (*verbum de his quae sunt communia naturalibus*) Avicenna refers to the discourse on the principles of natural things, i.e. matter and form, the four causes, etc.

3 i.e.: *Samā' ṭabī'ī*, which corresponds to Aristotle's *De physico auditu* or *Physica*.

4 i.e.: *Samā' wa-'Ālam*, which corresponds to Aristotle's *De Caelo*.

5 i.e.: *Kawn wa-Fasād*, which is the third section (*fann*), and corresponds to Aristotle's *De generatione et corruptione*.

6 i.e.: *Af'āl wa-Infi'ālāt*, which is the fourth section and corresponds to Aristotle's *Meteorologica*, IV.

than them to elementary generation, and we dealt with that [issue] in the fifth section.[7]

[1.2 The subject of the present inquiry: the form (i. e. soul) of all perishable living beings]
What remained to us of [natural] science is to investigate the matters concerning plants and animals. Since plants and animals are rendered subsistent as to [their] essences through a form, that is the soul, and a matter, that is body and limbs, and [since] it is more appropriate that what is science of something is [science] [**R2**] with respect to its form, it seemed to us [more convenient] to deal firstly with the soul.

[2. Methodological remarks]

[2.1 The unity of the inquiry into the soul]
It did not seem [convenient] to us to sever the science of the soul so as to deal firstly with the vegetative soul and plants, then with the animal soul and animals, [and] then with the human soul and human being.

[2.1.1 Two reasons for a unitary inquiry into the soul]
[2.1.1.1 First reason: a fragmentary inquiry into it contrasts with its intrinsic unity]
And we did not do that for two reasons: [(i)] the first [reason] is that this severing is among the things that render difficult grasping the science of the soul which relates one of its parts to another.

[2.1.1.2 Second reason: what is perceived of souls are the activities they share; their peculiar features are, by contrast, difficult to grasp]
[(ii)] The second [reason] is that plants share with animals the soul to which the activity of growth, nutrition, and reproduction belongs. It is unquestionably necessary that [animals] be separated from plants with respect to the psychic faculties that are proper to their genus and, then, proper to their species. And what we can deal with as regards the soul of plants is what is shared by animals, but we are not much aware of the *differentiae* that render this generic notion in plants specific. If this is the case, the relation of this part of the investigation to the fact of its being a discourse on plants has no greater claim than [its relation] to the fact of its being a discourse on animals, since the relation of animals to this (*sc.* vegetative) soul is the [same] relation as that of plants to it. And the state of the animal soul stands in similar relation to the human being and to other animals. And since we want to deal with the vegetative and the animal soul only insofar as it is shared – for there is no science of what is particular except [that which comes] after the science of what is shared

7 i. e.: *Maʿādin wa-Āṯār ʿulwiyya*, which corresponds to Aristotle's *Meteorologica*, I-III.

– and [since] we are little engaged in the essential *differentiae* of each soul, of each plant, and of each animal because that is difficult for us,[8] it is better that we deal with the soul in one single book. Then, if we can deal specifically with plants [**R3**] and animals, we shall do so, but the majority of what we can do of that depends on their bodies and the properties of their bodily activities.

[2.2 The priority of the inquiry into the soul over the inquiry into the body]
Therefore, we certainly bring forward the acquaintance with the issue concerning the soul and postpone the acquaintance with the issue concerning the body as a better way of teaching than that of bringing forward the acquaintance with the issue concerning the body and postponing the acquaintance with the issue concerning the soul. For, with respect to the knowledge of the bodily states, the help of knowing the issue concerning the soul is greater than the help of knowing the issue concerning the body with respect to the knowledge of the psychic states, even though each of them is helpful to the other, and it is not necessary to bring forward one of them.[9] Still, we prefer to bring forward the discourse on the soul because of the excuse we have put forward [before]. Then, whoever wishes to change this order can do that without our arguing with him.

[3. Announcement of the following exposition]

This is, then, the sixth section. Then, we will follow it in the seventh section with the investigation of the states of plants,[10] and in the eighth section with the investigation of the states of animals,[11] and there we shall conclude the natural science. Then, we will follow it (*sc.* the natural science) with the mathematical sciences [which will be divided] into four sections.[12] Then, we will follow all that with the divine science, and

8 In *Ilāhiyyāt*, V, 4, 220.13–18 [255.70–256.78], in dealing with the *differentia* that specifies the genus, Avicenna says that we cannot grasp what is proper to the specific difference of every genus with respect to every species, nor what is proper to the specific differences of the species of a single genus, because this knowledge goes beyond our cognitive capacities; rather, we can grasp the rule in virtue of which a *differentia* enters a genus and specifies it.
9 Lit.: one of the two extremes.
10 i.e.: *Nabāt*, which corresponds to the first book of Ps.-Aristotle's *De plantis.*
11 i.e.: *Ḥayawān*, which corresponds to Aristotle's *Historia animalium*, *De partibus animalium*, and *De generatione animalium.*
12 It is a cumulative reference to *Riyāḍiyyāt*, namely to the third part (*ǧumla*) of the *Šifāʾ*, which is entirely devoted to mathematics. It is divided into four sections (*funūn*): *Geometry* (*Uṣūl al-handasa*), whose model is Euclid's *Elements*; *Astronomy* (*ʿIlm al-hayʾa*), whose model is Ptolemy's *Almagest*; *Arithmetic* (*Ḥisāb*), whose model is Nicomachus of Gerasa's *Introduction to Arithmetic; Music* (*Ǧawāmiʿ ʿilm al-mūsīqà*), whose model is Ptolemy's *Harmonics.*

complement it with something about ethics,[13] and with that we shall conclude this our book.

[(**I.1**)]
[**R4**] [Chapter] on establishing the [existence of the] soul and defining it insofar as it is soul

[1. Topic of the present chapter]

We say: the first thing we must deal with is establishing the existence of the thing that is called *soul*. Then, we shall deal with what follows that.

[2. Proof of the existence of the soul as the principle of the vegetative and animal activities in living bodies]

[2.1 The vegetative and animal activities in living bodies are evident]
We thus say: we do sometimes see bodies that sense and move at will; indeed, we see bodies that nourish themselves, grow, and generate the like.

[2.2 The principle of these activities is the soul]
And this does not belong to them due to their corporeality; therefore, it remains that in these themselves there are principles for that other than their corporeality, that is, the thing from which these activities derive. In general, whatever is a principle for the derivation of activities that are not in the same manner [as if they were] devoid of will, we call it *soul*.

[2.3 *Soul* does not designate the essence of the principle for vital activities, but an accident belonging to it]
This expression is a name for this thing not with respect to its substance, but in virtue of a certain relation it has, namely, in virtue of its being the principle for these activities.

[2.4 The present investigation refers to the thing as far as it has a certain accident; the investigation of its essence will be made later on]
We shall seek for its substance and the category under which it falls later on.[14] Now, however, we have established only the existence of something which is a principle for what we have mentioned, and we have established the existence of something in virtue of its having a certain accident. [**R5**] We need to arrive from this accident

13 It is a reference to *Ilāhiyyāt*, the fourth part (*ǧumla*) of the *Šifāʾ*, which is entirely devoted to metaphysics with an appendix (X treatise) on practical science and Islamic law.
14 This is a reference to *Nafs*, I, 3.

belonging to it at an ascertaining of its essence in order to know its quiddity, just as if we had already come to know that something which is in motion has a certain mover, but we do not know from that what the essence of this mover is.

[3. Proving that the soul is the part of the living being's subsistence through which it is what it is in actuality]

[3.1 The soul is part of the living beings' subsistence]
We say: if the things to which we believe the soul belongs are bodies, and their existence insofar as they are plants or animals is completed only through the existence of this thing for them, this thing is, then, part of their subsistence.

[3.2 There are two parts in the thing's subsistence: a) the part through which the thing is what it is in actuality; b) the part through which the thing is what it is in potentiality[15]]
The parts of the subsistence [of something], as you have learned elsewhere,[16] are two[17]: [(a)] a part through which the thing is what it is in actuality, and [(b)] a part through which the thing is what it is in potentiality, which is equivalent to the subject.

[3.2.1 First argument: *reductio ad absurdum*][18]
If the soul belongs to the second division – and there is no doubt that the body belongs to that division – animals and plants, then, are not completed as animals and plants either by the body or by the soul. Therefore, they need another perfection, which is the principle in actuality for what we said. But that would be the soul, and it is [the topic] on which our discourse is. Indeed, the soul ought to be that by which plants and animals are plants and animals in actuality. And if [the principle belonging to the second division] is a body, then the form of the body is what we said.[19]

---

15 Avicenna shows that the soul is the part in virtue of which something is what it is in actuality [(a)] by ruling out the possibility that it is the part in virtue of which something is what it is in potentiality [(b)] by using two arguments.

16 This is a reference to *Samāʿ ṭabīʿī*, I, 2. Here Avicenna is referring to form and matter.

17 Lit.: two divisions.

18 Outline of the first argument:

i. Avicenna supposes that the soul belongs to the case [(b)], like the body;
ii. if so, the existence of living things needs something else, belonging to case [(a)], besides the soul and the body, in order to be complete;
iii. this thing will be the soul, but it has been accepted that the soul belongs to case [(b)] -> contradiction.

19 i.e.: the soul.

[3.2.2 Second argument: *regressus ad infinitum*][20]
If it is a body with a certain form, then it would not be that principle insofar as it is a body, but its being a principle is in virtue of that form, and the derivation of those states would be from that form itself, even though it happens through the mediation of this body. Therefore, the first principle would be that form and its first actuality would be by means of this body. And this body would be part of the body of the animal, but it is the first part to which the principle is connected. However, inasmuch as it is body, it is but [part] of the whole subject.

[3.3 Conclusion: the soul is not a body, but is a form, or like a form, or like a perfection]
It is, therefore, clear that the soul itself is not a body, but is a part of the animal [**R6**] and the plant: it is a form, or like the form, or like the perfection.

[4. Several terms by which one can refer to the soul]

[4.1 Soul as power. Two senses of power]
[4.1.1 First sense: power as faculty]
Now we say that it would be correct to call the soul *power* in relation to the activities that derive from it.

[4.1.2 Second sense: power as potentiality]
Similarly, it can be called *power* in another sense, in relation to what it receives in terms of sensible and intellectual forms.

[4.2 Soul as form]
It would also be correct to call it *form* in relation to the matter in which it inheres so that a material substance, be it vegetative or animal, is made of them.[21]

[4.3 Soul as perfection]
It would also be correct to call it *perfection* in relation to the perfection of the genus through it as a realized species in the higher or lower species. For the nature of the

---

20 Outline of the second argument:
i. Avicenna supposes that the soul is a body;
ii. if so, the soul will have a form;
iii. therefore, it will be the principle of the vital functions of the living being not as far as it is a body, but as far as it has a certain form;
iv. the living being will be a composite of: A) the form of the soul (= first principle); B) the body of the soul (= first, bodily part); C) the body of the composite of body-of-the-soul + soul-of-the-soul;
v. consequently, the body of the soul and the body of the composite will be the subject of the form of the soul.

21 i.e.: of the combination of matter and form.

genus is incomplete and undefined unless the nature of the simple or non-simple *differentia* is added to it;[22] once it is added to it, the species becomes perfect. For the *differentia* is the perfection of the species inasmuch as it is species. However, not every species has a simple *differentia* – you have already learned that[23] – but it belongs only to the species that are themselves composed of matter and form, and of these the form is the simple *differentia* of that for which it is the perfection.

[4.4 The notions of *form* and *perfection* do not completely overlap]

Moreover, every form is a perfection, but not every perfection is a form: for the king is the perfection of the city, and the steersman is the perfection of the ship, but each is not the form [respectively] of the city and of the ship. Therefore, whatever perfection is itself separate is not in reality a form for matter, nor in matter. For the form which exists in matter is the form impressed in it and subsisting through it, unless it is agreed to call the perfection of the species the form of the species.

[4.5 The soul is form, end/perfection, and agent in different respects]

In reality, convention has settled that [**R7**] the thing[24] in relation to matter is form, in relation to the whole is end and perfection, and in relation to setting in motion is an efficient principle and a motive power.

If this is the case, then the form requires a relation to something remote from the very substance resulting from it, to something by means of which the resulting substance is what it is in potentiality, to something to which the activities are not ascribed. This thing is matter, since the former is form with regard to its existence for matter.

[4.6 *Perfection* is the most appropriate term with which to define the soul]

[4.6.1 It is preferable to *form*]

Perfection requires a relation to the complete thing from which activities derive, since it is perfection in accordance with its consideration in terms of the species.[25] From this it is clear that, if in determining the soul we say that it is perfection, this is most indicative of its meaning. It would also include all species of soul in all their respects, the soul separable from matter not being an exception to this.

---

22 The simple *differentia* is the form or nature of the essence, whereas the non-simple (or logical) *differentia* is the predicate, which is derived by paronymy from the form (or nature) and is predicated of the species. For instance, "rationality" is a simple *differentia*, whereas "rational" is a non-simple *differentia*.

23 For the distinction between simple and non-simple *differentia*, see *Maqūlāt*, III, 2, 101.12–102.9. In *Maqūlāt*, IV, 1, 133.18–134.12, Avicenna says that the discrete quantity and the continuous quantity are examples of species having only a non-simple *differentia*.

24 i.e.: the soul.

25 Here Avicenna wants to distinguish *form* from *perfection:* the former is said of the matter in which it inheres, whereas the latter is said of the species.

[4.6.2 It is preferable to *power*]
And, likewise, if we say that the soul is perfection, it is better than our saying that it is power. For some of the things deriving from the soul belong to the category of motion, while some [belong] to the category of sensation and perception. And perception belongs to it more properly not inasmuch as it has a power which is a principle of activity, but a principle of receptivity. Setting in motion, by contrast, belongs to it more properly not inasmuch as it has a power which is a principle of receptivity, but a principle of activity. But it is not that one of the two things is ascribed to it,[26] because it is a power for one [of them] more than [it is a power] for the other. So, if it is said [to be] power, and both things together are meant by it,[27] this would be [said] by equivocation.[28] [**R8**] If, by contrast, it is said [to be] power, and [power] is limited to one of the two respects, then from that what we have said would occur, and another thing, namely that it would not include the indication of the essence of the soul insofar as it is soul absolutely, but in one respect and not another. And we have already shown in the logical books[29] that this is neither good nor right. Moreover, if we say perfection, [it] would include both meanings. For the soul with respect to the power by means of which the perception of the animal is perfected is perfection and, with respect to the power from which the activities of the animal derive, is also perfection. And both the separable soul and the soul that does not separate are perfection.

[5. The aforementioned denominations do not indicate whether the soul is a substance or not]

[5.1 Perfection does not indicate whether the soul is a substance or not]
However, if we say [that the soul is] perfection, from this one does not yet know [whether] it is a substance or not a substance. For the meaning of perfection is: the thing through whose existence the animal becomes animal in actuality, and the plant becomes plant in actuality. But from this one does not yet understand whether it is a substance or not a substance.

[5.2 The denomination *form*]
[5.2.1 The soul is not substance in the sense in which the subject/matter and the composite are substance]
However, we say: there is no doubt for us that this thing is not a substance in the sense in which the subject is substance nor, similarly, in the sense in which the com-

26 i.e.: to the soul.
27 i.e.: power as a principle of receptivity, and power as a principle of activity.
28 This is because *quwwa* as principle of receptivity (potentiality) and *quwwa* as principle of activity (faculty) are irreducible to each other, and the term *quwwa* cannot be applied to them both except by equivocation.
29 Avicenna is here probably referring to *Ǧadal*, IV, 1, 214.3–215.11, which corresponds to *Topics*, II, 1, 109 a16–21.

posite is substance. As for [its being] substance in the sense of form, let us look into this [case].

[5.2.2 The claim according to which the soul is substance insofar as it is a form]
If someone says: "I call the soul substance, and I mean by it[30] the form, and I do not mean by it a meaning more general than form, but the meaning that it is substance is the meaning that it is form" – and this is what some people have said, then there would be no room for discussion and disagreement with them at all. The meaning of their saying that the soul is substance is that the soul is form. Rather, their saying that the form is substance is like their saying that the form is form or configuration, or that man is man or human being, which is [**R9**] a senseless discourse.

[5.2.3 Avicenna's interpretation of the criterion of substantiality provided in Aristotle's *Categories*, that is, *not being in a subject at all*]
If someone means by *form* what is not in a subject at all, namely what is not in any respect subsisting in the thing that we have called for you subject, then not every perfection would be a substance. For many perfections are unquestionably in a subject, even though these many [perfections] are not in a subject in relation to the composite and insofar as they are in it: for their being a part of the composite does not prevent them from being in a subject, and their being in it not as the thing in a subject does not render them substance, as some have thought. For substance is not what is not in relation to something as if it were in a subject, such that the thing is a substance in virtue of its not being in this thing as if it were in a subject. Rather, it is substance only if it is not in anything as if it were in a subject. This sense does not disprove its being in something, existing not in a subject: for this [sense] does not belong to it in relation to everything, such that, if it is brought into relation with something in which it is not just as the thing that is in a subject, it becomes a substance, even though in relation to another thing it is such as to be an accident. Rather, it is a consideration belonging to it in itself. For, if you consider the thing itself and examine it and then there is no subject at all for it, it would be in itself a substance. And if it is found in a thousand things not in a subject, after having been found in one thing in the manner of the thing's existence in the subject, it is, then, in itself an accident.[31]

[5.3 If something is not an accident, it is not necessary that it be a substance][32]

---

30 i.e.: by substance.

31 Avicenna's conclusion seems to be that the substantiality or the accidentality of something should be evaluated in itself, and not in relation to something else, for instance in relation to the function performed by something in virtue of which it is defined.

32 The soul is defined in virtue of its relation to the body; therefore, it can be established whether this relation is substantial or accidental, not whether it is in itself a substance or an accident, which depends on its quiddity considered in itself.

It is not the case that, if [something] is not an accident in a thing, [**R10**] then it is a substance in it. For the thing can be neither an accident in the thing nor a substance in it, just as the thing can be neither one nor many in a thing,[33] but it is in itself either one or many. Substantial and substance are not one [thing]; nor is the accident in the sense of accidental that is in the *Isagoge* the accident that is in the *Categories*. We have already shown to you these matters in the discipline of logic.[34] It is, therefore, clear that the soul's being in the composite like a part does not remove its accidentality. Rather, it must be in itself not in a subject at all.[35] You have already learned what the subject is.[36]

[5.4 Three cases of perfection from which the substantiality of the soul *qua* perfection cannot be ascertained]
[(a)] If every soul exists not in a subject, then every soul is substance.
[(b)] If some soul is self-subsisting, while each of the remaining souls is in the *hyle*, not in a subject, then, every soul is a substance.[37]
[(c)] If some soul subsists in a subject and, nevertheless, is part of the composite, it is an accident.

All these [aforementioned entities] are perfection. However, by our positing that the soul is a perfection, it has not become clear yet for us whether the soul is a substance or not a substance. Thus, those who thought that this[38] was sufficient for them to render the soul a substance like the form made a mistake.[39]

[6. The definition of the soul]

[6.1 *Soul* is a relational term and, consequently, the reference to the body is included in its definition]

---

33 Reading *fī šay'* instead of *fī l-šay'*, like all the mss.
34 See *Madḫal*, I, 14, in part. 85.7–86.3 where Avicenna distinguishes accident from accidental, and 86.4–87.19 where Avicenna criticizes Porphyry and his followers because they did not explain satisfactorily the difference between accident and accidental. On the same issue, see also *Maqūlāt*, I, 6, 49.13–50.11.
35 Only in the case in which it is in itself not in a subject at all the soul would be a substance.
36 See *Samāʿ ṭabīʿī*, I, 2.
37 Here Avicenna seems to have in mind a distinction between the celestial and, possibly, the human rational souls and the sublunary souls of plants and animals: the former are substance because they exist independently of the body, i.e. are self-subsisting substances, whereas the latter are substances *qua* form, i.e. are Aristotelian substantial forms, inhering in matter, not in a subject. The expression *wa-in kānat nafs mā qā'ima bi-ḏātihā* to designate the self-subsisting soul echoes *Nafs*, I, 3, 27.16 (*anna nafsan mā yaṣiḥḥu lahā l-infirād bi-qiwām ḏātihā*). See the beginning of §1 of my translation of *Nafs*, I, 3.
38 i.e.: positing the soul as a perfection.
39 Here Avicenna is referring to the position held by Baghdad Aristotelians. See Chapter 4, n. 37.

Then we say: when we know that the soul is perfection, by whatever clarification and distinction we designated the perfection, we would not know yet the soul and its quiddity; rather, we would know it insofar as it is soul. The term *soul* does not apply to it with respect to its substance, but insofar as it governs bodies and is related to them. For this reason the body is included in its definition, just as the building, for example, is included in the definition of the builder, even though it is not included [**R11**] in his definition insofar as he is a human being. For this reason the investigation of the soul is part of natural science, because the investigation of the soul insofar as it is soul is an investigation of it insofar as it has a certain connection with matter and motion. However, we must devote another inquiry to our acquaintance with the essence of the soul. If we had come to know through this[40] the essence of the soul, then it would not have been obscure to us into which category it falls.[41] For whoever knows and understands the essence of something and then presents to himself the nature of something essential belonging to it, its existence for it[42] would not be obscure to him, as we have explained in logic.[43]

[6.2 First perfection, second perfection]
Perfection, however, [can] be of two ways: [(a)] first perfection, and [(b)] second perfection.

[(a)] The first perfection is that by means of which the species becomes species in actuality,[44] like shape for the sword.

[(b)] The second perfection is one of the things that follow the species of the thing in terms of its activities and affections,[45] like cutting for the sword, and like discernment, deliberation, sensation, and motion for the human being. For these are unquestionably perfections of the species, but are not first [perfections]: for, in order to become what it is in actuality, the species does not need these things to occur for it in actuality. Rather, when the principle of these things[46] occurs for it[47] in actuality so that these things[48] become for it in potentiality after having not been in potentiality – except in a remote potentiality that needs something to occur before them so that they become in reality in potentiality – then the animal becomes animal in actuality. The soul is, therefore, a first perfection. And, since the perfection is perfection of something, the soul is the perfection of something,

40 i.e.: the investigation conducted so far.
41 Lit.: the fact that it falls into any category in which it falls.
42 i.e.: the existence of that essential feature for the thing to which it belongs.
43 See *Madḫal*, I, 6, 34.13–35.5.
44 It is noteworthy that by using this formula in § 5.1 Avicenna referred to the notion of perfection.
45 By referring to the activity, in § 4.6.1 Avicenna referred to the notion of perfection without qualification.
46 i.e.: of the second perfections, that is, activities and affections.
47 i.e.: for the species.
48 i.e.: the aforementioned activities and affections.

this something being the body. The body must be taken in the [**R12**] generic, not material sense, as you have learned in the discipline of demonstration.[49] And this body of which the soul is the perfection is not every body: for the soul is not the perfection of the artificial body, like the bed, the chair, etc., but the perfection of the natural body. Nor [is the soul the perfection] of every natural body: for the soul is not the perfection of fire, nor of earth, but in our world[50] it is the perfection of a natural body from which its second perfections derive by means of organs of which it makes use in the activities of life, the first of which are nutrition and growth. Then, the soul we find[51] [in our world] is the first perfection of a natural, organic body, having the capacity of performing the activities of life.

[7. Objections to the definition of the soul that Avicenna has formulated, and their refutation]

[7.1 Presentation of the two main objections]
[7.1.1 First objection: the aforementioned definition of the soul excludes the celestial soul. Two possible solutions and their refutations]
In this place, however, one might raise doubts about some things. For instance, one could say that this definition [of the soul] does not include the celestial soul, for it[52] acts without organs.

[(sol_1)][53] Even if you abstain from mentioning the organs and limit yourself to mentioning life, that would not be of any use to you: for the life that belongs to the celestial soul does not consist of nutrition and growth, nor even sensation. And this is what you mean by life[54] in the definition [of the soul].

And [(sol_2)][55] if by life you mean that which belongs to the celestial soul in terms of perception, for example intellectual conceptualization, and the [capacity for] setting in motion for a voluntary goal, then you would exclude plants from the group of what has a soul. Moreover, if nutrition constitutes life, why do you not call the plants animals?

[7.1.2 Second objection: the unnecessariness of the notion of soul]
Also, one could say: what compelled you to establish [the existence] of a soul, and why was it not sufficient for you to say that life [**R13**] itself is this perfection? Life would, then, be the notion from which derives that whose derivation you ascribe to the soul.

---

49 See *Burhān*, I, 10. For the distinction between genus and matter, see also *Ilāhiyyāt*, V, 3.
50 i.e.: in the sublunary realm.
51 I read *naǧidu* (*we find*), instead of *naḥuddu* (*we define*). On this issue, see Chapter 4 of this book.
52 i.e.: the celestial soul.
53 Solution 1: to leave off the reference to the organs.
54 i.e.: nutrition, growth, and sensation.
55 Solution 2: to leave off the reference to the vegetative soul.

[7.2 Two opinions about the celestial bodies, and Avicenna's answer to the first objection]
[7.2.1 First opinion]
Let us, then, begin by answering these [objections] one by one, and solving them. We say: as for the heavenly bodies, there are two doctrines about them. [(i)] The doctrine of those who believe that every planet and several spheres which are governed by its[56] motion combine to form a whole body like one single animal.[57] Then, the activity of each sphere is completed by means of several parts that have motion, which are like organs. But this statement does not apply to every sphere.[58]

[7.2.2 Second opinion]
[(ii)] The doctrine of those who believe that every sphere has in itself a solitary life, in particular as they believe that there is a ninth body,[59] that body being one in actuality, since there is no multiplicity in it.[60] These must believe that [(a)] the term *soul*, when it is applied to the celestial soul and to the vegetative soul, is applied [to these entities] only by equivocation, that [(b)] this definition pertains only to the soul existing in what is composed, and that [(c)], when a stratagem is used so that animals and the celestial sphere share in the meaning of the term *soul*, the notion of plant is excluded from that group. Even so this stratagem is difficult. For animals and the celestial sphere do not share in the meaning of the term *life* nor, likewise, the meaning of the term *rationality*, because rationality here[61] applies to the existence of a soul that has **[R14]** the two material intellects, and this is not among the things that it is correct [to apply] there,[62] as you will see.[63] For the intellect there is an intellect in actuality, and the intellect in actuality is not a constituent of the soul that is part of the definition of *rational*.[64] Similarly, *sensation* here applies to the faculty by means of which sensible things are perceived by way of receiving what is similar to them and being affected by them. And this also is not among the things that it is correct [to apply] there, as you will see.[65] Moreover, if by making an effort one ren-

56 i.e.: of the planet.
57 Lit.: from every planet and several spheres, which are governed by its motion, is combined a whole body like one single animal.
58 The exception must be the orb/sphere of the fixed stars.
59 This is a unique sphere embracing all the other spheres. It is the ninth from the bottom to the top, namely from the centre to the periphery.
60 There is no multiplicity in it because this body is a planetless and starless orb.
61 i.e.: in the terrestrial, sublunary realm.
62 i.e.: in the celestial realm.
63 The reference is to *Ilāhiyyāt*, IX, 2
64 In *Ilāhiyyāt*, IX, 2 Avicenna clearly distinguishes the celestial soul from the celestial intellect. Consequently, there is no reference to the soul in the definition of the celestial intellect, which is an intellect always in actuality. In the sublunary realm, by contrast, intellect refers to a faculty of the soul, namely of the human *rational* soul. Therefore, *rational* is part of the definition of that soul.
65 The reference is to *Ilāhiyyāt*, IX, 2.

ders the soul a first perfection for what moves at will and perceives among the bodies, so that animals and the celestial soul are included in this [definition], plants would be excluded from this group. And this is the statement validated [through this investigation].

[7.3 Avicenna's answer to the second objection]
As for the matter of life and soul,[66] the solution to the doubt concerning this is as we say: it has already turned out to be true that bodies must have a principle for the known states, related to life in actuality. And if one were to name this principle *life*, there would be no dispute with him.

[7.3.1 Two meanings of *life* according to the multitude]
As for what is understood by the multitude by the expression *life* said of the animal, there are two things: [(i)] one of them is that in the species there is a principle from which those states derive; or [(ii)] [the second is that] the body is such that the derivation of these activities from it is admissible.

[(i)] As for the first [thing], it is known that it is not in any respect the meaning of *soul*. [(ii)] As for the second, it indicates a meaning that likewise is other than the meaning of *soul*. For a thing's being such that it is admissible that something derives from it or that it is characterized by some attribute functions in two ways. [(ii.i)] One of these is that [**R15**] in existence there would be something different from that being itself from which what derives derives, as the ship being such that naval benefits derive from it, and this is among the things that require the steersman[67] so that this being [of the ship] comes into existence. The steersman and this being are not one single thing with respect to subject. [(ii.ii)] The second [way] is that there is nothing different from this being in the subject, as the body being such that the combustion derives from it according to those who make this very being the heat[68] so that the existence of the heat in the body is the same [thing] as the existence of this being. Similarly, the existence of the soul is the existence of this being, as appears outwardly. However, this in the [case of the] soul is not right: for what is understood by this being and by the soul is not one thing. And how is this not the case, whereas what is understood by the described being does not prevent it from being by itself preceded by a perfection and a principle, and then to the body belongs this being? But what is understood by the first perfection that we have described, prevents it from being preceded by itself by another perfection, because the first perfection does not have a principle, nor a first perfection. Hence, what is understood by *life* and *soul* is not one [thing], if by *life* we mean what the multitude understands. If, by contrast, by

66 Here Avicenna is referring to the second objection mentioned in § 7.1.2 above, i.e. that according to which the notion of soul is unnecessary because that of life is sufficient.
67 Here the steersman corresponds to "something different from the being itself" mentioned at the beginning of 15.
68 There is no need for a further principle: the body is hot by itself.

life we mean that it is a synonymous expression with *soul* in indicating the first perfection, we would not argue, and *life* would be a name for what we endeavour to establish of this first perfection.

[8. The thought-experiment of the *Flying Man*]

[8.1 Introduction to the experiment]

We have now come to know the meaning of the term that applies to the thing called *soul* in virtue of a relation belonging to it. We ought, then, to engage ourselves in grasping the quiddity of this thing which, through the aforementioned consideration,[69] has become soul. Here we must point out a manner of establishing the existence of the soul belonging to us by way of pointing and reminding [**R16**], giving an indication that is adequate for someone who has the capacity for noticing the truth itself, with no need of being educated, constantly prodded, and diverted from errors.

[8.2 The experiment, which is arranged *quasi*-syllogistically]

We say: one of us must imagine himself as if he is created all at once and perfect, but his sight has been impeded from observing external things, and [as if] he is created floating in the air or in the void in such a way that the air resistance does not hit him in a manner that compels [him] to sense [it], and with his limbs separated from each other so that they neither meet nor touch. Then, he considers whether he will affirm that he exists. He will not have doubts about whether or not to do so. However, he will not affirm [the existence of] any of his limbs, any of his internal organs, [his] heart, [his] brain, or any external thing. Rather, he affirms [the existence of] himself, though he does not affirm his having height, breadth, and depth. If, in that [aforementioned] state, he were able to imagine a hand or some other limb, he would imagine it neither as part of himself nor as condition for [the existence of] himself.[70]

You know that what is affirmed is different from what is not affirmed, and what is acknowledged is different from what is not acknowledged.[71]

Hence, the self, whose existence [this human being] has affirmed as something proper to him[72] because this [self] is [identical to] himself, is different from his body and his limbs whose existence has not been affirmed.[73]

---

69 i.e.: in virtue of its being principle of activities in the body (operational principle).

70 This argument echoes the soul's experience of the separation from the body described in Plotinus' *Enneads*, which Avicenna might have read in the pseudo-*Theology of Aristotle*. On this as a possible source, see Bertolacci, *Il pensiero filosofico di Avicenna*, 553, n. 49. For the passage in question, see Plotino, *La discesa dell'anima nei corpi* (*Enn.* IV 8 [6]). *Plotiniana Arabica* (*Pseudo-Teologia di Aristotele, capitoli 1 e 7; "Detti del Sapiente Greco"*), C. D'Ancona ed., Il Poligrafo, Padova 2003, 229.10–230.1.

71 Reading *wa-l-muqarr bihī ġayr allaḏī lam yuqarri bihī*, as it is printed in the Cairo edition.

72 i.e.: to the human being engaged in the thought-experiment.

73 Reading *lam tuṯbat*.

[8.3 Conclusion of the experiment]
Hence, the recipient of the pointing has a way to be alerted to the existence of the soul as something other than the body, indeed other than body,[74] and [a way] to be directly acquainted with it and aware of it. However, if he is distracted from it, he would need educative prodding.

[(**I.3**)]

[**R27**] [Chapter] concerning the fact that the soul falls under the category of substance

[1. Two criteria of substantiality compared: independent existence vs. being a form]

We ourselves say: you know from what has preceded that the soul is not body.[75] And if it is established for you that it rightly occurs for some soul to be isolated [from the body] because of its self-subsistence, you will not doubt that it is a substance. This, however, is established for you only in the case of something that is said to be soul. In the case of other things, such as the vegetative and the animal soul, that has not been established for you [yet]. But the proximate matter for these souls to exist in it is what [**R28**] it is only because of a specific temperament and a specific configuration, and [the proximate matter] remains existing in actuality with that specific temperament only as long as the soul is in it. And the soul is what renders it[76] as having that temperament: for the soul is unquestionably the cause for the plant and the animal to exist according to the temperament belonging to them,[77] since the soul is the principle for reproduction and nurturing,[78] as we have said.

[2. The soul (of plants and animals) is a substance insofar as it is a form]

[2.1 The soul does not exist as something in a subject]
Hence, it is impossible for the proximate subject of the soul to be what it is in actuality, except by means of the soul, which would be a cause for its[79] being as such. It cannot be said that the proximate subject exists in its nature, and that this happens by a cause other than the soul, and then the soul unites with it in some way which thereafter has no part in its preservation, constitution, and nurturing, as is the case with accidents whose existence necessarily follows the existence of their subject but are not constituents of their subject in actuality. As for the soul, it is a constituent of

74 i.e.: incorporeal.
75 This is a general reference to *Nafs*, I, 1. See, in particular, 5.3–6.1.
76 i.e.: the proximate matter.
77 I disagree with Rahman's emendation of the pronoun *-hā* with *-hū*, since I think that the pronoun *-hā* attested by all mss. perfectly fits the reference to "plant and animal" mentioned at 28.3.
78 Here reproduction and nurturing, together with nutrition, which will be mentioned in the following pages, in all likelihood refer to the minimal vital activities for which the soul is responsible.
79 i.e.: of the proximate subject.

its proximate subject, bringing it into existence in actuality, as you will learn how things are concerning this when we deal with animals. As for the remote subject, there are between it and the soul other forms that render it subsistent.[80]

If the soul separates [from its subject], it necessarily follows that its separation occurs because of something predominant that makes the subject [endowed] with another state, and brings about in it an inanimate form as the counterpart of the temperamental form appropriate for the soul and for that form.[81] Therefore, after the soul['s separation] matter does not remain at all of its own species [**R29**]; rather, either its species and its substance by means of which a subject for the soul came to be cease [to be], or a form replaces the soul in it[82] which preserves matter in actuality in its nature. Therefore, that natural body would not be as it was, but it would have [another] form and other accidents. Likewise, some of its[83] parts would have been replaced and separated together with the change of everything in the substance. Thus, matter there will not be preserved in itself after the separation from the soul, [matter] which has been a subject for the soul, but now is a subject for something else. Therefore, the existence of the soul in the body is not like the existence of the accident in the subject. Then, the soul is a substance because it is a form not in a subject.

[2.2 An objection to the aforementioned criterion of substantiality]

[2.2.1 The vegetative soul is the cause for the subsistence of the proximate matter in which, as if it were in a subject, the animal soul inheres]

However, one could say: "Let us concede that this is the form of the vegetative soul: for it is a cause for the subsistence of its proximate matter. As for the animal soul, it seems that the vegetative [soul] renders its (*sc.* of the animal soul) matter subsistent. Then, it necessarily follows that this animal soul comes after it (*sc.* the vegetative soul) in that matter. The animal [soul] would, therefore, be attained in a matter that had been rendered subsistent by itself,[84] and it (*sc.* this matter) is a cause for the subsistence of that which came to inhere in it, that is, the animal [soul]. The animal [soul] would hence not subsist except in a subject".

[2.2.2 Avicenna's answer to the objection]

In answering this [objection] we say: from the vegetative soul, inasmuch as it is vegetative soul, nothing necessarily follows except a body that is nourished absolutely.[85]

80 In all likelihood here Avicenna is referring to the forms of the elements that render the proximate subject of the soul subsistent. The elements are the remote subject of the soul.

81 i.e.: the inanimate, inorganic form.

82 i.e.: in the matter.

83 i.e.: in the matter.

84 That is, the matter in which the animal soul inheres has been rendered subsistent by the vegetative soul and not by the animal soul itself, which supervenes.

85 i.e.: without other qualifications.

And the vegetative soul absolutely[86] [taken] does not have an existence except the existence of a generic meaning, which is only in the [faculty of] estimation. As for what exists in concrete individuals, this is its (*sc.* of the generic meaning) species. And that for which the vegetative soul must be said to be a cause is a thing likewise general, universal, not realized [in actuality], namely the body that is nourished and grows [**R30**], absolute, generic, not specific. As for the body possessing the organs of sensation, discernment, and voluntary motion, it does not derive from the vegetative soul inasmuch as it is vegetative soul, but inasmuch as another *differentia* is joined with it, by means of which it becomes another nature. This will not happen unless it becomes an animal soul.

[3. Three meanings of *vegetative soul*]

However, we must begin by adding this as an explanation. We say: *vegetative soul* [(a)] either means[87] the specific soul which is proper to plants and not animals; [(b)] or it means the general meaning which encompasses the vegetative and the animal soul in virtue of the fact that both nourish [themselves], generate [the like], and grow. For this[88] might be called *vegetative soul*, but this is a metaphorical saying. For the vegetative soul does not exist except in plants, whereas the meaning that encompasses the soul of plants and that of animals would be in animals as well as in plants, and its existence would be as the general meaning exists in things. [(c)] Or *vegetative soul* means one of the faculties of the animal soul from which the activities of nutrition, nurturing, and reproduction derive.

[3.1 The first meaning]
[(a)] If someone means by it the vegetative soul that, in relation to the soul performing [the activity of] nutrition, is specific, then this would be exclusively in plants, not in animals.

[3.2 The second meaning]
[(b)] If someone means by it the general meaning, then a general meaning, not a specific meaning, must be ascribed to it. For the general producer is the one to whom a general product is ascribed; the specific producer, like the carpenter, is the one to whom a specific product is ascribed; and the determined producer is the one to whom a determined product is ascribed. This [**R31**] is something whose verification has already been put forward to you.[89] Thus, what is ascribed to the general, vegetative soul in terms of the state of the body is that it grows, and is general. As for the fact that the body grows such that it is suitable or not suitable for the reception of

86 i.e.: without other qualifications.
87 Lit.: "by *vegetative soul* either is meant…". This applies also to sentence [(b)] and [(c)].
88 i.e.: the general meaning that encompasses both the vegetative and the animal soul.
89 See *Samāʿ ṭabīʿī*, I, 12, and *Madḫal*, II, 1. See also *Nafs*, V, 7, 260.

sensation, this is not ascribed to the vegetative soul insofar as it is general, nor does this meaning[90] follow the vegetative soul.

[3.3 The third meaning]
[(c)] As for the third division, it is impossible, as it is thought that the vegetative faculty comes along alone and produces an animal body. If what is alone in managing [the body] were that faculty,[91] then it would have completed a vegetative body. But that is not the case.[92] Rather, it only completes an animal body with the organs of sensation and motion. Therefore, it[93] would be a faculty of a soul having other faculties [besides that]. And this among its (*sc.* of the soul) faculties acts after the pattern that leads to the disposition of the organ [to the reception of] the second perfections belonging to that soul of which this is a faculty. This soul is the animal [soul].

[4. Conclusion]

It will become clear later on that the soul is one and that these are faculties branching off from it into the limbs, and that the activity of some of them is delayed or comes early in accordance with the disposition of the organ.[94]

Thus, the soul belonging to every animal gathers the elements of its body,[95] and composes them and combines them in the manner that renders it[96] suitable to be a body for it (*sc.* for the soul). The soul preserves this body according to the arrangement that it ought to [have], so the external changes do not take control of it[97] as long as the soul exists in it; otherwise, it would not remain in its[98] healthy state.

Due to the soul's control of the body is what occurs in terms of the strengthening of the faculty of growth or its weakening, when the soul is aware of propositions that it detests or loves with an aversion [**R32**] and a love that are not at all bodily. This happens when what comes to the soul is some assent, and this is not one of the things that cause an impression on the body inasmuch as it is a belief; rather,

90 i. e.: the meaning of the body being such that it is suitable or not suitable for the reception of sensation.
91 i. e.: the vegetative faculty (it is the only faculty mentioned within the previous lines).
92 Here Avicenna is discussing the meaning of *vegetative soul* as faculty of the animal soul, which performs the activities of nutrition, growth, and reproduction in the animal body.
93 i. e.: vegetative soul.
94 See *Nafs*, I, 4. See also *Nafs*, V, 7, where Avicenna uses the thought-experiment of the *Flying Man* to show that the soul is the unifying principle of the different faculties (and activities) observable in bodies.
95 i. e.: of the body of the animal.
96 i. e.: the body of the animal.
97 i. e.: of the body.
98 I agree with the correction suggested in Rahman's edition. Here the reference is to the body (masculine pronoun suggested by the editor), not the soul (feminine pronoun attested in all the manuscripts).

that belief is followed by an affection of joy or sadness. And this is among the things perceived by the soul, but which does not occur to the body inasmuch as it is a body. Then, this causes an impression on the faculty of growth and nutrition so that there comes to be in it from an accident occurring firstly to the soul – let it be rational happiness – an intensification and an effectiveness in its activity, whereas [there comes to be] from the accident contrary to this – let it be the rational sadness in which there is no bodily pain – a weakening and an inability so that its activity corrupts, and sometimes [its] temperament is completely destroyed.

All these are among the things that will persuade you that the soul gathers the two faculties of perception and of the use of nourishment,[99] being [the soul] one for them, this [faculty] not being isolated from that [faculty].[100] It is thus clear that the soul renders perfect the body in which it is, and preserves it according to its arrangement for which it is more appropriate to [have its parts] distinguished and separated since every part of the body deserves a different place[101] and requires a separation from its cognate. Only a thing external to its nature preserves it in the way it is, and this thing is the soul in the animal.

Consequently, when the soul is the perfection of a subject, that subject is rendered subsistent by it, and it (*sc.* the perfection) is also what renders perfect the species and makes it. For the things that have different souls become different species through them, and they differ in species, not in individuals.[102] The soul, therefore, is not among the accidents through which the species do not differ, and which do not enter the constitution of the subject. The soul is, then, perfection as substance, not as accident,[103] but it does not necessarily follow **[R33]** from this that perfection is either separable or inseparable. For not every substance is separable. For neither is matter separable, nor is form, but you have already learned that things are this way.[104] Let us now indicate in a concise way the faculties of the soul and their activities and then we will submit them to a close scrutiny.

[(**I.5**)][105]

[Chapter] containing the enumeration of the faculties of the soul by way of classification

---

99 i.e.: nutrition.

100 Perhaps here Avicenna is also hinting at the primacy of the nutritive faculty, without which all the other faculties cannot be found in a living being.

101 i.e.: other than the one occupied by another part.

102 Lit: and their differentiation is in species, not in individual.

103 Reading *ka-l-ǧawhar lā ka-l-ʿaraḍ* as attested in mss. ABDFG in Rahman's edition.

104 See § 2.1 above. See also *Samāʿ ṭabīʿī*, I, 2.

105 *Nafs*, I, 5, 41.4–43.1 corresponds to *Naǧāt*, 321.1–323.7 (ed. Dānišpažūh, 1985); *Nafs*, I, 5, 43.1–45.16 corresponds to *Naǧāt*, 327.5–330.1; *Nafs*, I, 5, 45.17–50.12 corresponds to *Naǧāt*, 330.7–336.8; *Nafs*, I, 5, 50.13–51.16 corresponds to *Naǧāt*, 341.10–343.9.

[1. General subdivision of the psychic faculties]

[1.1 First, traditional subdivision]

Let us now enumerate the faculties of the soul by way of convention; then we shall engage in the clarification of the state of every faculty. We say, thus, that the psychic faculties are divided, according to the primary division, into three parts.

[1.1.1 First division: the vegetative soul]

One of them is the vegetative soul, which is the first perfection of a natural, organic body in virtue of the fact that it generates [the like], grows, and nourishes itself. The nourishment is a body such that it becomes like the nature of the body of which it is said to be the nourishment. It[106] adds to the body the [exact] quantity of what has been dissolved, or more or less.[107]

[1.1.2 Second devision: the animal soul]

The second [division] is the animal soul, which is the first perfection of a [**R40**] natural, organic body in virtue of the fact that it perceives particulars and moves at will.

[1.1.3 Third division: the human soul]

The third [division] is the human soul, which is the first perfection of a natural, organic body in virtue of the fact that to it is ascribed [the capacity for] performing activities that come about by choice based on thinking,[108] and the deduction based on opinion, and in virtue of the fact that it perceives universal things.[109]

[1.2 Alternative subdivision of the psychic faculties]

If there were not [such a] custom,[110] it would be best to make every [perfection coming] first a condition that is mentioned in the description of the following [perfection], if we want to describe the soul, not the psychic faculty belonging to the soul in accordance with the activity for which it is responsible.[111] For *perfection* is included in the definition of the soul, not in the definition of the faculty of the soul. You will learn the difference between the animal soul and the faculty of perception and of setting in motion, and the difference between the rational soul and the faculty

---

106 i.e.: the nourishment.

107 Here Avicenna is saying that the ingested nourishment balances what the body has lost by performing its natural activities.

108 i.e.: by means of deliberation. The deliberation is what distinguishes human from divine action, for in the latter there is no deliberation, and no distinction between thinking and acting.

109 As opposed to the particular things, which are perceived by the animal soul.

110 i.e.: the custom of distinguishing three souls, namely the vegetative, the animal, and the human soul, on the basis of the faculties ensuing from them.

111 Lit.: in accordance with that activity.

concerning the aforementioned things with respect to discernment, etc.[112] If you want a close scrutiny,[113] the right thing [to do] would be to make the vegetative [soul] a genus for the animal [soul], and the animal [soul] a genus for the human [soul], and to include the more general in the definition of the more specific. However, if you take into consideration the souls insofar as they have specific faculties in their animality and in their humanity, then you may be satisfied with what we have mentioned.[114]

[2. The three faculties of the vegetative soul: nutrition, growth, reproduction]

The vegetative soul has three faculties.

[(i)] The nutritive [faculty], which is a faculty that transforms a body different from the body in which it is into something similar to the body in which it is, and attaches it to the body [in which it is] as a compensation of what dissolves from it.

[(ii)] The faculty of growth, which is a faculty that makes in the body in which it is, by means of the assimilated body,[115] a proportionate increase in its dimensions in terms of length, width, and depth, so that the body [in which it is] reaches by means of it[116] the perfect development.[117]

[(iii)] The faculty of reproduction, which is [**R41**] a faculty that takes from the body in which it is, a part similar to it in potentiality. Then, it produces in it, by drawing on other bodies that resemble it in terms of constitution and mixture, something that will become similar to it in actuality.

[3. The two faculties of the animal soul: locomotion and perception]

By means of the first division,[118] the animal soul has two faculties: [(i)] the locomotive [faculty], and [(ii)] the perceptive [faculty].

112 Cf. § 1.1.3 above. Here Avicenna is distinguishing between the soul and the faculties belonging to it. What Avicenna might be saying here is that, besides the classification of the souls based on their faculties, which can be arranged according to the ruling/serving scheme (see the end of this chapter), the different souls could be arranged according to a sort of genus-species scheme with respect to their level of generality (the nutritive soul is more general since, unlike the animal or the rational soul, it belongs to all living beings and can be found alone).

113 *Close scrutiny* (*istiqṣāʾ*) might refer to the distinction between soul and faculties belonging to the soul, instead of considering the two approaches as equivalent.

114 i.e.: with the first traditional subdivision mentioned in § 1.1 above.

115 i.e.: by means of nutrition.

116 i.e.: by means of the assimilated body.

117 Lit.: the perfection of [its] development.

118 Avicenna refers here to the first traditional subdivision (§ 1.1.2) according to which the faculties belonging to the animal soul are firstly divided into two main faculties, that is, locomotion and perception. These two faculties will be the object of further internal subdivisions.

[3.1 The locomotive faculty and its two subdivisions]
[(i)] The locomotive [faculty] exists according to two divisions: either [(i.i)] [it is] locomotive because it incites motion; or [(i.ii)] [it is] locomotive because it enacts [motion].

[(i.i)] The [faculty which is] locomotive because it incites [motion] is the appetitive or desiderative faculty, which is the faculty that, when in the imaginative faculty, which we will mention later on,[119] is impressed a form which is sought after or shunned, incites the other locomotive faculty, which we will mention,[120] to set [something] in motion. It has two branches: [(i.i.i)] one branch is called the concupiscible faculty, which is a faculty that incites to set [something] in motion, [a setting in motion] by means of which it gets close[121] to imagined things, being necessary or useful in the quest for pleasure. [(i.i.ii)] The [other] branch is called the irascible faculty, which is a faculty that incites to set [something] in motion, [a setting in motion] by means of which it repels[122] the imagined thing, being harmful or destructive in the quest for predominance.

[(i.ii)] As for the locomotive faculty because it enacts [motion], it is a faculty, emitted in the sinews and muscles, such that it contracts the muscles and then attracts the tendons and the ligaments that are connected to the limbs, in the direction of the principle [of the motion], either loosening them or stretching them lengthwise, so that the tendons and the ligaments are contrary to the direction of the principle [of the motion].

[3.2 The perceptive faculty and its two subdivisions]
[(ii)] As for the perceptive faculty, it is divided into two parts: among them [(ii.i)] there is a faculty that perceives from outside, and [(ii.ii)] there is a faculty that perceives from within.

[3.2.1 External senses]
[(ii.i)] The perceptive [faculty] from outside are the five or eight senses.[123]

[3.2.1.1 Sight]
Among the external senses there is sight. It is a faculty located in the concave nerve,[124] which perceives the form of whatever is impressed in the vitreous

---

119 See § 3.2.2.3.4 below. See also *Nafs*, IV, 2.
120 i.e.: the locomotive faculty that actually sets in motion. See [(i.ii)] below.
121 Reading *taqrubu* instead of *yaqrubu.*
122 Reading *tadfaʿu* instead of *yadfaʿu.*
123 This double enumeration refers to the possibility of detecting, within the sense of touch, four subspecies, each of which is capable of perceiving a pair of contraries. If such species were considered as so many external senses, the number of the latter would rise from five to eight.
124 Here *al-ʿaṣaba al-muǧawwafa* refers to the optic nerve. The same expression occurs in *Nafs*, II, 3, 72.6 [139.13]; III, 7, 144.2 [257.50]; III, 8, 151.17 [268.43]; V, 8, 267.9 [181.57–8]. In *Nafs*, III, 8 Avicenna

humor[125] of the apparitions of the bodies possessing a color, which are led through the actually transparent bodies to the surfaces of [**R42**] polished bodies.

[3.2.1.2 Hearing]
Among them there is [also] hearing, a faculty located in the nerve dispersed over the surface of the auditory meatus, which perceives the form of what is led to it[126] through the vibration of the air compressed between what strikes and what is struck, the latter resisting violently the former, from which a sound comes into being. Its[127] vibration is led to the stagnant air confined in the cavity of the auditory meatus and moves it in the manner of its motion. Then, the waves of this motion touch the nerve,[128] and so someone hears.[129]

[3.2.1.3 Smell]
Among them there is [also] smell, a faculty located in two outgrowths of the front part of the brain, resembling the two nipples of the breast. It perceives what the inhaled air brings to it of the odor existing in the vapor mixed with it or of the odor impressed in it because of the alteration [caused] by a body having odor.

[3.2.1.4 Taste]
Among them there is [also] taste, a faculty located in the nerve spread over the body of the tongue, which perceives the tastes dissolved from the bodies which are in contact with it[130] and mixed with the sweet humor on it[131] in a manner that transforms [them].

[3.2.1.5 Touch]
Among them there is [also] touch, a faculty located in the nerves of the skin of the whole body and of its flesh. It perceives what touches it and causes an impression on it because of the opposition that transforms the temperament, or [because of the opposition] that transforms the configuration of the composition. It seems that for a

explicitly defers the discussion of the physiology of the two optic nerves to medicine (*wa-humā ʿaṣabatāni nubayyinu laka ḥālahumā ḥīna natakallamu fī l-tašrīḥ*, 151.18–19 [*...qui sunt duo nervi, quorum dispositionem assignabimus cum loquemur de chirurgia*, 268.43–4]). Avicenna deals with the optic nerve in *Qānūn*, III, iii, I, 1 where he deals with the physiology of the eye. This chapter is reproduced almost verbatim in *Ḥayawān*, XII, 13.

125 It is the crystalline lens.

126 i.e.: to the nerve dispersed over the surface of the auditory meatus.

127 i.e.: of the air compressed between what strikes and what is struck.

128 i.e.: the nerve dispersed over the surface of the auditory meatus.

129 Or: a sound is heard.

130 i.e.: with the body of the tongue.

131 See the previous footnote. Sweet humor (*ruṭūba ʿaḏba*) refers to the saliva. Cf. *Nafs*, II, 4, 75.8 [143.80], where the salivary humor (*ruṭūba luʿābiyya* [*humor salivae*]) is said to be the medium of the sense of taste.

group of people this faculty is not a final species, but a genus for four or more faculties, disseminated together all over the skin. [(i)] One [of these supposed faculties] makes judgements on the contrariety between hot and cold; [(ii)] the second makes judgements on the contrariety between moist and dry; [(iii)] the third makes judgements on the contrariety between hard and soft; [(iv)] the fourth makes judgements on the contrariety between rough and smooth; except [**R43**] that their being gathered in one single organ gives the impression that they are one in essence.

[3.2.2 Internal senses]
[3.2.2.1 General introduction to the object of the internal senses and their activity]
[(ii.ii)] As for the perceptive faculties from within, some of them are faculties that perceive the forms of sensible things, whereas some [others] perceive the meanings of sensible things. And among the perceptive [faculties from within] some perceive and act at the same time, whereas some [others] perceive, but do not act. And among them some perceive in a primary way, while some perceive in a secondary way.

[3.2.2.2 Form and meaning]
[3.2.2.2.1 Perception of the form]
The difference between the perception of the form and the perception of the meaning is that the form is the thing that the internal sense and the external sense perceive together. However, the external sense perceives it first, then brings it to the internal sense, like the sheep's perception of the form of the wolf, that is, its shape, its configuration, and its color. For the internal sense of the sheep perceives it,[132] but its external sense perceives it first.

[3.2.2.2.2 Perception of the meaning]
As for the meaning, it is the thing that the soul perceives of the sensible thing without the external sense perceiving it first, like the sheep's perception of the hostile meaning in the wolf, or of the meaning necessitating the sheep's fearing it, and its fleeing from it, without the [external] sense perceiving it at all.

[3.2.2.2.3 What is meant by form, and what is meant by meaning]
Thus, what firstly the external sense, then the internal sense, perceives of the wolf is assigned here the name *form*. What, by contrast, the internal faculties – not the [external] sense – perceive is assigned here the name *meaning*.

[3.2.2.2.4 Perception with activity, perception without activity]
The difference between perception with activity and perception without activity is that among the activities of some internal faculties there is [the activity to] combine

132 i.e.: the form of the wolf.

some perceived forms and meanings with some [others], and to separate [some of] them from some [others]. Therefore, [these internal faculties] have already perceived and also acted upon what they have perceived. As for perception without activity, it [consists] in having the form or the meaning being only impressed in the thing [receiving them] without its[133] acting freely upon it at all.

[3.2.2.2.5 First perception, second perception]
The difference between first perception and second perception is that first perception **[R44]** consists in that the occurrence of the form in a certain manner has already happened to the thing[134] by itself, whereas second perception consists in that the occurrence of the form for the thing[135] happens in virtue of another thing that brought the form to it.

[3.2.2.3 List of the internal senses][136]
[3.2.2.3.1 *Phantasia*, or common sense]
Then, among the internal perceptive faculties of the animal there is the faculty [called] *fantasia*,[137] that is, the common sense. It is a faculty located in the first cavity of the brain, which receives in itself all the forms impressed in the five senses and [then] brought to it.

[3.2.2.3.2 Imagery, or form-bearing faculty]
Then there is the imagery and the form-bearing [faculty]. It is a faculty also located in the rear part of the front cavity of the brain, which retains what the common sense has received from the five particular senses, where it[138] remains after the disappearance of those sensible things. Know that the reception belongs to a faculty different from the faculty through which retention occurs.[139] Consider that about water: it has the faculty of receiving engraving, imprinting and, in general, the figure, but it does not have the faculty of retaining it; however, we will add to this a verification for you later on.[140]

---

133 i.e.: of the thing receiving them.
134 i.e.: to the subject of perception.
135 See the previous footnote.
136 A similar, though more detailed, presentation of the internal senses can be found in *Nafs*, IV, 1. For the analysis of this chapter, and its entire English translation, see T. Alpina, "Retaining, Remembering, Recollecting".
137 *banṭāsiyā* is a calque of the Greek term φαντασία, by means of which in *De an.*, III, 3 Aristotle refers to both retentive and compositive imagination. In *Nafs*, I, 5, 51.5–6 is also attested the form *fanṭāsiyā*.
138 i.e.: what the common sense has received from the five external senses.
139 Cf. *Nafs*, IV, 1, 165.9–18 [5.60–6.72].
140 See *Nafs*, IV, 1–2.

[3.2.2.3.3 The difference of perception among external senses, common sense, and imagery]

If you want to know the difference between the activity of the external sense in general,[141] the activity of the common sense, and the activity of the form-bearing [faculty], consider the state of the drop that descends from the rain, and then is seen as a straight line, and [consider] the state of the straight thing that rotates, and then its extremity is seen as a circle. It is not possible for a thing to be perceived as a line or a circle unless it is seen several times. The external sense, however, cannot see it twice; on the contrary, it sees it where it is. But when it is impressed in the common sense and vanishes [externally] before the form is effaced from the common sense, the external sense would perceive it where it is, whereas the common sense would perceive it as though being where it was and [simultaneously] as being where it has come to be. Then it sees a circular or a [**R45**] straight extension. But this cannot be ascribed to the external sense at all. As for the form-bearing [faculty], it perceives both things, and conceive them both, even though the thing ceases [to be] and disappears.

[3.2.2.3.4 The imaginative or the cogitative faculty]

Then [there is] the faculty which is called imaginative in relation to the animal soul, and cogitative in relation to the human soul. It is a faculty located in the central cavity of the brain, near the worm,[142] such that it combines some [things stored] in the imagery with some [others] and separates some [things] from some [others] at will.

[3.2.2.3.5 Estimation]

Then [there is] the estimative faculty, which is the faculty located at the end of the central cavity of the brain. It perceives the non-sensible meanings (*al-maʿānī l-ġayr al-maḥsūsa*) existing in sensible, particular things, like the faculty existing in the sheep which judges that this wolf is to be shunned, and that this offspring is to be favourably disposed to. It seems also to be [the faculty] that acts on the imaginative things by combining and separating [them].

[3.2.2.3.6 Retentive and recollective faculty]

Then [there is] the retentive, remembering faculty, which is a faculty located in the rear cavity of the brain. It retains what the estimative faculty perceives of the non-

141 The reference is to the five external senses considered as a whole. The same reference occurs at line 15–6. For a similar use of *ḥiss*, see *Nafs*, II, 2, 59.11; IV, 1, 165.2.

142 The vermiform substance (*dūda*, *vermis*) is a piece of brain substance, similar to a worm, which acts as a door to close the passageway connecting the front cavity with the rear cavity of the brain, in order to prevent the pneuma (*rūḥ*, *spiritus*) from going any further than the middle cavity. On the fact that the forms retained in imagery penetrate the rear cavity of the brain, i.e. the seat of memory, upon the decision of estimation, which opens at will the vermiform substance, and on the physiology of this transfer, which occurs through the mediation of the pneuma of the imaginative/cogitative faculty, see *Nafs*, III, 8, 153.9–154.11 [270.77–272.2].

sensible meanings in particular sensible things. The relation of the retentive faculty to the estimative faculty is like the relation of the faculty that is called imagery to the [common] sense; and the relation of that faculty[143] to meanings is like the relation of this faculty[144] to the sensible forms.

Thus, these are the faculties of the animal soul.

[4. The rational soul and its two faculties]

As for the human rational soul, its faculties are divided into a practical faculty and a cognitive faculty, both of which are called *intellect* by equivocation or by its similarity.[145]

[4.1 The practical faculty and its threefold consideration]

The practical is a faculty which is a principle that moves the body of the human being towards the particular activities characterized by deliberation in accordance with what is required by opinions which are conventionally proper to them.[146] There belongs to it [**R46**] a consideration in relation to the animal appetitive faculty, a consideration in relation to the animal imaginative and estimative faculty, and a consideration in relation to itself.

[4.1.1 The relation of the practical faculty to the appetitive faculty]

Its consideration in accordance with relation to the animal appetitive faculty is the kind from which configurations proper to the human being come into being in it, through which he is quickly prepared to act and being affected,[147] like shame, shyness, laughter, weeping, and the like.

[4.1.2 The relation of the practical faculty to the imaginative and estimative faculty]

Its consideration in accordance with relation to the animal imaginative and estimative faculty is the kind that joins with the practical faculty when it engages in discovering the devices in the generable and corruptible things and in inventing the human arts.

[4.1.3 The relation of the practical faculty to itself]

Its consideration in accordance with relation to itself is the kind in which between the practical and the theoretical intellect[148] are generated the opinions which are

143 i.e.: the retentive faculty.

144 i.e.: of the imagery that, like the retentive faculty, performs a storage activity with respect to the sensible forms brought from the five external senses to the common sense.

145 The similarity of the word *intellect* when applied to both these faculties.

146 i.e.: to those particular activities.

147 Lit.: is prepared to the quickness of activity and affection.

148 i.e.: from the collaboration of the practical and the theoretical intellect.

connected with actions, and are spread as widespread and generally accepted [opinions], such as, lying is repugnant, and injustice is repugnant – not by way of demonstration – and what is similar [to these opinions] among the premises defined [as for their] separation from the pure intellectual principles in the books of logic, even though, if demonstrated, they also become of the sort of intellectual [principles], as you have come to know in the books of logic.[149]

[4.1.4 The relation of the practical intellect to the bodily faculties]
This faculty must control the rest of the faculties of the body in accordance with what the judgments of the other faculty, which we will mention,[150] require, so that it will not be affected by them[151] at all but, rather, those [faculties] will be affected by it, and tamed under it, lest there come into being in it from the body submissive configurations, acquired from natural things, which are called vile characters (*sc.* vices). Rather, it must not be affected [**R47**], nor subdued at all, but controlling, so that it would have virtuous characters (*sc.* virtues). Characters may be related also to the bodily faculties. If, however, these [bodily faculties] are predominant, they will have an active configuration, whereas this intellect[152] will have a passive configuration. Let us call each configuration *character*, thus from one thing there comes into being a character in this [active configuration], and a character in that [passive configuration]. If they[153] are the vanquished, they will have a passive configuration, whereas to it[154] an active configuration will not be foreign. Therefore, that will also be two configurations and two characters, or the character will be one with two relations.

[4.2 The substance of the human soul and its two faces. End of the discourse about the practical faculty]
The characters that are in us are ascribed only to this faculty because the human soul, as will become evident later on,[155] is one substance, but it has a relation and a reference to two sides, a side below it and a side above it, and in accordance with each side it has a faculty by means of which the connection between it and that side is regulated. Thus, this practical faculty is the faculty belonging to it[156] for the sake of [its] connection to the side below it, that is, the body and its guidance. As for the theoretical faculty, it is the faculty belonging to it for the sake of [its] connection with the side above it so that it would be affected [by it], would acquire from

149 See *Burhān*, I, 4.
150 i.e.: the theoretical intellect. See § 4.3 below.
151 i.e.: by the bodily faculties.
152 i.e.: the practical intellect.
153 i.e.: the bodily faculties.
154 i.e.: the practical intellect.
155 See *Nafs*, V, 1, 208.10 – 13.
156 i.e.: to the substance of the human soul.

it, and would receive from it. So it is as though our soul has two faces, [(i)] a face oriented towards the body, and this face must not be receptive at all of any impression of a kind required by the nature of the body; and [(ii)] a face oriented towards the high principles, and this face must be [in a state of] perpetual reception of what is there and of perpetually receiving an impression from it. Therefore, from the downward direction characters are engendered, whereas from the upward direction sciences are engendered. This is the practical faculty.

[4.3 The theoretical faculty and its object]
[**R48**] As for the theoretical faculty, it is a faculty such that it is impressed with the universal forms abstracted from matter. If they are abstracted in themselves, the faculty's grasping of their form in itself is easier. If, by contrast, they are not [in themselves abstracted from matter], they become abstracted by the faculty's abstraction of them so that nothing of the material appurtenances[157] remains in them. We will explain how this [happens] later on.[158]

[4.3.1 The relationship between the theoretical faculty and its forms]
This theoretical faculty has different relations to these forms, because the thing, which is such that it receives something, sometimes is capable of receiving it in potentiality, and sometimes is capable of receiving it in actuality.

[4.3.2 Three senses of *potentiality*]
Potentiality is spoken of in three senses according to priority and posteriority. [(i)] *Potentiality* is spoken of the absolute disposition from which nothing will proceed to actuality, nor likewise will occur that by means of which [something] proceeds [to actuality], like the potentiality of the child for writing. [(ii)] *Potentiality* is spoken of this disposition when there has occurred for the thing only that by which it can arrive at the acquisition of actuality with no intermediary, like the potentiality for writing of the boy who has grown up and has come to know [how to use] the inkpot, the pen and the elements of letters. [(iii)] *Potentiality* is spoken of this disposition when it is completed by the instrument and with the instrument the perfection of the disposition has also come to be, since it can act whenever it wishes with no need for acquisition; rather, it is sufficient only to aim [at it], like the potentiality of the writer who is perfect in the art [of writing] when he is not writing.

The first potentiality is called *absolute* and *material*, the second potentiality is called *possible potentiality*, and the third potentiality is called *perfection of the potentiality*.

---

157 Lit.: connections of matter.

158 Here Avicenna might refer to *Nafs*, II, 2 where the issue of the degrees of abstraction belonging to all the perceptive faculties (intellect included) is dealt with, or to *Nafs*, V, 5 where the manner in which human intellection occurs is dealt with. I think that here any reference to *Nafs*, V, 2, which has been suggested in Reisman-McGinnis's anthology (184, n. 46), can be excluded.

[4.3.3 The four relationships between the human intellect and the intellectual forms]
[4.3.3.1 The material intellect]
The relation of the theoretical faculty to the abstracted forms that we have mentioned is sometimes the relation of what exists in the absolute potentiality. And this [happens] when [**R49**] this faculty belonging to the soul has not yet received anything of the perfection that is in accordance with it,[159] and then it is called *material intellect*. This faculty which is called material intellect, exists in every individual of the [human] species, and it is called material only because of its resemblance to the disposition of primary matter, which in itself has no [particular] form, but is a subject for every form.

[4.3.3.2 The dispositional intellect]
Sometimes [the relation of the theoretical faculty to the abstracted forms] is the relation of what exists in possible potentiality, that is when there have already occurred in material potentiality[160] the primary intelligibles from which and by which it arrives at the secondary intelligibles. By *primary intelligibles* I mean the premises to which assent is granted with no acquisition and without the one assenting to them being aware that he could ever be free from assenting to them at any time, like our belief that the whole is greater than the part, and [our belief] that things which are equal to one thing are equal to one another. So, as long as there is still only a notion at that amount of actuality in it, it is called *dispositional intellect*, and this [potentiality] can be called *intellect in actuality* in relation to the first [potentiality, i.e. the material intellect], because the first potentiality cannot think of anything in actuality, whereas this [potentiality] can think when it begins to investigate in actuality.

[4.3.3.3 The actual intellect]
Sometimes [the relation of the theoretical faculty to the abstracted forms] is the relation of what exists in perfect potentiality, that is when also the intellectual forms that have been acquired after the primary intelligibles occur in it, except that it does not inspect them and does not return to them in actuality; rather, it is as if they are stored in it.[161] Therefore, whenever it wishes, it will inspect those forms

159 It is worth noticing that this passage in the translation provided in Reisman-McGinnis' anthology is rendered as "through its body" (184); nonetheless, the Arabic text has *bi-ḥasabihā* (and not *bi-ǧismihā*) and no variants are attested in the manuscripts.

160 i.e.: in the material intellect.

161 Here *maḫzūna* (*repositae*) points at the fact that these intellectual forms are retrievable. It is noteworthy that these intellectual forms cannot be present in the intellect at this stage in the proper sense, because they are present in it only when the intellect is actually thinking of them. For this reason, this stage of the intellect cannot be conceived as temporally prior to the stage of acquired intellect. Avicenna is presenting here all the stages of the relation of the theoretical intellect to the intellectual forms, starting from the lowest one, i.e. the one in absolute potentiality, and progressing to the highest one, i.e. the one in complete actuality, only for the sake of exposition.

in actuality, and then think of them, and think itself already to have thought of them.[162] It is called *intellect* [**R50**] *in actuality* because it is an intellect that thinks, whenever it wishes, without the effort of acquisition, even though it can be called *intellect in potentiality* in relation to what comes after it.

[4.3.3.4 The acquired intellect]

Sometimes the relation [of the theoretical faculty to the abstracted forms] is the relation of what is in absolute actuality, that is when intellectual forms are present in it and it inspects them in actuality. Then, it thinks of them and thinks itself to be thinking of them in actuality. What occurs to it is, therefore, an *acquired intellect*, and it is called *acquired intellect* only because it will become clear to us[163] that the intellect in potentiality proceeds to actuality only by means of an intellect which exists always in actuality and that, when the intellect in potentiality comes into a sort of contact with that intellect which exists in actuality, a species of the forms acquired from outside is impressed in it.

Thus, these are also the degrees of the faculties that are called theoretical intellects, and at the stage of the acquired intellect the genus *animal* and its species *human* are complete, and there the human faculty will resemble the first principles of all existence.

[5. The hierarchical arrangement of all the psychic faculties]

Consider now and examine the state of these faculties, how some of them rule some [others], and how some of them serve some [others]. For you will find the acquired intellect, which is the ultimate goal, at the head, and all [the rest of the faculties] serving it. Then, the intellect in actuality is served by the dispositional intellect, whereas the material intellect, inasmuch as it contains some disposition, serves the dispositional intellect. Thereafter, the practical intellect serves all of this,[164] because the bodily connection, as will become clear later on,[165] exists for the sake of perfecting the theoretical intellect, purifying it, and cleansing it, and the practical intellect is what governs that connection. Then, estimation serves the practical intellect, whereas estimation is served by two faculties, a faculty after it and a faculty be-

---

162 It is worth noticing that this passage in the translation provided in Reisman-McGinnis' anthology is translated as "intellects that it is intellecting them"; nonetheless, this is the correct translation of what follows (*wa-yaʿqilu annahū yaʿqiluhā bi-l-fiʿl*, 50.4), whereas here Avicenna says *wa-ʿaqala annahū qad ʿaqalahā*, aiming at distinguishing the actual intellect, which does not possess the intellectual forms in itself when it is not actually thinking of them, although whenever it wishes it can retrieve them since it has already thought of them, from the acquired intellect, which thinks the intellectual forms in actuality and is aware of itself thinking of them.

163 See *Nafs*, V, 5, 234.14 – 18, where Avicenna re-states this general rule. See § 1.1 of my translation of *Nafs*, V, 5.

164 i.e.: the theoretical intellect in its entirety.

165 See *Nafs*, V, 1. In the *Avicenna Latinus* it is interpreted as a joint-reference to *Nafs*, V, 1 and V, 6.

fore it. The faculty after it is the faculty that retains what estimation brings to it, that is, the remembering [faculty] [**R51**], whereas the faculty before it is all the animal faculties. So then, the imaginative [faculty] is served by two faculties, different with respect to [their] manner of acting: the appetitive faculty serves it through counsel, because it incites it by a sort of incitement to set [something] in motion, whereas the imagery serves it through its presentation [to it] of the forms stored in it, which are prepared to receive combination and separation. Then, these two [faculties] are at the head of two groups. As for imagery, it is served by the *fantasia*, whereas the *fantasia* is served by the five [external] senses. As for the appetitive faculty, it is served by the concupiscible and the irascible [faculty], whereas the concupiscible and the irascible [faculty] are served by the locomotive faculty, which is in the muscles. Here the animal faculties come to an end.

Then, the animal faculties are served by the vegetative [faculties], the first and head of them being the generative [faculty]. The [faculty] of growth serves the generative [faculty], and the nutritive [faculty] serves them both together. Then, the four natural faculties[166] serve this [nutritive faculty]:[167] among them, the digestive [faculty] is served, on the one hand, by the retentive [faculty], whereas on the other hand, by the attractive [faculty]. The expulsive [faculty], by contrast, serves them all. Then, the four [elementary] qualities serve all of this.[168] However, coldness serves heat: for, it either prepares a matter for heat or preserves what heat has prepared, but coldness does not have any rank in the potentialities included in the natural accidents, except as a benefit of what follows and succeeds. These two [elementary qualities] are served by dryness and moistness together.

Here is the last rank of the [psychic] faculties.

[(**V.2**)][169]

[Chapter] on establishing that the rational soul does not subsist as something impressed in corporeal matter

[1. The receptacle of the intelligibles is neither a body nor a form of or a faculty in a body]

166 i.e.: the digestive, the retentive, the attractive, and the expulsive faculty.

167 I interpret *hāḏihi* as referring to the nutritive faculty, which is immediately served by the four natural faculties acting upon nourishment. On the faculty of nutrition in Avicenna, see T. Alpina, "Is Nutrition a Sufficient Condition for Life?".

168 i.e.: the four natural faculties as a whole.

169 *Nafs*, V, 2, 209.17–216.8 corresponds to *Naǧāt*, 356.10–364.13 (ed. Dānišpažūh, 1985); *Nafs*, V, 2, 216.18–221.12 corresponds to *Naǧāt*, 364.15–371.11.

One thing about which there is no doubt is that in the human being there is a thing, that is,[170] a certain substance that obtains intelligibles by receiving [them]. We say that the substance which is the receptacle of intelligibles [**R210**] is in no way a body, nor subsists in a body, either as a faculty in it or as a form belonging to it.[171]

[2. First demonstration *a parte subiecti. Reductio ad absurdum:* if the receptacle of the intelligibles is a body, this body will be either indivisible or divisible]

For if the receptacle of the intelligibles were a body or a magnitude, the intellectual form would either [(i)] inhere in a single, indivisible thing of it,[172] or [(ii)] inhere in a divisible thing of it. The thing, [being part] of the body, which is indivisible is unquestionably a punctiform extremity.

[2.1 [(i)] First alternative: the receptacle of the intelligibles is an indivisible body]
[2.1.1 [(i.i)] The receptacle of the intelligibles is a point]
[(i.i)] Let us firstly examine whether its[173] receptacle can be an indivisible extremity. We say that this is impossible, because the point is a limit which is not distinct from the line with respect to position, nor from the magnitude that terminates with it, in such a way that the point would be for it something in which a thing is settled without being in something of that magnitude.[174] Rather, just as the point is not isolated in itself, but is only an essential extremity of what is in itself a magnitude, similarly it can only be said in a certain way that in the point inheres the extremity of something inhering in the magnitude of which the point is the extremity. Then, it[175] is determined by that magnitude accidentally; and just as it[176] is determined by it accidentally, similarly it[177] terminates accidentally with the point. Therefore, a limit by accident would be together with a limit by essence, just as an extension by accident would be together with an extension by essence.

[2.1.2 [(i.ii)] The receptacle of the intelligibles is an atom]
If the point were an isolated thing that receives anything, it would have a distinct essence. The point would then have two sides: a side that is adjacent to the line from which it is distinguished, and a side that is different from and opposite to

170 I interpret the *-wa* as epexegetical. For in the following sentence Avicenna directly speaks of *substance* (*ǧawhar*).
171 In *Ilāhiyyāt*, I, 1, 6–7 Avicenna refers the same characterization to God; however, unlike the human soul, God is not a substance.
172 i.e.: of the body.
173 i.e.: of the intellectual form.
174 The point cannot be the thing in which something of the magnitude is settled, i.e. its limit, without being a part of that magnitude.
175 i.e.: the something that inheres in the magnitude of which the point is the extremity.
176 See n. 175.
177 See n. 175.

it.[178] Further, [the point] would subsist [by itself] as separate from the line, and the line that is separate from it[179] would unquestionably have a limit different from it, which encounters it.[180] Therefore, that point would be the limit of the line, not this [one].[181] However, the discourse about it and this point[182] is one [and the same]. **[R211]** This leads to [the conclusion] that points could be paired in the line either finitely or infinitely. The impossibility of this matter has already become clear to us in other places.[183] It has already become clear that no body is composed by means of pairing points.[184] Similarly, it has become clear that points do not have a specific, distinct position.[185]

However, there is no harm in pointing out some of these [arguments]. We then say that two points that are adjacent to one single point from its two sides,[186] [are such that] either [(i)] the middle point[187] interposes between the two [other points], so that they do not touch each other. It would then necessarily follow that the intermediary is divisible according to the fundamental principles that you have learned, but this is impossible.[188] Or [(ii)] the middle [point] would not hinder the contact of the two [points] that surround it on both sides. Hence, the intellectual form would inhere in all the points, all the points being like one single point. But we have already posited this single point as separate from the line. Then the line, in virtue of being separate from the point, would have an extremity different from it,[189] through which it is separated from that point. That point is then different from this [point][190] in terms of position. However, all the points have been already posited as sharing the [same] position. This is therefore a contradiction. It is therefore false that the receptacle of the intelligibles is something indivisible of the body. Hence, it remains that their receptacle is something divisible of the body, if their receptacle is in the body.

178 i.e.: opposite to the line from which the point is distinguished.
179 i.e.: from the point.
180 The line would therefore have a limit different from the limit represented by the point, which is thus self-subsisting and separate from the line. As a consequence, the limit of the line will be adjacent to the point and touch it.
181 i.e.: the point that is the actual limit of the line, not the self-subsisting point, separate from the line, which the limit of the line touches.
182 i.e.: the discourse about the point which is the limit of the line, and the self-subsisting point, which is separate from the line.
183 Lit.: This is a matter whose impossibility has already become clear to us in other places.
184 See Avicenna's criticism of atomism in *Samāʿ ṭabīʿī*, III, 4.
185 Lit: no specific position is distinguished for points. See § 2.1.1 above.
186 The case that Avicenna has in mind can be represented as follows: xyz,
x and *z* being two points adjacent to a third point *y*, one from one side and the other from the other side.
187 *y* in the scheme provided in n. 186 above.
188 Atomists, to whom Avicenna is referring here, claimed that the atom is indivisible. Hence, a contradiction would ensue from their position. See *Samāʿ ṭabīʿī*, III, 3.
189 i.e.: from the point.
190 i.e.: the point that is the limit of the line.

[2.2 [(ii)] Second alternative: the receptacle of the intelligibles is a divisible body]
[2.2.1 The intellectual form would then be divided into similar parts or dissimilar parts]
Let us assume an intellectual form in something divisible. If we assume divisions in the divisible thing, it will happen that the form [itself] will be divisible. Therefore, the two parts [into which the form is divisible] will be either [(ii.i)] similar or [(ii.ii)] dissimilar.

[2.2.1.1 [(ii.i)] The intellectual form is divided into similar parts]
[(ii.i)] If the two [parts] are similar, then how from these two [parts] would there be combined something which is not the two [parts] [**R212**], since the whole, insofar as it is whole, is not the part, unless that whole is something resulting from the two [parts] in virtue of an increase in magnitude or [in virtue of] an increase in number, but not in virtue of the form? In that case, the intellectual form would be a certain shape or a certain number, but no intellectual form is a shape or a number, [otherwise] the form would become imaginative, not intellectual. You know that it cannot be said that each of the two parts is itself the whole. How could it be, whereas the second [part] is both included in the notion of the whole, and external to the notion of the other part? It is clear and manifest that one of the two [parts] alone does not indicate the notion itself of what is complete.

[2.2.1.2 [(ii.ii)] The intellectual form is divided into dissimilar parts. Several absurdities derive from this alternative]
[(ii.ii)] If, by contrast, [the two parts] are dissimilar, let us investigate how this could be, and how the intellectual form could have dissimilar parts. For there cannot be dissimilar parts [in the intellectual form] except the parts of the definition, which are genera and *differentiae*. However, some absurdities necessarily follow from this [alternative].

Among them: [(a)] every part of the body would also receive a potentially infinite division; therefore, genera and *differentiae* must be potentially infinite. This is impossible: it has already turned out to be true that essential genera and *differentiae* for one thing are not potentially infinite.[191]

[(b)] [This is an absurdity] also because it is not possible that imagining[192] the division would [actually] set apart the genus and the *differentia*. Rather, there is no doubt that, when here a genus and a *differentia* must be distinct in the receptacle, this distinction does not rest on imagining the division. Therefore, genera and *differentiae* must be also infinite in actuality. [**R213**] But it has already turned out to be

191 Avicenna seems to claim that the essential *genus* and *differentia* are not potentially infinite in *Burhān*, III, 6 ([*Chapter*] *on the account of what has been said in the First Teaching with respect to the fact that the parts of the syllogisms are finite* [*in number*] *and on the intermediate* [*elements*] *of affirmation and negation*).
192 Lit.: having an estimation (*tawahhum*).

true that the genera, the *differentiae*, and the parts of the definition are, for one thing, finite in every respect.[193] If genera and *differentiae* had been infinite in actuality, then they could not have been combined in the body in a certain way according to this form. For this would require that one single body be separated into infinite parts in actuality. [But this is impossible].

[(c)] Moreover, let the division be among the things that have already occurred in some way, then [it] sets apart a genus on one side, and a *differentia* on [another] side. If we were to change the division, then it would either be [(ca)] [the case] that from it[194] half a genus and half a *differentia* will occur on every side; or [(cb)] the transfer of the genus and of the *differentia* to one of the two parts [respectively] will be necessary, and thus the genus and the *differentia* will incline each one to a part of the division. This being the case, our estimative assumption or our assumed division would invert the place of the genus and the *differentia* and each of them would join a certain side at the will of any external individual.[195] Even that would not be enough: for we could introduce a division within a division [*ad infinitum*].

[(d)] Moreover, not every intelligible can be divided into intelligibles simpler than it: for here there are intelligibles which are the simplest intelligibles, which are the principles for the combination of the rest of the intelligibles. These do not have genera nor *differentiae* and are divisible neither in quantity, nor in notion.

Hence, the assumed parts cannot be similar, each of them being in the notion of the whole (the whole only results from [their] combination); and, similarly, [they] cannot be dissimilar. Therefore, the intellectual form cannot be divisible.

[**R214**] If the intellectual form cannot be divided, nor can it inhere in an indivisible extremity of magnitudes, but [it] must have a recipient in us, then we must judge that the receptacle of the intelligibles is a substance that is not body, and also that what is within us which obtains them is not a faculty in a body. For then what attaches to the body in terms of divisions would attach to it, and the rest of the absurdities would follow. Rather, what is within us which obtains the intellectual form must be an incorporeal substance.

[3. Second demonstration *a parte obiecti*]

We will demonstrate this[196] by means of another demonstration.

We say: the intellectual faculty is that which abstracts the intelligibles from defined quantity, place, position, and the rest of what has been said earlier.[197] Concerning this form itself that is abstracted from position, we must investigate how it is abstracted from it, whether in relation to the thing from which it is grasped, or in

193 See n. 191 above.
194 i.e.: from the division.
195 Lit.: in accordance with the will of one who exercises his will on it from outside.
196 i.e.: that the human rational soul is an incorporeal substance.
197 See *Nafs*, II, 2, 61.5–17 [120.26–41].

relation to the thing that grasps [it]. That is, does the existence of this intellectual essence abstracted from position exist in the external[198] existence or does it exist in the existence conceptualized in the intellecting substance? It is impossible for us to say that it is so in external existence. Therefore, it remains for us to say that it is separated with respect to position and place only when it exists in the intellect.[199] When [the intellectual essence] exists in the intellect, it does not have any position, nor exists in such a manner that a particularizing sign, or a division, or anything that is similar to this notion, occurs to it. Consequently, [the intellectual essence] cannot be in a body.

Moreover, if the singular indivisible form which belongs to indivisible things in notion is impressed in a divisible matter, which has dimensions,[200] then either [(a)] [**R215**] none of its parts which are assumed in matter in accordance with its dimensions has a relation to the intelligible thing, single in itself, indivisible, and abstracted from matter; or [(b)] each part that is assumed [in matter] has [that relation]; or [(c)] some [of the parts assumed in matter] have it, while some [others] do not.

[(a)] If none of its parts [has that relation], then the whole does not have [the relation] either; for what is combined of different things is itself different.

[(c)] If some parts have it, while some [others] do not, then those parts having no relation [to the intelligible thing] are not part of its notion at all.

[(b)] If every part that is assumed [in matter] has a relation [to the intelligible thing], then either [(ba)] each part that is assumed in it has a relation to the essence as it is,[201] or [(bb)] to a part of the essence.

[(ba)] If every part that is assumed has a relation to the essence as it is, then the parts [of the divisible matter] are not parts of the notion of the intelligible; rather, each of them is intelligible in itself separately. However, if every part has a relation [to the essence] different from the relation of the other part to the essence, then it is known that the essence is divisible in the intelligible, but we already posited it as indivisible. This is a contradiction.

[(bb)] If the relation of each [part assumed in matter] is to something of the essence, different from that to which the relation of the other [part] is, then the division of the essence is even more evident. It becomes clear from this that the forms impressed in the bodily matter are nothing but apparitions of the particular, divisible things, and every part of them has a relation to a part of it either in actuality or in potentiality.

Moreover, the thing having multiple parts in its definition, with respect to the completeness, is an indivisible unity. Let us investigate how that single existence, in-

198 i.e.: extramental.

199 Here Avicenna is saying that the intellectual form is universal only in mental existence, because in extramental existence it is particularized by material accidents, like position, place, and the like, which befall it as a consequence of its inhering in matter. On this issue, see *Ilāhiyyāt*, V, 1–2.

200 Here Avicenna is referring to a physical, three-dimensional body.

201 i.e.: in its entirety, undivided.

sofar as it is some single thing, [**R216**] is impressed in something divisible. However, the discourse on it and on what is not divisible in the definition is one.

[4. The theoretical faculty does not act by means of a bodily organ]

[4.1 If the theoretical faculty makes use of a bodily organ, it will not think of itself, nor of its organ, nor of its thinking activity]

Similarly, it has already turned out to be true for us that the assumed intelligibles, which the rational faculty is capable of thinking one by one in actuality, are infinite in potentiality. And it has already turned out to be true for us that the thing that is able to manage infinite things in potentiality cannot be a body or a faculty in a body. This has already been demonstrated in the previous sections.[202] Therefore, the essence conceptualizing the intelligibles cannot subsist in a body at all, nor [can] its activity be in a body or by means of a body. No one could say: "Imaginative things are like that". This is a mistake. For the animal faculty cannot imagine any infinite thing at any time, unless the direction of the rational faculty is associated with it. No one could say, either: "This faculty, namely the intellective [faculty], is receptive, not active. You have only established the finitude of the active faculty, but people do not doubt that an infinite receptive faculty like the one belonging to prime matter can exist". We then reply: "You will learn that the rational soul's reception of many infinite things is a reception [occurring] after an active mode of acting".[203]

Let us cite as evidence of what we have shown the discourse investigating the substance of the rational soul and its most specific activity[204] by [providing] indications [taken] from the states of the other activities belonging to it, which relate to what we mentioned. We say: if the intellectual faculty were to think by means of a bodily organ, so that its specific activity is completed only by the use of this bodily organ, [**R217**] it would necessarily follow that it does not think itself, that it does not think the organ, and that it does not think to have thought. For it has no organ between it and itself, nor has it an organ between it and its organ, nor has it an organ between it and its having thought, but it thinks itself, the organ that is claimed for it,[205] and that it has thought. Therefore, it thinks by itself, not by means of an organ. However, we will ascertain [this].

[4.2 Three possible alternatives]

We say: the intellectual faculty's intellection of its organ is either [(a)] due to the existence of that form itself of its organ; or [(b)] due to the existence of another form,

202 That in the body, which is finite, there cannot be an infinite power, has been demonstrated in *Samāʿ ṭabīʿī*, III, 10.

203 See *Nafs*, V, 5.

204 That intellection, i.e. the conceptualization of universal, intellectual forms, is the most specific activity of the rational soul is stated in *Nafs*, V, 1, 206.11–12.

205 i.e.: the brain.

numerically different from the one belonging to the organ, which is both in it and in its organ; or [(c)] due to the existence of another form, different in species from that form of its organ, which is both in it and in its organ.

[4.2.1 Refutation of the first alternative: the intellective faculty thinks of its organ because the form of its organ exists in itself]
If [(a)] [the intellectual faculty's intellection of its organ] is due to the existence of the form of its organ, then the form of its organ is always in its organ and in it through partnership. Hence, [the intellectual faculty] must always think of its organ, since it thinks of it only due to the form's arrival to it.

[4.2.2 Refutation of the second alternative: the intellective faculty thinks of its organ because of the existence of a form numerically different from that of its organ, which is in itself and in its organ]
If [(b)] [the intellectual faculty's intellection of its organ] is due to the existence of a form belonging to its organ, numerically different from that form,[206] that is false. Firstly, [this is so] because the difference among things that are included in one single definition is either [(i)] due to the difference of matters, states, and accidents; or [(ii)] due to a difference between the universal and the particular, that is, [between] what is abstracted from matter and what exists in matter. But here there is no difference of matters and accidents: for, the matter is one, and the accidents existing [in matter] are one. Nor is there any difference of abstraction and existence in matter: for both are in matter. Nor is there any difference of specificity and generality, because if one of them acquires particularity, it acquires particularity only due to the particular matter and the attributes that attach to it[207] in virtue of the matter in which it exists. This notion is not peculiar to one of the two to the exclusion of the other, and this does not necessarily follow from the soul's perception of itself. For it always perceives itself, even though it perceives it in most cases associated with the bodies that are with it, as we have shown.[208]

[4.2.3 Refutation of the third alternative: the intellective faculty thinks of its organ because of the existence of a form different in species from that of its organ, which is in itself and in its organ]
And you [**R218**] know that [(c)] [the intellectual faculty's intellection of its organ] cannot be due to the existence of another form, different [in species] from the form of its organ. For, this is even more absurd because, when the intellectual form inheres in an intellecting substance, the intellectual form makes the substance intellect that of which that form is the form, or that to which that form is related. Then the form of

206 i.e.: from the form of the organ itself.
207 i.e.: with one of the two forms.
208 It could be a reference to the thought-experiment of the *Flying Man*. See *Nafs*, I, 1 (for another formulation of this experiment, see *Nafs*, V, 7).

what is related [to this form] would be included in this form. But this intellectual form is not the form of this organ, nor similarly is the form of something related to it by itself, because the essence of this organ is a substance, whereas we grasp and consider only the form of its essence, and the substance in itself is not related [to it] at all.

[4.2.4 Conclusion of this demonstration]

This demonstration makes clear that what perceives by means of an organ cannot perceive its organ while it is perceiving. For this reason, the sense senses only something external, but it does not sense itself, nor its organ, nor its sensing. Likewise, imagery does not imagine itself or its activity at all. Rather, if it imagines its organ, it imagines it not in the manner proper to it, nor [does it imagine] that this organ unquestionably belongs to it and to no other, unless the sense brings to it[209] the form of its organ, if this were possible. Then it would only imitate an image taken from the sense, not related for it to anything, so that, if it were not its organ, it would not imagine it.

[4.3 First corollary: the intellectual faculty does not make use of a bodily organ because, unlike all the other perceptive faculties, the perception of intense intelligibles does not fatigue it]

Likewise, one of the things that confirm this for us, and that persuade about it, is that the faculties that perceive by means of organs happen to be fatigued by prolonged action, because prolonged motion fatigues the organs and corrupts their temperament, which is their substance and their nature. Intense things, difficult to perceive, weaken the organs and might corrupt them, and the organs cannot perceive what comes after them,[210] which is weaker than them, because the organs are plunged into the affection [caused] by what is difficult [to perceive], like in the case of the sense. For sensible things, which are difficult [to perceive] and reiterated, weaken the sense and might corrupt it, like the [intense] light for sight, [**R219**] and the violent thunder for hearing, and after the perception of what is intense, the sense is not able to perceive what is weak. For the one who sees a strong light does not see with it, nor after it a weak light, and the one who hears a strong sound does not hear with it and after it a weak sound, and the one who tastes an intense sweetness does not sense after it a weak [sweetness].

The case of the intellectual faculty is the reverse. For its prolonged [activity of] intellection and its conceptualization of things that are more intense make it acquire the capacity and the ease with which to receive what comes after them among the things that are weaker than them. For if in some moments weariness or fatigue happen to it, that is because the intellect uses imagery, which makes use of the organ

209 i.e.: to imagery.

210 i.e.: intense things, difficult to perceive.

that becomes fatigued. Then [this organ] does not serve the intellect. If [weariness] occurred for a different reason, it would happen always or for the most part, but the matter is contrary [to this].

[4.4 Second corollary: the intellectual faculty does not make use of a bodily organ because, unlike all the other perceptive faculties, the strengthening of the intellectual faculty is directly proportional to the aging of the body]
Likewise, all the parts of the body begin to weaken in terms of their powers after the end of the development and [its] stopping. This [happens] before forty or at forty [years of age]. On the contrary, this faculty that perceives the intelligibles becomes stronger, for the most part, only after that [age]. If this faculty were among the bodily faculties, it would be always necessary for it to weaken in every state at this point. But this is not necessary, except in [some] states, and when some impediments appear, but not in all states. Therefore, it is not among the bodily faculties.

[4.5 General conclusion of § 4]
From these things it has become clear that [(i)] every faculty that perceives by means of an organ, does not perceive itself, nor its organ, nor its [act of] perceiving; that [(ii)] the multiplication of activity weakens it; and that [(iii)] it does not perceive what is weak right after [perceiving] what is intense, what is intense weakens it, and its activity is weakened by the weakening of the organs of its activity. The intellectual faculty is contrary to all of this.

As for the fact that, when the soul forgets its intelligibles and does not perform its activity when the body is ill[211] and in old age, this is believed to happen because its activity is not complete except by the body, [this is] an assumption neither necessary nor true. For [**R220**] it might be possible that the two things[212] are combined together; thus, the soul has an activity by itself, when nothing[213] impedes [it], and nothing[214] averts the soul from it, and nonetheless, the soul might forsake its proper activity together with a state that occurs to the body; thus, it does not perform its activity and averts itself from it. However, the two statements remain [valid] without contradiction; and, if this is the case, no attention should be paid to this objection.

[5. The two faculties of the rational soul: the guidance of the body and the intellection of the intellectual forms]

However, we say that the substance of the soul has two activities: [(a)] an activity belonging to it in relation to the body, which is the guidance [of the body], and [(b)] an

211 Lit.: together with the illness of the body.
212 i.e.: the soul's forgetfulness of the intelligibles and the illness of the body.
213 Lit.: no impediment.
214 Lit.: nothing averting.

activity belonging to it in relation to itself and its principles, which is perception by means of the intellect.

[5.1 These two faculties oppose each other]
These two [activities] oppose and obstruct each other. For, when [the substance of the soul] engages in one of them, it relinquishes the other, and it is difficult for it to combine the two things. Its occupations with respect to the body are sensing, imaging, desires, anger, fear, sadness, and pain; and you know this because, when you begin to think about an intelligible, everyone of these [occupations] is suspended for you unless they subdue the soul and subjugate it by bringing it back to their side. You know that sensation prevents the soul from intellection: for, when the soul dedicates itself to the sensible thing, it is distracted from the intelligible with no damage having befallen the organ of the intellect or the intellect itself in any way. And you know that the cause for this is the soul's occupation with an activity, but not with [another] activity. Similarly, [this is] the state and the cause when it happens that the activities of the intellect are suspended during illness. For if the acquired intellectual disposition were to have ceased and corrupted due to the organ, then the organ's returning to its [healthy] state would need an acquisition anew. But this is not the case. For the soul returns to its disposition and configuration, intellecting all that it had thought in its state, once the body has returned to its well-being. Therefore, what the soul had acquired already existed with it in some way, except that it has been distracted [**R221**] from it.

[5.2 Each of these two faculties can be obstructed by its own activities]
It is not only the difference of the two sides of the activity of the soul that entails mutual obstruction in its activities. Rather, the multiplicity of the activities of one single side [of the soul] may entail this very thing. For fear makes [the soul] disregard pain, desire obstructs anger, and anger averts from fear, and the cause for all this is one, namely the soul's devoting itself totally to one single thing.

It is clear from this that it does not necessarily follow that, if something does not perform its activity when it is occupied with something [else], it will perform its activity only when that thing with which it is occupied exists.

[6. Conclusion of the discourse]

We could talk at great length about the clarification of this topic, except that devoting all efforts to what is sought after once it has been sufficiently attained[215] might be accused of needless effort. It has already become evident from the fundamental principles that we have established that the [human] soul is not impressed in the body, nor subsists through it. Therefore, the fact that the soul is peculiar to the body must

215 Lit.: after the attainment of what is sufficient [to the purpose].

be by a way that requires a particular configuration in the soul, which pulls [it] to occupy itself with guiding the particular body, due to an essential providence peculiar to it.[216] According to this [configuration] the soul becomes as it is together with the existence of its body, which is characterized by its [own] configuration and temperament.

[(**V.5**)]

[Chapter] on the Intellect Active upon our souls and the intellect that is affected through our souls

[1. In search of a cause that brings the human soul's capacity for intellection from potentiality to actuality]

[1.1 The cause for human soul's proceeding from potentiality to actuality is an intellect that is always in actuality]
We say that the human soul is sometimes intellecting in potentiality, then it comes to intellect in actuality. And whatever has proceeded from potentiality to actuality proceeds [from potentiality to actuality] only by a cause in actuality that brings it [into actuality]. Thus, there is here a cause that brings our souls from potentiality to actuality with respect to intelligibles; and since it is the cause for giving the intellectual forms, it can only be an intellect in actuality in which are the principles of intellectual forms in an abstracted way[217] [from matter].[218]

[1.2 The analogy of light]
[1.2.1 The relation of the Active Intellect to human soul is similar to the relation of the Sun to sight]
Its relation to our souls is [like] the relation of the Sun to our sights. For, just as the Sun is visible [**R235**] by itself in actuality and through its luminosity[219] makes visible in actuality what is not visible in actuality; likewise is the state of this intellect with respect to our souls.

[1.2.2 Human intellection is a process consisting of two movements: [(i)] human intellect's inspection of the imaginative particulars; [(ii)] the Active Intellect's shining light on those particulars. Intellectual forms are neither the imaginative particulars

216 i.e.: to the body.
217 The Latin translation seems to read (or, at least, to intend): *ʿindahū mabādiʾ al-ṣuwar al-ʿaqliyya al-muǧarrada* (*penes quam sunt principia formarum intelligibilium abstractarum*). On the contrary, the Arabic text is: *ʿindahū mabādiʾ al-ṣuwar al-ʿaqliyya muǧarradatan*. See Avicenna Latinus, *Liber de anima*, 127, n. 35.
218 For a parallel passage, see *Nafs*, I, 5, 50.4–9.
219 i.e.: by lending its luminosity to things potentially visible.

themselves nor their reduplication in the intellect; rather, they are the imaginative particulars' abstracted counterparts]
For, [(i)] when the intellectual faculty looks at the particulars that are in the imagery and [(ii)] the luminosity of the Intellect Active upon us, which we have mentioned, shines on them, [these particulars] turn into things abstracted from matter and its appurtenances and are impressed in the rational soul, not in the sense that the particulars themselves move from the imaginative faculty to our intellect, nor in the sense that the notion submerged in the [material] appurtenances – [the notion] that in itself and considered from the point of view of its essence is abstracted [from matter] – produces something similar to itself; rather, in the sense that their inspection prepares the soul so that what is abstracted flows onto it from the Active Intellect. For thoughts and reflections are motions that prepare the soul for the reception of the effluence, just as middle terms prepare in the most reliable way the reception of the conclusion, although in the first case in one way, while in the second in another way, as you will come to understand. For, when to the rational soul there occurs a certain relation to this form through the mediation of the illumination of the Active Intellect, from it there comes to be in the rational soul something that on the one hand is of its genus, while on the other hand it is not of its genus: just as light, when it falls on colored things, produces from them in the sight an impression that cannot be in every respect [corresponding] to all of them; [likewise] the imaginative things, which are intelligible in potentiality, become intelligible in actuality, not themselves, but what is collected from them. Rather, just as the impression resulting from the sensible forms by means of the light is not those forms themselves, but another thing corresponding to them, which is engendered through the mediation of the light in the opposite recipient[220]; likewise, when the rational soul inspects those imaginative forms and the luminosity of the Active Intellect comes into a mode of contact with them, [the rational soul] is prepared [**R236**] so that in it from the light of the Active Intellect come to be [the counterparts] of those forms, abstracted from [their] imperfections.[221]

[2. Unifying and multiplying: the activities peculiar to the human intellect]

The first thing that is distinguished in the human intellect is the essential and the accidental condition of these [abstracted counterparts of the forms], as well as that in virtue of which those imaginative things are similar and that in virtue of which they are different; therefore the notions in virtue of which those [things] are not different, become one single notion in the intellect itself in relation to [their] similarity, whereas in relation to that in virtue of which they are different, [those notions]

220 Cf. *Nafs*, III, 7, 141.11–142.9.
221 The passage corresponding to "[the counterparts]...imperfections" in the Latin translation is: *ipsae formae nudae ab omni permixtione*. See Avicenna Latinus, *Liber de anima*, 128.63.

become in it many notions. Thus, the intellect has the capacity for multiplying one single notion and for unifying many [notions]. As for the unification of the many, [that happens] in two ways: one of them is that when many notions, which are numerically different in imaginative things, are not different in definition, they become one single notion; the second way is to combine from the notions of *genera* and *differentiae* one single notion in definition. The way of multiplying [a single notion] is the reverse of these two ways. This [capacity for multiplying and unifying notions] is among the properties of the human intellect, and it does not belong to any other faculty [of the soul]. For they perceive the many as many as it is and the one as one as it is, and they cannot perceive the simple one; rather, [they perceive] the one insofar as it is a whole composed of things and their accidents; nor they can separate the accidental [aspects] and extract them from the essential [aspects].

Thus, when the sense presents a certain form to the imagery and the imagery [presents it] to the intellect, the intellect grasps from it a notion. However, if it[222] presents another form of that species to it,[223] which is another only numerically, the intellect by no means grasps from it a form different from what it has [previously] grasped, except in virtue of the accident which, insofar as it is that accident, is proper to this [form], because [the intellect] grasps it once as abstracted [from that accident], and once along with that accident. And for this [reason] it is said [**R237**] that Zayd and ʿAmr have one single notion with respect to humanity, not in the sense that the humanity associated with the properties of ʿAmr is in itself the humanity that is associated with the properties of Zayd, as though one single essence belongs to Zayd and ʿAmr, as happens in the case of friendship, or ownership, and so forth. Rather, humanity is multiple with respect to [external] existence, and there is no existence belonging to one single humanity that is shared in the external existence so that it is in itself the humanity of Zayd and ʿAmr: we shall make this clear in the sapiential discipline.[224]

The meaning of this is that when the preceding of these [forms][225] bestows the form of humanity upon the soul, the second [of these forms][226] does not bestow anything at all [upon the soul]; rather, the notion impressed from these two [forms] in the soul is one, namely that [deriving] from the first image, whereas the second image does not cause any impression. For either of these two [forms] can precede [the other] and thus produce this same impression in the soul; and this is not [what happens] in the case of two individuals, these being a man and a horse.[227]

---

222 i.e.: the imagery.

223 i.e.: to the intellect.

224 The reference is to *Ilāhiyyāt*, V, 1–2, where Avicenna deals with his doctrine of universals.

225 e.g.: that of Zayd.

226 e.g.: that of ʿAmr.

227 As for the meaning of this last sentence, I suggest correcting the Arabic text provided in Rahman's edition by expunging the comma before *hāḏā* (*this*) and considering *hāḏā* the subject of *laysa*. This correction seems to provide a better sense.

[3. Time in human intellection]

The intellect is such that when it perceives things in which there are priority and posteriority, it necessarily conceives time along with them; this, however, does not [happen] in time, but in an instant. And the intellect conceives time in an instant. As for its composition of syllogism and definition, it unquestionably happens in time, except that its conceptualization of the conclusion and the thing defined occurs all at once.

[4. Human intellect's conceptualization of things at the highest and the lowest degree of existence]

[4.1 The human intellect's immersion in the body prevents its achievement of the most excellent of its perfections in this life]
The inability[228] of the intellect to conceptualize things that are at the highest degree of intelligibility and abstraction from matter is neither due to something [that is] in those things themselves, nor to something [that is] in the natural disposition of the intellect; rather, [the inability of the intellect] is due to the fact that the soul is occupied in the body with the body and, then, it needs the body in many things; therefore, the body removes the soul from the most excellent of its perfections. And the eye is not able to look at the Sun not because of something [that is] in [**R238**] the Sun, nor [because] it is not clear; rather, [it is not able to look at the Sun] because of something [that is] in the constitution of its body.[229] Thus, when this immersion [in the body] and this impediment [caused by the body] cease in our soul, the soul's intellection of these [things] is the most excellent of the soul's intellections, its clearest and its most pleasant.

However, since our discourse here concerns only the state of the soul insofar as it is soul, namely insofar as it is associated with this matter, we ought not to deal with the matter of the return of the soul [to the celestial realm] while we are dealing with nature until we move to the sapiential discipline and there investigate the separate entities.[230] As for the investigation in the natural discipline, it is peculiarly concerned

---

228 On the topic of the *inability* (*ʿağz*) of the intellect to conceptualize things at the highest degree of intelligibility and abstraction from matter, see *Ilāhiyyāt*, I, 3, 21.6 – 8. For the Aristotelian background of this topic with the famous simile of the eyes of bats in the daylight, see *Metaph.* II, 1, 993 b9 – 11. The first author to introduce this topic (together with the Aristotelian simile) in the psychological context was Philoponus.

229 The sentence "because...its body" is missing in the Latin translation. See Avicenna Latinus, *Liber de anima*, 132.14.

230 The reference is to *Ilāhiyyāt*, IX, 7, where Avicenna deals with the soul's afterlife and its return (*maʿād*) to the celestial realm.

with what is appropriate to natural things, namely the things having a relation to matter and motion.[231]

[4.2 The human intellect's conceptualization differs in accordance with the degree of existence of things]
Rather, we say that the conceptualization of the intellect differs in accordance with the existence of things: [as for] the things [whose existence is] extremely strong, the intellect falls short of perceiving them because of their predominance, whereas the conceptualization of things whose existence is extremely weak, like motion, time, and prime matter, is difficult because they have a weak existence. [As for] privations, the intellect, being absolutely in actuality, does not conceptualize them, for privation is perceived insofar as [the possession of a] disposition is not perceived. Therefore, what is perceived of privation insofar as it is privation and of evil insofar as it is evil is something in potentiality and the privation of a perfection. Then, if an intellect perceives it, it perceives it only because it stands in relation to it in potentiality. Hence, the intellects with which there is not mixed what is in potentiality do not conceive privation and evil insofar as they are privation and evil and do not conceptualize them, there being in existence nothing that is absolutely evil.[232]

231 For a parallel passage, see *Nafs*, I, 1, 11.1–3.
232 For Avicenna's discussion of evil, see *Ilāhiyyāt*, IX, 6.

Bibliography

Bibliographical Catalogues and Lexica

G. C. Anawati, *Essai de bibliographie avicennienne*, Dār Al-Maʿārif, Cairo 1950

H. Bonitz, *Index Aristotelicus*, Akademische Druck- u. Verlagsanstalt, Graz 1955 (repr. or. ed. Berlin 1870)

C. Brockelmann, *Geschichte der Arabischen Litteratur*, vols. I-II, Brill, Leiden, 1943–1949[2]; suppl. vols. I-III, Brill, Leiden 1937–1942

O. Ergin, "Ibni Sina Bibliografyasi", in *Büyük Türk Filozof ve Tıb Üstadı Ibn Sina*. Şahsiyeti ve Eserleri Hakkında Tetkikler, İstanbul 1937, 3–80

A.-M. Goichon, *Lexique de la langue philosophique d'Ibn Sīnā*, Desclée de Brouwer, Paris 1938

J. L. Janssens, *An Annotated Bibliography on Ibn Sīnā (1970–1989)*, Leuven University Press, Leuven 1991

id., *An Annotated Bibliography on Ibn Sīnā: First Supplement (1990–1994)*, Fédération Internationale des Institute d'études médiévales, Louvain-la-Neuve 1999

E. W. Lane, *Arabic-English Lexicon*, 2 vols., Islamic Texts Society, Cambridge 1984 (repr. or. ed. Williams and Norgate, London-Edinburgh 1863–1893)

H. G. Liddell-R. Scott, *A Greek-English lexicon*. Rev. and augm. throughout by Sir H. S. Jones, with the assistance of R. McKenzie, and with the cooperation of many scholars, Clarendon press, Oxford 1996

Y. Mahdavī, *Fihrist-i nusḫahā-yi muṣannafāt-i Ibn-i Sīnā*, Intišārāt-i Dānišgāh-yi Tihrān, Tehran 1333H/1954

Primary sources

Alexander of Aphrodisias, *Praeter commentaria scripta minora. De anima liber cum mantissa, Quaestiones, De Fato, De Mixtione*, ed. I. Bruns, Reimer, Berlin 1887–1892

Alexander of Aphrodisias, *In Aristotelis Metaphysica commentaria*, ed. M. Hayduck, *Commentaria in Aristotelem Graeca*, vol. 1, Reimer, Berlin 1891

Alexander of Aphrodisias, *In Aristotelis Meteorologicorum libros commentaria*, ed. M. Hayduck, *Commentaria in Aristotelem Graeca*, vol. 3.2, Reimer, Berlin 1899

Alexander of Aphrodisias, *In librum De sensu commentarium*, ed. P. Wendland, *Commentaria in Aristotelem Graeca*, vol. 3.1, G. Reimer, Berlin 1901

Alexander of Aphrodisias, *Commentaire sur les Météores d'Aristote. Traduction de Guillaume de Moerbeke*, edition critique par A. J. Smet, Publications universitaires, Louvain 1968

Alexander of Aphrodisias, *Commentaire perdu à la* Physique *d'Aristote (livres IV-VIII). Les scholies byzantines: édition, traduction et commentaire par* M. Rashed, Commentaria in Aristotelem Graeca et Byzantina 1, De Gruyter, Berlin 2011

Ammonius, *In Aristotelis Categorias commentarius*, ed. A. Busse, *Commentaria in Aristotelem Graeca*, vol. 4.4, Reimer, Berlin 1895

Aristotle, *Metaphysics. A Revised Text with Introduction and Commentary*, ed. W. D. Ross, Clarendon Press, Oxford 1924

Aristotle, *Physics. A Revised Text with Introduction and Commentary*, ed. W. D. Ross, Oxford University Press, Oxford 1936

Aristotle, *Parts of Animals*, with an English translation by A. L. Peck, foreword by F. H. A. Marshall, *Movement of animals, Progression of animals*, with an English translation by E. S.

https://doi.org/10.1515/9783110706840-011

Forster, The Loeb classical library, Harvard University Press, London – Cambridge (Mass.) 1945

Aristotle, *Categoriae et Liber de interpretatione* recognivit brevique adnotatione critica instruxit L. Minio-Paluello, Oxford Classical Texts, Oxford 1949

Aristotle, *Prior and Posterior Analytics. A Revised Text with Introduction and Commentary.* ed. W. D. Ross, Clarendon Press, Oxford 1949, 1965[2]

Aristotle, *De Anima, with Introduction and Commentary*, ed. W. D. Ross, Clarendon Press, Oxford 1961

Aristotle, *The Arabic version of Aristotle's* Parts of Animals. *Book XI-XIV of the* Kitāb al-Ḥayawān. *A critical edition with introduction and selected glossary*, ed. R. Kruk, Verhandelingen der Koninklijke Nederlandse Akademie van Wetenschappen. Afd. Letterkunde. Nieuwe Reeks 97, North Holland Publ. Co., Amsterdam-Oxford 1979

Aristotle, *Fī l-Nafs* [...]. *Rāǧa'ahā 'alà uṣūlihā al-yūnāniyya wa-šaraḥahā wa-ḥaqqaqahā wa-qaddama lahā* 'A. Badawī, coll. " Dirāsāt Islāmiyya " 16, Cairo 1954, reprinted Bayrūt 1980

Aristotle, *Météorologiques. Texte etabli et traduit par* P. Louis, 2 vols., Les Belles Lettres, Paris 1982

Aristotle, *De anima with translation, introduction and notes*, ed. R. D. Hicks, Ayer Company, Salem 1988 (repr. or. ed. University Press, Cambridge 1907)

Aristotle, *Topiques. Texte établi et traduit par* J. Brunschwig, 2 vols., Les Belles Lettres, Paris 2007[2]

Aristotle, *De Anima. A Critical Commentary*, ed. R. Polansky, Cambridge University Press, Cambridge 2010

Asclepius, *In Aristotelis Metaphysicorum libros A-Z commentaria*, ed. M. Hayduck, *Commentaria in Aristotelem Graeca*, vol. 6.2, Reimer, Berlin 1888

Avicenna (Ibn Sīnā), *Maqāla fī l-nafs 'alà sunnat al-iḫtiṣār* (*Compendium on the Soul*), in S. Landauer, "Die Psychologie des Ibn Sīnā", *Zeitschrift der Deutschen Morgenländischen Gesellschaft*, 29, 1875, 339–372

Avicenna, *Le livre des théorèmes et des avertissements*, ed. J. Forget, W. J. Brill, Leiden 1892

Avicenna, *Manṭiq al-mašriqiyyīn*, ed. M. al-Ḫaṭīb, 'A. al-Qatlā, al-Maktaba al-Salafiyya, Cairo 1328H/1910

Avicenna, *Naṣṣ Kitāb al-Mubāḥaṯāt*, in 'A. Badawī ed., *Arisṭū 'inda l-'Arab*, Maktabat al-nahḍa al-miṣriyya, Cairo 1947, 1978[2], 122–239

Avicenna, *Risāla ilà Abī Ǧa'far Ibn al-Marzabān al-Kiyā*, in 'A. Badawī ed., *Arisṭū 'inda l-'Arab*, Maktabat al-nahḍa al-miṣriyya, Cairo 1947, 1978[2], 119–122

Avicenna, *Šarḥ Kitāb Uṯūlūǧiyā al-mansūb ilà Arisṭū*, in 'A. Badawī ed., *Arisṭū 'inda l-'Arab*, Maktabat al-nahḍa al-miṣriyya, Cairo 1947, 1978[2], 35–74

Avicenna, *al-Ta'līqāt 'alà ḥawāšī kitāb al-nafs li-Arisṭāṭālīs*, in 'A. Badawī ed., *Arisṭū 'inda l-'Arab*, Maktabat al-nahḍa al-miṣriyya, Cairo 1947, 1978[2], 75–116

Avicenna, *Manṭiq-Ṭabī'iyyāt. Dānešnāme-ye 'Alā'ī*, ed. M. Meškāt, Anǧoman-e Āṯār-e Mellī, Tehran 1331H/1951

Avicenna, *Ilāhiyyāt. Dānešnāme-ye 'Alā'ī*, ed. M. Mu'īn, Anǧoman-e Āṯār-e Mellī, Tehran 1331H/1951

Avicenna, *Riyāḍiyyāt. Dānešnāme-ye 'Alā'ī*, ed. M. Mīnovī, Anǧoman-e Āṯār-e Mellī, Tehran 1331H/1951

Avicenna, *Al-Šifā', al-Manṭiq, al-Madḫal*, eds. G. Š. Qanawatī, M. al-Ḫuḍayrī, A. F. al-Ahwānī, Al-Maṭba'a al-amīriyya, Cairo 1952 (repr. Ibn Sīnā, *Kitāb al-Shifā'*, ed. I. Madkour, Thawi al-Qorba, Tehran 2010)

Avicenna, *al-Ma'ād* [*al-aṣġar*] (*Ḥāl al-nafs al-insāniyya*), in A. F. al-Ahwānī ed., *Aḥwāl al-nafs*, Dār iḥyā' al-kutub al-'arabiyya, Cairo 1371H/1952, 43–142

Avicenna, *R. fī l-kalām ʿalà l-nafs al-nāṭiqa*, in A. F. al-Ahwānī ed., *Aḥwāl al-nafs*, Dār iḥyāʾ al-kutub al-ʿarabiyya, Cairo 1371H/1952, 195–199

Avicenna, *ʿUyūn al-Ḥikma*, ed. ʿA. Badawī, Cairo, Publications de l'Institut Français d'Archeologie Orientale, 1954; Dār al-Qalam, Beirut, Wakālat al-Maṭbūʿāt, Kuwait, 1980[2]

Avicenna, *Al-Šifāʾ, al-Manṭiq, al-Burhān*, ed. A. ʿAfīfī, Al-Maṭbaʿa al-amīriyya, Cairo 1956

Avicenna, *Al-Šifāʾ, al-Riyāḍiyyāt, Ǧawāmiʿ ʿilm al-mūsīqà*, ed. Z. Yūsuf, al-Hayʾa al-miṣriyya al-ʿāmma li-l-kitāb, Cairo 1956

Avicenna, *Psychologie d'Ibn Sīnā (Avicenne), d'après son oeuvre al-Shifāʾ*, Texte arabe vol. I, traduction annotée vol. II, ed. J. Bakoš, Travaux de l'Académie Tchécoslovaque des Sciences. Section de linguistique et de littérature, Prague 1956

Avicenna, *De Anima [Arabic Text], being the Psychological Part of Kitāb al-Shifāʾ*, ed. F. Rahman, Oxford University Press, London-New York-Toronto 1959, 1970[2]

Avicenna, *Al-Šifāʾ, al-Manṭiq, al-Maqūlāt*, eds. G. Š. Qanawatī, M. al-Ḫuḍayrī, A. F. al-Ahwānī, S. Zāyid, al-Hayʾa al-ʿāmma li-šuʾūn al-maṭābiʿ al-amīriyya, Cairo 1959

Avicenna, *Al-Šifāʾ, al-Ilāhiyyāt (1)*, eds. G. Š. Qanawatī, S. Zāyid, al-Hayʾa al-ʿāmma li-šuʾūn al-maṭābiʿ al-amīriyya, Cairo 1960; *Al-Šifāʾ, al-Ilāhiyyāt (2)*, eds. M. Y. Moussa, S. Dunyā et S. Zayed, al-Hayʾa al-ʿāmma li-šuʾūn al-maṭābiʿ al-amīriyya, Cairo 1960

Avicenna, *Al-Išārāt wa-l-tanbīhāt maʿa Šarḥ Naṣīr al-Dīn al-Ṭūsī*, ed. S. Dunyā, 4 parts in 3 vols., Dār al-maʿārif, Cairo 1960–68

Avicenna, *Al-Šifāʾ, al-Manṭiq, al-Ǧadal*, ed. A. F. al-Ahwānī, al-Hayʾa al-ʿāmma li-šuʾūn al-maṭābiʿ al-amīriyya, Cairo 1965

Avicenna, *Al-Šifāʾ, al-Ṭabīʿiyyāt, al-Maʿādin wa-l-Āṯār al-ʿulwiyya*, eds. ʿA. Ḥ. Muntaṣir, S. Zāyid, ʿA. Ismāʿīl, I. Madkūr, al-Hayʾa al-ʿāmma li-šuʾūn al-maṭābiʿ al-amīriyya, Cairo 1965

Avicenna, *Al-Šifāʾ, al-Ṭabīʿiyyāt, al-Samāʾ wa-l-ʿĀlam, al-Kawn wa-l-Fasād, al-Afʿāl wa-l-Infiʿālāt*, ed. M. Qāsim, Dār al-kitāb al-ʿarabī li-l-ṭibāʿa wa-l-našr, Cairo 1969

Avicenna, *Risāla Aḍḥawiyya fī l-maʿād* (*Epistola sulla vita futura*), ed. F. Lucchetta, Antenore, Padova 1969

Avicenna, *Al-Šifāʾ, al-Ṭabīʿiyyāt, al-Ḥayawān*, eds. ʿA. Muntaṣir, S. Zāyid, ʿA. Ismāʿīl, al-Hayʾa al-miṣriyya al-ʿāmma li-l-taʾlīf wa-l-našr, Cairo 1970

Avicenna, *Kitāb al-Hidāya*, ed. M. ʿAbduh, Maktaba al-Qāhira al-ḥadīṯa, Cairo 1974

Avicenna and Abū ʿUbayd al-Ǧūzǧānī, *The Life of Ibn Sina. A Critical Edition and Annotated Translation*, ed. W. E. Gohlman, Studies in Islamic Philosophy and Science, State University of New York Press, Albany-New York 1974

Avicenna, *Al-Šifāʾ, al-Ṭabīʿiyyāt*, vol. 6: *al-Nafs*, eds. G. C. Anawati, S. Zayed, revised edition by I. Madkūr, al-Hayʾa al-miṣriyya al-ʿāmma li-l-kitāb, Cairo 1975

Avicenna, *Rasāʾil fī l-ḥikma wa-l-ṭabīʿiyyāt*, 2 vols., Dār al-ʿarab, Cairo 1980[2]

Avicenna, *Al-Šifāʾ, al-Ṭabīʿiyyāt, al-Samāʿ al-ṭabīʿī*, ed. S. Zāyid, al-Hayʾa al-miṣriyya al-ʿāmma li-l-kitāb, Cairo 1983

Avicenna, *Al-Naǧāt min al-ġaraq fī baḥr al-ḍalālāt*, ed. M. T. Dānišpažūh, Dānišgah-i Tehran, Tehran 1985

Avicenna, *Kitāb al-Naǧāt*, ed. M. Faḫrī, Dār al-afāq al-ǧadīda, Beirut 1985

Avicenna, *Al-Mubāḥaṯāt*, ed. M. Bīdārfar, Entešārāt-e Bīdār, Qum 1992

Avicenna, *al-Ḥikma al-mašriqiyya. al-Ṭabīʿiyyāt*, ed. A. Özcan, in *İbn Sīna'nın el-Hikmetuʾl-meşrikiyye adlı eseri ve tabiat felsefesi*, PhD thesis, Marmara Üniversitesi Sosyal Bilimler Enstitüsü, İslam Felsefesi Bilim Dalı, Istanbul 1993

Avicenna, *Kitāb al-Maǧmūʿ aw al-Ḥikma al-ʿArūḍiyya*, ed. M. Ṣāliḥ, Dār al-Hādī, Beirut 1428H/2007

Avicenna, *Commentaire sur le livre lambda de la* Metaphysique *d'Aristote (chapitres 6–10) par Ibn Sīnā (Avicenne)*. Edition critique, traduction et notes par M. Geoffroy, J. Janssens et M. Sebti, Vrin, Paris 2014

Avicenna Latinus, *Liber de anima seu sextus de naturalibus IV-V.* Édition critique de la traduction latine médiévale par S. van Riet. Introduction sur la doctrine psychologique d'Avicenne par G. Verbeke, Peeters-Brill, Louvain-Leiden 1968

Avicenna Latinus, *Liber de anima seu sextus de naturalibus I-II-III.* Édition critique de la traduction latine médiévale par S. van Riet. Introduction sur la doctrine psychologique d'Avicenne par G. Verbeke, Peeters-Brill, Louvain-Leiden 1972

Avicenna Latinus, *Liber de Philosophia prima sive Scientia divina I-IV.* Édition critique de la traduction latine médiévale par S. van Riet. Introduction doctrinale par G. Verbeke, E. Peeters-Brill, Louvain-Leiden 1977

Avicenna Latinus, *Liber de Philosophia prima sive Scientia divina V-X.* Édition critique de la traduction latine médiévale par S. van Riet. Introduction doctrinale par G. Verbeke, E. Peeters-Brill, Louvain-Leiden 1980

Avicenna Latinus, *Liber de Philosophia prima sive Scientia divina, I-X.* Lexiques par S. van Riet, E. Peeters-Brill, Louvain-la-Neuve–Leiden 1983

Avicenna Latinus, *Liber tertius naturalium de generatione et corruptione.* Édition critique de la traduction latine médiévale et lexiques par S. van Riet. Introduction doctrinale par G. Verbeke, Peeters-Brill, Louvain-la-Neuve–Leiden 1987

Avicenna Latinus, *Liber quartus naturalium de actionibus et passionibus qualitatum primarum.* Édition critique de la traduction latine médiévale et lexiques par S. Van Riet. Introduction doctrinale par G. Verbeke, Peeters-Brill, Louvain-la-Neuve–Leiden 1989

Avicenna Latinus, *Liber primus naturalium. Tractatus primus. De causis et principiis naturalium.* Édition critique de la traduction latine médiévale par S. van Riet. Introduction doctrinale par G. Verbeke, Peeters-Brill, Louvain-Leiden 1992

Avicenna Latinus, *Liber primus naturalium. Tractatus secundus. De motu et de consimilibus.* Édition critique de la traduction latine médiévale par S. van Riet, J. Janssens, A. Allard. Introduction doctrinale par G. Verbeke, Académie Royale de Belgique, Bruxelles 2006

Avicenna Latinus, *Liber primus naturalium. Tractatus tertius. De His Quae Habent Naturalia Ex Hoc Quod Habent Quantitatem*, Édition critique de la traduction latine médiévale par J. Janssens, Académie Royale de Belgique, Bruxelles 2017

David, *Prolegomena et in Porphyrii Isagogen commentarium,* ed. A. Busse, *Commentaria in Aristotelem Graeca,* vol. 18.2, Reimer, Berlin 1904

Elias, *In Porphyrii Isagogen et Aristotelis Categorias commentaria,* ed. A. Busse, *Commentaria in Aristotelem Graeca,* vol. 18.1, Reimer, Berlin 1900

Euclid, *Elementa,* post I.L. Heiberg edidit E.S. Stamatis, B.G. Teubner, Leipzig 1972

al-Fārābī, *Iḥṣāʾ al-ʿulūm*, ed. ʿU. Amīn, Dār al-Fikr al-ʿArabī, Cairo 1931, 1949[2] (repr. in al-Fārābī, *Texts and Studies,* IV, ed. F. Sezgin, Institut for the History of Arabic-Islamic Science at the J. W. Goethe University, Frankfurt am Main 1999, 1–148), Maktaba al-Anǧlū al-Miṣriyya, Cairo 1968[3]

al-Fārābī, *De Platonis philosophia (Falsafat Aflāṭūn)*, eds. F. Rosenthal, R. Walzer, The Warburg Institut, London 1943

al-Fārābī, *Philosophy of Aristotle (Falsafat Arisṭūṭālīs).* Arabic Text, Edited with an Introduction and Notes by M. Mahdi, Dār Majallat Šiʿr, Beirut 1961

al-Fārābī, *Kitāb Taḥṣīl al-saʿāda,* ed. Ǧ. Āl-Yāsīn, Dār al-Andalus, Beirut 1981

al-Fārābī, *Über die Wissenschaften De scientiis. Nach der lateinischen Übersetzung Gerhards von Cremona. Mit einer Einleitung und kommentierenden Anmerkungen herausgegeben und übersetzt von* Franz Schupp, Felix Meiner Verlag, Hamburg 2005

al-Ḥasan Ibn Mūsā al-Nawbaḫtī, *Commentary on Aristotle* De generatione et corruptione. *Edition, translation and commentary by* M. Rashed, Collection " Scientia Graeco-Arabica " 19, Walter De Gruyter, Berlin-Boston 2015

Ibn Abī Uṣaybiʿa, *ʿUyūn al-anbāʾ fī ṭabaqāt al-aṭibbāʾ*, ed. A. Müller, 2 vols., al-Maṭbaʿa al-Wahbiyya, Cairo, 1882
Ibn Ǧulǧul, *Ṭabaqāt al-aṭibbāʾ wa-l-ḥukamāʾ*, ed. F. Sayyid, Cairo 1955
Ibn al-Nadīm, *Kitāb al-Fihrist*, G. Flügel, J. Rodiger, A. Müller eds., 2 vols., Leipzig 1871–1872
Ibn al-Qifṭī, *Taʾrīḫ al-ḥukamāʾ*, ed. J. Lippert, Leipzig 1903
al-Kindī, *Fī l-qawl fī l-nafs al-muḫtaṣar min kitāb Arisṭū wa-Flāṭūn wa-sāʾir al-falāsifa*, in *Rasāʾil al-Kindī al-falsafiyya*, ed. M. ʿA. Abū-Rīda, vol. I, Dār al-fikr al-ʿarabī, Cairo 1950–53, 270–281
al-Kindī, *Kalām li l-Kindī fī l-nafs muḫtaṣar waǧīz*, in *Rasāʾil al-Kindī al-falsafiyya*, ed. M. ʿA. Abū-Rīda, vol. I, Dār al-fikr al-ʿarabī, Cairo 1950–53, 281–282
al-Kindī, *Risālat fī Kammiyyat kutub Arisṭāṭālīs wa-mā yuḥtāǧu ilayhi fī taḥṣīl al-falsafa*, in *Rasāʾil al-Kindī al-falsafiyya*, ed. M. ʿA. Abū-Rīda, vol. I, Dār al-fikr al-ʿarabī, Cairo 1950–53, 363–384 (Italian translation and commentary in M. Guidi, R. Walzer, "Studi su al-Kindī I: Uno Scritto Introduttivo allo Studio di Aristotele", *Memorie della Reale Accademia Nazionale dei Lincei. Classe di Scienze Morali, Storiche e Filosofiche*, ser. VI, vol. VI, fasc. V, 1940, 375–419)
Olympiodorus, *In Aristotelis Meteora commentaria*, ed. G. Stuve, *Commentaria in Aristotelem Graeca*, vol. 12.2, Reimer, Berlin 1900
Olympiodorus, *Prolegomena et in Categorias commentarium*, ed. A. Busse, *Commentaria in Aristotelem Graeca*, vol. 12.1, Reimer, Berlin 1902
Philoponus, *In Aristotelis Physicorum libros tres priores (1–3) commentaria*, ed. H. Vitelli, *Commentaria in Aristotelem Graeca*, vol. 16, Reimer, Berlin 1887
Philoponus, *In Aristotelis Physicorum libros quinque posteriores (4–8) commentaria*, ed. H. Vitelli, *Commentaria in Aristotelem Graeca*, vol. 17, Reimer, Berlin 1888
Philoponus, *In Aristotelis libros De generatione et corruptione commentaria*, ed. H. Vitelli, *Commentaria in Aristotelem Graeca*, vol. 14.2, Reimer, Berlin 1897
Philoponus, *In Aristotelis De anima libros commentaria*, ed. M. Hayduck, *Commentaria in Aristotelem Graeca*, vol. 15, G. Reimer, Berlin 1897
Philoponus, (*olim Ammonii*) *In Aristotelis Categorias commentarium*, ed. A. Busse, *Commentaria in Aristotelem Graeca*, vol. 13.1, Reimer, Berlin 1898
Philoponus, *In Aristotelis Meteorologicorum librum primum commentarium*, ed. M. Hayduck, *Commentaria in Aristotelem Graeca*, vol. 14.1, Reimer, Berlin 1901
Plotinus, *Plotini Opera, Tomus II: Enneades IV-V*, ed. P. Henry et H.-R. Schwyzer, Desclée de Brouwer-L'Edition Universelle, Paris-Bruxelles 1959
Plotinus, *La discesa dell'anima nei corpi* (*Enn.* IV 8 [6]). *Plotiniana Arabica* (*Pseudo-Teologia di Aristotele, capitoli 1 e 7; "Detti del Sapiente Greco"*), a cura di C. D'Ancona, Il Poligrafo, Padova 2003
Simplicius, *In libros Aristotelis De anima commentaria*, ed. M. Hayduck, *Commentaria in Aristotelem Graeca*, vol. 11, G. Reimer, Berlin 1882
Simplicius, *In Aristotelis Physicorum libros quattuor priores commentaria*, ed. H. Diels, *Commentaria in Aristotelem Graeca*, vol. 9, Reimer, Berlin 1882
Simplicius, *In Aristotelis Physicorum libros quattuor posteriores commentaria*, ed. H. Diels, *Commentaria in Aristotelem Graeca*, vol. 10, Reimer, Berlin 1895
Simplicius, *In Aristotelis Categorias commentarium*, ed. C. Kalbfleisch, *Commentaria in Aristotelem Graeca*, vol. 8, G. Reimer, Berlin 1907
Themistius, *In libros Aristotelis De anima paraphrasis*, ed. R. Heinze, *Commentaria in Aristotelem Graeca*, vol. 5.3, G. Reimer, Berlin 1899
Themistius, *Kitāb al-nafs li-Arisṭūṭālīs. An Arabic Translation of Themistius' Commentary on Aristotle's* De Anima, ed. M. Lyons, Oriental Studies II, Cassirer, Oxford 1973

Secondary literature

P. Accattino, P. Donini, Alessandro di Afrodisia, *L'anima*. Traduzione, introduzione e commento a cura di P. Accattino, P. Donini, Laterza, Roma-Bari 1996

M. Achena, H. Massé, Avicenne. *Le Livre de science*, traduit par M. Achena, H. Massé, Les Belles Lettres, Paris 1955, 1958²; Les Belles Lettres/Unesco 1986³

P. Adamson, "Two Early Arabic Doxographies on the Soul: al-Kindī and the *Theology of Aristotle*", *The Modern Schoolman*, 77, 2000, 105–125

P. Adamson, "Aristotelianism and the Soul in the Arabic Plotinus", *The Journal of the History of Ideas*, 62, 2001, 211–232

P. Adamson, *The Arabic Plotinus. A Philosophical Study of the* Theology of Aristotle, Duckworth, London 2002

P. Adamson, "Correcting Plotinus: Soul's Relationship to Body in Avicenna's Commentary on the *Theology of Aristotle*", in P. Adamson, H. Baltussen, M.W.F. Stone eds., *Philosophy, Science and Exegesis in Greek, Arabic and Latin Commentaries*, in honor of Richard Sorabji, 2 vols., Supplement to the Bulletin of the Insititute Of Classical Studies 83.1–2, London 2004, 59–75

P. Adamson, "Non-Discoursive Thought in Avicenna's Commentary on the *Theology of Aristotle*", in *Interpreting Avicenna: Science and Philosophy in Medieval Islam. Proceedings of the Second Conference of the Avicenna Study Group*, ed. J. McGinnis with the assistance of D. C. Reisman, Brill, Leiden – Boston 2004, 87–111

P. Adamson, *Al-Kindī*, Oxford University Press, Oxford-New York 2007

P. Adamson, "The Kindian Tradition: the Structure of Philosophy in Arabic Neoplatonism", in C. D'Ancona ed., *The Libraries of the Neoplatonists*, Brill, Leiden 2007, 351–70

"Al-Kindī", The Stanford Encyclopedia of Philosophy (Fall 2010 Edition), http://plato.stanford.edu/archives/fall2010/entries/al-kindi/

P. Adamson, (with G. Endress), "Abū Yūsuf al-Kindī", in U. Rudolph, R. Würsch eds., *Grundriß der Geschichte der Philosophie begründet von F. Überweg, völlig neu bearbeitete Ausgabe heraugegeben von H. Holzhey. Philosophie in der islamischen Welt (8.–10. Jahrhundert)*, Schwabe&Co., Basel 2012, 92–147

P. Adamson, (with P. E. Pormann), *The Philosophical Works of al-Kindī*, Oxford University Press, Karachi 2012

P. Adamson, (with R. Wisnovsky), "Yaḥyā Ibn ʿAdī on the Location of God", *Oxford Studies in Medieval Philosophy*, 1, 2013, 205–28

P. Adamson, *Into Thin Air–Avicenna on the Soul*, in *Philosophy in The Islamic World. A History of Philosophy without Any Gaps*, Volume 3, Oxford University Press, Oxford 2016

P. Adamson, (with F. Benevich), "The Thought Experimental Method: Avicenna's *Flying Man* Argument", *Journal of the American Philosophical Association*, 4.2, 2018, 147–164

P. Adamson, "From Known to Knower: Affinity Arguments for the Mind's Incorporeality in the Islamic World", forthcoming

A. Q. Ahmed, "The *Shifāʾ* in India I: Reflections on the Evidence of the Manuscripts", *Oriens*, 40, 2012, 199–222

M. Alonso Alonso, "Notas sobre los traductores toledanos Domingo Gundisalvo y Juan Hispano", *Al-Andalus*, 8, 1943, 155–188

T. Alpina, "Intellectual Knowledge, Active Intellect and Intellectual Memory in Avicenna's *Kitāb al-Nafs* and Its Aristotelian Background", *Documenti e studi sulla tradizione filosofica medievale*, 25, 2014, 131–183

T. Alpina, "Al-Ǧūzǧānī's Insertion of *On Cardiac Remedies* in Avicenna's *Book of the Soul* : the Latin Translation as a Clue to his Editorial Activity on *the Book of the Cure?*", *Documenti e studi sulla tradizione filosofica medievale*, 28, 2017, 365–400

T. Alpina, (with A. Bertolacci), *Documenti e studi sulla tradizione filosofica medievale*, 28, 2017 (special issue: The Latin Translations of Avicenna's *Kitāb al-Šifā'* [*Book of the Cure/Healing*])
T. Alpina, "Knowing the Soul from Knowing Oneself. A Reading of the Prologue to Avicenna's *Kitāb al-Nafs* (*Book of the Soul*)", *Atti e Memorie dell'Accademia Toscana di Scienze e Lettere 'La Colombaria'*, 82 (68), 2018, 443–458
T. Alpina, "The *Soul of*, the Soul *in itself*, and the *Flying Man* Experiment", *Arabic Sciences and Philosophy*, 28.2, 2018, 187–224
T. Alpina, "Is Nutrition a Sufficient Condition for Life? Avicenna's Position between Natural Philosophy and Medicine", in R. Lo Presti, G. Korobili eds., *Nutrition and Nutritive Soul in Aristotle and Aristotelianism*, De Gruyter – Topics in Ancient Philosophy, Berlin-Boston 2020, 221–258
T. Alpina, "Retaining, Remembering, Recollecting. Avicenna's Account of Memory and Its Sources", in V. Decaix, C. Thomsen Thörnqvist eds., *Aristotle's* De memoria et reminiscentia *and Its Reception*, Brepols Publishers, Studia Artistarum, Turnhout, forthcoming
T. Alpina, "Is the Heaven an Animal? Avicenna's Celestial Psychology at the Intersection between Cosmology and Biology", in R. Salles ed., *Biology and Cosmology in Ancient Philosophy: from Thales to Avicenna*, Cambridge University Press, forthcoming
T. Alpina, "Exercising Impartiality to Favor Aristotle: Avicenna and "the accomplished anatomists" (*aṣḥāb al-tašrīḥ al-muḥaṣṣilūna*) in *Ḥayawān*, III, 1", *Arabic Sciences and Philosophy*, forthcoming
A. Alwishah, "Ibn Sīnā on Floating Man Arguments", *Journal of Islamic Philosophy*, 9, 2013, 32–53
M. Aouad, (with R. Goulet), "Alexandros D'Aphrodisias", in *Dictionnaire des Philosophes Antiques*. Publié sous la direction de R. Goulet, avec une Préface de P. Hadot, Editions du Cnrs, Paris 1994, 125–139
R. Arnzen, *Aristoteles'* De anima. *Eine verlorene spätantike Paraphrase in arabischer und persischer Überlieferung. Arabischer Text nebst Kommentar, quellengeschichtlichen Studien und Glossaren*, Brill, Leiden 1998
R. Arnzen, "*De anima*. Paraphrase arabe anonyme", in *Dictionnaire des Philosophes Antiques*. Publié sous la direction de R. Goulet. Supplement, avec la collaboration de J.-M. Flamand, M. Aouad, Editions du Cnrs, Paris 2003, 359–365
A. Bäck, "The Islamic background: Avicenna (b. 980; d. 1037) and Averroes (b. 1126; d. 1198)", in J.E. Gracia ed., *Individuation in Scholasticism. The Later Middle Ages and the Counter-Reformation 1150–1650*, State University of New York Press, Albany (N.Y.) 1994, 39–67
O. Balleriaux, "Eugénios, père de Thémistius et philosophe néoplatonicien", *L'Antiquité Classique*, 65, 1996, 135–160
J. Barnes, *The Complete Works of Aristotle. The revised Oxford translation*, ed. J. Barnes, 2 vols., Princeton University Press, Princeton 1984
F. Benevich, "Fire and Heat: Yaḥyà B. 'Adī and Avicenna on the Essentiality of Being Substance or Accident", *Arabic Sciences and Philosophy*, 27, 2017, 237–67
F. Benevich, *Essentialität und Notwendigkeit: Avicenna und die Aristotelische Tradition*, Islamic Philosophy, Theology and Science. Texts and Studies, Brill, Leiden-Boston 2018
M. Bergeron, R. Dufour, Alexandre d'Aphrodise, *De l'âme*. Texte grec introduit, traduit et annoté, " Textes & Commentaires ", Vrin, Paris 2008
E. Berti, "Il libro *Lambda* della *Metafisica* di Aristotele tra fisica e metafisica", in G. Damschen, R. Enskart und A. Vigo eds., *Platon und Aristoteles – sub ratione veritatis. Festschrift für Wolfgng Wieland zum 70. Geburgstag*, Vandenhoek & Ruprecht, Gottingen, 2003, 177–193 (repr. id., *Nuovi studi aristotelici. II – Fisica, antropologia e metafisica*, Morcelliana, Brescia 2004, 471–487)

A. Bertolacci, "Some Texts of Aristotle's *Metaphysics* in the *Ilāhīyāt* of Avicenna's *Kitāb al-Šifā'*", in D. C. Reisman, A. H. al-Rahim eds., *Before and After Avicenna. Proceedings of the First Conference of the Avicenna Study Group,* Brill, Leiden 2003, 25–45

A. Bertolacci, "Il pensiero filosofico di Avicenna", in C. D'Ancona ed., in *Storia della filosofia nell'Islam medievale,* 2 voll., Einaudi, Torino 2005, 522–626

A. Bertolacci, *The Reception of Aristotle's* Metaphysics *in Avicenna's* Kitāb al-Šifā'. *A Milestone of Western Metaphysical Thought,* Brill, Leiden-Boston 2006

A. Bertolacci, "Avicenna and Averroes on the Proof of God's Existence and the Subject-Matter of *Metaphysics*", *Medioevo,* 32, 2007, 61–97

A. Bertolacci, Avicenna (Ibn Sīnā). *Libro della Guarigione. Le cose divine,* a cura di A. Bertolacci, Unione Tipografico-Editrice Torinese (Utet), Torino 2007

A. Bertolacci, "A Community of Translators: The Latin Medieval Versions of Avicenna's *Book of the Cure*", in C. J. Mews, J. N. Crossley eds., *Communities of Learning: Networks and the Shaping of Intellectual Identity in Europe 1100–1500,* Brepols, Turnhout 2011, 37–54

A. Bertolacci, "The 'Ontologization' of Logic. Metaphysical Themes in Avicenna's Reworking of the *Organon*", in M. Cameron, J. Marenbon eds., *Methods and Methodologies. Aristotelian Logic East and West 500–1500,* Brill Leiden-Boston 2011, 27–51

A. Bertolacci, "The Distinction of Essence and Existence in Avicenna's *Metaphysics:* The Text and Its Context", in F. Opwis, D. C. Reisman eds., *Islamic Philosophy, Science, Culture, and Religion. Studies in Honor of Dimitri Gutas,* Brill, Leiden 2012, 257–288

A. Bertolacci, "A Hidden Hapax Legomenon in Avicenna's *Metaphysics.* Considerations on the Use of *Anniyya* and *Ayyiyya* in the *Ilāhiyyāt* of the *Kitāb al-Šifā'*", in A. M. I. van Oppenraay ed., with the collaboration of R. Fontaine, *The Letter before the Spirit. The Importance of Text Editions for the Study of the Reception of Aristotle,* Brill (Aristoteles Semitico-Latinus 22), Leiden-Boston 2012, 289–309

A. Bertolacci, "How Many Recensions of Avicenna's *Kitāb al-Šifā'?*", *Oriens,* 40.2, 2012, 275–303

A. Bertolacci, "The Metaphysical Proof of Prophecy in Avicenna", in A. Palazzo, A. Rodolfi eds., *Il profeta e la profezia tra XI e XIV secolo,* forthcoming

H. H. Biesterfeldt, "Medieval Arabic Encyclopedias of Science and Philosophy", in S. Harvey ed., *The Medieval Hebrew Encyclopedias of Science and Philosophy,* Kluwer, Boston 2000, 77–98

H. H. Biesterfeldt, "Arabisch-islamische Enzyklopädien : Formen und Funktionen", in C. Meier ed., *Die Enzyklopädie im Mittelalter vom Hochmittelalter bis zu frühen Neuzeit,* Wilhelm Fink, München 2002, 43–83

D. L. Black, "Estimation (*Wahm*) in Avicenna: The Logical and Psychological Dimensions", *Dialogue,* 32, 1993, 219–258

D. L. Black, "Avicenna on the Ontological and Epistemic Status of Fictional Beings", *Documenti e studi sulla tradizione filosofica medievale,* 8, 1997, 425–453

D. L. Black, "Estimation and Imagination: Western Divergences from an Arabic Paradigm", *Topoi,* 19, 2000, 59–75

D. L. Black, "Psychology: soul and intellect", in *The Cambridge Companion to Arabic Philosophy,* P. Adamson, R. C. Taylor eds., Cambridge University Press, Cambridge 2005, 308–326

D. L. Black, "Avicenna on Self-Awareness and Knowing that One Knows", in S. Rahman, T. Street, H. Tahiri eds., *The Unity of Science in the Arabic Tradition. Science, Logic and Epistemology and their Interactions,* Springer, Dordrecht 2008, 63–87

D. L. Black, "Rational Imagination: Avicenna on the Cogitative Power", in L. X. Lopéz-Farjeat, J. A. Tellkamplack eds., *Philosophical Psychology in Arabic Thought and the Latin Aristotelianism of the 13th Century,* Vrin, Paris 2013, 59–81

D. Blank, "Ammonius", Stanford Encyclopedia of Philosophy, 2011 http://plato.stanford.edu/entries/ammonius/

H. J. Blumenthal, "John Philoponus and Stephanus of Alexandria: Two Neoplatonic Christian Commentators on Aristotle?", in D. J. O'Meara ed., *Neoplatonism and Christian Thought*, State University of New York Press, Albany 1982, 54–63
H. J. Blumenthal, "Body and Soul in Philoponus", *The Monist*, 69/3, 1986, 370–82
H. J. Blumenthal, "Simplicius (?) on the first book of Aristotle's *De anima*", in I. Hadot ed., *Simplicius. Sa vie, son oeuvre, sa survie. Actes du colloque international de Paris (28 sept.–1er oct. 1985) organisé par le centre de recherche sur les oeuvres et la pensée de Simplicius (RCP 739 – CNRS)*, De Gruyter, Berlin-New York 1987, 91–112
H. J. Blumenthal, "Themistius: the last Peripatetic commentator on Aristotle?", in *Aristotle Transformed. The Ancient Commentators and their Influence*, R. Sorabji ed., London, Duckworth, 1990, 113–123
H. J. Blumenthal, *Aristotle and the Neoplatonism in Late Antiquity. Interpretations of the* De anima, Duckworth, London 1996
H. J. Blumenthal, "Were Aristotle's Intentions in writing the *De anima* forgotten in Late Antiquity?", *Documenti e studi sulla tradizione filosofica medievale*, 8, 1997, 143–157
R. Bolton, "Aristotle's definitions of the soul: *De Anima* II, 1–3", *Phronesis*, 23, 1978, 258–278
G. Bos, *Aristotle's* De Anima, translated into Hebrew by Zeraḥyah Ben Isaac ben Shealtiel Ḥen. A critical edition with an introduction and index by G. B., coll. " Aristoteles Semitico-latinus " 6, Brill, Leiden 1994
F. Bossier, C. Steel, "Priscianus Lydus en de '*In De anima*' van pseudo(?)-Simplicius", *Tidschrift voor Filosofie*, 34, 1972, 761–822
R. Brague, Thémistius, *Paraphrase de la* Métaphysique *d'Aristote: livre lambda*, traduit de l'hébreu et de l'arabe, introduction, notes et indices par R. Brague, Vrin, Paris 1999
S. Broadie, "*Nous* and Nature in *De anima* III", in J. J. Cleary ed., *Proceedings of the Boston Area Colloquium in Ancient Philosophy*, 12, 1996, 163–76
J. Brunschwig, "*Metaphysics* Λ 9: A Short-Lived Thought-Experiment?", in M. Frede and D. Charles eds., *Aristotle's* Metaphysics *Lambda. Simposium Aristotelicum*, Clarendon Press, Oxford 2000, 245–306
C. Burnett, "The Coherence of the Arabic-Latin Translation Program in Toledo in the Twelfth Century", *Science in Context*, 14 (1/2), 2001, 249–288
C. Burnett, "Arabic into Latin: the reception of Arabic philosophy into Western Europe", in P. Adamson – R. C. Taylor eds., *The Cambridge Companion to Arabic Philosophy*, Cambridge University Press, Cambridge 2004, 370–404
M. Burnyeat, "Is an Aristotelian Philosophy of Mind Still Credible? A Draft", in M. C. Nussbaum, A. O. Rorty eds., *Essays on Aristotle's* De anima, Clarendon Press, Oxford 1992, 15–26
M. Burnyeat, "Aristotle and the foundation of sublunary physics", in J. Mansfeld, F. J. de Haas eds., *Aristotle. On Generation and Corruption*, I. *Proceeding of the 15th Symposium Aristotelicum*, Oxford University Press, Oxford 2004, 7–24
G. Cambiano, *Storiografia e dossografia nella filosofia antica*, Tirrenia Stampatori, Torino 1986
L. M. Castelli, "Manifestazioni somatiche e fisiologia delle 'affezioni dell'anima' in ps.Arist., *Problemata*", in B. Centrone ed., *Studi sui Problemata Physica aristotelici*, Elenchos LVIII, Bibliopolis, Napoli 2011, 239–274
V. Caston, Alexander of Aphrodisias, *On the Soul: Soul as form of the body, parts of the soul, nourishment, and perception*. Translated with an introduction and commentary by V. Caston, Ancient commentators on Aristotle 94, Bloomsbury Academic, London – New York 2012
C. Cerami, *Génération et Substance. Aristote et Averroès entre physique et métaphysique*, Scientia Graeco-Arabica 18, De Gruyter, Berlin – Boston 2015
W. Charlton, "Aristotle's Definition of Soul", *Phronesis*, 25, 1980, 170–186

W. Charlton, "Aristotle on the place of mind in nature", in A. Gotthelf and J. G. Lennox eds., *Philosophical Issues in Aristotle's Biology,* Cambridge University Press, Cambridge 1987, 408–423

W. Charlton, Philoponus, *On Aristotle On the intellect.* De Anima 3. 4–8; translated by W. Charlton, with the assistance of F. Bossier, Duckworth, London 1991

W. Charlton, Philoponus, *On Aristotle On the soul* 3.1–8, translated by W. Charlton, Duckworth, London 1999

W. Charlton, Philoponus, *On Aristotle On the soul* 3.9–13, translated by W. Charlton, Duckworth, London 2000

W. Charlton, Philoponus, *On Aristotle On the soul* 2.1–6, translated by W. Charlton, Duckworth, London 2005

W. Charlton, Philoponus, *On Aristotle On the soul* 2.7–12, translated by W. Charlton, Duckworth, London 2005

A. Code, J. Moravcsik, "Explaining various forms of living", in M. Nussbaum, A. Rorty eds., *Essays on Aristotle's* De anima, Clarendon Press, Oxford 1992, 129–145

K. Corcilius, (with Pavel Gregoric), "Separability vs. Difference: Parts and Capacities of the Soul in Aristotle", Oxford Studies in Ancient Philosophy, 39, 2010, 81–119

A. Cortabarria Beitia, "La classification des sciences chez al-Kindī", *Melanges de l'Institut Dominicain d'Etudes Orientales du Caire*, 11, 1972, 49–76

M.-Th. D'Alverny, "Avendauth?", in *Homenaje a Millas-Vallicrosa,* I, Barcelona, 1954, 19–43 (repr. in M.-Th. D'Alverny, *Avicenne en Occident. Recueil d'articles de Marie-Thérèse d'Alverny réunis en hommage à l'auteur,* Vrin, Paris 1993, n. VIII)

M.-Th. D'Alverny, "*Anniyya – Anitas*", in *Mélanges offerts à Etienne Gilson,* Ed. Pontifical Institute of Medieval Philosophy, Toronto – Paris 1959, 9–81 (rist. in *Avicenne en Occident. Recueil d'articles de Marie-Thérèse d'Alverny réunis en hommage à l'auteur,* Vrin, Paris 1993, n. X)

M.-Th. D'Alverny, (with S. van Riet, P. Jodogne) *Avicenna Latinus. Codices*, E. Peters – E. J. Brill, Louvain-la-Neuve – Leiden 1994

C. D'Ancona Costa, "Avicenna and the *Liber de Causis:* A Contribution to the Dossier", *Revista Española de Filosofía Medieval*, 7, 2000, 95–114

C. D'Ancona Costa, "Commenting on Aristotle. From Late Antiquity to the Arab Aristotelianism", in W. Geerlings, C. Schulze eds., *Der Kommentar in Antike und Mittelalter.* Vol. 1. *Beiträge zu seiner Erforschung,* Brill, Leiden 2002, 200–251

C. D'Ancona Costa, "The *Timaeus'* Model for Creation and Providence: An Example of Continuity and Adaptation in Early Arabic Philosophical Literature", in G. J. Reydams-Schils ed., *Plato's* Timaeus *as Cultural Icon*, University of Notre Dame Press, Notre Dame (IN) 2003, 206–237

C. D'Ancona Costa, "Degrees of Abstraction in Avicenna. How to Combine Aristotle's *De Anima* and the *Enneads*", in S. Knuuttila, P. Kärkkäinen eds., *Theories of Perception in Medieval and Early Modern Philosophy*, Springer, Helsinki 2008, 47–71

C. D'Ancona Costa, "Man's Conjunction with Intellect: A Neoplatonic Source of Western Muslim Philosophy", *Proceedings of the Israel Academy of Sciences and Humanities*, 8 2008, 57–89

C. D'Ancona Costa, "Aux origines du *dator formarum.* Plotin, l'*Épître sur la science divine* et al-Farabi", in E. Coda, C. Martini Bonadeo eds., *De l'Antiquité tardive au Moyen Age. Études de logique aristotélicienne et de philosophie grecque, syriaque, arabe et latine offertes à Henri Hugonnard-Roche*, J. Vrin, Paris 2014, 381–414

H. Daiber, "Qosṭā ibn Lūqā (9. Jh.) über die Einteilung der Wissenschaften", *Zeitschrift für die Geschichte der arabisch-islamischen Wissenschaften*, 6, 1990, 93–129

H. Daiber, *Salient Trends of the Arabic Aristotle*, in G. Endress, R. Kruk eds., *The Ancient Tradition in Christian and Islamic Hellenism: Studies on the Transmission of Greek Philosophy and Sciences* dedicated to H. J. Drossaart Lulofs on his ninetieth birthday, Brill, Leiden 1997, 29–41

H. Daiber, "The Limitations of Knowledge According to Ibn Sīnā: Epistemological and Theological Aspects and the Consequences", in M. Lutz-Bachmann, A. Fidora, P. Antolic eds., *Erkenntnis und Wissenschaft. Probleme der Epistemologie in der Philosophie des Mittelalters*, Akademie Verlag, Berlin 2004, 25–34

H. A. Davidson, "Alfarabi and Avicenna on the Active Intellect", *Viator*, 3, 1972, 109–178

H. A. Davidson, *Alfarabi, Avicenna and Averroes, on Intellect: Their Cosmologies, Theories of the Active Intellect, and Theories of the Human Intellect*, Oxford University Press, New York – Oxford 1992

A. Dhanani, "The Impact of Ibn Sīnā's Critique of Atomism on Subsequent Kalām Discussions of Atomism", *Arabic Sciences and Philosophy*, 25, 2015, 79–104

B. Dodge, Ibn al-Nadīm, *The Fihrist. A Tenth-century Survey of Muslim Culture*, ed. and transl. by B. Dodge, New York-London 1970

P. Donini, "Testi e commenti, manuali e insegnamento. La forma sistematica e i metodi della filosofia in età postellenistica", in W. Haase, H. Temporini eds., *Aufstieg und Niedergang der römischen Welt*, II 36.7, Berlin – New York 1994, 5027-5100

P. Donini, *La* Metafisica *di Aristotele. Introduzione alla lettura*, La Nuova Italia Scientifica, Roma 1995

G. Dragon, *L'Empire Romain d'Orient au Ive Siècle et les Traditions Politiques de l'Hellénisme: Le Témoignage de Thémistius*, Travaux et Memoirs du Centre de Recherche d'Hist. et Civ. Byz. 3, Paris 1968, 1–235

T.-A. Druart, "The Soul and Body Problem: Avicenna and Descartes", in T.-A. Druart ed., *Arabic Philosophy and the West. Continuity and Interaction*, Georgetown University, Washington 1988, 27–49

T.-A. Druart, "The Human Soul's Individuation and Its Survival after the Body's Death: Avicenna on the Causal Relation between Body and Soul", *Arabic Sciences and Philosophy*, 10, 2000, 259–273

T.-A. Druart, "*Shay'* or *Res* as Concomitant of 'Being' in Avicenna", *Documenti e studi sulla tradizione filosofica medievale*, 12, 2001, 125–42

J. Dudley, "Johannes Grammaticus Philoponus Alexandrinus, " *in Aristotelis De anima proemion* ". Translated from the Greek", *Bulletin de philosophie médiévale édité par la société internazionale pour l'étude de la philosophie médiévale*, 16–17, 1974–1975, 62–85

I. Düring, *Aristotle in the Ancient Biographical Tradition*, Erlauders Boktryckeri, Göteborg 1957

H. Eichner, "*Endoxa* and the *Theology of Aristotle* in Avicenna's "Flying Man": Contexts for Similarities with Sceptical and Cartesian Arguments in Avicenna" in G. Veltri, R. Haliva, S. Schmid, E. Spinelli eds., *Sceptical Paths. Enquiry and Doubt from Antiquity to the Present*, De Gruyter, Berlin-Boston 2019, 67–82

A. Elamrani-Jamal, "*De anima*. Tradition arabe", in *Dictionnaire des Philosophes Antiques*. Publié sous la direction de R. Goulet. Supplement, avec la collaboration de J.-M. Flamand, M. Aouad, Editions du Cnrs, Paris 2003, 346–358

G. Endress, "La 'Concordance entre Platon et Aristote'. L'Aristote arabe et l'émancipation de la philosophie en Islam médiéval", in B. Mojsisch and O. Pluta eds., *Historia Philosophiae Medii Aevi*. Studien zur Geschichte der Philosophie des Mittelalters (Festschrift K. Flash), Amsterdam – Philadelphia 1991, 237–257

G. Endress, "'Der erste Lehrer'. Der arabische Aristoteles und das Konzept der Philosophie im Islam", in U. Tworuschka ed., *Gottes ist der Orient. Gottes ist der Okzident. Festschrift für Abdoldjavad Falaturi zum 65. Geburtstag*, Böhlau, Köln-Wien 1991, 151–181

G. Endress, "L'Aristote arabe. Réception, autorité et transformation du Premier Maître", *Medioevo*, 23, 1997, 1–42

G. Endress, "The Cycle of Knowledge : Intellectual Traditions and Encyclopædias of the Rational Sciences in Arabic Islamic Hellenism", in G. Endress ed., preface by A. Filali-Ansary,

Organizing Knowledge. Encyclopædic Activities in the Pre-Eighteenth Century Islamic World, Brill, Leiden – Boston 2006, 103 – 133

A. Falcon, *Aristotle and the Science of Nature. Unity without Uniformity,* Cambridge University Press, New York, 2005

A. Falcon, "Aristotle on the Scope and Unity of the *De anima*", in G. Van Riel and P. Destrée eds., *Ancient Perspectives on Aristotle's* De anima, Leuven University Press, 2010, 167 – 181

R. Fontaine, "Abraham Ibn Daud", *The Stanford Encyclopedia of Philosophy* (Spring 2015 Edition), Edward N. Zalta ed., URL = http://plato.stanford.edu/archives/spr2015/entries/abraham-daud/

R. Frank, "Some Fragments of Isḥāq's Translation of the *De Anima*", *Cahiers de Byrsa*, 9, 1958 – 59, 231 – 51

M. Frede, "The definition of sensible substances", in D. Devereux, P. Pellegrin eds., *Biologie, logique et métaphysique chez Aristote*, Les Editions du CNRS, Paris 1990, 113 – 129

M. Frede, "On Aristotle's Conception of the Soul", in M. C. Nussbaum, A. O. Rorty eds., *Essays on Aristotle's* De anima, Clarendon Press, Oxford 1992, 93 – 107

M. Frede, "La théorie aristotélicienne de l'intellect agent", in G. Romeyer-Dherbey ed., *Corps et âme. Sur le De anima d'Aristote*, études réunies par C. Viano, Vrin, Paris 1996, 377 – 390

M. Frede, "Introduction", in M. Frede and D. Charles eds., *Aristotle's* Metaphysics *Lambda. Simposium Aristotelicum,* Clarendon Press, Oxford 2000, 1 – 52

G. Freudenthal, "Abraham Ibn Daud, Avendauth, Dominicus Gundissalinus and Practical Mathematics in Mid-Twelfth Century Toledo", *Aleph*, 16.1, 2016, 61 – 106

G. Galluzzo, "Il problema dell'oggetto della definizione nel commento di Tommaso d'Aquino a *Metafisica* Z 10 – 11", *Documenti e studi sulla tradizione filosofica medievale,* 12, 2001, 417 – 465

G. Galluzzo, (with M. Mariani), *Aristotle's Metaphysics Book Z: the Contemporary Debate,* Edizioni della Scuola Normale Superiore, Pisa 2006

E. Gannagé, "Jean Philopon. Tradition arabe", in *Dictionnaire des Philosophes Antiques.* Publié sous la direction de R. Goulet, CNRS Editions, Paris 2012, 503 – 563

H. Gätje, *Studien zur Überlieferung der aristotelischen Psychologie im Islam,* coll. " Annales Universitatis Saraviensis, Philosophische Fakultät ", 11, Winter, Heidelberg 1971

M. Geoffroy, "La tradition arabe du *Περὶ νοῦ* d'Alexandre d'Aphrodise et les origines de la théorie farabienne des quatres degrés de l'intellect", in C. D'Ancona, G. Serra eds., *Aristotele e Alessandro di Afrodisia nella tradizione araba.* Atti del colloquio *La ricezione araba ed ebraica della filosofia e della scienza greche* (Padova, 14 – 15 maggio 1999), Il Poligrafo, Padova 2002, 191 – 231

N. Germann, "Avicenna and Afterwards", in J. Marenbon ed., *The Oxford Handbook of Medieval Philosophy,* Oxford University Press, Oxford 2012, 83 – 105

G. R. Giardina, "'Se l'anima sia entelechia del corpo alla maniera di un nocchiero rispetto alla nave'. Plotino IV 3, 21 su Aristotele *De anima* II. 1, 413 a8 – 92", in M. Di Pasquale Barbanti, D. Iozzia eds., *Anima e libertà in Plotino. Atti del Convegno Nazionale (Catania, 29 – 30 gennaio 2009)*, CUEM, Catania 2009, 70 – 112

G. R. Giardina, (et alii) "Jean Philopon", in ed., *Dictionnaire des Philosophes Antiques.* Publié sous la direction de R. Goulet, CNRS Editions, Paris 2012, 455 – 502

E. Gilson, "Les sources gréco-arabes de l'augustinisme avicennisant", *Archives d'Histoire Doctrinale et Littéraire du Moyen Age*, 5, 1930, 1 – 107

A.-M. Goichon, Ibn Sīnā (Avicenne), *Livre des Directives et Remarques* (*Kitāb al-Išārāt wa-l-tanbīhāt*), traduction avec introduction et notes par A.-M. Goichon, Commission internationale pour la traduction des chefs-d'oeuvre, Vrin, Beirut-Paris 1951, repr. 1999

A. Gonzáles Palencia, *Al-Farabi, Catálogo de las ciencias*, Consejo Superior de Investigaciones Científicas, Patronato Menéndez y Pelayo – Instituto Miguel Asín, Madrid 1932, 1953[2]

L. E. Goodman, "A Note on Avicenna's Theory of the Substantiality of the Soul", *The Philosophical Forum*, 1, 1969, 547–562

J.-B. Gourinat, "L'Intellect divin d'Aristote est-il cause efficiente?", *Bollettino filosofico. Università della Calabria*, 20, 2004, 54–81

P. Gregoric, C. Pfeiffer, "Grasping Aristotle's intellect", *Documenti e Studi sulla Tradizione Filosofica Medievale*, 26, 2015, 13–31

D. Gutas, "Paul the Persian on the Classification of the Parts of Aristotle's Philosophy: A Milestone between Alexandria and Baghdad", *Der Islam*, 60, 1983, 231–267

D. Gutas, "The Starting Point of Philosophical Studies in Alexandrian and Arabic Aristotelianism", in W. W. Fortenbaugh, P. M. Huby, A. A. Long eds., *Theophrastus of Eresus. On His Life and Works*, Transaction Books, New Brunswick and Oxford 1985, 115–123

D. Gutas, "Philoponos and Avicenna on the Separability of the Intellect", *The Greek Orthodox Theological Review*, 31, 1986, 121–129

D. Gutas, "Avicenna. Mysticism", in, E. Yarshater ed., *Encyclopaedia Iranica*, vol. III, Routledge and Kegan Paul, London – Boston 1987, 79–83

D. Gutas, *Avicenna and the Aristotelian Tradition. Introduction to Reading Avicenna's Philosophical Works*, E. J. Brill, Leiden-Boston 1988; *Second, Revised and Enlarged Edition, Including an Inventory of Avicenna's Authentic Works*, Brill, Leiden-Boston 2014

D. Gutas, "Aspects of Literary Form and Genre in Arabic Logical Works", in C. Burnett ed., *Glosses and Commentaries on Aristotelian Logical Texts. The Syriac, Arabic and Medieval Latin Traditions*, The Warburg Institute of the University of London, London 1993, 29–76

D. Gutas, "Ibn Tufayl on Ibn Sīnā's *Eastern Philosophy*", *Oriens*, 34, 1994, 222–41

D. Gutas, "Avicenna, *De anima* (V 6). Über die Seele, über Intuition und Prophetie", in K. Flasch ed., *Hauptwerke der Philosophie. Mittelalter*, Stuttgart 1998, 90–107

D. Gutas, *Greek thought, Arabic culture. The Greek-Arabic translation movement in Baghdad and early Abbasid society* (2nd-4th/8th-10th centuries), Routledge, London 1998 (trad. it. *Pensiero greco e cultura araba*, C. D'Ancona ed., Einaudi, Torino 2002)

D. Gutas, "The 'Alexandria to Baghdad' Complex of Narratives. A Contribution to the Study of Philosophical and Medical Historiography among the Arabs", *Documenti e studi sulla tradizione filosofica medievale*, 10, 1999, 155–193

D. Gutas, "Avicenna: Die Metaphysik der rationale Seele", in T. Kobusch ed., *Philosophen des Mittelalters*, Primus Verlag, Darmstadt, 2000, 27–41

D. Gutas, "Avicenna's *Eastern ("Oriental") Philosophy*. Nature, Contents, Transmission", *Arabic Sciences and Philosophy*, 10, 2000, 159–80

D. Gutas, "Filosofia greca, filosofia araba", in S. Settis ed., *I Greci. Storia Cultura Arte Società*, vol. 3, *I Greci oltre la Grecia*, Einaudi, Torino 2001, 767–796

D. Gutas, "Intuition and Thinking: The Evolving Structure of Avicenna's Epistemology", in *Aspects of Avicenna*, R. Wisnovsky ed., Markus Wiener Publishers, Princeton 2001, 1–38

D. Gutas, "The Study of Arabic Philosophy in the Twentieth Century. An Essay on the Historiography of Arabic Philosophy", *British Journal of Middle Eastern Studies*, 29, 2002, 5–25

D. Gutas, "Medical Theory and Scientific Method in the Age of Avicenna", in *Before and After Avicenna. Proceedings of the First Conference of the Avicenna Study Group*, ed. D. C. Reisman, with the assistence of A. H. al-Rahim, Brill, Leiden – Boston 2003, 145–162

D. Gutas, "Avicenna's Marginal Glosses on *De Anima* and the Greek Commentatorial Tradition", *Philosophy, Science and Exegesis in Greek, Arabic and Latin Commentaries*, vol. 2, 2004, 77–88

D. Gutas, "Geometry and the Rebirth of Philosophy in Arabic with al-Kindī", in R. Arnzen, J. Thielmann eds., *Words, Texts and Concepts Cruising the Mediterranean Sea. Studies on the sources, contents and influences of Islamic civilization and Arabic philosophy and science dedicated to G. Endress on his sixty-fifth birthday*, Peeters-Department Oosterse Studies, Leuven-Paris-Dudley (Mass.) 2004, 195–209

D. Gutas, "The Greek and Persian Background of Early Arabic Encyclopedism", in G. Endress ed., preface by A. Filali-Ansary, *Organizing Knowledge. Encyclopædic Activities in the Pre-Eighteenth Century Islamic World*, Brill, Leiden – Boston 2006, 91–101

D. Gutas, "Intellect without limits: the absence of mysticism in Avicenna", in M. C. Pacheco – J. F. Meirinhos eds., *Intellect et imagination dans la Philosophie médiévale. Actes du XIe Congrès International de Philosophie Médiévale de la Société Internationale pour l'Études de la Philosophie Médiévale (S.I.E.P.M.) – Porto, du 26 au 31 août 2002*, Brepols Publishers, Turnhout 2006, 351–372

D. Gutas, "Imagination and transcendental knowledge in Avicenna", in J. E. Montgomery ed., *Arabic Theology, Arabic Philosophy. From the Many to the One: Essays in Celebration of Richard M. Frank*, Uitgeverij Peeters en Departement Oosterse Studies, Leuven – Paris – Dudley, MA 2006, 337–354

D. Gutas, "Avicenna: The Metaphysics of the Rational Soul", *The Muslim World* (Special Issue: *The Ontology of the Soul in Medieval Arabic Thought*), 102/3–4, 2012, 417–425

D. Gutas, "The Empiricism of Avicenna", *Oriens*, 40, 2012, 391–436

I. Hadot, *Le problème du néoplatonisme alexandrin: Hiéroclès et Simplicius*, Etudes Augustiniennes, Paris 1978

I. Hadot, *Arts libéraux et philosophie dans la pensée antique*, Etudes Augustiniennes, Paris 1984 (second edition: Vrin, Paris 2005)

I. Hadot, Simplicius, *Commentaire sur les Catégories. Traduction commentée sous la direction de* Ilsetraut Hadot, *Fascicule I, Introduction, Première partie. Traduction de* Ph. Hoffmann *(avec la collaboration de* I. *et* P. Hadot*). Commentaire et notes à la traduction par* I. Hadot *avec des appendices de* P. Hadot *et* J.-P. Mahé, Philosophia Antiqua, E. J. Brill, Leiden 1990

I. Hadot, "Simplicius or Priscianus? On the Author of the Commentary on Aristotle's *De anima*", *Mnemosyne*, 55/2, 2002, 159–199

R. E. Hall, "Intellect, Soul and Body in Ibn Sina: Systematic Synthesis and Development of the Aristotelian, Neoplatonic and Galenic Theories", in *Interpreting Avicenna: Science and Philosophy in Medieval Islam. Proceedings of the Second Conference of the Avicenna Study Group*, ed. J. McGinnis with the assistance of D. C. Reisman, Brill, Leiden – Boston 2004, 62–86

O. Hamelin, Aristote, *Physique II*. Traduction et commentaire par O. Hamelin, Vrin, Paris 1931

D. W. Hamlyn, *De Anima. Books II and III (with passages from Book I)*, Translated with Introduction and Notes by D. W. Hamlyn, with a Report on Recent Work and a Revised Bibliography by C. Shields, Clarendon Aristotle Series, Clarendon Press, Oxford 1993 (first published 1963)

R. E. Hansberger, *The Transmission of Aristotle's* Parva naturalia *in Arabic*, Unpublished DPhil diss., University of Oxford 2007

R. E. Hansberger, "How Aristotle Came to Believe in God-given Dreams: The Arabic Version of *De divinatione per somnum*", in ed. L. Marlow, *Dreaming Across Boundaries: The Interpretation of Dreams in Islamic Lands*, Ilex Foundation and Center for Hellenic Studies, Washington and Cambridge, Mass., 2008, 50–77

R. E. Hansberger, "*Kitāb al-Ḥiss wa-l-maḥsūs:* Aristotle's *Parva Naturalia* in Arabic Guise", in eds. C. Grellard and P.-M. Morel, *Les* Parva naturalia *d'Aristote: Fortune antique et médiévale*, Paris, 2010, 143–62

R. E. Hansberger, "Plotinus Arabus Rides Again", *Arabic Sciences and Philosophy*, 21, 2011, 57–84

R. E. Hansberger, "Length and Shortness of Life Between Philosophy and Medicine: The Arabic Aristotle and his Medical Readers", in *Philosophy and Medicine in the Islamic World*, ed. by P. Adamson and P. E. Pormann, The Warburg Institute, London, 2018

R. E. Hansberger, "Representation of Which Reality? "Spiritual Forms" and "*ma'ānī*" in the Arabic Adaptation of Aristotle's *Parva naturalia*", in eds. B. Bydén, F. Radovic, *The Parva naturalia in Greek, Arabic and Latin Aristotelianism. Supplementing the Science of the Soul*, Springer, 2018, 99–121

A. Hasnawi, "La conscience de soi chez Avicenne et Descartes", in J. Biard, R. Rashed eds., *Descartes et le Moyen Âge*, Vrin, Paris 1997, 283–291

D. N. Hasse, "Das Lehrstück von den vier Intellekten in der Scholastik: von den arabischen Quellen bis zu Albertus Magnus", *Recherches de Théologie et Philosophie Médiévales*, 66, 1999, 21–77

D. N. Hasse, *Avicenna's* De Anima *in the Latin West. The Formation of a Peripatetic Philosophy of the Soul 1160–1300*, The Warburg Institute – Nino Aragno Editore, London – Turin 2000

D. N. Hasse, "Avicenna on Abstraction", in R. Wisnovsky ed., *Aspects of Avicenna*, Markus Wiener Publishers, Princeton 2001, 39–72

D. N. Hasse, "The social conditions of the Arabic-(Hebrew-)Latin translation movements in medieval Spain and in the Renaissance", in A.Speer, L. Wegener eds., *Wissen über Grenzen. Arabisches Wissen und lateinisches Mittelalter*, Miscellanea Mediaevalia 33, Berlin-New York 2006, 68–86

D. N. Hasse, "Avicenna's 'Giver of Forms' in Latin Philosophy, Especially in the Works of Albertus Magnus", in D. N. Hasse, A. Bertolacci eds., *The Arabic, Hebrew and Latin Reception of Avicenna's Metaphysics*, "Scientia Graeco-Arabica", 7, De Gruyter, Berlin 2012, 225–249

D. N. Hasse, "Avicenna's epistemological optimism", in P. Adamson ed., *Interpreting Avicenna. Critical Essays*, Cambridge University Press, Cambridge 2013, 109–119

C. Hein, *Definition und Enteilung der Philosophie. Von der spätantiken Einleitungsliterature zur arabischen Enzyklopädie*, Peter Lang, Frankfurt a. M.-Bern-New York 1985

P. Huby, Priscian, *On Theophrastus on Sense-Perception*, within Simplicius, *On Aristotle's On the Soul* 2.5–12, trans. by P. Huby and C. Steel, in collaboration with J. O. Urmson; notes by P. Lautner, Duckworth, London 1997

A. L. Ivry, "The Arabic Text of Aristotle's *De anima* and Its Translator", *Oriens*, 36, 2001, 59–77

D. Janos, "Moving the Orbs: Astronomy, Physics, and Metaphysics, and the Problem of Celestial Motion according to Ibn Sīnā", *Arabic Sciences and Philosophy*, 21, 2011, 165–214

J. Janssens, "L'Avicenne latin: un témoin (indirect) des commentateurs (Alexandre d'Aphrodise – Thémistius – Jean Philopon)", in R. Beyers, J. Brams, D. Sacré, K. Verrycken eds., *Tradition et traduction. Les textes philosophiques et scientifiques grecs au Moyen Age latin. Hommage à Fernand Bossier*, Leuven University Press, Leuven 1999, 89–105

J. Janssens, ""Experience" *(tajriba)* in Classical Arabic Philosophy (al-Fārābī – Avicenna)", *Quaestio*, 4, 2004, 45–62

J. Janssens, "The Notions of *Wāhib al-ṣuwar* (Giver of Forms) and *Wāhib al-'aql* (Bestower of intelligence) in Ibn Sīnā", in M. C. Pacheco – J. F. Meirinhos eds., *Intellect et imagination dans la Philosophie médiévale. Actes du XIe Congrès International de Philosophie Médiévale de la Société Internationale pour l'Études de la Philosophie Médiévale (S.I.E.P.M.) – Porto, du 26 au 31 août 2002*, Brepols Publishers, Turnhout 2006, 551–62

J. Janssens, "Ibn Sīnā on Substance in Chapter Two of the *Maqūlāt (Categories)* of the Shifā'", in P. Fodor, G. Mayer, M. Monostori, K. Svozák, L. Takács, eds., *More modoque. Die Wurzeln der europäischen Kultur und deren Rezeption im Orient und Okzident. Festschrift für Miklós Maróth zum siebzigsten Geburtstag*, Forschungszentrum für Humanwissenschaften der Ungarischen Akademie der Wissenschaften, Budapest 2013, 353–360

T. K. Johansen, *The Powers of Aristotle's Soul*, Oxford Aristotle Studies, Oxford University Press, Oxford 2012

J. Jolivet, *L'Intellect selon Kindī*, E. J. Brill, Leiden 1971

J. Jolivet, "Classifications of the sciences", in R. Rashed, J. Morelon eds., *Encyclopedia of the History of Arabic Science,* vol. 3, Routledge, London – New York 1996, 1008–1025

J. Jolivet, "L'*Êpître sur la quantité des livres d'Aristote* par al- Kindī (une lecture)", in R. Morelon, A. Hasnawi eds., *De Zénon d'Elée à Poincaré. Recueil d'études en hommage à Roshdi Rashed,* Peeters, Louvain – Paris 2004, 665–683

L. Judson, "Aristotle and Crossing the Boundaries between the Sciences", *Archiv für Geschichte der Philosophie,* 101.2, 2019, 177–204

G. Karamanolis, "Porphyry's notion of *empsychia*", *Bulletin of the Institute of Classical Studies,* 50, 2007, 91–109

J. Kaukua, *Self-Awareness in Islamic Philosophy. Avicenna and Beyond,* Cambridge University Press, Cambridge 2015

J. Kaukua, "Avicenna's Outsourced Rationalism, Journal of the History of Philosophy", 58.2, 2020, 215–240

W. Kutsch, "Ein Arabisches Bruchstück aus Porphyrios (?) und die Frage des Verfassers der " *Theologie des Aristoteles* "", *Mélanges de l'Université St. Joseph*, 31, 1954, 263–286

A. Laks, "*Metaphysics* Λ 7", in M. Frede and D. Charles eds., *Aristotle's* Metaphysics *Lambda. Simposium Aristotelicum,* Clarendon Press, Oxford 2000, 207–243

A. Lammer, *The Elements of Avicenna's Physics. Greek Sources and Arabic Innovations*, Scientia Graeco-Arabica, 20, De Gruyter, Berlin – Boston 2018

P. Lautner, "Philoponus, *In De Anima* III: Quest for an author", *Classical Quarterly,* 42, 1992, 510–522

P. Lautner, "Status and Method of Psychology according to the Late Neoplatonists and their Influence during the Sixteenth Century", in C. Leijenhorst, C. Lüthy, J. M. M. H. Thijssen eds., *The Dynamics of Aristotelian Natural Philosophy from Antiquity to the Seventeenth Century,* Brill, Leiden-Boston-Köln 2002, 81–108

J. Lennox, "The Place of Mankind in Aristotle's Zoology", *Philosophical Topics*, 27/1, 1999, 1–16

J. Lennox, Aristotle, *On the Parts of Animals.* Translated with a Commentary by J. G. Lennox, Clarendon Press, Oxford 2001

J. Lennox, "Aristotle's Nature Science: the Many and the One", *Apeiron* (Special issue: *From Inquiry to Demonstrative Knowledge. New Essays on Aristotle's* Posterior Analytics, J. H. Lesher ed.), 43, 2010, 1–23

M. Lenzi, *Anima, forma e sostanza: filosofia e teologia nel dibattito antropologico del XIII secolo,* coll. " Uomini e mondi medievali ", Fondazione Centro Italiano di Studi sull'Alto Medioevo (CISAM), Spoleto 2011

O. Lizzini, "La metafisica del *Libro della Guida.* Presentazione e traduzione della terza parte (*bāb*) del *Kitāb al-Hidāya* di Avicenna", *Le Muséon*, 108, 1995, 367–424

O. Lizzini, Avicenna (Ibn Sīnā). *Metafisica. Le* Scienza delle cose divine (al-Ilāhiyyāt) *dal* Libro della Guarigione (Kitāb al-Šifāʾ), a cura di O. Lizzini e P. Porro, Bompiani, Milano 2002

O. Lizzini, "L'*Epistola sulle divisioni delle scienze intellettuali* di Avicenna: alcune note sulla definizione e la collocazione della profetologia e della psicologia", in S. Caroti, R. Imbach, Z. Kaluza, G. Stabile, L. Sturlese, eds., *Ad Ingenii Acuitionem. Studies in Honour of Alfonso Maierù*, Brepols, 2006, 221–248.

O. Lizzini, "L'âme chez Avicenne: quelques remarques autour de son statut épistémologique et de son fondament métaphysique", *Documenti e studi sulla tradizione filosofica medievale,* 21, 2010, 223–242

O. Lizzini, *Fluxus (fayḍ). Indagine sui fondamenti della metafisica e della fisica di Avicenna,* Edizioni di Pagina, Bari, 2011

O. Lizzini, *Avicenna*, Carocci, Roma 2012

A. C. Llyod, "Genus, species and ordered series in Aristotle", *Phronesis*, 7, 1962, 67–90

G. E. R. Llyod, "Aspects of the Relationship between Aristotle's Psychology and his Zoology", in M. Nussbaum, A. Rorty eds., *Essays on Aristotle's* De anima, Clarendon Press, Oxford 1992, 147–167

M. J. Loux, *Primary Ousia. An Essay on Aristotle's Metaphysics Z and H*, Cornell University Press, Ithaca – London 1991

M. J. Loux, *Nature, Norm and Psyche. Explorations in Aristotle's Philosophical Psychology*, Pubblicazioni della Classe di Lettere e Filosofia, 32, Edizioni della Scuola Normale Superiore, Pisa 2004

M. C. Lyons, "Ibn Sīnā and Aristotle: A Study in Technique", in R. Arnzen, J. Thielmann eds., *Words, Texts and Concepts Cruising the Mediterranean Sea. Studies on the sources, contents and influences of Islamic civilization and Arabic philosophy and science dedicated to G. Endress on his sixty-fifth birthday*, Peeters-Department Oosterse Studies, Leuven-Paris-Dudley (Mass.) 2004, 95–110

M. Mahdi, *Alfarabi's Philosophy of Plato and Aristotle*. Translated with an introduction by M. Mahdi, The Free Press of Glencoe, New York 1962; rev. ed. 1969; rev. ed., with a Foreword by C. E. Butterworth and T. L. Pangle, Cornell University Press, Ithaca (N.Y.) 2001

J. Mansfeld, *Prolegomena. Questions to be settled before the study of an author, or a text*, Brill, Leiden 1994

S. Mansion, "Soul and Life in Aristotle's *De anima*", in G. E. R. Lloyd, G. E. L. Owen eds., *Aristotle on Mind and the Senses. Proceedings of the Seventh Symposium Aristotelicum*, Cambridge University Press, Cambridge – London – New York – Melbourne 1978, 1–20

M. E. Marmura, "Avicenna and the problem of the infinite number of souls", *Mediaeval Studies*, 22, 1960, 232–9

M. E. Marmura, "Avicenna's Chapter on Universals in the *Isagoge* of his *Shifā'*", in A. T. Welch, P. Cachia eds., *Islam: Past Influence and Present Challenge*, Edinburgh University Press, Edinburgh 1979, 34–56

M. E. Marmura, "Avicenna's "Flying Man" in Context", *The Monist*, 69, 1986, 383–395

M. E. Marmura, "Ghazali and the Avicennan proof from personal identity for an immaterial self", in R. Link-Salinger, ed., *A Straight Path. Studies in Medieval Philosophy and Culture. Essays in Honor of Arthur Hyman*, Catholic University of America Press, Washington (D.C.) 1988, 195–205

M. E. Marmura, "Fakhr al-Dīn ar-Rāzī's Critique of an Avicennan *Tanbīh*", in *Historia Philosophiae Medii Aevi*, B. Mojsisch and O. Pluta eds., Amsterdam 1991, 627–37

M. E. Marmura, "Plotting the Course of Avicenna's Thought", *Journal of the American Oriental Society*, 111/2, 1991, 333–342

M. E. Marmura, Avicenna, *The Metaphysics of* the Healing. A parallel English-Arabic text translated, introduced, and annotated by M. E. Marmura, Brigham Young University Press, Provo (Utah) 2005

C. Martini Bonadeo, (with C. Ferrari), "Al-Fārābī", in C. D'Ancona ed., *Storia della filosofia nell'Islam medievale*, vol. 1, Einaudi, Torino 2005, 380–448

J. McGinnis, "Making Abstraction less Abstract: The Logical, Psychological, and Metaphysical Dimensions of Avicenna's Theory of Abstraction", *Proceedings of the American Catholic Philosophical Association*, 80, 2007, 169–183

J. McGinnis, "Avicenna's Naturalized Epistemology and Scientific Method", in S. Rahman, T. Street, H. Tahiri eds., *The Unity of Science in the Arabic Tradition. Science, Logic and Epistemology and their Interactions*, Springer, Berlin 2008, 129–152

J. McGinnis, Avicenna, *The Physics of* the Healing. A parallel Arabic-English text translated, introduced and annotated by J. McGinnis, Brigham Young University Press, Provo (Utah) 2009

J. McGinnis, *Avicenna*, Oxford University Press, Oxford 2010

J. McGinnis, "New Light on Avicenna: Optics and Its Role in Avicennian Theories of Vision, Cognition and Emanation", in L. X. Lopéz-Farjeat, J. A. Tellkamplack eds., *Philosophical Psychology in Arabic Thought and the Latin Aristotelianism of the 13th Century*, Vrin, Paris 2013, 41–57

J. McGinnis, "Avicenna's natural philosophy", in P. Adamson ed., *Interpreting Avicenna. Critical Essays*, Cambridge University Press, Cambridge 2013, 71–90

T. McTighe, "Further Remarks on Avicenna and Descartes", in T.-A. Druart ed., *Arabic Philosophy and the West. Continuity and Interaction*, Georgetown University, Washington 1988, 51–54

S. Menn, "Aristotle and Plato on God as Nous and as the Good", *The Review of Metaphysics*, 45/3, 1992, 543–73

S. Menn, "Aristotle's definition of soul and the programme of the *De Anima*", *Oxford Studies in Ancient Philosophy*, 22, 2002, 83–139

Ph. Merlan, *From Platonism to Neoplatonism*, Martinus Nijhoff, The Hague 1968

J. Michot, "Les sciences physiques et metaphysiques selon la *Risālah fī Aqsām al-ʿulūm* d'Avicenne. Essai de traduction critique", *Bulletin de philosophie médiévale*, 22, 1980, 62–73

J. Michot, *La destinée de l'homme selon Avicenne. Le retour à Dieu (maʿād) et l'imagination*, Lovanii Aedibus Peeters, Louvain 1986

J. Michot, "Avicenne. *La Définition de l'âme.* Section I de l'*Épître des états de l'âme.* Traduction critique et lexique", in A. de Libera, A. Elamrano-Jamal, A. Galonnier eds., *Langages et philosophie. Hommage à Jean Jolivet*, Vrin, Paris 1997, 239–256

L. Minio-Paluello, "Le texte du *De Anima* d'Aristote: la tradition latine avant 1500", in *Autour d'Aristote : recueil d'études de philosophie ancienne et medievale offert à Monseigneur A. Mansion*, coll. " Bibliothèque philosophique de Louvain " 16, Publications Universitaire de Louvain, Louvain 1955, 217–243; reprinted in *Opuscula. The latin Aristotle*, A. M. Hakkert, Amsterdam 1972, 250–276

P. Moraux, *Les listes anciennes des ouvrages d'Aristotle*, Éditions Universitaires de Louvain, Louvain 1951

P. Moraux, *Der Aristotelismus bei den Griechen von Andronikos bis Alexander von Aphrodisias*, vol. I, De Gruyter, Berlin-NewYork 1973

P. Moraux, "Le *De Anima* dans la tradition grecque. Quelques aspects de l'interpretation du traité, de Théophraste à Thémistius", in *Aristotle on mind and the senses. Proceedings of the Seventh Symposium Aristotelicum*, G. E. R. Lloyd, G. E. L. Owen eds., Cambridge University Press, Cambridge – London – New York – Melbourne 1978, 281-324

S. N. Mousavian, S. H. S. Mostafavi, "Avicenna on the Origination of the Human Soul", *Oxford Studies in Medieval Philosophy*, 5, 2017, 41–86

L. Muehlethaler, "Ibn Kammūna (d. 683/1284) on the argument of the *Flying Man* in Avicenna's *Ishārāt* and in al-Suhrawardī's *Talwīḥāt*" in Y. T. Langermann ed., *Avicenna and his Legacy. A Golden Age of Science and Philosophy*, Brepols, Turnhout 2009, 179–203

S. R. Ogden, "Avicenna's Emanated Abstraction", *Philosophers' Imprint*, forthcoming

G. E. L. Owen, "Logic and Metaphysics in Some Earlier Works of Aristotle", in J. Barnes, M. Schofield, R. Sorabji eds., *Articles on Aristotle*, vol. 3 (Metaphysics), Duckworth, London 1979, 13–32 [first published in I. Düring, G. E. L. Owen eds., *Aristotle and Plato in the Mid-Fourth Century*, Göteburg 1960]

J. Owens, "Aristotle's Definition of Soul", in R. Palmer, R. Hamerton-Kelly eds., *Philomathes. Studies and Essays in the Humanities in Memory of Philip Merlan*, Martinus Nijhoff, The Hague 1971, 125–145

P. Pellegrin, "Le *De anima* et la vie animale. Trois remarques", in *Corps et âme. Sur le* De anima *d'Aristote*, sous la direction de G. Romeyer-Dherbey, études réunies par C. Viano, Vrin, Paris 1996, 465–492

F. E. Peters, *Aristoteles Arabus. The Oriental translations and commentaries on the Aristotelian Corpus*, coll. " Monographs on Mediterranean Antiquity " 2, Brill, Leiden 1968

S. Pines, "La 'Philosophie Orientale' d'Avicenne et sa polémique contre les Bagdadiens", *Archives d'Histoire Doctrinale et Littéraire au Moyen Age*, 27, 1952, 5–37

S. Pines, "La conception de la conscience de soi chez Avicenne et chez Abu' l-Barakat al-Baghdadi", *Archives d'Histoire Doctrinale et Littéraire au Moyen Age*, 1954, 21–98

N. Polloni, "Elementi per una biografia di Dominicus Gundisalvi", *Archives d'histoire doctrinale et littéraire du Moyen Âge*, 1, 2015, 7–22

N. Polloni, "Gundissalinus and Avicenna: Some Remarks on an Intricate Philosophical Connection", *Documenti e studi sulla tradizione filosofica medievale*, 28, 2017, 515–552

N. Polloni, "The Toledan Translation Movement and Gundissalinus: Some Remarks on His Activity and Presence in Castile", in Y. Beale-Rivaya, J. Busic eds., *A Companion to Medieval Toledo. Reconsidering the Canons*, Brill, Leiden-Boston 2018, 263–280

A. Preus, "Man and Cosmos in Aristotle: *Metaphysics* and the Biological Works", in D. Devereux, P. Pellegrin eds., *Biologie, logique et métaphysique chez Aristote*, Les Editions du CNRS, Paris 1990, 471–90

D. Quarantotto, *Causa finale, sostanza, essenza in Aristotele. Saggio sulla struttura dei processi teleologici naturali e sulla funzione del* telos, Bibliopolis, Napoli 2005

D. Quarantotto, "Che cosa fa di una forma un'anima: L'organizzazione anatomo-fisiologica dei viventi e la sede della *psuche*", in A. Fermani, M. Migliori eds., *Attività e virtù: anima e corpo in Aristotele* (Macerata, 24–6 marzo 2004), Vita e Salute, Milano 2009, 367–381

D. Quarantotto, "Aristotle on the Soul as a Principle of Biological Unity", in S. Föllinger ed., *Was ist Leben? Aristoteles' Anschauungen zur Entstehung und Funktionsweise von Leben*, Franz Steiner Verlag, Stuttgart, 2010, 35–54

F. Rahman, *Avicenna's Psychology* (English translation of Book 2, Chapter 6), Oxford University Press, London 1952

F. Rahman, *Prophecy in Islam: Philosophy and Orthodoxy*, Allen and Unwin, Chicago – London 1958

C. Rapp, "Interaction of Body and Soul: What the Hellenistic Philosophers Saw and Aristotle Avoided", in R. A. H. King ed., *Common to Body and Soul. Philosophical Approaches to Explaining Living Behaviour in Greco-Roman Antiquity*, Walter de Gruyter, Berlin – New York 2006, 187–208

M. Rashed, "Textes inédits transmis par l'Ambr. Q 74 sup. Alexandre d'Aphrodise et Olympiodore d'Alexandrie", *Revue des Sciences Philosophiques et Historiques*, 81, 1997, 219–238

M. Rashed, "Alexandre d'Aphrodise lecteur du *Protreptique*", in J. Hamesse ed., *Les prologues médiévaux : actes du Colloque international organisé par l'Academia belgica et l'École française de Rome avec le concours de la FIDEM : Rome 26–28 mars 1998*, Brepols, Turnhout 2000, 1–37

M. Rashed, "Théodicée et approximation: Avicenne", *Arabic Sciences and Philosophy*, 10, 2000, 223–257

M. Rashed, "La préservation (σωτηρία), objet des *Parva Naturalia* et ruse de la nature", *Revue de philosophie ancienne*, 20, 2002, 35–59

M. Rashed, "Agrégat de parties ou *vinculum substantiale?* Sur une hésitation conceptuelle et textuelle du corpus aristotélicien", in A. Laks, M. Rashed eds., *Aristote et le mouvement des animaux. Dix études sur le* De motu animalium, Presses universitaires du septentrion, Villeneuve d'Ascq 2004, 185–202

M. Rashed, "Ibn ʿAdī et Avicenne: sur les types d'existants", in V. Celluprica, C. D'Ancona, R. Chiaradonna eds., *Aristotele e i suoi esegeti neoplatonici. Logica e ontologia nelle interpretazioni greche e arabe. Atti del convegno internazionale, Roma, 19–20 ottobre 2001*, Bibliopolis, Napoli 2004, 107–171

M. Rashed, "Priorité de l'ΕΙΔΟΣ ou du ΓΕΝΟΣ entre Andronicos et Alexandre : vestiges arabes et grecs inédits", *Arabic Sciences and Philosophy*, 14, 2004, 9–63

M. Rashed, "Imagination astrale et physique supralunaire selon Avicenne", in G. Federici-Vescovini, V. Sorge, C. Vinti eds., *Corpo e anima, sensi interni e intelletto dai secoli XIII-XV ai post-cartesiani e spinoziani*, Brepols, Turnhout 2005, 103–117

M. Rashed, *Essentialisme. Alexandre d'Aphrodise entre logique, physique et cosmologie*, De Gruyter, Berlin 2007

M. Rashed, *L'Héritage Aristotélicien. Textes inédits de l'Antiquité*, Les Belles Lettres, Paris 2007 (Nouvelle édition revue et augmentée 2016)

M. Rashed, "Chose, *item* et distinction: l'"homme volant" d'Avicenne avec et contre Abū Hāšim al-Ǧubbā'ī", *Arabic Sciences and Philosophy*, 28.2, 2018, 167–185

D. C. Reisman, *The Making of the Avicennan Tradition. The Transmission, Contents, and Structure of Ibn Sīnā's* al-Mubāḥaṯāt (*The Discussions*), Brill, Leiden 2002

D. C. Reisman, "al-Fārābī and the philosophical curriculum", in P. Adamson, R. Taylor eds., *The Cambridge Companion to Arabic Philosophy*, Cambridge University Press, Cambridge 2005, 52–71

L. Repici, *Uomini capovolti. Le piante nel pensiero dei Greci*, Editori Laterza, Roma-Bari 2000

G. Rodier, Aristote, *Traité de l'Ame*. Traduit et annoté par G. Rodier, Ernest Leroux Editeur, Paris 1900

M.-D. Roland-Gosselin, O.P., "Sur les relations de l'âme et du corps d'après Avicenne", in *Mélanges Mandonnet*, vol. II, Vrin, Paris 1930, 47–54

U. Rudolph, "Abū Naṣr Muḥammad al-Fārābī", in U. Rudolph, R. Würsch eds., *Grundriß der Geschichte der Philosophie begründet von F. Überweg, völlig neu bearbeitete Ausgabe heraugegeben von H. Holzhey. Philosophie in der islamischen Welt (8.–10. Jahrhundert)*, Schwabe&Co., Basel 2012, 363–457

H. D. Saffrey, "Olympiodoros D'Alexandrie", in *Dictionnaire des philosophes antiques IV*, R. Goulet ed., CNRS Editions, Paris 2005, 769–771

G. Saliba, "Avicenna's *Shifā'* (*Sufficientia*): in Defense of Medieval Latin Translators", *Der Islam. Journal of the History and Culture of the Middle East*, 94.2, 2017, 423–433

F. Sanagustin, *Avicenne (XIe siècle) théoricien de la médecine et philosophe. Approche épistemologique*. 2 Tome, Institut Français du Proche-Orient, Damas 2009

P. L. Schoonheim, "Météorologiques. Tradition syriaque, arabe et latine", in *Dictionnaire des philosophes antiques. Supplément*, R. Goulet ed., CNRS Editions, Paris 2003, 324–328

M. Sebti, "La signification de la définition avicennienne de l'âme comme "perfection première d'un corps naturel organique" dans le livre I du *Traité de l'âme* du *Šifā*"", *Bulletin d'Études Orientales*, 51, 1999, 299–312

M. Sebti, *Avicenne. L'âme humaine*, Presses universitaires de France, Paris 2000

M. Sebti, "La distinction entre intellect pratique et intellect théorique dans la doctrine de l'âme humaine d'Avicenne", *Philosophie*, 77, 2003, 23–44

M. Sebti, "Le statut ontologique de l'image dans la doctrine avicenniene de la perception", *Arabic Sciences and Philosophy*, 15, 2005, 109–140

M. Sebti, "L'analogie de la lumière dans la noétique d'Avicenne", *Archives d'histoire doctrinale et littéraire du Moyen Âge*, 73/1, 2006, 7–28

M. Sebti, "La question de l'authenticité de l'*Épître des états de l'âme* (Risāla fī aḥwāl al-nafs) d'Avicenne", " Studia Graeco-Arabica ", 2, 2012, 331–354

M. Sebti, "Avicenna's "Flying Man" Argument as a Proof of the Immateriality of the Soul", in E. Coda, C. Martini-Bonadeo eds., *De l'Antiquité Tardive au Moyen Âge. Études de logique aristotélicienne et de philosophie grecque, syriaque, arabe et latine offertes à Henri Hugonnard-Roche*, Vrin, Paris 2014, 531–543

D. Sedley, "Is Aristotle's teleology anthropocentric?", *Phronesis*, 36/2, 1991, 179–96

R. W. Sharples, "Common to Body and Soul: Peripatetic Approaches After Aristotle", in R. A. H. King ed., *Common to Body and Soul. Philosophical Approaches to Explaining Living Behaviour in Greco-Roman Antiquity*, Walter de Gruyter, Berlin – New York 2006, 165–186

R. W. Sharples, Alexandri Aphrodisiensis *De anima libri mantissa*. A new edition of the Greek text with introduction and commentary, ed. R. W. Sharples, Walter de Gruyter, Berlin 2008

A. Shihadeh, "From al-Ghazālī to al-Rāzī: 6th/12th century Developments in Muslim Philosophical Theology", *Arabic Sciences and Philosophy*, 15, 2005, 141–179

A. Shihadeh, *Doubts on Avicenna. A Study and Edition of Sharaf al-Dīn al-Masʿūdī's Commentary on the* Ishārāt, Islamic Philosophy, Theology and Science. Texts and Studies 95, Brill, Leiden-Boston 2015

R. Sorabji, *Philoponus and the rejection of Aristotelian science*, Duckworth, London 1987

R. Sorabji, *Aristotle's Transformed. The Ancient Commentators and Their Influence*, R. Sorabji ed., Duckworth, London 1990

R. Taylor, "Al-Fārābī and Avicenna: Two Recent Contributions", *MESA Bulletin*, 39, 2005, 180–2

R. Taylor, "Avicenna and the Issue of the Intellectual Abstraction of Intelligibles", in *Philosophy of Mind in the Early and High Middle Ages*, ed. M. Cameron, Routledge, Oxford – New York 2019, 56–82

S. Tlili, *Animals in the Qurʾan*, Cambridge University Press, Cambridge 2012

R. B. Todd, Themistius, *On Aristotle On the soul*, translated by R. B. Todd, Duckworth, London 1996

Th. Tracy, "The soul/boatman analogy in Aristotle's *De anima*", *Classical Philology*, 77/2, 1982, 97–112

A. Treiger, "Avicenna's Notion of Transcendental Modulation of Existence (*taškīk al-wuǧūd, analogia entis*) and Its Greek and Arabic Sources", *Documenti e studi sulla tradizione filosofica medievale*, 21, 2010, 165–198

J. Tricot, Aristote, *Organon. 1. Categories. 2. De l'interprétation*. Traduction nouvelle et notes par J. Tricot, Vrin, Paris 1959

O. Urmson, Simplicius, *On Aristotle On the Soul 1.1–2.34*. Translated by J. O. Urmson, notes by P. Lautner, Duckworth, London 1995

P. Vallat, *Farabi et l'école d'Alexandrie. Des prémisses de la connaissance à la philosophie politique*, Vrin, Paris 2004

P. J. van der Eijk, Philoponus, *On Aristotle On the soul* 1.1–2, translated by Philip J. van der Eijk, Duckworth, London 2005

P. J. van der Eijk, Philoponus, *On Aristotle On the soul* 1.3–5, translated by Philip J. van der Eijk, Duckworth, London 2006

G. Vajda, "Les notes d'Avicenne sur la 'Theologie d'Aristote'", *Revue Thomiste*, 51, 1951, 346–406

J. Vanderpoel, *Themistius and the Imperial Court: Oratory, Civic Duty, and* Paideia *from Constantius to Theodosius*, University of Michigan Press, Ann Arbor 1998

G. Verbeke, Jean Philopon, *Commentaire sur le De anima d'Aristote*. Traduction de Guillaume de Moerbeke, ed. G. Verbeke, Editions Béatrice-Nauwelaerts, Paris 1966

G. Verbeke, "Levels of human thinking in Philoponus", in C. Laca, J. A. Munitiz, L. van Rompay eds., *After Chalcedon. Studies in Theology and Church History offered to Professor Albert von Roey for his Seventieth Birthday*, Peeters, Louvain 1985, 451–70

K. Verrycken, "The development of Philoponus' thought and its chronology", in R. Sorabji ed., *Aristotle Transformed. The Ancient Commentators and their Influence*, Duckworth, London, 1990, 233–274

R. Walzer, "New Light on the Arabic Translations of Aristotle", *Oriens*, 6, 1953, 91–142

R. Walzer, "Al-Fārābī", in *Encyclopaedia of Islam*, New edition, vol. 2, E. J. Brill, Leiden 1965, 797–800

P. Ward, "Souls and figures. Defining the soul in the *De anima* II 3", *Ancient Philosophy*, 16, 1996, 113 – 28

M. V. Wedin, *Mind and Imagination in Aristotle*, Yale University Press, New Heaven and London 1988

L. G. Westerink, "The Alexandrian commentators and the introductions to their commentaries", in R. Sorabji ed., *Aristotle's Transformed. The Ancient Commentators and Their Influence*, Duckworth, London 1990, 325 – 348

R. Wisnovsky, "Yaḥyā al-Naḥwī (John Philoponus)", in *L'Encyclopédie de l'Islam*, [16], vol. XI, ed. H. A. R. Gibbs, Brill, Leiden – Paris, 1977 – 1996, 251 – 253

R. Wisnovsky, "Notes on Avicenna's concept of *thingness* (*shayʾiyya*)", *Arabic Sciences and Philosophy*, 10.2, 2000, 181 – 221

R. Wisnovsky, *Avicenna's Metaphysics in Context*, Cornell University Press, Ithaca – New York 2003

R. Wisnovsky, "Towards a history of Avicenna's distinction between immanent and transcendent causes", in in D. C. Reisman, A. H. al-Rahim eds., *Before and After Avicenna. Proceedings of the First Conference of the Avicenna Study Group*, Brill, Leiden 2003, 49 – 68

R. Wisnovsky, *Avicenna's Islamic reception*, in P. Adamson ed., *Interpreting Avicenna. Critical Essays*, Cambridge University Press, Cambridge 2013, 190 – 213

M. S. Zarepour, "Avicenna's Notion of Fiṭrīyāt: A Comment on Dimitri Gutas' Interpretation", *Philosophy East and West*, 70.3, 2020, 819 – 833

F. W. Zimmermann, "The Origins of the so-called *Theology of Aristotle*", in J. Kraye, W. F. Ryan, C. B. Schmitt eds., *Pseudo-Aristotle in the Middle Ages. The* Theology *and Other Texts*, Warburg Institute, London 1986, 110 – 240

M. Zonta, "La *divisio scientiarum* presso al-Farabi: dalla "introduzione alla filosofia" tardoantica all'enciclopedismo medievale", in G. d'Onofrio ed., *La Divisione della Filosofia e le sue Ragioni. Lettura di testi medievali. Atti del Settimo Convegno della Società Italiana per lo Studio del Pensiero Medievale (S.I.S.P.M.) – Assisi, 14 – 15 novembre 1997*, Avagliano Editore, Cava de' Tirreni 2001, 65 – 78

Index

Index of concepts

abstraction (tağrīd) 2–3, 122n, 131–144, 148, 157, 161, 176, 177n, 187, 220, 230, 237
accident (ʿaraḍ) 26n, 31, 48, 49n, 63, 70, 75, 76n, 90n, 105–106, 116–117, 123, 125, 145n, 172, 186, 194, 199–200, 206–207, 210, 223–224, 228n, 230, 236
accidental (ʿaraḍī) 33n, 105, 140–141, 199–200, 235–236
accidentality 106, 186, 199n, 200
Active Intellect (ʿaql faʿʿāl) 2, 11, 50, 126n, 131–139, 144–147, 150, 152–157, 162–163, 166–167, 172–173, 176, 187, 234–235
activity (ἐνέργεια, fiʿl) 1–2, 5, 7, 9–11, 29, 32–33, 35–39, 49–53, 56, 58–59, 62–63, 67, 73, 75, 77–82, 85–87, 91, 93–104, 106–112, 114–125, 127, 129–131, 138n, 139, 144, 146–147, 150, 152, 157, 160–163, 165, 167, 174–176, 177n, 182–184, 186–189, 191–194, 196–198, 201–204, 205n, 206n, 208–211, 215–218, 229, 231–233, 235
actuality (ἐντελέχεια, fiʿl) 1, 37–39, 56–57, 59, 79n, 80n, 88n, 92n, 98, 100–102, 107–108, 112, 125, 127, 135n, 144, 150–154, 156, 195–196, 198, 201, 203–204, 206–208, 212, 220–222, 226–229, 234–235, 238
affection (πάθος, infiʿāl) 7, 11, 31, 48n, 108, 125, 147, 182, 191, 201, 210, 218n, 231
afterlife 88–91, 94, 130, 160, 183, 185, 237n
animals 7, 10, 14n, 21n, 31–32, 34–35, 36n, 42–44, 46–50, 53, 56, 65–67, 70n, 75, 77–78, 80n, 81, 86–89, 91–92, 98n, 99n, 106n, 108, 109n, 116–118, 121–122, 148, 159, 161, 182–185, 191n, 192–193, 195–196, 198, 200n, 201–204, 206–210, 216, 222
appurtenance (ʿalāqa) 84, 118, 122, 140–143, 145, 149, 220, 235
argument 31n, 35, 54n, 55n, 64n, 68–78, 82n, 83, 89n, 91n, 92, 98, 113n, 114n, 116, 121–122, 124, 153n, 170, 185, 195–196, 205n, 225
assent (taṣdīq) 78n, 121, 209, 221
atom 24, 83, 224–225
attribute (lāḥiqa) 32n, 48n, 60, 69, 85, 107, 115, 140–142, 204, 230

body (badan, ğism) 1–4, 7, 10, 14, 29, 32–33, 35, 37–38, 40–41, 45–46, 48–54, 56–64, 66n, 69–94, 96–112, 114–117, 119–131, 134n, 139, 141n, 143–144, 150–151, 156–157, 163, 167, 173–175, 181–189, 191–196, 199n, 200–212, 214, 218–220, 221n, 223–230, 232–234, 237
botany 7, 32n, 49, 53, 55–56, 58n, 65, 174, 182, 188
brain 69, 125, 205, 214, 216–217, 229n

cause (sabab, ʿilla) 7, 15, 23n, 34, 45–46, 53n, 97, 101, 106, 108n, 111, 117, 120, 123, 126–127, 132–134, 144–145, 148n, 151–152, 154–155, 167–168, 172, 181, 185, 187–188, 191, 206–210, 214, 233–234, 236
celestial sphere 79, 87, 88n, 94n, 203
certainty 153–154, 157
cogitation 10, 149n, 160–161, 165, 217
color 10, 13, 118n, 141n, 150–152, 214–215
common sense 14, 160–161, 163, 165, 216–218
conceptualization (taṣawwur) 2, 5, 77–78n, 82, 109n, 118, 121, 149, 182–183, 202, 229, 231, 237–238
concupiscible faculty 160–161, 165, 213, 223
configuration 105, 108, 110n, 111, 120–121, 124–126, 199, 206, 214–215, 218–219, 233–234
constituent 33, 61n, 88n, 92, 203, 206
corporeality 63n, 98, 171, 194
corruption 7, 24, 40n, 48n, 51n, 59, 90n, 103, 126–127, 182–183, 191

Dator formarum see Active Intellect
definition (ḥadd) 1–2, 5, 26n, 36n, 37, 57, 70, 84, 88n, 95–97, 100, 102, 106–108, 111–117, 119n, 128, 149, 158, 160, 169, 186–188, 200–204, 211–212, 226–230, 236–237

https://doi.org/10.1515/9783110706840-012

demonstration 15, 73–79, 83–85, 87n, 89n, 106n, 111n, 116, 153n, 160, 162–163, 167, 172, 185–186, 202, 219, 224, 227, 231
desiderative faculty 118n, 213
differentia (faṣl) 60n, 66, 67n, 72, 84, 99–100, 192–193, 197, 208, 226–227, 236

elements 7, 13, 42, 48n, 89n, 111, 173–174, 181–182, 191, 207n, 209
emanation (fayḍ) 2–3, 131–133, 135n, 136–137, 139, 144, 146, 157, 176, 187
equivocation (ištirāk al-ism) 36, 88n, 99, 198, 203, 218
essence (ḏāt) 1, 24, 29, 31–32, 53, 55, 60, 62–64, 66n, 68–70, 71n, 73–74, 76n, 77–79, 82, 89n, 91–93, 97, 99, 106–107, 111–112, 116–117, 124–125, 127, 130, 137n, 140n, 145, 147–149, 152, 169, 175, 182, 187–188, 192, 194–195, 197n, 198, 201, 215, 224, 228–229, 231, 235–236
estimation 3, 10, 69n, 87, 140, 141n, 156n, 160–161, 163, 165, 208, 217–218, 222–223, 226n, 227
existence (wuǧūd) 9, 15, 37, 60–63, 68–73, 75–77, 82n, 83–86, 87n, 88n, 90–95, 98n, 107, 108n, 115–116, 117n, 120, 122, 124, 126–127, 130, 132, 140n, 141n, 142, 147–149, 156, 166, 171–172, 174, 184–185, 188, 194–195, 197–199, 201–208, 222, 228–230, 234, 236–238
experience 153–155

faculty (quwwa) 2–3, 5, 9–11, 14–15, 20, 21n, 23n, 32, 39n, 53, 59, 62, 67n, 69n, 78–85, 87–89, 91–93, 95, 97–98, 109n, 115–121, 124n, 125, 127, 130–131, 138–146, 149–150, 153n, 156, 159–161, 163, 165, 167, 172–176, 177n, 182–183, 187–188, 192, 196, 198n, 203, 208–224, 227, 229–233, 235–236
form (εἶδος, ṣūra) 2, 13n, 15, 29, 32n, 33, 40, 42n, 44, 51, 54, 56, 59, 61, 64–66n, 74–75, 78–80, 82–87, 90n, 92n, 93–94, 96n, 98–104, 105–106n, 108–112, 114n, 116–117, 118n, 122–124, 128–158, 160, 165, 167–168, 172, 175–176, 181–182, 184–187, 191–192, 195–200, 203, 206–207, 210, 213–218, 220–232, 234–236
form-bearing faculty 10, 156, 161, 165, 216–217

generation 7, 34n, 40n, 48n, 51n, 182, 191–192
genus 49, 60, 66, 67n, 73–74, 84, 98, 99n, 119, 146–147, 192, 193n, 196–197, 202, 212, 215, 222, 226–227, 235–236
Giver of forms (Wāhib al-ṣuwar) see Active Intellect
God 45, 62n, 63n, 79n, 87n, 95, 142, 148n, 185, 191, 224n
growth 32, 35–36, 38, 67n, 111n, 159, 161, 175, 192, 202, 209–210, 212, 223

heart 14n, 69, 205
human beings 4, 11, 15, 30n, 32n, 36n, 48, 50, 66–67, 69, 71–72, 75–79, 82–84, 86n, 89–91n, 92, 94n, 100, 105–106, 108, 109n, 118, 120, 122, 130, 133n, 134, 136, 139, 152, 157–158, 160–161, 176, 182–183, 185, 187, 191n, 192, 199, 201, 205, 218, 224

imagery 85, 140–141n, 145, 147, 149–150, 156, 163, 165, 216–218, 223, 231, 235–236
imagination 14, 23, 52, 87, 91n, 118, 121, 133n, 140, 141n, 149n, 150, 160–161, 165, 172, 176, 213, 216n, 217–218, 223, 235
immateriality 34n, 55–56, 59n, 70, 71n, 73–74, 78–80, 84–85, 90, 92–93, 125, 136n, 139, 141n, 142–144, 157, 183
immortality 15, 57, 71n, 90, 120, 126, 166
incorporeality 46n, 49–50, 68, 71n, 72, 74–75, 76n, 77–78, 80n, 82n, 83n, 84–85, 89–90n, 92–93, 125, 160, 162, 165, 172, 185, 206n, 227
independence 1–2, 4, 29, 32, 62, 71n, 72, 74–76, 90, 104, 111, 126, 130–131, 157, 163, 167, 185, 187, 189, 200n, 206
individuation 120–127, 186
induction 153, 154n
intellect (νοῦς, ʿaql) 2–3, 11, 23n, 34, 36, 38–39n, 40, 47, 49–52, 59n, 79, 80–81n, 82, 86–90n, 96, 102n, 109n, 118n, 122n, 125, 130, 133–140, 141n, 142–147, 149–150, 152–157, 160–162, 165, 167, 173, 176, 185, 191n, 203, 218–222, 228–231–238
intellection 2–3, 5, 29, 36n, 38, 79n, 90, 97, 109n, 120, 122, 130–131, 133–139, 142–145, 147, 149–150, 152–157, 162, 176, 187–188, 220n, 229–234, 237
irascible faculty 160–161, 165, 213, 223

life 21n, 22, 23n, 29–32, 35–36, 40, 43–44, 50, 53n, 58–59, 63–65n, 79n, 88, 94n, 100, 107, 111–112n, 114, 117n, 119n, 128, 160, 173–174, 183, 188, 202–205, 223n, 237
light 10, 13, 54n, 138, 145–147, 150–156, 231, 234–235
limbs 66n, 69n, 92n, 192, 205, 209, 213
locomotion 10, 31n, 118n, 160–161, 165, 182–183, 197, 212–213, 223

mathematics 6, 13–14n, 37, 51, 53, 54n, 57, 60, 65, 142n, 159, 163–164, 166, 193
matter (mādda) 11, 32n, 33–34, 52, 54, 59, 61, 64, 65–66n, 75–80, 84, 86, 87n, 89n, 90–91, 96, 98, 99, 101, 104, 105n, 106–108, 110n, 115, 117, 118n, 122–127, 132, 136, 139–145, 153–154, 163, 165, 181, 185, 191n, 192, 195n, 196–198, 200n, 201, 202n, 206–207, 210, 220–221, 223, 228–230, 234–235, 237–238
meaning (as object of estimation, maʿnan) 141, 156n, 165, 215–218
medicine 3–4, 14, 22, 23n, 58, 169n, 214n
memory 14, 22, 69, 125, 134, 136–137, 155–157, 161–163, 165, 217–218, 223
method 8, 27n, 63n, 65, 71–72, 77, 170–171
motion 4, 21, 45, 61, 63–64, 75, 80n, 82n, 86–87, 90–91, 96, 99, 106–108, 109n, 115, 118, 119n, 142n, 143, 146, 174, 181, 185, 191, 195, 197–198, 201–203, 208–209, 211, 213–214, 223, 231, 235, 238

natural faculties 23n, 223
nature 1–2, 4, 7, 8n, 15, 24, 30–31, 35n, 36, 39n, 42, 45–46, 49, 53–56, 63–64n, 65–66, 68, 72, 78, 83, 88, 90–91, 94n, 99n, 100, 102n, 107, 125, 130, 133, 141, 145, 147–148n, 149, 155–156, 175, 177n, 181–183, 191, 196–197, 201, 206–208, 210–211, 220, 231, 237
nutrition 23, 32, 35–36, 38, 50n, 58n, 63n, 67n, 111n, 116, 118, 159, 161, 175, 192, 202, 206n, 208–210, 212, 223n

observation, direct 63, 71, 77, 93, 154, 184
operational principle 2, 59, 62, 64, 73–75, 77, 95, 97, 109–110, 115–117, 119–120, 129, 186, 188, 205n
organ 2, 10, 21n, 22, 29, 56, 69–70, 80n, 85, 92n, 111, 112n, 162–163, 165, 167, 173, 202–203, 205, 208–209, 215, 229–233

part 1, 5, 21, 34, 35–36n, 38, 40, 42–44n, 48, 51, 54n, 66–67, 69n, 70, 76n, 79–80, 81n, 82–84, 86n, 88n, 91, 92n, 95, 98, 102, 105–106, 108n, 119n, 125, 156, 184–185, 192, 195–196, 199–200, 203, 205, 207, 210–214, 216, 221, 224, 226–228, 232
particulars 2, 131, 137n, 138–139, 144–147, 149–150, 152–156, 187, 211, 234–235
perception (idrāk) 9, 13n, 14, 21, 31n–33, 35–36, 38, 53, 63n, 69n, 80n, 82, 88f., 89n, 99, 108, 109n, 118–119n, 122, 133n, 138n, 139–140, 149, 151–152, 153n, 161, 163, 165, 171, 173, 191, 194, 198, 201–203, 205, 208–212, 215–217, 230–231, 233
perfection (τελειότης, kamāl) 1–2, 9n, 26n, 54n, 86n, 87, 89, 95–117, 119, 121–122, 124, 128–129, 152, 158, 173, 186–188, 195–202, 204, 210–211, 212n, 220–221, 237–238
– first (k. awwal) 88, 96, 107–108, 110–112, 114, 116–117, 120, 124n, 186–187, 201–202, 204–205, 211
– second (k. ṯānī) 107–108, 110, 111n, 117, 186–187, 201–202, 209
– inseparable (k. ġayr mufāriq) 103, 104, 117, 187–188, 210
– separable (k. mufāriq) 101n, 103–104, 117, 124n, 187–188, 210
plants 7, 31–32, 42–43, 44n, 46–50, 53, 56, 58, 65–67, 70n, 75, 77–78, 81, 86–89n, 91, 92n, 98n, 106n, 116–118, 159, 161, 173, 182–185, 191n, 192–193, 195, 200n, 202, 204, 206, 208
pneuma 14, 91n, 130, 217n
point (as geometrical entity) 83, 224–225
potentiality (δύναμις, quwwa) 37–38, 59n, 79–80n, 92n, 98–100, 108, 127, 135n, 137, 144, 151–152n, 154, 157, 195–197, 198n, 201, 212, 220–222, 228–229, 234–235, 238
power (quwwa) 31n, 38, 49–50, 81n, 85, 98, 99n, 125, 137–138, 139n, 196–198, 229n, 232
principle 2, 4, 7–8, 12, 24, 29–31, 33n, 36n, 37–38, 43, 46n, 47–50, 52, 55–56,

58–65, 67, 73–75, 77, 79n, 81–82, 86, 87n, 89, 91–99, 102n, 106, 108–111, 114–118, 120–124, 128–129, 137, 145, 152–154, 164, 166, 170, 174, 182–183, 185–188, 191n, 194–198, 201, 204–206, 209n, 213, 218–220, 222, 225, 227, 233–234
priority 8, 35n, 65–66, 144n, 186, 193, 220, 237
proof 63, 76n, 77, 164, 171, 174, 194
prophecy 10, 15, 87n, 177n
providence 120–121, 234

quality 7, 10, 49, 53n, 140, 141n, 150, 182, 191, 223
quiddity (māhiyya) 15, 53n, 61–62, 63n, 70–71, 73, 75–76, 86, 89, 90n, 94–98, 106–108, 110–111, 115, 122–123, 129, 147n, 172, 184–186, 195, 199n, 201, 205

rationality 88, 99n, 100, 197n, 203
receptacle (maḥall) 75, 78, 80n, 84, 103n, 165, 167, 175, 184, 223–227
reception (qubūl) 2, 98, 104, 117, 123, 128, 131, 133n, 146, 172, 187, 189, 208–209, 216, 220, 229, 235
receptivity see potentiality
recollection 10, 22, 139, 144, 153n, 155–157, 217
relation (iḍāfa, nisba) 2, 37, 46n, 59, 60, 61n, 62, 64, 67n, 70, 75, 79, 81n, 82, 86n, 87–88, 90, 93, 97, 99n, 100, 104, 106–107, 109n, 117, 120–126, 128–131, 141, 145–146, 149, 150, 152n, 157, 165, 185–187, 189, 192, 194, 196–197, 199, 205, 208, 217–222, 227–228, 232–235, 238
reproduction 14n, 32, 67n, 118, 159, 161, 175, 192, 206, 208, 209n, 212
retentive faculty (as the faculty that stores maʿānin) see memory

self-subsistence (qiwām al-ḏāt) 3, 54–55, 74–77, 86n, 93, 117, 127, 134n, 175, 185, 187, 189, 206
sensation, sense perception see perception
sense (ḥāssa) 3, 9–11, 13–14, 21–22, 52, 56, 63, 69n, 116, 139–141, 149, 160–161, 163, 165, 167–168, 171, 176, 194, 205, 213–217, 218n, 223, 231, 236
separability 1, 45, 101–102, 128
shape (σχῆμα, šakl) 104, 108, 110n, 141n, 201, 215, 226
soul (ψυχή, nafs) *passim*
species 35, 48, 53, 66f., 73f., 98–101, 108, 116f., 119, 122f., 125, 140, 192f., 196f., 201, 204, 207f., 210, 212f., 215, 221f., 230, 236
state (ḥāl) 10, 61, 69n, 78n, 82n, 88–90, 94, 98n, 118, 123–124, 140n, 173, 182–184, 191, 193, 196, 204–205, 207, 211, 217, 222, 229–230, 232–234
steersman (κυβερνήτης, rubbān) 59n, 101–102, 104, 123, 197, 204
subject (ὑποκείμενον, mawḍūʿ) 33n, 75–76, 92n, 98n, 101–106, 116–117, 147n, 148, 184–185, 195–196, 198–200, 204, 206–207, 210, 216n, 221
substance (οὐσία, ǧawhar) 2–3, 9, 12, 24, 26n, 32–33, 35n, 36, 39n, 42n, 49–51, 54–55, 59n, 61–62, 63n, 70–71n, 74–86, 87n, 89–94, 96–97, 99, 100–106, 108–111, 114, 116–117, 123, 127–129, 165, 172, 175, 183–187, 189, 191n, 194, 196–201, 206–207, 210, 217n, 219, 224, 227–233
substantial (ǧawharī) 33n, 36, 45–46, 104–105, 110n, 111, 117, 187, 199n, 200
substantiality 2, 63, 70–71n, 75–76, 78, 80, 93–94, 104, 106n, 112n, 116, 185–186, 199–200, 206–207
Sun 13n, 54n, 138, 150–152, 162, 164n, 176, 234, 237

temperament 120, 125–127, 171, 174, 206, 210, 214, 231, 234
thought-experiment 58n, 59, 67–72, 85, 89n, 91–93, 97, 205, 209n, 230n

unity 1–2, 5, 29, 30n, 32n, 35n, 36, 38, 48, 56–57, 62, 66, 87n, 91–93, 120, 122, 129, 133n, 142n, 150, 157–158, 166, 184–187, 192, 228
universality 78, 94n, 148–149, 156
universals 81n, 133n, 137n, 148, 236n

vision 8n, 12–13, 14n, 22n, 138, 150–151, 152n, 155, 161, 163, 165, 167, 176, 177n

zoology 4, 7, 14, 31, 48–49, 53, 55–56, 65, 174, 182–183, 188

Index of names

Abraham Ibn Daūd see Ibn Daūd, Abraham
Abū Bišr Mattà ibn Yūnus see Ibn Yūnus, Abū Bišr Mattà
'Alā' al-Dawla 158, 166
Alexander of Aphrodisias 19, 20n, 22n, 32n, 36n, 42–44, 46, 51n, 57, 100–102, 104, 128n, 131, 137n, 184
Alexandrians 16, 19
Ammonius 41n, 45–46, 54n, 128n
Aristotle 1–4, 6–9, 12–21, 22n, 23, 28–38, 39n, 40–46, 48–60, 61n, 66, 75, 76n, 81n–82n, 85, 93, 96, 97n, 100–106, 107n, 108n, 109n, 110–111, 113n, 115, 118–119, 127–128, 132, 149–150, 151n, 153n, 156, 167–168, 176, 182, 184–187, 191n–193n, 199, 216n
'Arūḍī, Abū l-Ḥasan al- 158–159
Asclepius 45
Aṯāwālīs 16, 19
Atomists 83, 225n
Avendauth Israelita see Ibn Daūd, Abraham
Averroes 18, 28

Baghdad Aristotelians 200n
Ba'labakkī, Qusṭā ibn Lūqā al- 55–56

David (Élias) 41n
Descartes, René 68
Dominicus Gundisalvi see Gundisalvi, Dominicus

Euclid 7n, 51n, 193n

Fārābī, Abū Naṣr Muḥammad ibn Muḥammad ibn Ṭarḫān ibn Awzaluġ (or Uzluġ) al- 21n, 22n, 24, 41n, 45, 47–50, 57, 109n, 131, 184

Galen 14n, 22, 23n
Gundisalvi, Dominicus 27
Gundissalinus see Gundisalvi, Dominicus
Ǧūzǧānī, Abū 'Ubayd 'Abd al-Wāḥid ibn Muḥammad al- 6, 12n, 14n, 27n, 115n, 162, 164, 166

Ḥen, Zeraḥyah Ben Isaac ben Shealtiel 18n, 19
Homer 188
Ḥunayn ibn Isḥāq see Ibn Isḥāq, Ḥunayn

Iamblichus 54n
Ibn Abī Uṣaybi'a 128n
Ibn 'Adī, Yaḥyà 16, 18n
Ibn al-Biṭrīq, Yaḥyà 16, 19–20, 103
Ibn Daūd, Abraham 27
Ibn Ǧulǧul, Sulaymān ibn Ḥassān 17n
Ibn al-Ḫammār, al-Ḥasan ibn Suwār 105n
Ibn Ḥunayn, Isḥāq 16–19
Ibn Isḥāq, Ḥunayn 16
Ibn Kammūna, 'Izz al-Dawla 73
Ibn Muḥammad al-Šayḫ al-Mufīd, Abū 'Abd Allāh Muḥammad 55
Ibn al-Nadīm, Abū l-Farağ Muḥammad ibn Isḥāq 15–17, 19–20, 21n
Ibn al-Qifṭī, 'Alī ibn Yūsuf 17, 19n, 128n
Ibn Suwār ibn al-Ḫammār, al-Ḥasan see Ibn al-Ḫammār, al-Ḥasan ibn Suwār
Ibn al-Ṭayyib, Abū l-Farağ 105n
Ibn Yūnus, Abū Bišr Mattà 21
Ibn Zur'a, Abū 'Alī 'Isā ibn Isḥāq 18n
Isḥāq ibn Ḥunayn see Ibn Ḥunayn, Isḥāq

John of Castellmoron 28
John Peckham 132

Kindī, Abū Yūsuf Ya'qūb ibn Isḥāq al- 20–22, 24, 52–57, 127n, 131, 184

Mağd al-Dawla 115n
Mu'tazilites 24

Nawbaḫtī, Abū Muḥammad al-Ḥasan ibn Mūsā al- 24, 55
Nicolaus of Damascus 7

Olympiodorus 16, 19, 41n, 45–47, 54n, 57, 128n

Peripatetics 9
Philoponus 1, 15, 20, 35n, 37n, 40n, 41n, 45–46, 54n, 57, 59n, 82n, 102–104, 109n, 128, 184, 237n
Plato 30n, 45, 46n, 48, 60n, 128
Platonists 30n
Plotinus 23, 102n, 128n, 205n
Porphyry 23n, 50n, 60n, 105, 173, 200n
Priscianus 19n
Proclus 7n, 23, 51n, 128n
Ps.-Aristotle 182, 193n

Ps.-Simplicius 51–52, 57
Ptolemy 12n, 193n

Qusṭā ibn Lūqā al-Baʿlabakkī see Baʿlabakkī, Qusṭā ibn Lūqā al-

Raymond de La Sauvetat 28
Rāzī, Faḫr al-Dīn al- 160
Roger Bacon 132

al-Šayḫ al-Mufīd, Abū ʿAbd Allāh Muḥammad ibn Muḥammad see Ibn Muḥammad al-Šayḫ al-Mufīd, Abū ʿAbd Allāh Muḥammad
Simplicius 16, 19, 41n, 50, 51n, 52n, 53n, 57, 100n, 128n, 184

Ṭabarī, Abū ʿAmr (or Abū ʿUmar) al- 21
Ṯāmisṭiyūs see Themistius
Themistius 16–20, 23, 24n, 42n, 57, 61n, 101n, 133n
Theophrastus 32n

William of Auvergne 132

Yaḥyà ibn ʿAdī, see Ibn ʿAdī, Yaḥyà

Zeraḥyah Ben Isaac ben Shealtiel Ḥen see Ḥen, Zeraḥyah Ben Isaac ben Shealtiel

www.ingramcontent.com/pod-product-compliance
Lightning Source LLC
Chambersburg PA
CBHW081001180426
43192CB00041B/2727